Using

Microsoft®
Home
Essentials®
98

Faithe Wempen

A Division of Macmillan Computer Publishing, USA
201 W. 103rd Street
Indianapolis, Indiana 46290

Contents

Using Microsoft® Home Essentials® 98

Library of Congress Catalog No.: 98-84375

ISBN: 0-7897-1652-6

01 00 99 98   6 5 4 3 2 1

Interpretation of the printing code: The rightmost double-digit number is the year of the book's printing; the rightmost single-digit number, the number of the book's printing. For example, a printing code of 98-1 shows that the first printing of the book occurred in 1998.

Composed in Formata and Janson by Macmillan Computer Publishing.

Printed in the United States of America.

Trademarks

Credits

Executive Editor
Angela Wethington

Acquisitions Editor
Stephanie J. McComb

Development Editor
Lorna Gentry

Technical Editor
Mark Hall

Managing Editor
Thomas F. Hayes

Project Editor
Heather E. Butler

Copy Editors
Krista Hansing
Julie McNamee

Indexer
Tim Tate

Book Designers
Nathan Clement
Ruth Harvey

Cover Designers
Dan Armstrong
Ruth Harvey

Production Team
Cyndi Davis-Hubler
Terri Edwards
Donna Martin

Contents

About the Author

Faithe Wempen, MA, operates Your Computer Friend, a computer training and troubleshooting business in Indianapolis that specializes in helping beginning users with their PCs. A self-avowed hardware geek, she loves tinkering with computers, and especially enjoys helping new computer owners learn to operate and maintain their PCs. Her eclectic writing credits include more than 20 computer books, including the best-selling titles *Microsoft Office Professional 6-in-1* and *Learn Word 97 in a Weekend*, plus articles, essays, poems, training manuals, and OEM documentation. Her hobbies include surfing the Internet, doing cross-stitch, being an active member of Broadway United Methodist Church in Indianapolis, and raising Shetland sheepdogs.

Dedication

To Margaret.

Acknowledgments

Thanks to everyone at Macmillan Computer Publishing who helped turn this manuscript into a book in record time. Stephanie McComb was great about turning around the needed contracts and files quickly. Lorna Gentry offered great development suggestions and helped trim back the fat to make it a lean, mean manuscript. Mark Hall made sure all the steps worked as advertised, and Julie McNamee and Krista Hansing tightened up the wording and made sure everything was consistent. Good job, everyone!

About the Technical Editor

Mark Hall has been a technical editor for the past 7 years, and has worked on more than 57 computer titles. Mark has a master's degree in computer science education and is a Novell Certified Network Engineer. He coauthored two books: *PC Magazine: Webmasters Ultimate Resource Guide* and *Windows NT RAS Server 4*. Mark has also written test banks for MCSE training guides for New Riders Publishing.

We'd Like to Hear from You!

Que Corporation has a long-standing reputation for high-quality books and products. To ensure your continued satisfaction, we also understand the importance of customer service and support.

Tech Support

If you need assistance with the information in this book or you have feedback for us about the book, please contact Macmillan Technical Support via email at support@mcp.com.

Orders, Catalogs, and Customer Service

To order other Que or Macmillan Computer Publishing books, catalogs, or products, please contact our Customer Service Department:

Phone: 1-800-858-7674

Order Line: 1-800-428-5331

Fax: 1-800-882-8583

International Fax: 1-317-228-4400

Or visit our online bookstore: http://www.mcp.com/.

CONGRATULATIONS ON CHOOSING Microsoft Home Essentials! If you're looking for versatile software that will handle what you need to do on your home PC, you've picked the right program. Home Essentials is exactly what you need.

Although Microsoft Office is the best-selling suite of applications for business, it's not always appropriate for home use. It contains dozens of expensive features that many home users will never need, and lacks such home-management basics as a home finance program.

Home Essentials is the right tool for the home. It contains the most-used component of Office—Word, the *word processor*—as well as several special programs geared specifically for the home. With Home Essentials, you're armed with the best available tools to tackle any computer project, from the family Christmas newsletter to your retirement planning.

Home Essentials Includes...

Microsoft put a lot of thought into the makeup of Home Essentials 98. It contains programs that you, the home user, said you wanted, and leaves out the stuff that you don't need. Here's what you get:

- **Word.** A full version of the #1 best-selling word processor in the world.

- **Works.** A fully integrated suite for home users, consisting of a *word processor*, a *spreadsheet program*, a *database program*, and a *communications program*.

- **Money.** A home financial management program that helps you keep your checkbook balanced and your stock prices updated, plus much more.

- **Internet Explorer.** A top-quality *Web browser*, so you can explore the online world of the Internet.

- **Greetings Workshop.** A really cool, easy-to-use program that creates greeting cards, posters, invitations, and more. (You'll want a color printer for this one.)

- **Encarta.** A full-service encyclopedia, complete with sound and video clips and interactive learning games.

- **Entertainment Pack: The Puzzle Collection.** Great non-violent brain-teasing puzzles that emphasize skill and thought, rather than shoot-em-up action.

About the Book

Home Essentials doesn't come with very much documentation—only one slim book about Word. For the rest of the programs, you're on your own, unless you want to read the online Help files (which can be somewhat awkward when you are trying to use the program at the same time). That's where this book comes in! It provides easy-to-follow step-by-step instructions for using all the important parts of Home Essentials. Here's what you'll find in the upcoming pages.

Part I covers Works, including all the main components. You'll discover how to use Works' simple but powerful word processor to create common documents, perform calculations and what-if analysis with the spreadsheet, and keep large quantities of data organized with the database. There's even a special section on using the components together—for example, to *merge* addresses from the database with form letters from the word processor. If you're a beginner to computing or word processing, Works is a great warm-up program.

Part II deals with Word, a very powerful, yet easy-to-use, word processor. You'll learn how to create and format documents, including sophisticated ones that include columns and graphics.

You'll even learn how to create your own Web page to establish your presence on the *Internet*.

In Part III, we'll tackle Money. You'll learn how to set up and track all your bank accounts, schedule payments, pay bills online, and plan for the future with Money's top-notch budgeting feature.

In Part IV, you'll learn about the Internet, featuring the Internet Explorer Web browser. If you have been curious about the Internet and are ready to see what it offers, you should pay special attention to this section!

Part V is a compilation of the best of the other Home Essentials components. We'll pay visits to Greetings Workshop and Encarta, I'll give you some tips for playing the games in the Entertainment Pack, and you'll see what the Essential Web Site has to offer.

Along the way, special hints and helps will keep you on track. Step-by-step sections lay out complex procedures in easy-to-follow numbered instructions.

This book contains a thorough index where tasks, features, and procedures are listed in a number of ways; you should be able to find the information you seek, whether or not you look under the "proper" term for that item.

Conventions Used in This Book

Commands, directions, and explanations in this book are presented in the clearest format possible. The following items are some of the features that will make this book easier for you to use:

- *Menu and dialog box commands and options.* You can easily find the onscreen menu and dialog box commands by looking for bold text like you see in this direction: Open the **File** menu and click **Save**.

- *Hotkeys for commands.* The underlined keys onscreen that activate commands and options are also underlined in the book as shown in the preceding example.

- *Combination and shortcut keystrokes.* Text that directs you to hold down several keys simultaneously is connected with a plus sign (+), such as Ctrl+P.

- *Graphical icons with the commands they execute.* Look for icons like this ✂ in text and steps. These indicate buttons onscreen that you can click to accomplish the procedure.

- *Cross-references.* If there's a related topic that is prerequisite to the section or steps you are reading, or a topic that builds further on what you are reading, you'll find the cross-reference to it after the steps or at the end of the section like this:

SEE ALSO

➤ *To learn how to install Greetings Workshop, see page 524.*

- *Glossary terms.* For all the terms that appear in the glossary, you'll find the first appearance of that term in the text in *italic* along with its definition.

- *Sidebars.* Information related to the task at hand, or "inside" information from the author, is offset in sidebars as not to interfere with the task at hand and to make it easy to find this valuable information. Each of these sidebars has a short title to help you quickly identify the information you'll find there. You'll find the same type of information in these that you might find in notes, tips, or warnings in other books, but here the titles should be more informative.

Your screen may look slightly different from some of the examples in this book. This is due to various options during installation and because of hardware setup.

Anything Else?

That's really all you need to know to get started! Armed with this book and Home Essentials, you're all set with the best tools available. So get ready to tackle your home computing projects with confidence!

Using Works

Introducing Microsoft Works

Starting and exiting Works

Using the Help system

Navigating the Task Launcher window

Understanding TaskWizards

What Is Microsoft Works?

Many home users have found that Works is all the software they need. Microsoft Works is an integrated software program that combines several capabilities into one easy-to-use interface. There's a word processor, a spreadsheet, a database, and a communications program. These programs, or *Works tools,* can be used separately or together to help you perform tasks.

SEE ALSO

➤ *For information on how to integrate the work you perform in the various Works tools, see page 149.*

Each program, or tool, is designed to perform a specific function:

- Use the Word Processor to write letters or other documents.

- Use the Spreadsheet tool to create documents that contain numbers in rows and columns, and to perform calculations on those numbers.

- Use the Database tool to keep track of lists of names and addresses or inventoried objects.

- Use the Communications tool to communicate with another computer, sending and receiving files (if you have a modem connected to your computer and if you have the rights to access the other computer).

Figure 1.1 shows the Works Task Launcher dialog box with the descriptions of the four tools found in Microsoft Works.

Program dèjá vu

Although Microsoft Works calls them *tools,* the Word Processing, Spreadsheet, and Database functions of Works are actually scaled-down computer programs that fall in the software program categories of *word processing, spreadsheet,* and *database.* Their function and design follow the basic function and design of other programs in the same category. For example, the Microsoft Works Word Processing tool is a similar program to Microsoft Word and Lotus WordPro. The Microsoft Works Spreadsheet tool is a similar program to Microsoft Excel and Lotus 1,2,3 spreadsheet programs. Basic skills that you will learn in these programs apply to other word-processing, database, and spreadsheet programs.

FIGURE 1.1

Microsoft Works has four tools that can work independently or together.

Starting Works

You can start Works in either of two ways:

- Double-click the **Works** shortcut icon on your desktop, if one is there. (When you ran the installation program, you were given the option of placing this shortcut.)

- Click the **Start** button, and then point to **P**rograms, and then **Microsoft Works**. Click on the **Microsoft Works** icon.

SEE ALSO

➢ *If you haven't installed Works yet, refer to page 523.*

Either way, the first thing you see is the Microsoft Works Task Launcher dialog box appears, as shown in Figure 1.2. The Task Launcher is the master control for Works. It provides an easy-to-use menu that displays all Works features in one window.

First time?

The first time you start Works, you'll see a box asking whether you want to see a demo of Works. Click **OK** to see it, and then return to this book when you're finished, or click **Cancel** to skip it. You can run the demo later by choosing **Help, Introduction to Works** from within any Works tool.

FIGURE 1.2
The Works Task Launcher greets you each time you start Works.

Understanding the Works Task Launcher

There are three tabs on the Task Launcher:

- **Tas_kWizards**. These mini-programs assist you in performing your task. For example, you can use the Letter TaskWizard to help you write a professional-looking letter.

SEE ALSO

➢ *TaskWizards are covered in more detail on page 13.*

Dialog box tabs

Tabs such as the ones in Figure 1.2 are common among Windows dialog boxes. Each tab page displays different options you can apply. To see the contents of a tab, click once on the tab name.

- **Existing Documents**. This tab displays a list of the documents you have created and saved. If you are using Works for the first time, this window will be empty. When you create Works documents you can reopen them by double-clicking on the document in the list.

- **Works Tools**. Through this tab you can access the Word Processor, Spreadsheet, or Database tools without the help of Wizards. This enables you to create your own documents without assistance, but it requires some knowledge in using these types of programs. The Communications tool is also accessed from this page and does have Wizards to help you in sending and receiving files to and from other computers.

These tabs look and act like an index tab in a notebook, and each contains different selections.

To view the selections on each tabbed page, click once on the tab. That tabbed page will then appear in front of the other tabbed pages.

Exiting Works

To exit Works, click the **Exit Works** button found in the Task Launcher, if the Task Launcher is displayed. If you are working with one of the Works tools, you can also exit by opening the **File** menu and choosing **Exit Works**.

An experienced Windows user may try to exit Works while the Task Launcher is displayed either by using the **Exit Works** option on the **File** menu or by clicking the **Close** button in the upper-right corner of the Window. However, these methods won't work if the Task Launcher is showing. That's because the Task Launcher is a dialog box, and a Windows dialog box must be closed before you can access the windows and menus behind it.

Getting Help

Help is on the way. There are a variety of ways to get help in Works, so you can access the Help system in whatever way works best for you. Let's take a look at the choices.

Using the What's This? Feature

The What's This? feature offers quick assistance for dialog box controls. Because the Works program starts with a dialog box (the Task Launcher), it's a good place to start checking out the Help system. When you activate What's This?, a pop-up window displays a short description of the dialog box control that you point to with your mouse.

Using What's This? Help

1. Click the **?** icon located in the upper-right corner of the Task Launcher dialog box. A question mark appears next to the mouse pointer (see Figure 1.3).

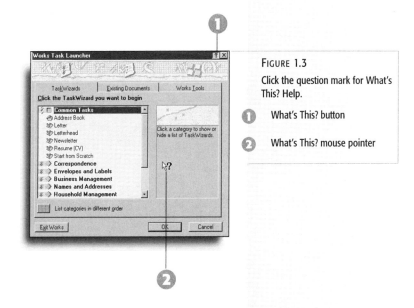

FIGURE 1.3

Click the question mark for What's This? Help.

1   What's This? button

2   What's This? mouse pointer

2. Click any list item, button, or area of the dialog box. A short description of that option or item is displayed, as shown in Figure 1.4.

3. To clear the screen of the Help box description, click outside the Help box anywhere on the screen, or press the Esc key.

FIGURE 1.4

What's This? describes the Common Tasks category.

Using the Help Menu

What's quicker than What's This?

In some cases, you can right-click a dialog box area, option, or list, and the Help box description activates. Another quick method is to press the **F1** key. The F1 key activates a description for whatever is currently highlighted in the dialog box.

To access the Help Menu, the Task Launcher dialog box must be closed. To close it, click the **Cancel** button. The Works Help window automatically appears, showing a list of topics for commonly used tasks such as how to create a document, how to open an existing document, and so on.

To access the Help Menu (and for more detailed help information), click **Help** on the menu bar or press Alt+H. The menu drops down, as shown in Figure 1.5.

FIGURE 1.5

The Help menu lists your help choices.

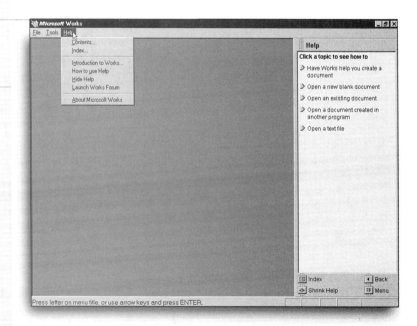

After you click the menu selection you want, a dialog box, window, or program will appear with the information you have requested. The following sections explain the primary Help features—Contents and Index. Table 1.1 lists some of the additional ones you may want to try out on your own.

TABLE 1.1 **Other help menu commands**

Menu Selection	Description
Introduction to Works	Activates a 10-minute introductory tour of Microsoft Works.
How to _use_ Help	Opens a Help Window with a list of Help features. Click an item in the list to learn more about that item.
_H_ide Help	Closes Help windows (but not dialog boxes).
_L_aunch Works Forum	Launches your Web browser and dials into the Works Forum at Microsoft.
_A_bout Microsoft Works	Displays the About dialog box, which contains information about the version of Works you are using and copyright information.

Using the Contents Feature

The Contents feature of Works helps lists the available help topics by category. It's most useful when you don't know the exact name of what you're trying to do, but you know in a general way what it's about. For example, suppose you want to know how to preview the printout onscreen before you actually print your document, but you don't know that this feature is called Print Preview. You could explore the Help system by topic and find the information fairly easily.

Exploring Help contents

1. Open the **Help** menu and select **Contents.** The Help Topics: Microsoft Works dialog box appears.

2. Expand a Help topic category by clicking it. A list of topics displays under the category, with file folder icons for each topic. Click a file folder once to expand the topic, as shown in Figure 1.6.

FIGURE 1.6

Click a folder to expand it.

1 Category

2 Folders

3 The Works help window

3. Continue opening file folders until you see a subject represented by a document icon, as shown in Figure 1.7. You can use the scroll bar to scroll through the menu choices. Click the document icon, and the Help information appears in the Help Window on the right of your screen (see Figure 1.7).

4. Expand as many file folders as you want, and read the documents in them. To collapse file folders, click the opened folder.

Using the Index Feature

The Index feature of Help enables you to type a word or phrase and search the Help file for that word or phrase. As with Contents, you don't necessarily have to know the proper or technical phrase for your topic to find it. For example, if you didn't know how to change the way paragraphs align on your page, you could search for *paragraphs*, or even *changing*.

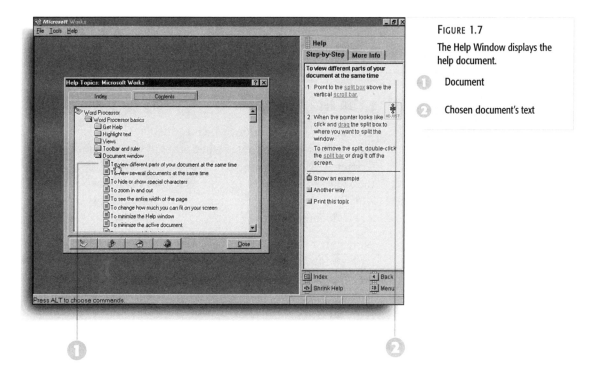

FIGURE 1.7
The Help Window displays the help document.

1   Document

2   Chosen document's text

Looking up a Help topic in the Help index

1. Choose **Help** and select **Index**.

2. Type the word you want to search for in the text box, as shown in Figure 1.8. As you type, the index entries in the bottom of the screen change, matching the word you type as closely as possible.

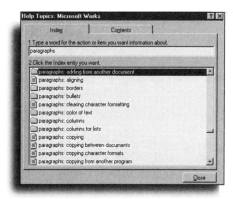

FIGURE 1.8
Use the Index feature of Help to search for particular topics.

3. Click the index entry you want to see. Works displays the selected topic information in the Help window.

4. To close the Index feature, click the **Close** button.

Using the Help Window

The Works Help window, which is the big window on the right side of the screen, activates when you are working in the Contents or Index features of Help. It displays the contents of the Help topics you choose. The Help window also activates when you do certain procedures for the first time, such as create a new document.

Notice that there are two tabs in the Help window. The Step-by-Step tab lists the steps necessary to perform a task. For example, Figure 1.9 shows the instructions found on the Step-by-Step tab page when the **To highlight text** document is selected in the Contents page of Help. The More Info tab contains overview, troubleshooting, and other information related to your topic. The Help window can also contain *hypertext* (green, underlined text). You will see a pop-up description of the word in hypertext when you click it.

The Help window is great, but it does take up quite a bit of the screen space. To minimize it, click the **Shrink Help** icon. When you minimize the Help window, you see two icons on the far right of the Works Windows: the Shrink Help button and the Index button. To restore the Help window, click again on the **Shrink Help** icon. Restoring the Window restores the last topic you viewed in the window.

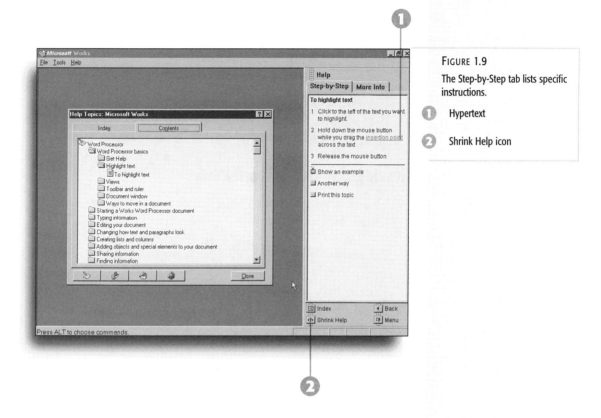

FIGURE 1.9
The Step-by-Step tab lists specific instructions.

1   Hypertext

2   Shrink Help icon

Using the Works TaskWizards

Have you ever wanted a personal secretary? With Works, you sort of have one in the TaskWizard feature. TaskWizards are the heart of the Works program. They do a lot of the upfront work for you in creating a new document so that you can create professional-looking results, even if you have little or no experience.

The TaskWizards page in the Works Task Launcher lists categories for types of tasks you can do with Works. Each task that you select runs a *wizard*, a Microsoft term for a mini-program that assists you in performing your task. For example, when you select Letterhead from the list of tasks, Works starts a program comprised of a series of questions that you must answer. The answers you provide instruct the program, and the program then designs the letterhead for you.

Viewing the TaskWizards Tab

When you first launch Works and click the TaskWizards tab, you'll see the wizards listed by category. To view a category's contents, click once on the icon on the left of the category, as shown in Figure 1.10. This expands the category. To collapse the category, click its icon again. If you'd like to change the way the Tasks are ordered in the list, click the **List categories in different order** button, and select a new ordering system—by category, by alphabetical order, by the most recently used task, or by the document type.

FIGURE 1.10

Categories can be expanded and collapsed by clicking their icons.

1 Expanded category

2 Collapsed category

3 Click here to choose a new ordering system

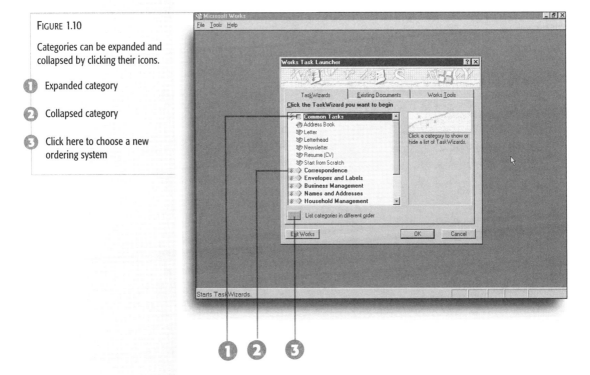

Icons found to the left of the document names indicate which Works tool will be used to create that document (see Table 1.2).

TABLE 1.2 Document type icons

	Word processing
	Spreadsheet
	Database

When you click one of the icons, a brief explanation of what you can do with that wizard appears in the right pane of the TaskWizards tab, as shown in Figure 1.11.

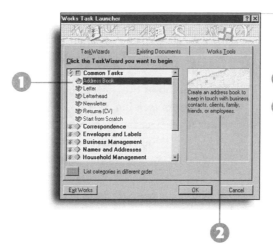

FIGURE 1.11

Select a wizard icon to learn more about it.

① Click a wizard icon

② A brief explanation of the wizard

TaskWizards, wizards, tasks

Much of what you can do in Works can be done in a TaskWizard. Throughout this book, you'll find the TaskWizards also referred to as Wizards, or simply Tasks. They all have the same meaning.

Document definition

In Works, a *document* is any data file you create: a word-processing project, a spreadsheet, or a database.

Starting a New Document

Starting a TaskWizard is easy—just double-click on the one you want. The TaskWizard starts, and you fill in the blanks and follow the directions to complete the document.

To start a blank document of whatever type you want (word processor, spreadsheet, or database), click the **Works Tools** tab in the Task Launcher (see Figure 1.12), and then click the button corresponding to the type you want.

FIGURE 1.12

Use the Works Tools tab to strike out boldly on your own with a blank document.

Opening an Existing Document

The final tab in the Task Launcher dialog box is **Existing Documents** (see Figure 1.13). We haven't talked too much about it yet because you probably don't have any existing documents yet if you are just starting out in Works. Keep in mind for future reference, however, that whenever you create a document

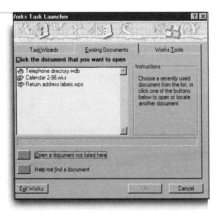

FIGURE 1.13

Double-click an existing document to reopen it.

in Works and save it, its name appears on this Existing Documents tab, and you can reopen it by double-clicking on its name there. Figure 1.13 shows an Existing Documents list with a few saved documents on it, so you can see what you'll be encountering later.

Now you have a basic idea of how Works works—at least the general, "lobby" portion of it. In the next chapter, we'll dive into the most popular tool in Works, the word processor. You'll pick up some essential skills that will carry you through not only the Word Processor but also the Spreadsheet and Database tools.

Task Launcher redux

Here's another little tip to file away for later use. From within any of the Works tools, you can close the tool to return to the Task Launcher. But you can also leave the tool that you're working with open and return to the Task Launcher to start a second, third, or fourth document (or however many you can juggle at once). Just click the **Task Launcher** button on the toolbar in the application with which you're working. You'll get a closer look at toolbars in the next chapter, but for now, just remember this button:

 Task Launcher icon

Introducing the Works Word Processor

Understanding the word processor controls

Typing and editing text

Creating a letter with a TaskWizard

Saving and printing your work

Checking your spelling

Launching the Word Processor

With the Works *word processor*, you can create all kinds of interesting documents, including reports, letters, résumés, envelopes, and so on. The method you use for starting the word processor depends largely on what you want to do with it after it's started. Starting from the Task Launcher (opening screen) in Works, your choices include the following:

- To start a new, blank document, click the **Works Tools** tab and then click the **Word Processor** button. A blank page appears in the word processor, as shown in Figure 2.1.

- To open an existing word processing document, click the **Existing Documents** tab and then double-click the document you want to open.

- To start a new document based on a TaskWizard, click the **TaskWizards** tab and then double-click the TaskWizard you want to use.

To follow along with the lessons in this chapter, you should create a new document. Your new document will look like Figure 2.1.

Here's what you're looking at as you stare at your screen or at Figure 2.1:

- *Title bar.* This bar displays the name of the open document and the word processor's Minimize, Maximize/Restore, and Close (**X**) buttons (in the top-right corner).

- *Menu bar.* A collection of menus that contains commands for doing everything from saving your document to changing fonts.

- *Toolbar.* This bar holds Works' tools—shortcut buttons that act in place of menu commands.

- *Margin guidelines.* These faint lines show the document's margin boundaries. A separate boundary marks the page header.

Hide the Help

If you still have that large Help window covering the right third of your screen, click the **Shrink Help** button at the bottom to get it out of the way.

Optional ruler

You can display a ruler across the top of the document window to help you set margins and lay out your document. To display the ruler, open the **View** menu and choose **Ruler**. (You can turn it off again just as easily with the same command.)

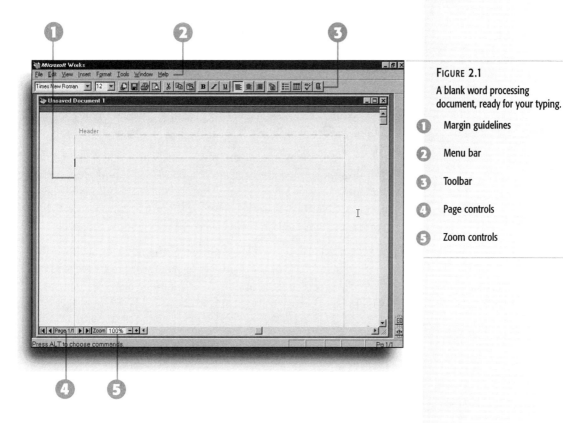

- *Zoom controls.* The zoom in (+) and zoom out (-) buttons control the amount of the document displayed in the Works window; zoom controls don't affect the size of the actual document.

- *Page controls.* Use these to jump quickly among pages in a large document. The arrow buttons move one page at a time; the arrow/line buttons move to the beginning or end of the document.

SEE ALSO

➤ *To learn more about the TaskWizards, see page 32.*

➤ *To insert headers and footers in Works documents, see page 61.*

Working with Menus

Most of the commands you issue in Works can be chosen from the menu system. The menus are organized into eight categories (**File**, **Edit**, and so on), each represented by a word on the menu bar. Click the menu name (for example, **File**) to open a menu of commands. Then select the command you want by clicking it.

Menu items may appear dimmed (sometimes called grayed out) at different times during the document-creation process. When a menu command is dimmed, it means that particular command is unavailable for use at the moment. Figure 2.2 shows the **Edit** menu, which contains some dimmed commands.

Take a few minutes to look at each of the menus in the word processor. Many of the commands are similar to those in the Works spreadsheet program. These similar menu structures make Works easy to learn and use.

Mouseless menus

To open a menu without using the mouse, hold down the Alt key and press and release the underlined letter in the menu name. Many menus also display key combinations next to some of the commands. You can use these shortcut keys in place of opening the menu. For example, instead of opening the **File** menu and choosing **Save**, you can press Ctrl+S.

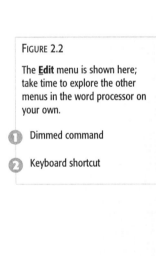

FIGURE 2.2

The **Edit** menu is shown here; take time to explore the other menus in the word processor on your own.

1 Dimmed command

2 Keyboard shortcut

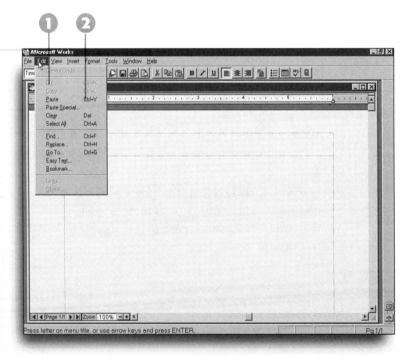

The Word Processor Toolbar

The word processor toolbar contains buttons that represent the most commonly used menu commands (many of the same buttons are found on all Works toolbars). Some of the buttons, such as the ones that control Bold, Italic, and Underline formatting, work like toggle switches; One click turns a feature on, a second click turns it off (when a *toggle button* is switched on, it looks like it's pressed in on the toolbar). Other toolbar buttons, such as **Save** and **Spell Check**, open a dialog box. Still others, such as the ones that control paragraph alignment, all work as a group; one of them is always on, and if you select another, the first one turns off.

The first two tools on the toolbar are *drop-down lists*. To see the list of alternatives, click the drop-down arrow. When you select an item from the list, it becomes the current setting, and it appears in the box to the left of the drop-down arrow. Figure 2.3 shows the Works word processor toolbar with one of these drop-down lists open.

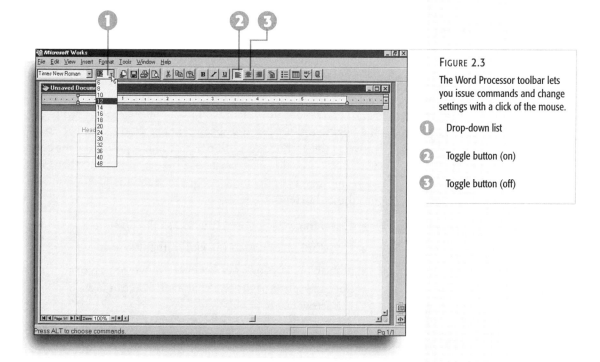

FIGURE 2.3

The Word Processor toolbar lets you issue commands and change settings with a click of the mouse.

1. Drop-down list

2. Toggle button (on)

3. Toggle button (off)

Typing Text

Typing begins at the *cursor*, also known as the *insertion point*. It's the short vertical line you see blinking on your blank page.

Some typing basics:

- Don't press Enter when your text is approaching the right margin. A feature called *Word Wrap* automatically moves your text to the next line when you reach the margin. Press Enter to start a new paragraph or to separate items in a vertical list.

- Use the arrow keys or the scrollbars (not Enter or Backspace or the Spacebar) to move around your page. The Enter key inserts a blank line every time you press it, the Spacebar inserts a blank space, and Backspace deletes a space or character.

- The Delete key erases the text to the right of the cursor.

- The Backspace key erases the text to the left of the cursor.

- Don't use letters (lowercase "l" and uppercase "o") in place of numbers. Works can't figure out that you intend for the letters "lO" to represent the number 10.

Moving Around in a Document

As you type your document, you may want to move quickly to the beginning of a previous paragraph, go to the next page, or move to the end of a line. To navigate and reposition your cursor within your document, you can use the scrollbars and then click your mouse on the document to place your cursor. You can also use these shortcuts:

- Ctrl+Home takes you to the top of the document.
- Ctrl+End takes you to the end of the document.
- The arrow keys on your keyboard move you up or down one line, and left or right one character. You can press and hold the arrow key to scroll.

- Press the Ctrl key while pressing the arrows, and you move up or down one full paragraph, and left or right one full word.

- The Home key takes you to the beginning of the line you're on.

- The End key takes you to the end of the line you're on.

- Press Page Up or Page Down to move up or down one full screen (a full screen doesn't always correspond to one printed page).

- Press Ctrl+G to open the Go To dialog box, and enter the page number to which you want to go. This feature works only on documents of more than one page.

You also can use the Page controls (bottom-left corner of the screen) to move through your document. The Page controls show you which page you're on and how many total pages exist. The Page controls buttons move you to the beginning of your document, one page up, one page down, or to the end of the document.

Positioning Your Cursor

Your cursor marks the place in the document where your keyboard actions—typing text, pressing Delete, pressing Enter, and so on—take effect. Using the scrollbars to view another section of your document does not move your cursor to a new insertion point. If you scroll to another section of the document, you must click your mouse in the new location to place your cursor there. Make sure you can see your cursor before you begin typing; otherwise, you may be adding or deleting text in the wrong place in your document.

Many beginners become frustrated when they try to use the arrow keys to move their cursor below the final line of text. Remember that the document ends at the last insertion point. To move below the last line of text, you need to press the Enter key to move the insertion point down. Every time you press the

Enter key, you insert a blank line and move your insertion point down two lines.

Editing Text

Typing text is only half the battle—you then have to read what you've written, realize that it's not quite right, and change your mind. At that point, you're ready to edit your document. To change a word or short phrase, you can just reposition the cursor, use the Backspace or Delete keys to remove the words you don't want, and then type your changes. To change more than a few words, however, take advantage of the Works word processor's more powerful editing features.

Selecting Text

Before you can act on blocks of typed text—whether that action is formatting, deleting, moving, or whatever—you must select the text. A big mistake that beginners often make is to forget to select the text they want to change. The word processor's editing features require the same structure as a common sentence: To structure an edit, you must define both a subject (what you're changing) and a verb (what action you desire).

You can select text with your mouse, the keyboard, or a combination of the two. When selecting text with the mouse, your mouse pointer will change depending on its location in the word processor window:

- When your mouse is within your existing text, the mouse pointer looks like a capital I, and is called an *I-beam*. You can use this pointer for selecting smaller portions of text, such as a word within a sentence, or a sentence within a paragraph.

- The mouse pointer turns to a right-pointing arrow when it's in the left margin of your document window. Use this mouse pointer for selecting large areas of text such as entire lines or paragraphs.

- Your mouse returns to a standard left-pointing arrow when it's on the menus, toolbar, scrollbars, or page/view controls.

Whether your mouse is an I-beam or a right-pointing arrow, clicking your mouse can select text:

- To select a single word, point to the word and double-click.
- To select a line of text, place your mouse pointer in the left margin next to the line and click once.
- To select an entire paragraph, place your mouse pointer in the left margin next to the paragraph and double-click.

To select text with the keyboard, use the Shift key and the arrow keys together:

- Use the Shift key with the left and right arrows to select text one character at a time.
- Press Ctrl+Shift plus the left or right arrows to select entire words.
- Use Shift with the up and down arrows to select text one line at a time.
- Press Ctrl+Shift plus the up or down arrows to select entire paragraphs.

If you want to add more text to text that you selected with either the mouse or the keyboard, press the Shift key and click the mouse at the end of the additional text you want to select.

Introducing the Clipboard

We're going to talk about moving and copying text momentarily, but to understand those processes, you need to understand the Clipboard. The *Clipboard* is a temporary holding area in your computer's memory. The Clipboard enables you to move or copy text, graphics, or data from one document to another, from one file to another, and from one application to another.

It works like this: When you select text and then issue either the **Cut** or **Copy** command, the material is placed on the Clipboard. Then you reposition your cursor and issue the **Paste** command, and whatever is on the Clipboard appears at the cursor.

Some "ground rules" for the Clipboard include

- You can place only one selection on the Clipboard at a time. When you place a new selection on the Clipboard, the previous selection is removed from its memory.

- You can use the Clipboard to move or copy between different Windows–based programs. You aren't restricted to just using the clipboard in Works; for example, you can copy text from Works and paste it into Microsoft Word or into an email program.

- Exiting Windows empties the Clipboard. If you accidentally exit Windows or shut down your computer, you will lose whatever is stored in the Clipboard. However, exiting an individual Windows program such as Works does not disturb the Clipboard contents.

Moving and Copying Text

Moving and copying are closely related. The only difference is that with moving, the original gets deleted, whereas with copying, the original stays put. You can move or copy selected text to another location in your current document, to another document, or to a completely different application.

No "Move" command exists per se; moving is a combination of two commands: **Cut** and **Paste**. You cut the selection from its original location and paste it into its new home, effectively moving it. When you copy, you issue the **Copy** command to copy the selection to the Clipboard, and then the **Paste** command to put the copy where you want it.

Moving or copying text

1. Select the text you want to move or copy.

2. Open the **Edit** menu, and then choose **Cut** to move or **Copy** to copy, or click the Cut button 🔲 or the Copy 🔲 button on the toolbar.

3. Position your cursor where you want to insert the selection (the target location). If your target location is in another

document, open the document and place your cursor where you want to insert the Clipboard's contents.

4. Open the **Edit** menu and choose **Paste**, or click the Paste button  on the toolbar.

Using Undo

You can reverse your last action with the Works **Undo** command. Open the **Edit** menu and choose **Undo Editing** or press Ctrl+Z. As soon as you've undone an action, that action will appear on the **Edit** menu as an action that you can **Redo**.

If you've just made a mistake, *you must use **Undo** immediately*. The **Undo** command applies only to the last action you took.

Finding and Replacing Text

Whether it's your car keys or a bit of text you've lost, it can be frustrating not to find what you're looking for. Fortunately, you can search for a particular word or phrase in your Works document to assist you with proofreading, and you can replace the text you find with another word or phrase.

Finding text in a document

1. Open the **Edit** menu and choose **Find** or press Ctrl+F. The Find dialog box opens (see Figure 2.4).

2. In the **Fi<u>n</u>d what** text box, enter the text you're looking for; then, click **Find Next**.

FIGURE 2.4

Use the Find dialog box to search for particular words and phrases.

3. If the text you're looking for appears more than once in the document, click **Find Next** again to go to the next occurrence.

4. When you've come to the last occurrence of the text, you will be prompted, Works did not find a match. Click **OK**, and then click **Cancel** in the Find dialog box.

Sometimes you just want to find things, but more often you want to find with a purpose: so that you can replace one thing with something else. For example, suppose that your company changed its name from Acme Corporation to Friendly Foods Corporation. You could use the Replace feature in Works to change all instances of the old name to the new name.

Replacing text

1. Open the **E**dit menu and choose **Replace** or press Ctrl+H; the Replace dialog box opens (see Figure 2.5).

2. In the **Fi**nd what box, enter the text you want to find.

3. Press Tab or click your mouse in the **Re**place with box. Enter the replacement text exactly as you want it to appear in the document.

Start at the top

If you start the Find program in the middle of your document, Works will stop at the end and ask you if you want to start looking again at the beginning of the document. To avoid this extra step, make sure your cursor is at the top of the document before you begin the Find process. You can get to the top of the document quickly by pressing Crtl+Home.

FIGURE 2.5

Use the Replace dialog box to replace one text string with another.

4. If you want to replace every occurrence of the text without seeing each one, click **Replace A**ll. Clicking **Replace** instead enables you to review each of the found items in case you don't want to replace all of them. To skip an item, click **Fi**nd **Next**.

5. When you're finished, click the **Cancel** button to close the dialog box.

As you may have already noticed, we haven't talked about all the controls in the Find and Replace dialog boxes yet. You can use the **Match** c**ase** check box to specify that your search match the case of the text that you enter in the **Fi**nd **what** box, and you can **Find** w**hole words only**. For example, a search that uses both of these options would keep you from finding "candy" when you're looking for "Andy."

You can also find and replace *tabs* and *paragraph codes* in your document by clicking the **Tab** (the arrow) and **Paragraph** (the paragraph symbol) buttons in the Find dialog box (Paragraph codes appear wherever you press Enter). The Tab code appears as ^T, and the Paragraph code appears as ^P.

Using Easy Text

Easy Text is a Works feature that can save you time typing words, phrases, or entire paragraphs that you use often. For example, if you use the same closing paragraph in all your business letters, you can save the paragraph as Easy Text and never have to type it again.

Create Easy Text

1. Type the name, phrase, or paragraph you want to save as Easy Text, and select the text.

2. Open the **Insert** menu and choose **Easy Text**. From the submenu, choose **New Easy Text**.

3. In the Easy Text dialog box, enter a short name for your Easy Text, such as "address" for your return address. You can see your selected text in the **Easy Text contents** box (see Figure 2.6).

4. Click **Done** to create your Easy Text and close the dialog box.

Viewing codes

You can choose to see tab, paragraph, and space mark codes onscreen by opening the **View** menu and choosing **All Characters**. These symbols (arrows for tabs, paragraph marks for hard returns, and dots for spaces) don't print, they just appear onscreen.

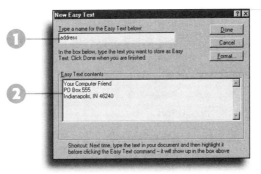

FIGURE 2.6

Create Easy Text from frequently used words, phrases, and paragraphs.

1 Easy Text name

2 Text it represents

To use your Easy Text, place your cursor where you want your text to appear, type the name you gave it, and press the F3 key (a quick alternative to opening the Insert menu, choosing Easy Text, and then choosing the name from the submenu).

Using the TaskWizard to Create a Basic Letter

As you know from our discussion in Chapter 1, "Introducing Microsoft Works," Works provides a variety of *TaskWizards* for common jobs. The Letter TaskWizard is one that most people will find useful because almost everyone has to write letters at one time or another.

Creating a letter with a TaskWizard

1. If the Task Launcher dialog box isn't currently displayed, click the Task Launcher button 🖻 on the toolbar to make it appear.

2. On the Task Launcher's **TaskWizards** tab, look in the **Common Tasks** category for **Letter**. (Click the **Common Tasks** category if needed, to open its list of tasks.) Then double-click **Letter** to select the wizard and close the Task Launcher.

3. The TaskWizard begins by offering you three types of letters: **Professional, Simple**, and **Formal** (see Figure 2.7). As you click each one, you see a brief description of that particular type of letter as well as a sample. Choose the **Professional** letter, and click **Next**.

4. In the next dialog box, shown in Figure 2.8, a series of five buttons offers you the chance to customize the letterhead, address, content, text style, and extras such as typist's initials and enclosure note. Click each of these buttons in turn to open additional controls, and plug in your answers for each prompt.

5. When you are finished with the controls in Figure 2.8, click **Create It!** The Wizard's Checklist appears, showing your choices.

Extra dialog box

When you run any TaskWizard, an extra Works Task Launcher dialog box appears that asks whether you want to run the TaskWizard or open an existing document. Choose **Yes, Run the TaskWizard** to continue with your task. If you don't want to see this dialog box every time you run a TaskWizard, deselect the **Always Display This Message** option.

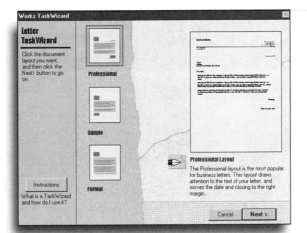

FIGURE 2.7

Choose the letter style that you prefer.

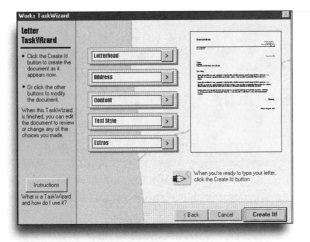

FIGURE 2.8

Click any of the TaskWizard's modification buttons to work with additional controls.

6. Click **Create Document** to accept the choices shown, or click **Return to Wizard** to go back to the wizard screen shown in Figure 2.8 and make some changes. When you click **Create Document**, the Wizard begins building the letter, and the resulting document opens in a new window (see Figure 2.9).

7. You can edit and customize the letter as you would any Works word processing document. You'll see some extra instructions at the bottom of the letter; make sure you read and then delete these before printing.

FIGURE 2.9

A letter created by the Letter TaskWizard contains standardized formatting.

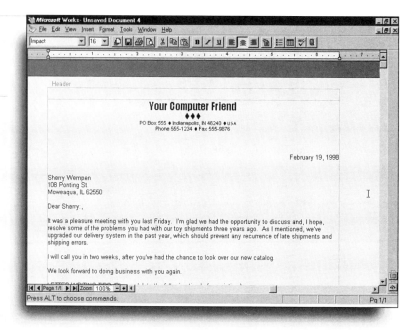

Running Spell Check

You can check your document for misspelled words by using the Works Spelling Check program. A spelling check can be performed at any point in your editing process and can be done more than once. You can add your own words, such as people's names, peculiar terminology, and abbreviations to the Works dictionary.

Proofread!

Spell-checking programs work on the basis of a spelling dictionary: If a word doesn't appear in that dictionary, Works flags it as a spelling error. It may not be an error though–it could be a proper name or jargon particular to your industry. Also, a spell checker will not catch misused words if they are spelled correctly (such as "form" when you meant "from"). It won't catch punctuation errors, either. You still need to proofread!

Checking your document's spelling

1. With your document open onscreen, open the **Tools** menu and choose **Spelling** or click the Spell Check button on the Standard toolbar.

   The Spelling dialog box opens and Works displays the first word that it doesn't find in its internal dictionary in the **Change to** box. A list of alternate spellings appears in the **Suggestions** box. Figure 2.10 shows the Spelling dialog box.

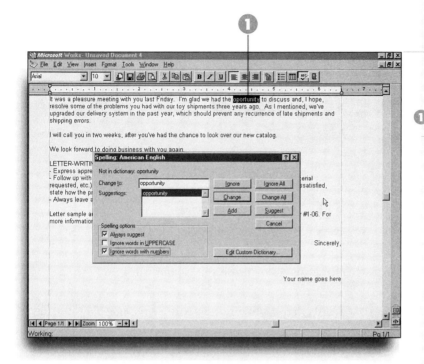

FIGURE 2.10
The Spelling dialog box identifies
words that may be misspelled.

1   Found word

2. Choose from any of the following options:

   • If one of the suggestions is appropriate, select it from
     the list and click **Change.** Click **Change All** if you've
     used the word more than once.

   • If none of the suggestions is appropriate or no sugges-
     tions are offered, type your own correction in the
     Change to box. Click **Change** or **Change All**.

   • If the word is spelled correctly, click **Ignore** or **Ignore
     All.** Choose **Ignore All** if all instances of the word
     should be ignored.

   • If the word is spelled correctly and you know you'll be
     using it in future documents, click **Add**. This will add
     the word to the Works custom dictionary, preventing it
     from appearing as misspelled the next time you use it.

   • To set up how the spelling check works, you can select
     one of the three **Spelling options** in the lower-left area
     of the dialog box.

3. When the spelling check is completed, a dialog box appears telling you Spelling check is finished. Click **OK** to return to your document.

Using the Thesaurus

You can use the Thesaurus to look up alternative words (synonyms) or words you feel you're using too often, and to get a word's definition by looking at other words that mean the same thing.

Finding a synonym with the Thesaurus

1. Select the word you want to look up.

2. Open the **Tools** menu and choose **Thesaurus**. The Thesaurus dialog box displays your word, and two lists:

   • A list of potential meanings for your word appears on the left. In Figure 2.11 you see the meanings for the word "opportunity."

   • A list of synonyms (alternate words) appears on the right in the **Replace with synonym** box. Depending on which meaning you choose, the list of synonyms changes.

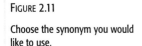

FIGURE 2.11

Choose the synonym you would like to use.

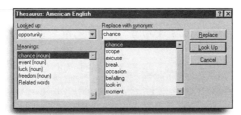

Thesaurus as dictionary

You can also use the Thesaurus to look up the meaning of a word of which you aren't sure. Just type the word and select it, and then open the Thesaurus. Note the meanings that appear, and then click **Cancel** to close the Thesaurus without making a change.

3. If multiple meanings exist for the word, choose the one that's appropriate for your context from the **Meanings** list.

4. Click the word you want to use from the **Replace with synonym** box.

5. Click **Replace**.

You can also use the Thesaurus to look up words that aren't in a document. In an open document with no text selected, open the

Tools menu and choose **Thesaurus**. In the dialog box, type the word you want to look up in the **Replace with synonym** box, and click **Look Up.** The word you inserted moves to the **Looked up** box. A list of meanings appears on the left, accompanied by synonyms on the right.

Handling Your Document Files

When you exit from Works, the valuable work you have done is lost forever—unless you save it to disk. That's why it's important to master the skills of saving, opening, and closing files before you go much further.

Saving a Document

It's a good idea to save your document as soon as you start typing it. Don't wait until you've finished the entire document. Too many things can happen while you're working—a power outage or some computer hardware malfunction—and you could lose your work.

Saving your work for the first time

1. From the **File** menu, choose **Save As**.

2. The **Save As** dialog box opens (see Figure 2.12), asking you to name your file and choose a location to store it.

FIGURE 2.12

Give your file a name that you will recognize later.

3. From the **Save in** box, choose the folder in which you want to save your file. You may need to open the drop-down list and choose a different drive.

Folder changing?

Don't be too eager to change the folder in step 3. Beginners do best when they save all their work to the same location, and the default one is as good as any.

4. In the **File name** box, type a descriptive name for your document. Although Windows 95 enables you to use up to 255 characters (including spaces) for a filename, keep your filenames short and relevant. This will make it easier to find them later. If you're going to share files with someone who doesn't use Windows 95, try to limit the name to eight characters.

5. Click the **Save** button. Your document is saved, and you can continue working on it. Notice that the title bar of your Works window has changed. It now displays the filename you just assigned to the file.

As you continue to work on your document, you must save your changes and additions. You have three options for updating your saved file to include any modifications: clicking the Save button 🖫 on the toolbar, opening the **File** menu and choosing **Save**, or pressing Ctrl+S.

To save your file and give it a different name or save it to a new location, open the **File** menu and choose **Save As**. This will open the Save As dialog box again, and you can assign a new name or choose a new folder or drive location for your file. Saving with a new name creates a new version of your file, and the original file is left intact. The latest changes become part of the new file, and the original file is closed.

Closing a Document

If you're ready to close Works and close your document at the same time, go ahead and exit from Works. You don't need to close the document separately. But there may be times when you want to close a document and then stay in Works to do something else. To close only the document, click the Close (X) button at the right end of the document's title bar (see Figure 2.13), or open the **File** menu and choose **Close**.

Opening a Document

You've already seen that you can open an existing file from the Task Launcher window, but you can also open one from within any of the Works tools. To open a previously saved and closed file, open the **File** menu and choose **Open**.

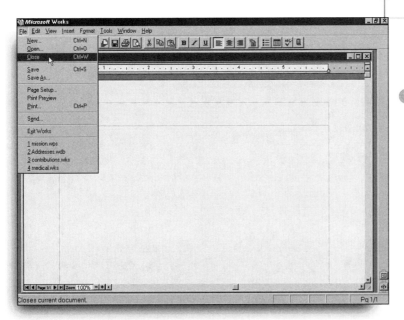

FIGURE 2.13

Use the document's **Close (X)** button or the **File** menu to close a document.

① Close button

You can also open a file in the following ways:

- Press Ctrl+O on the keyboard.

- Choose the file from the most recently used files at the bottom of the **File** menu (see Figure 2.14). The last four files that you saved appear in this list, below the E**x**it Works command.

- (You already know this one.) From the Task Launcher, click the **Existing Documents** tab. Double-click the document you want to open.

SEE ALSO

➤ *Opening an existing file from the Task Launcher is covered on page 20.*

FIGURE 2.14

You can select a recently used document from the File menu.

 Files

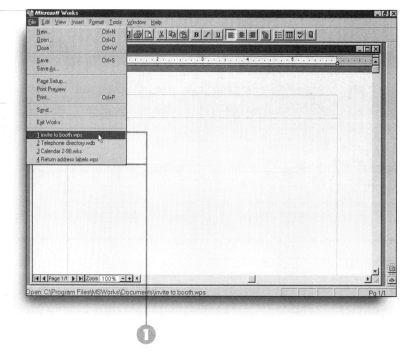

Previewing and Printing a Document

Is it already open?

In Works, you can have many files open at once and switch among them. To check whether a file is already open (but just not on top) open the **Window** menu. The bottom of this menu shows a list of the files that are already open, with a check mark next to the active file. Click any file on the list to bring it to the top.

Although the screen shows your document very much as the printed version appears, it's sometimes difficult to get a real sense of how your final document will look. To see a preview of your document before printing, open the **File** menu and choose **Print Preview**. Works shows you a reduced view of your document, and provides buttons for zooming in closer to your preview and viewing subsequent pages. Figure 2.15 shows the Print Preview window and tools.

If you want to print with the default options (default printer, one copy, all pages), you can just click the Print button on the toolbar or click the **Print** button from Print Preview.

If you need to customize your print settings, open the **File** menu and choose **Print.** The Print dialog box, shown in Figure 2.16, opens and presents the following options:

- You can print a range of pages by choosing **Pages** in the **Print range** section and then entering page numbers into the **from** and **to** boxes.

- Print multiple copies by changing the number in the **Number of copies** field. Enter a number or use the up- and down arrows to increase or decrease the number of copies.

- If you're printing multiple copies of a document with more than one page, you'll want to leave on the default **Collate** setting.

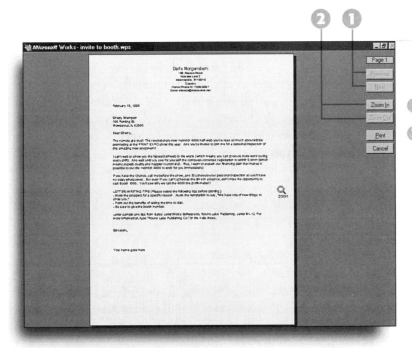

FIGURE 2.15

Use Print Preview to see how the document will look when printed.

1 Next and Previous buttons

2 Zoom controls

Two Kinds of Exiting

There's a difference between exiting one of Works' tools and exiting Works itself. You learned earlier in this chapter how to close a word processing document. When you close all the open documents for a tool, you exit that tool and return to the Task Launcher. In contrast, when you exit Works itself, Works closes down completely.

FIGURE 2.16

The Print dialog box enables you to specify the page range and number of copies, among other things.

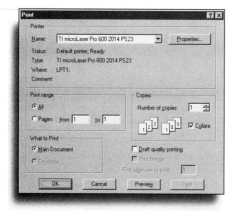

Getting back to the Task Launcher

You don't have to close all your open documents to get back to the Task Launcher. Just click the Task Launcher button on the toolbar.

To exit Works itself, click the Close (X) button in the Works title bar or open the **File** menu and choose **Exit Works.** If you've made changes to any open documents since you last saved them, Works will ask if you want to save the changes. Click **Yes** if you want to save the first one it asks about, **No** if you want to exit without saving the document, or **Cancel** if you decide not to exit Works at this time.

3

Creating Fancier Documents in Works

Changing the typeface and size of lettering

Setting tabs and indents

Changing page margins

Adding headers and footers

Creating tables

Formatting Text

The most basic, fundamental level of *formatting* is that which involves the actual characters. You can change the *typeface* (*font*) and size of the lettering, apply bold, italic, and underline attributes, and more. Changes like these can be used strategically to make headings stand out, to emphasize important words and phrases, and to make the document more readable.

Selecting a Font

Intelligent font choices

For the main body of a document, stay away from novelty fonts such as Freestyle Script or Jokerman. Stick with plain, easy-to-read fonts such as Arial and Times New Roman. These fonts look great both on printouts and on the screen. Don't use a broad mix of fonts in any single document; one or two fonts in a single document usually are enough. Choose a font that promotes the readability and spirit of your document. You can vary the size of the font, and apply bold, italic, or underline formatting to emphasize individual words or phrases.

The choice of font is probably the most important decision you make with each document. If the lettering is difficult to read, your reader may not make it through and may not receive your entire message! You want to pick a font that will attract readers and make people care about your message.

You can format your text by changing its font. You can also change the *font size* (that is, the size of each letter) and *font style* (in other words, the attributes applied to the text, such as bold or underline). These changes can be made from the toolbar or the **Format** menu.

Changing the font from the toolbar

1. With your document open, select the text you want to change. Or, if you're starting a new document, make the change before you start typing.

2. Click the drop-down arrow on the **Font** list box on the toolbar. A list of fonts drops down. The fonts appear graphically, so you can tell what they will look like in your document (see Figure 3.1).

3. Select a font that you like by clicking it in the list. Your selected text changes to that font.

The fonts on the list with TT next to them are *TrueType* fonts. These fonts are *scalable*, which means they can be used at any size. Any fonts that are missing the TT moniker are not TrueType; perhaps they are fonts built into your printer, or some other kind of font. Try to choose TrueType fonts whenever possible because they look good both on the screen and in print.

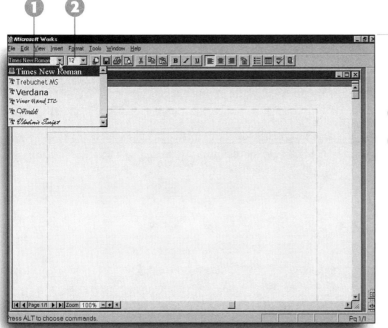

FIGURE 3.1

The **Font** drop-down list shows the available fonts installed on your computer.

1 **Font** drop-down list

2 **Font Size** drop-down list

Even though the font has changed, the text is still the same size. To increase or decrease the font size (measured in *points*), open the **Font Size** drop-down list. A list of point sizes drops down. The higher the number, the bigger your text will be. Select a point size by clicking the number in the list.

If you make your text Bold, Italic, or Underlined, you're changing the font style. The Bold, Italic, and Underline buttons on the toolbar work like toggle switches—one click and they're on, a second click and they're off. Figure 3.2 shows the toolbar with the Bold button turned on. To apply these styles to your text, select the text and then click the appropriate button. You can apply one, two, or all three styles to any text. To remove the attribute, select the text again and click the attribute button.

You can also change the text's font, size, and style by using the **Format** menu to open the Format Font and Style dialog box. This dialog box lets you set all the font formatting in one place, and it offers styles not available on the toolbar.

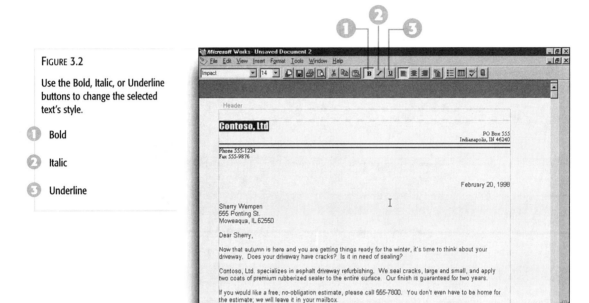

Use the Bold, Italic, or Underline buttons to change the selected text's style.

❶ Bold

❷ Italic

❸ Underline

To change your text's font, size, and style from the menu, open the **Format** menu and choose **Font and Style**. The Format Font and Style dialog box appears as shown in Figure 3.3. The dialog box provides one location for you to change all your text's visual attributes.

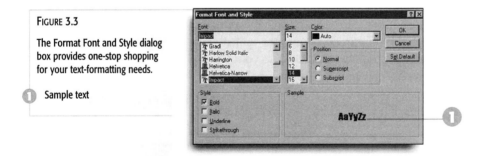

FIGURE 3.3

The Format Font and Style dialog box provides one-stop shopping for your text-formatting needs.

❶ Sample text

In addition to the font and style settings, the Format Font and Style dialog box also contains settings for the following:

- **Color**. Click the drop arrow and scroll through 15 color choices. **Auto** is the default black text.
- **Position**. Choose from **Normal**, **Superscript** (text shrunken and raised above the baseline), and **Subscript** (text shrunken and lowered slightly below the baseline).
- **Style**. You can choose to make your text **Bold**, **Italic**, **Underlined**, or use **Strikethrough** to put a line through the text. You can use any combination of these styles.

Figure 3.4 shows a sample report with character formatting applied, so you can see the dramatic effects you can create with simple text formatting.

SEE ALSO

➤ *To select text, see page 26.*

Changing the Default Font

Defaults are settings that are in effect automatically. Your default font in Works is Times New Roman, in 10 points. If you'd prefer to have a different font as your default, open the **Format** menu and choose **Font and Style**. Select your font, size, and style (you probably don't want colored text as a default), and click the **Set Default** button. Click **Yes** to change the default to your new settings.

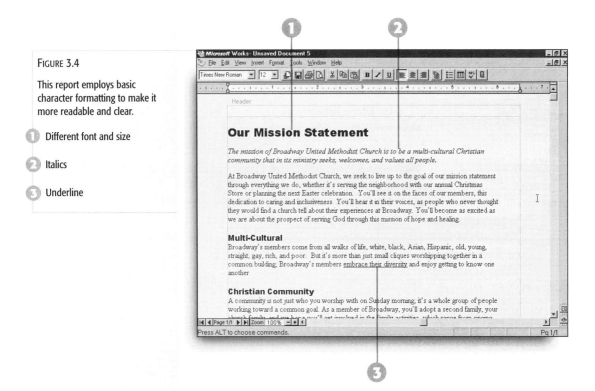

FIGURE 3.4

This report employs basic character formatting to make it more readable and clear.

1 Different font and size

2 Italics

3 Underline

Using WordArt

WordArt is an accessory program that runs within Works (and Word, too). It helps you dress up plain text, for headings, posters, and other special uses. You can add *textures* to the lettering, give them shadows, twist them into different shapes, and so on. Spend some time experimenting with these effects—they can add real impact and interest to your documents.

Inserting WordArt into an open document

1. Place your cursor where you want to place your WordArt text. Open the **Insert** menu and choose **WordArt**.

2. When WordArt is activated, its toolbar replaces the Works toolbar. Figure 3.5 shows the WordArt window and toolbar. A box appears in your document, with sample text that reads Your Text Here.

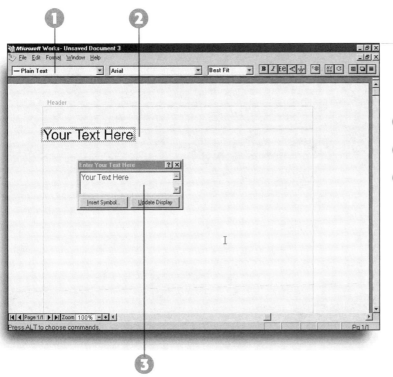

3. Type your text in the box, and click the **Update Display** button. The WordArt text appears in your document, and the WordArt tools and text box remain onscreen.

4. Apply any special effects by clicking the toolbar buttons.

5. When you're finished, close the Enter Your Text Here window by clicking its Close (X) button.

When you're finished formatting your WordArt text, click anywhere outside the WordArt text box to deactivate WordArt and return to Works.

After you've created WordArt you can

- Move the WordArt object by dragging it with your mouse.
- Resize your WordArt object by clicking once on the text and then grabbing one of the *handles* and dragging outward to increase the item's size, or inward to make it smaller (see Figure 3.6).

Using Best Fit

If you click the Font Size drop-down list on the WordArt toolbar, you'll see that the default is **Best Fit**. Using **Best Fit** means that if your text box is enlarged or reduced, the text size will be automatically adjusted to fit the box.

FIGURE 3.6

Resizing a WordArt object is as simple as dragging a corner of its box.

1 Handles are gray boxes that surround an object.

- Return to WordArt to reformat your text. Just double-click the WordArt object. The WordArt program is activated and the WordArt tools return to the screen.

- Delete a WordArt object by clicking it once to select it (the handles show) and then pressing the Delete key.

Formatting Paragraphs

So far in this chapter, we've been concentrating on the text itself. Now it's time to think about the paragraphs in which the text lies. Every time you press Enter, you create a new paragraph. Each of these paragraphs is a discrete unit that can be formatted separately from the others; each can have its own alignment, tabs, and indents.

Aligning Text

You can *align* your text by the left or right margin, or from the center of the page. By default, your text is left aligned, meaning that when you type your text starts on the left side of the page and the left side of your text stays even with the left margin. The right edge of the text doesn't have to stay even with the right margin (it's "ragged right").

Alignments can be applied to existing text, or set before you start typing. If you want to align existing text, select it first.

The easiest way to set alignment is with the toolbar buttons. In addition to the default left alignment ▤, you can choose

- ▤ **Center**. Text centered between margins; often used for titles and headings.

- ▤ **Right**. Text aligned to the right margin; often used for the date at the top of a letter.

You can also set alignment with the Format Paragraph dialog box, shown in Figure 3.7. Just open the **Format** menu, choose **Paragraph**, and make your selections from the Format Paragraph dialog box. This method has the advantage of having a fourth alignment method: *Justified*. Use Justified alignment to align a paragraph from both the left and the right, eliminating the ragged right edge. Justified alignment is often used to create smooth text columns in newsletters.

Showing the paragraphs

To display the end-of-paragraph symbols at the end of each paragraph (to make it easier to know where they are), open the **View** menu and choose **All Characters**.

FIGURE 3.7

The Format Paragraph dialog box contains four alignment types; the toolbar has only three.

Setting and Using Tabs

Tabs are places on your document ruler where you place a mark (called a *tab stop*) that will control the movement of the Tab key. In a new, blank document, tabs are set by default to every half-inch starting at the left margin. You can set custom tabs at any place on the ruler and use them to indent the first line of a paragraph or for typing multi-column lists.

The "normal" kind of tab stop is left-aligned with no *leader*. Most of the time you will want this kind of tab stop. However, other types may be useful in certain circumstances. Figure 3.8 shows some tab stop variations with text. *Decimal tabs*, for example, are particularly helpful for typing numbers with an irregular number of characters to the right of the decimal point, but can also be used for currency where dollars and cents are involved. Right alignment works well for aligning whole numbers or for positioning text in a column so it evenly lines up on its right edge.

Missing ruler?

If the ruler does not appear, open the **View** menu and choose **Ruler**.

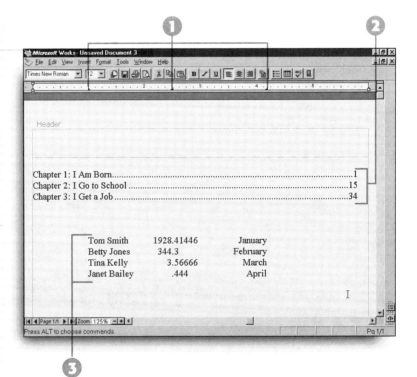

FIGURE 3.8

Notice the different kinds of tab stops at work.

 Tab stop markers on ruler.

2 These lines have a right-aligned tab stop with a leader.

3 These lines have a left stop, a decimal stop, and a right stop.

One way to set tabs is to click the ruler where you want a tab stop to appear. This is easy but is lacking somewhat in flexibility; all tab stops set this way are left-aligned with no leader.

Setting tabs

1. Double-click the ruler, or open the **Format** menu and choose **Tabs**, to open the Format Tabs dialog box as shown in Figure 3.9.

> **Follow the leader**
>
> A leader is a repeated character, usually a dot, which fills the blank space between text and a tab.

> **FIGURE 3.9**
>
> You can set tab stops with great accuracy and control from the Format Tabs dialog box.

2. Type a number in the **Tab stop position** text box to indicate at what spot on the ruler you want to place a tab stop.

3. Click a button in the **Alignment** area to choose how text will align with the tab stop.

4. Choose a leader from the **Leader** area. The default is **None**, which works with most tabbed text.

5. Click **Set**. If you need to set more tabs, repeat steps 1–3, clicking **Set** after each one, and then click **OK** to accept your settings and close the dialog box.

When tabs are set, they appear as small symbols on the ruler. Refer to Figure 3.8 to see a ruler with a series of tab stops. The stops on the ruler are for whatever paragraph the cursor is lying in at the moment. If you move the cursor to another paragraph, that paragraph's tab stops appear on the ruler instead.

You can change tab settings that you've made in your document by dragging the tab stops on the ruler with your mouse, or by making changes to your tab settings in the Format Tabs dialog box. If you want the change to apply to more than the current paragraph, you must select all the paragraphs to be involved *before* you make the change.

To remove a tab stop, click the tab stop marker on the ruler with your mouse, and drag it down and off the ruler. When you release your mouse, the tab stop is gone. To remove a tab when you're in the Format Tabs dialog box, select the tab from the **T̲ab stop position** list box and click **Cl̲ear**. Click **Clear A̲ll** to remove all the tab stops and return to the default tab stops.

Indenting Paragraphs

Indenting a paragraph increases the distance between the text and the margin. You can set a variety of indent types, indenting the text from the left, right, or both. For example, you might indent a quotation from the rest of a report to make it stand out, or you might indent a list of items from the regular paragraphs.

Paragraphs have two parts: a first line and a body (the rest of the lines). You can indent one or both of these parts. For example, some people like to have the first line of every paragraph indented five spaces. You can also indent the body and leave the first line flush with the left margin; this is called a *hanging indent* and it's used to create bulleted lists. (To do that, you set the Left indent to a positive number, for example, 1.0, and the First Line indent to a negative one, for example, 0.5.) When you set an indent to a negative number, it's called an *outdent*.

Setting paragraph indents

1. In your open document, place your cursor in the paragraph you want to indent. You don't need to select text unless you want to apply the indents to more than one existing paragraph.

2. Open the **Fo̲rmat** menu and choose **P̲aragraph**. The Format Paragraph dialog box opens.

3. In the **I̲ndents and Alignment** tab (see Figure 3.10), type a value in the text box for the indentation you want, or click the *increment buttons* to increment the number up or down:

- **L̲eft**. The left edge of all the lines in the paragraph move to the left by an amount you specify.

Can't I just change it at the beginning?

As you are initially typing your text, you can set tab stops for your first paragraph, and then each time you press Enter to start a new paragraph, those same tab stops are used.

- **Right**. The right edge of all the lines in the paragraph move in a specified distance from the right margin.

- **First line**. The first line of the paragraph is indented by a distance you specify. The body of the paragraph remains at the left margin.

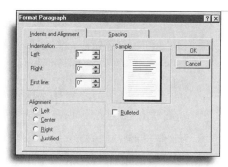

FIGURE 3.10
Use the format Paragraph dialog box to change the indents.

4. The **Sample** area of the dialog box shows how your indent settings will look in your document. Click the **OK** button to accept your settings and close the dialog box. Figure 3.11 shows some sample indents.

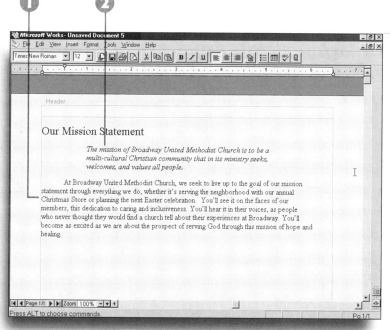

FIGURE 3.11
Some things you can do with indents are shown here.

① This paragraph uses a first-line indent.

② This quote is both left and right indented.

SEE ALSO

> *For more detail about how bulleted lists work, see page 56.*

Creating Bulleted Lists

Bullets are small symbols used to mark the beginning of all paragraphs within a list, or to add emphasis to a single, inset paragraph. Notice that there are many bulleted lists in this book!

The Bullets feature in Works makes creating a bulleted list easy. This feature adds a bullet character in front of the selected paragraphs *and* sets the indents appropriately, all in one step. You can place bullets in existing paragraphs, or you can add them as you type. The choice is yours.

Typing bulleted paragraphs

1. Position the cursor where you want to begin the first bulleted paragraph.
2. Click the Bullets button ▤ on the toolbar. A bullet appears before the current line.
3. Type the paragraph, and press Enter. A bullet automatically appears in front of the following paragraph, too.
4. Keep repeating step 3 until you are finished with the bulleted list. Then click the Bullets button again to turn off the bullet feature.

Adding bullets to existing paragraphs

1. Select the paragraphs to which you want to add bullets.
2. Click the Bullets button ▤ on the toolbar. A bullet appears before each selected line.
3. Click anywhere away from the paragraphs to deselect them.

If there were blank lines between your lines or paragraphs that are now bulleted, click each line individually and click the Bullet button on the toolbar. This will turn the bullet off for that line.

The default bullet is a generic dot. If you want to choose from a group of other symbols for your bullets, highlight your text, open the **Format** menu, and then choose **Bullets**. The Format Bullets dialog box appears as shown in Figure 3.12. Click the bullet symbol you want to use, and set a size for it in the **Bullet size** text box. Then click **OK** to accept your selection and close the dialog box. Your selection now becomes the default. To return to the generic dot, you'll have to go back and choose it from the Format Bullets dialog box.

FIGURE 3.12

The Format Bullets dialog box enables you to choose the bullet character you prefer.

SEE ALSO

➤ *In Word, you can use any character in any font, not just the 24 characters that Works provides. See page 178 for details.*

Formatting Pages

So far in this chapter, you have learned about formatting individual characters and individual paragraphs. Now let's move one step further and talk about formatting that applies to entire pages or documents. You can use such formatting to affect the overall, larger picture that your document presents.

Inserting Page Breaks

Page breaks occur naturally every time your text exceeds the length of a page. As you're entering text and you reach the bottom margin of the page, Works creates a new page and the rest of the text flows onto it. This is known as a *soft page break*. However, you may need to force a page break where one would not occur naturally to keep text on a particular page or move the following text to the next page. This is a *hard or manual page break*.

To manually create a page break, position your cursor where you want the page break to occur and press Ctrl+Enter.

A hard page break is different from a soft one. A soft page break doesn't control where the text breaks between the preceding page and the subsequent page. It just happens to occur. If you delete text on the first page, text flows back from the second page. In the case of a hard page break, however, a code is inserted into the document, and the text that follows the page break always starts on a new page unless the page break code is deleted.

You can only see and delete page breaks in Normal view (open the **View** menu and choose **Normal**). Page breaks appear as dotted lines running horizontally on the page. To delete your break, place the mouse in the left margin, on the same line as the dotted break line. Click the mouse to select the page break and press the Delete key.

Adding Page Numbers

It's a good idea to add page numbers to any documents that are longer than one page. Page numbers can make your collating job easier if you're producing multiple copies of the document, and they make it easier for your readers to keep the document pages in order. It's also a lifesaver for reassembling your work after you have accidentally dropped all the printed pages on the floor and they have scattered every-which-way! (I speak from sad personal experience here.)

Adding page numbers

1. In an open, multi-page document, place your cursor in the header or footer area. It doesn't matter which page you're on. If you can't see the header and footer sections, open the **View** menu and choose **Page Layout**.

2. Open the **Insert** menu and choose **Page Number**. The word *page* (between asterisks) appears on your document, in the upper-left corner. This is a page number code, also

---

Page Layout versus Normal view

Works lets you view your word processing documents in two ways. The Page Layout view (the default view) shows you the edge of your pages, columns, footnotes, all pictures and objects, and headers and footers in the same position as they will appear on the printed page. Page Layout view is good for assessing the "look" of the page, but it may be faster to type in Normal view because you don't have to wait as long for the screen to refresh. Open the **View** menu to change views.

known as a *placeholder*. When the document is printed, the actual page number will replace the code.

3. To center or right-align your page number, highlight the code and click the appropriate alignment button on your toolbar.

4. To remove your page number from the first page of your document, open the **File** menu and choose **Page Setup**. Click the **Other Options** tab, and select the **No header on first page** and **No footer on first page** check boxes. Then click **OK.** Figure 3.13 shows the Page Setup dialog box.

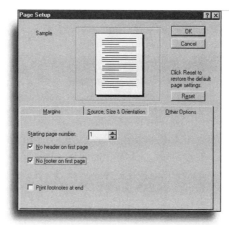

FIGURE 3.13

You can use the Page Setup dialog box to suppress the header or footer on the first page.

5. To start your page numbering with a number other than 1, open the **File** menu and choose **Page Setup**. Click the **Other Options** tab, and enter a number in the **Starting page number** box (or use the up- and down-arrows to change the number). Click **OK.**

SEE ALSO

➤ *For information about alignment buttons, see page 51.*

Changing Margins

Your document margins are the areas around the edge of the page—top, bottom, and both sides—where there is no text. Works' default margins are 1 inch from the top and bottom, and 1 1/4 inches from the left and right sides of the page.

Don't number the cover

If your page 1 is a cover page, you can make page 2 into page 1 by setting the starting page number to 0. The starting page number can also be set to negative numbers, so you can count the number of unnumbered pages that precede the page you want to be page 1, and set the starting page number to that negative number. This can be useful if your document will have several introductory pages or a table of contents. For example, if you have a cover and a 3-page table of contents, set the starting page number to -3 (counting backward, that's 0, -1, -2, -3).

Changing page margins

1. Open the **File** menu and choose **Page Setup**. Click the **Margins** tab as shown in Figure 3.14.

FIGURE 3.14

Change the document margins here.

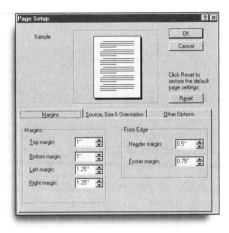

FIGURE 3.14

Change the document margins here.

Header and footer margins

In the Page Setup dialog box, you can also set how far from the edge of the paper you want to put the header or footer. In the **From Edge** section, specify an amount in the **Header margin** or **Footer margin** text box.

2. You'll see a series of four boxes for the **Top margin**, **Bottom margin**, **Left margin**, and **Right margin** of your page. Use the up- and down-increment buttons next to each field to increase or decrease the defaults, or select the contents of the boxes and type the new measurement. You don't need to type the inch marks.

3. Click **OK** to accept your changes and close the dialog box.

Setting the Paper Size and Orientation

Most business and personal documents are "letter size," or 8 1/2 by 11 inches, and this is the default paper size for a Works word processing document. Also by default, Works prints documents in *portrait orientation*, where the long edge of the paper is vertical. If you want to print on another size paper or in *landscape* orientation (with the long edge of the paper horizontal), you can do so through the Page Setup dialog box. For example, you might want to print on special stationery for party invitations or formal announcements (such as enclosures for a wedding invitation). You can also use the Page Setup dialog box to choose a different paper source if your printer has more than one paper tray.

Changing the Paper Size, Orientation, and Source in Works

1. Open the **File** menu and choose **Page Setup**. This opens the Page Setup dialog box.

2. Click the **Source, Size & Orientation** tab (see Figure 3.15).

Printing envelopes

You don't have to change the paper size to print on an envelope. Instead, open the **Tools** menu and choose **Envelopes** and follow the prompts there to set up to print on an envelope.

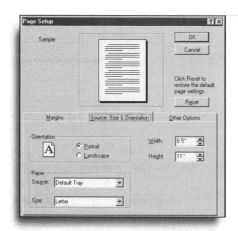

FIGURE 3.15
You can change information about the paper you are using with these controls.

3. Choose the appropriate paper size, orientation, and paper tray. Click **OK** to accept your settings and close the dialog box.

Using Headers and Footers

Just as page numbers help readers see which page they're on, headers and footers provide information to assist the reader in following long documents. A *header* is text that appears at the top of every page in your document, and a *footer* is text that appears at the bottom of every page in your document. You can place title, date, copyright, and other information in your header and footer. Figure 3.16 shows a sample header. (This page has a footer too, but you can't see it onscreen right now. You can scroll down in your own document to see the footer area.)

FIGURE 3.16

This document header will print the same useful information on every page.

1 Center-aligned tab stop

2 Page number code

3 Right-aligned tab stop

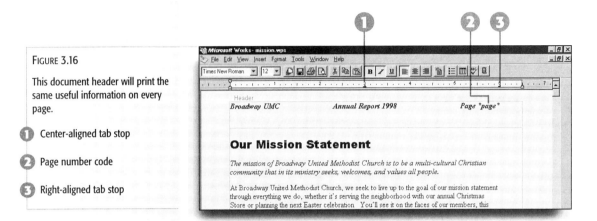

You can see headers and footers only in Works' Page Layout view, not in Normal view. If you have switched over to Normal view, change back by opening the **View** menu and choosing **Page Layout**. In Page Layout view, the header and footer areas appear at the top and bottom of the document page.

By default, each header and footer has two tab stops: a center-aligned one in the middle of the line and a right-aligned one at the right edge. (Take a look at the ruler in Figure 3.16 and see for yourself.) This makes it easy to enter text at any or all of the three positions in the header: left, center, and right. For example, in Figure 3.16, I typed the first phrase, pressed Tab, typed the second (Annual Report 1998), pressed Tab again, and typed Page. Then I opened the **Insert** menu and chose the **Page Number** command to insert the *page* code.

Creating a header or footer

1. Click your mouse to place your cursor in the header or footer area of your document. (You can also open the **View** menu and then choose **Header** or **Footer**.)

2. Type your text. You can format this text as you would any other text in the body of the document.

3. (Optional) To insert codes in the header or footer, such as a page number code or a code that produces the current date, open the **Insert** menu and choose the code you want to

insert. Some common codes used in headers and footers include the ones shown in Table 3.1.

4. To switch between the header area and the footer area, use your scrollbars and reposition your cursor by clicking your mouse in the header or footer area, or open the **View** menu and choose **Header** or **Footer**.

TABLE 3.1   **Codes to insert in headers and footers**

Insert Menu Command	Code Placed	Result
Page Number	*page*	Numbers pages
Document Name	*filename*	Places document name (same one) on every page
Date and Time	Varies	Opens a dialog box where you can choose a date/time format, then places a code for it

Just as page numbers shouldn't be placed on the first page of a business or personal letter, headers and footers shouldn't appear on the first page, either.

Suppressing the header and footer on the first page

1. Open the **File** menu and choose **Page Setup**.

2. Click the **Other Options** tab (see Figure 3.17).

FIGURE 3.17

Use the **No header on first page** and **No footer on first page** check boxes to suppress header and footer information on page 1.

3. Check **No header on first page** to remove the header from the first page. Check **No footer on first page** to remove the footer.

4. Click **OK** to accept your settings and close the dialog box.

Creating Columns

When you create a newsletter or similar document, you can divide your page into columns like a newspaper. Although you can set up many columns per page, two or three columns are the easiest for you to use and for your audience to read.

Column settings apply to your entire document. You can format existing text in columns or set up columns in a blank document before you begin typing.

Creating multiple columns

1. Open the **View** menu and choose **Page Layout.** You won't be able to see your columns unless you're in Page Layout view.

2. Place your cursor anywhere in the body of an open document. Open the **Format** menu and choose **Columns**. This opens the Format Columns dialog box shown in Figure 3.18. In this dialog box, you can change any or all of these three settings:

   - **Number of columns**. You can enter up to seven columns for portrait, letter-size paper. If you choose a higher number, Works will advise you that your number of columns and the paper size don't match.

   - **Space between**. This setting controls the space between columns. The default is 0.5 inch. You may have to print your document before you can judge if this distance is too small or too large. Then adjust the gap between the columns by changing this measurement.

   - **Line between columns**. Vertical lines serve two purposes—they can add a polished look to a newsletter, and they can help the reader follow the text.

Don't forget the TaskWizards

When creating something complicated like a newsletter that involves multiple columns, it's a lot easier to start with a TaskWizard than it is to try to build from scratch. The special Newsletter TaskWizard is highly worth your while to check out.

3. After entering your selections, click **OK** to close the dialog box.

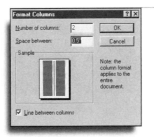

FIGURE 3.18
Specify the number of columns and the space between them, and choose whether to have a vertical line between columns.

Working with Tables

A *table* is a group of rows and columns added to a document for storing and organizing text. The intersections of the columns and rows in a table are called *cells*. Tables can be used to create multi-column lists, parallel paragraphs, and fill-in forms.

SEE ALSO

➤ *For more information about spreadsheets, see page 74.*

Creating a Table

A Works word processing table is actually a simple spreadsheet that is added to your document.

To create a table in an open document

1. Place your cursor at the point in your document where you want to place the table.

2. Open the **Insert** menu and choose **Table,** or click the Table button 🖽 on the toolbar. The Insert Table dialog box appears (see Figure 3.19).

3. Enter the number of rows and columns you want in the **Number of rows** and **Number of columns** text boxes.

4. (Optional) Choose one of the predesigned formats if desired from the **Select a format** list. The **Example** area shows what the format will look like.

5. Click **OK** to accept your settings and close the dialog box.

Using a spreadsheet

If your table is going to contain a lot of calculations and will be filled with numbers rather than text, you're better off creating a spreadsheet in Works' spreadsheet program. If you need to include the spreadsheet in your word processing document, you can always copy the spreadsheet to the Clipboard and then paste it into the document.

FIGURE 3.19

Choose your table settings from the
Insert Table dialog box.

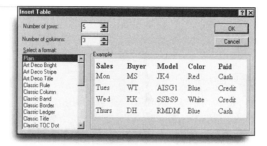

FIGURE 3.19

Choose your table settings from the
Insert Table dialog box.

Entering Text into a Table

Context-sensitivity

When you're working in a table, your
menus (all except **File**, **Window**,
and **Help**) change to contain
spreadsheet-related commands. This
is called *context-sensitivity*. If you
click your mouse outside the table,
your menus return to normal. Click
back inside the table and the spreadsheet commands reappear.

After you've inserted your table, you see a large rectangle appear
on your screen. The first cell is *active*, and your cursor is blinking in the cell. To enter text into the cell, type as you would any
other text (see Figure 3.20). Press the Tab key to move to the
next cell (press Shift+Tab to move to the previous cell). You
can also use the arrow keys to move from cell to cell or click in
a cell to place the cursor there. *Do not* press Enter to move
from cell to cell. Pressing Enter begins a new paragraph within
the cell.

FIGURE 3.20

Type text in a cell as you would in a
regular paragraph.

❶ Active cell

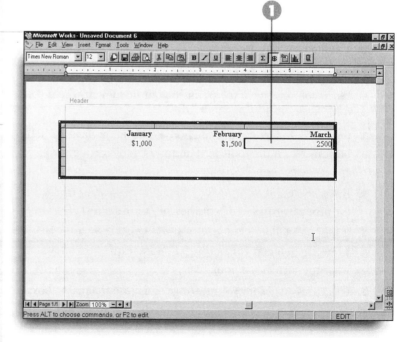

Selecting Table Cells

To format your table cells or the text in your table, you have to select the cells first. To select cells in your table, click in the first cell you want to select, and drag your mouse through the remaining cells you want to select. You can also press the Shift key and use the arrow keys to select cells in any direction.

If you want to select an entire column or row, click the control cell at the top of each column or at the beginning of each row. The control cells are not really cells—they're gray rectangles that act like buttons. Click one to select the entire row or column at once. Figure 3.21 shows the table control cells and a group of selected cells.

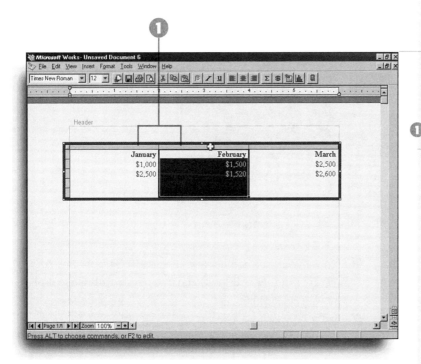

FIGURE 3.21

Select cells by dragging across them or highlighting with Shift+arrow keys.

❶   Control cells (thin gray boxes)

Formatting Text in a Table

You can format text in table cells like any other text—you can change the text's alignment, fonts, style, and size. You can type paragraph text into a cell (the text wraps within the horizontal dimensions of the cell) and set indents for the text. The only thing you can't do in a table cell is use the Tab key to indent text, because the Tab key moves you to the next cell.

In addition to character and paragraph formatting, you can format any numbers in your table. Choose from formats such as currency (adds a dollar sign and a comma between thousands), percentages (multiplies the number by 100 and adds a percent sign), fractions (changes decimals to fractions), or dates (lets you change 1/23/97 to January 23, 1997).

Formatting numbers in a table

1. Select the cell or group of cells you want to format.

2. Open the **Format** menu and choose **Number** to open the Format Cells dialog box, then click the **Number** tab (see Figure 3.22).

Having trouble navigating your table?

Turn on your gridlines so that you can see each individual cell. To turn gridlines on or off, open the **View** menu and choose **Gridlines**.

FIGURE 3.22

You can choose from among 12 number formats, just like in the spreadsheet tool in Works.

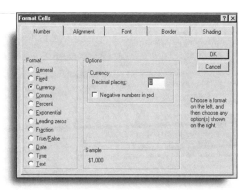

3. Choose your numeric format (check the **Sample** box to see how the number will look) and the number of decimal places you want to display.

4. Click **OK** to accept your settings and close the dialog box.

Quick formatting for currency

Use the Currency button **$** on the toolbar to format your cells that contain money amounts. Select the cells first, and then click the button.

SEE ALSO

➤ *For more information about formatting text in or out of a table, see page 44.*

➤ *For more information about the Spreadsheet tool, see page 74.*

Changing Table Dimensions

Before you create your table, you should think about what will go into it. For example, if the table will contain a list of employees and the hours they worked on a given day, think about how many columns that will require—one column each for the employee name, date, and hours worked. That's three columns. The number of employees plus your column headings will tell you how many rows you'll need.

Even if you plan ahead, you might need to make changes. After you've created the table and entered the text, you may decide that you want to add a column for their Social Security numbers. If you forget to put in an employee and his hours, you'll need to add a row.

To add a column, place your cursor in any cell in the column to the right of where you want to add your new column. Open the **Insert** menu and choose **Column** (or right-click the cell and choose **Insert Column** from the pop-up menu). A new column appears, sized to fit within your current table dimensions.

To add a row, click to place your cursor in any cell in the row below where you want to add your new row. Open the **Insert** menu and choose **Row** from the menu (or right-click the cell and choose **Insert Row** from the pop-up menu).

Changing Column Width

Does the text you type into a cell not fit into a single row? If you're not happy with the appearance of your table due to weird widths, you can change the width of your columns to accommodate the width of the text in your cells.

Adjusting column widths with the mouse

1. Move your mouse pointer to the gray cells at the top of the column you want to widen or narrow.

2. Point to the seam between the column you want to adjust and the column to its right. You'll know you're in the right place because your mouse pointer will change to the word "Adjust."

3. Hold down the left mouse button and drag to the right to widen the column or to the left to narrow it.

You can also change column width from the Column Width dialog box. This method has the advantage of giving you more precise control, but it's a bit more trouble. Use it when the exact width is important to you (and not just an eyeball guesstimate.)

Adjusting column widths with a dialog box

1. Place your cursor in any cell in the column to be adjusted. Open the **Format** menu and choose **Column Width**.

2. In the **Column Width** dialog box, enter the number of characters wide your column should be. The default is 15.

3. Click **OK** to accept your setting and close the dialog box.

If you're not sure how wide to make your column, click the **Best Fit** button in the Column Width dialog box. Your column width will be based on the widest entry.

Applying Table Borders and Shading

Adding borders and shading to your table will enhance its appearance and help to draw your readers' attention to specific columns, rows, or cells. Works supplies a series of preformatted table shading and border designs, which can make the process of enhancing a table much easier.

AutoFormatting a table

1. Place your cursor anywhere in the table. If you've clicked outside the table, double-click the table to reactivate it.

2. Open the **Format** menu and choose **AutoFormat**. This opens the AutoFormat dialog box (see Figure 3.23).

3. Scroll through the list of formats, and preview them by clicking them once. The **Example** area shows you a preview of the selected format. When you find one you like, click **OK** to accept your selection and close the dialog box.

If you'd prefer to apply your own borders and shading on a cell-by-cell basis, you can use the separate **Border** and **Shading** commands in the **Format** menu. (You might start with an AutoFormat and then use the controls to fine-tune.)

Row height

Although the row height adjusts automatically depending on the size of type in the row, you can adjust the row height manually by dragging the seam between the gray cells at the beginning of the rows. You can also open the **Format** menu and choose **Row Height** to open the Format Row Height dialog box where you can specify the exact row height you want, click **Standard** to return to the standard row height, or click **Best Fit** to let Works fit the row height to the contents of the row. Click **OK** to exit the dialog box.

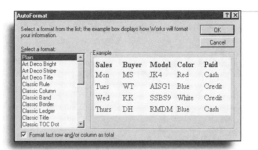

FIGURE 3.23

AutoFormat makes it easy to create professional-looking tables.

Manually placing borders and shading in a table

1. Select the cell or cells you want to shade or border.

2. Choose one of the following menu commands:

   - To apply shading, open the **Format** menu and choose **Shading**. Figure 3.24 shows the **Shading** tab in the Format Cells dialog box. Choose the shading pattern, and foreground and background colors you want.

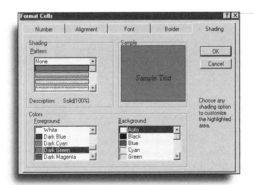

FIGURE 3.24

You can apply your own shading choices to the selected cells.

   - To apply a border, open the **Format** menu and choose **Border**. Figure 3.25 shows the **Border** tab in the Format Cells dialog box. Choose the border type, color, and line style you want for your table.

Format cells

You'll notice that the **Border** and **Shading** commands both take you to the Format Cells dialog box, just on different tabs. You can click the **Border** or **Shading** tab to do both jobs from one place, with one original command.

FIGURE 3.25

You can apply borders to one or more sides of the selected block of cells.

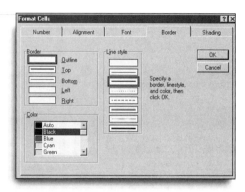

3. Click **OK** to accept your settings and close the dialog box.

If you decide you don't need the table in your document, select the table by clicking it once. The table displays gray handles (if a solid border shows, click outside the table and the gray handles will appear). Press the Delete key.

Using the Works Spreadsheet

Starting a Spreadsheet

A *spreadsheet program* is a software application that organizes data into *rows* and *columns*. Numeric values can be calculated, and text can be sorted in a spreadsheet program. The pages or documents these programs create are called *spreadsheets* or *worksheets*. They work great for organizing material into rows and columns, much like tables in the word processor but with more precision and features.

The TaskWizards included with Works offer dozens of great spreadsheet ideas, from price lists to business forms, such as invoices.

You can start a spreadsheet in much the same way you start a word processing document:

- From the **TaskWizards** tab on the Task Launcher dialog box, double-click one of the TaskWizards with a spreadsheet icon next to it.

- From the Task Launcher's **Works Tools** tab, start a new spreadsheet document by clicking the **Spreadsheet** button.

If you want to follow along with this chapter's activities, do the latter—start a blank spreadsheet.

SEE ALSO
➤ *For information about TaskWizards, see page 13.*
➤ *If you've forgotten what the spreadsheet icon next to a TaskWizard looks like, see Table 1.2 on page 15.*

Déjà vu?

Some of the skills you'll use while working with spreadsheets are the same in every Works tool. Rather than repeat information here for such things as starting new documents, opening and closing documents, saving, printing, and so on, I'll reference you to the full descriptions of those skills given in earlier chapters.

Understanding the Spreadsheet Window

The Spreadsheet window has a lot in common with the Word Processing window you saw in Chapter 3, "Creating Fancier Documents in Works." The main difference is the area where you enter your work. There, you have a series of rows and columns that intersect to form *cells*. Figure 4.1 points out the important features and the following list describes them.

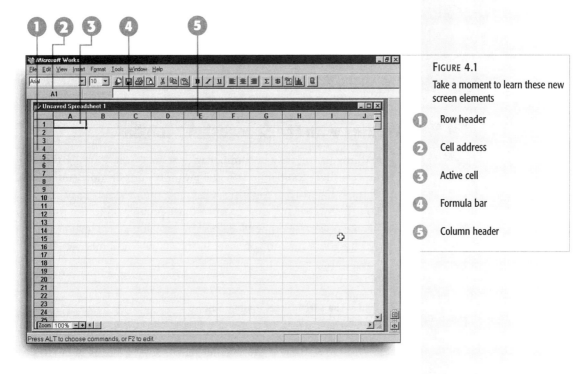

FIGURE 4.1

Take a moment to learn these new screen elements

1 Row header

2 Cell address

3 Active cell

4 Formula bar

5 Column header

- *Formula bar*. Displays any formula that is in the active cell. The cell itself displays the results of the formula.

- *Row header*. Lists the numbers that label each row.

- *Column header*. Lists the letters that label each column.

- *Active cell*. This cell is marked by a black border (called a *cell cursor*). Any characters or commands you type act upon the active cell.

- *Cell address area*. This area shows the address of the active cell (refer to Figure 4.1). The cell address identifies the column and row in which a cell occurs. The address "A1," for example, identifies the cell in the first column and first row of the spreadsheet.

A *cell* occurs at the intersection of a column and a row. Columns are identified by letters of the alphabet (A through IV). Rows are identified by numbers (1 through 16384). Because each cell address consists of the column name plus the row name, the cell address of the top cell in the first column is A1; the cell address of the last cell on the spreadsheet is IV16384.

SEE ALSO

➤ *For more information about some of the common features in Works tools such as the toolbar, menu bar, and Zoom control, see page 20.*

Working with the Spreadsheet Toolbar

Although you may be familiar with some of the tools on the spreadsheet toolbar, it also includes tools not found elsewhere in Home Essentials. You can see a name and description of any tool on the toolbar by resting your mouse pointer on it; the tool's name (a *ToolTip*) appears below the tool and a brief explanation of the tool's function appears in the status bar. Table 4.1 describes some of the spreadsheet tools.

TABLE 4.1 **The spreadsheet toolbar buttons**

Tool	Name	Description
🗗	**Task Launcher**	Brings up the Task Launcher dialog box that gives you access to TaskWizards, existing documents, and Works tools
Σ	**AutoSum**	Inserts the SUM function in the current cell and proposes a range of cells to total
$	**Currency**	Applies the currency format to numbers in the selected cell
🖩	**Easy Calc**	Starts Easy Calc, which helps you create formulas
📊	**New Chart**	Creates a new chart

Working with Spreadsheet Files

You probably already know how to handle files in Works, because we covered it in some detail in Chapter 2, "Introducing the Works Word Processor." In case you need a refresher, turn back to one of these sections:

SEE ALSO

➤ *Saving Your Work—see page 37.*

➤ *Closing a Spreadsheet—see page 38.*

➤ *Opening an Existing Spreadsheet—see page 38.*

➤ *Previewing and Printing—see page 40.*

Moving Around the Spreadsheet

To designate the active cell (in other words, to position your cursor in a specific cell) click it with the mouse. The cell cursor appears as a black border around the active cell. If you can't see the cell you want to work with, you need to scroll the display to bring the needed cell into view.

As you place information into the cells, you may put so much in that you won't be able to see it all onscreen at once. You can use the *scrollbars* to move around the spreadsheet, just as you would with a document. Notice that the spreadsheet has both a vertical (on the right) and horizontal (on the bottom) scrollbar, so you can move in two dimensions. You can also move around by using keyboard shortcuts, as shown in Table 4.2.

TABLE 4.2 **Keyboard shortcuts for moving around the spreadsheet**

Press...	To...
←	Move one cell to the left
→	Move one cell to the right
↑	Move one row up
↓	Move one row down
Tab	Move one cell to the right
Shift+Tab	Move one cell to the left

continues...

TABLE 4.2 **Continued**

Press...	To...
Home	Move to beginning of row
End	Move to end of row (last cell containing data)
Page Down	Move one screen down the spreadsheet
Page Up	Move one screen up the spreadsheet
Ctrl+Home	Go to A1 (the first cell on the spreadsheet)
Ctrl+End	Go to the last cell in the spreadsheet that contains data

Entering Your Data

Building a spreadsheet has a natural process flow to it. First, enter the text labels for the rows and columns. Then enter the data (the text or numbers that you're tracking). Finally, enter any formulas or functions that you'll use to calculate the results.

Entering Text

The first thing you will probably want to do is enter some text into some of the cells. For example, if you are setting up a spreadsheet that keeps track of your diet plan for the day, you need enter a title for the list and then some column labels, as shown in Figure 4.2.

Skipping the Enter

If you're entering information in a series of cells, you don't need to press Enter after each entry. Instead, press the arrow key pointing in the direction of the next cell. Works accepts the entry and moves to the next cell all in one motion. If you're entering data into adjacent cells in a row, you can press Tab after each entry to accept the data and then move one cell to the right.

Entering text into a cell

1. Click the cell (or use the keyboard shortcuts to go to the cell) in which you want the text to appear. That cell then becomes the *active cell*.

2. Type the text. As you type, the text appears in both the cell and in the formula bar at the top of the spreadsheet.

3. Press Enter or click the check mark next to the formula bar to accept your text entry.

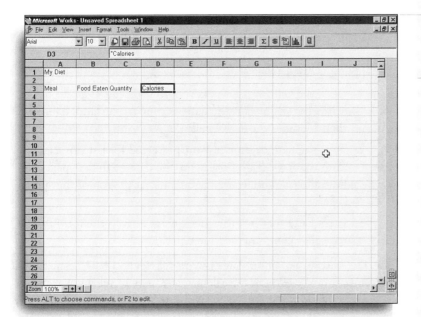

FIGURE 4.2
Most spreadsheets start out with some text.

Entering Numbers

Entering numbers works the same as entering text; just position the cell cursor in the cell in which you want to enter, and then type the numbers. If the numbers you are entering require special symbols, such as currency or percentage, you can enter them now if you like, or you can format the cells with a special formatting that applies those symbols automatically. (You'll learn about that later in this chapter.)

Entering Dates and Times

Dates and times are considered "numbers" by the spreadsheet, and it can perform calculations on them. For example, if you have 7/7/98 in one cell and 7/1/98 in another, and you ask the spreadsheet (through a formula) to subtract the second from the first, the result will be 6 (for 6 days).

A date's number is the number of days between it and January 1, 1900. So, for example, January 1, 1900 would be 1, and December 31, 1999 would be 36,525. Times are measured in decimal points after the whole number. So, for example, if 1 is midnight on January 1, 1900, then 1.5 would be noon on that day, and 1.75 would be 6:00 p.m.

What happened to my zeros?

If you're typing figures with decimal points, your trailing zeros will disappear. For instance, the number 55.10 will appear as 55.1. This is normal. It happens because the spreadsheet is automatically set in the General format. Later in this chapter, you'll learn how to apply different number formats. Meanwhile, don't worry—the calculations will still be correct even without the zero.

However, you don't see these raw numbers on your spreadsheet because Works formats dates in a more readable date format, such as 1/1/00 or 6:00 p.m.

Entering a date or time

1. Click the cell (or use the keyboard shortcuts to go to the cell) where you want the date or time to appear. That cell then becomes the active cell.

2. Type the date or time in your preferred format (for example, xx/xx/xx or xx:xx). As you type, the date or time appears in both the cell and in the formula bar at the top of the spreadsheet.

3. Press Enter or click the check mark next to the formula bar to accept your date or time entry.

The best way to enter dates is with slashes (1/12/97), especially if you want to use them for calculations such as figuring ages or length of employment. You can always format it later to appear in some other format (such as January 12, 1998). Avoid entering the date with dashes (such as 1-12-97) because Works treats that as text and won't recognize it as a date for calculations.

When entering times, add AM or PM for morning or afternoon (10:00 PM) or use the 24-hour or military clock (22:00). You can specify time to the second (10:00:03 PM).

Using Undo

If you make a mistake in an entry as you are typing it, just backspace and enter the correct text. Don't use the arrow keys to move back and forth, because you'll end up in one of the cells next to the one in which you wanted to enter the data, and your mistake will appear in the original cell.

After you accept the entry, the fastest way to fix it is to undo the mistake. Open the **Edit** menu and choose **Undo Entry.** (Ctrl+Z is the keyboard shortcut for **Undo**). You must use Undo immediately after making the error because you can undo only the last thing you did.

SEE ALSO
➤ *To choose different date and time formats, see page 105.*

Selecting Cells and Ranges

Before you can delete, move, copy, or format data, you must
select the cells to be involved in the operation. The active cell is
automatically selected, but you also can select a range of cells. A
range is a rectangular group of cells connected either horizontally or vertically. It can be as small as one or two cells or as large
as the entire spreadsheet.

The range is referenced by the first cell in the upper-left corner
of the range and the last cell in the lower-right corner of the
range. When written, a range reference always has a colon
between the cell addresses that define it, such as A1:C9.

The selected cells in a range are surrounded by a thick border
and all but the first cell in the selection appear in reverse highlighting (see Figure 4.3). The range reference appears in the Cell
Address area.

Table 4.3 lists the methods (both keyboard and mouse) for highlighting cells in your spreadsheet.

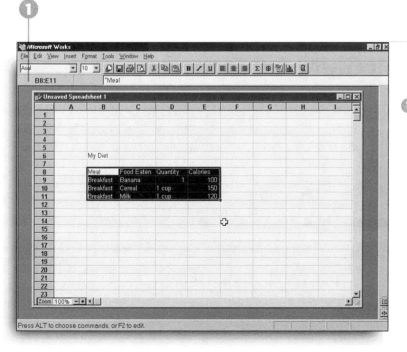

FIGURE 4.3

A range of selected cells is shown
in this spreadsheet.

❶ Range reference

Entering a large block of data quickly

When you have to enter data in a large block of cells, highlight the cells first. Then starting in the first cell in the upper-left corner of the block, enter the data and press Enter. Works automatically moves you to the next cell, first going down one column, then moving to the top of the next column to the right, down that column, then to the next column on the right, and so on.

TABLE 4.3   **How to highlight (select) cells**

To Highlight...	Mouse Method	Keyboard Method
A cell	Click the cell.	Press an arrow key.
A group of cells	Click first cell, hold down the mouse button, and drag to the last cell in the group.	Position cursor in the first cell in the upper-left corner of the group, press F8, and then use the arrow keys to highlight the rest of the cells.
A row	Click the row header.	Highlight one cell in the row and then press Ctrl+F8.
A column	Click the column header.	Highlight one cell in the column and press Shift+F8.
The entire spreadsheet	Click the corner header cell in which the column headers and row headers meet (upper-left corner of spreadsheet).	Press Ctrl+Shift+F8.

Modifying Cell Contents

These next few sections deal with ways to make changes to what you've entered in your cells, short of wiping it all out and starting over. Changes are inevitable, even if you carefully planned ahead of time! You may need to change the data in a cell, move or copy it, clear it out completely, or any of several other operations.

Editing Data

If you've entered data incorrectly and it's too late to undo the entry with the **Undo** command, you can correct it by replacing the entry or by editing the entry. To replace information in a cell, click the cell containing the information you want to replace, type the new information, and press Enter. The new entry wipes out the old one.

To edit a cell, click it and then press F2 or click in the formula bar to move the insertion point into that cell for changes. Use the Backspace or Delete key to remove what's there as needed, and type your changes. Press Enter when you're done.

Deleting Cell Content

To delete data from a cell or group of cells, highlight the cell or cells that contain the data, and then press the Delete key on the keyboard or open the **Edit** menu and choose **Clear**.

If you accidentally delete data in the wrong cell, quickly open the **Edit** menu and choose **Undo Clear**.

Moving or Copying Cell Content

You can move or copy data from one part of a spreadsheet to another, or from one spreadsheet to another spreadsheet. For example, perhaps you have decided that the column on the left side would look better on the right? Or that the rows are in the wrong order? Or maybe you want a copy of a particular row to appear on a different spreadsheet?

To move or copy cells, you can either cut and paste them, as you learned how to do with text in Chapter 2, or you can use a different technique called *drag and drop*.

Moving or copying with drag and drop

  1. Select the cell you want to move or copy.

  2. Point to the edge of the highlighted cell or group of cells, so the word "DRAG" appears on the mouse pointer (see Figure 4.4).

  3. Hold down the left mouse button and drag the highlighted cell to a new location. If you want to copy (as opposed to move), hold down the Ctrl key too. An outline of the cells appears as you drag, and the word "MOVE" or "COPY" replaces "DRAG" under the mouse pointer. Release the mouse button and the data is relocated.

SEE ALSO

➤ *For a reminder about how to use the cut-and-paste method, see page 28.*

Have a clear destination in mind

When you move cells, the destination cells must be blank. If you move cells onto cells with existing content, the existing content goes away. So before you move cells, you may have to insert some blank ones. See "Inserting Columns and Rows" later in this chapter to learn how to do that.

Move versus copy

As you drag, make sure the mouse pointer says the right thing. If you are trying to copy, but the mouse pointer says "Move," you didn't press and hold the Ctrl key before pressing and holding the mouse button. Release both buttons and try again.

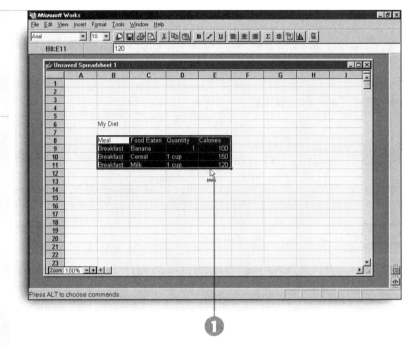

Finding and Replacing Data

The spreadsheet tool uses the same Find and Replace procedures as the word processor, which you learned about in Chapter 2. Turn back to "Finding and Replacing Text" in that chapter and try out the same steps on your spreadsheet, just to reinforce the skills.

Working with Formulas

A *formula* is an algebraic expression using numbers, *functions*, and cell addresses that tell a spreadsheet program what operations to perform on those numbers or the contents of the designated cells. A formula can be as simple as 1+1. The result of that formula, of course, is 2.

In a spreadsheet, formulas are often written using cell references rather than actual numbers. For example, a formula in cell C1 might be =A1+B1. (The equal sign preceding the formula tells Works that it is a formula and not regular text.) Such a formula would add up whatever numbers happened to be in cells A1 and B1 at the moment and place the answer in cell C1. For example, in Figure 4.5, cell A1 contains 10 and cell B1 contains 12. The formula in cell C1 (=A1+B1) results in an answer of 22.

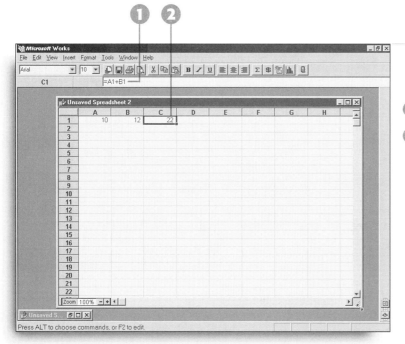

FIGURE 4.5

The simple formula in cell C1 sums A1 and B1.

❶ Formula appears in formula bar.

❷ Result in cell

Formulas are always written with no spaces, and they start with an equal sign. To indicate the type of operation you want the spreadsheet to perform, you need to use *operators* in a formula. You assign, modify, or combine values into new values by using operators. The most common operators are *arithmetic operators*, as listed in Table 4.4.

TABLE 4.4   **Arithmetic operators**

Operator	Use to...	Example
+	Add two numbers or cell addresses	=C5+C9
–	Subtract two numbers or cell addresses	=C5-C9
*	Multiply two numbers or cell addresses	=C5*C9
/	Divide two numbers or cell addresses	=C5/C9

A formula is calculated from left to right. For example, if the formula is =C6+C9-C10, the contents of cell C6 are added to the contents of cell C9 and the contents of cell C10 are then subtracted from that result.

Arithmetic operators evaluate in the following order: exponents, multiplication and division, and then addition and subtraction. Therefore, the result of the formula =6+4/2 is 8 because the division (4/2) is evaluated first and then added to the 6.

If the formula contains an *exponent*, it's calculated first so the result of the formula =6+4^2/2 is 14. The exponent (4^2) is calculated first, the result of 16 is then divided by 2 for an answer of 8, and that answer is added to 6.

If your formula is more complicated, you might want to group expressions by using parentheses. For example, in algebra a formula might be (x*y)/(z-y). When parentheses are used in a formula, the calculation within the parentheses is performed first. In this formula, you would calculate the answer to x*y first and then divide it by the answer to z-y. So in a spreadsheet formula such as =(C5*C9)-(D11/D12), the answer to C5*C9 is calculated first, then the answer to D11/D12 is calculated, and finally the two answers are subtracted.

For example, the formula =6+4/2 results in 8 but the formula (6+4)/2 results in 5 because the addition in the parentheses is calculated first and then the division occurs.

Entering a formula in a cell

1. Click the cell in which you want the result of the formula to appear.

2. Type an equal sign to indicate that you're entering a formula.

3. Type the values, cell addresses, range references, and operators you need to create your formula.

4. Press Enter or click the check mark next to the formula bar. The formula results appear in the cell and the formula itself appears in the formula bar.

Using AutoSum

One of the most common formulas involves adding a column or row of numbers. Works provides a special function called AutoSum that handles such activities very efficiently.

For example, suppose you want to add the numbers for each quarter in Figure 4.6. You should place formulas that sum each column in row 11. For example, in cell B11 you could enter =B7+B8+B9+B10. That's a bit tedious, however, because you have to type all those cell references. There is a better way.

Using point and paint

When you want to use a range reference in a formula, enter the formula up to the point where you need the range reference, and then highlight the range of cells you want to reference. Works automatically displays the cell reference on the formula bar. Type the next character of the formula or press Enter, and the range reference becomes part of the formula. If you've assigned a name to that range of cells, the range name automatically appears in place of the cells addresses.

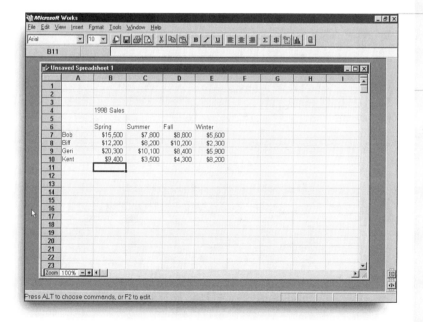

FIGURE 4.6

Columns and rows of numbers like these can be easily added with AutoSum.

Using AutoSum to sum a column of numbers

1. Enter the numbers in your spreadsheet that you want to sum. For example, from Figure 4.6 we'll sum the values in B7 through B10.

2. Click in the cell in which you want the result to appear (for example, B11 in Figure 4.6.)

3. Click the **AutoSum** Σ button on the toolbar.

4. Works makes a guess at what you want to sum (see Figure 4.7). If the range outlined is correct, press Enter. If not, drag across the cells that you actually want to sum, and then press Enter.

FIGURE 4.7

AutoSum makes its best guess about what you want to sum, based on the position of the cell.

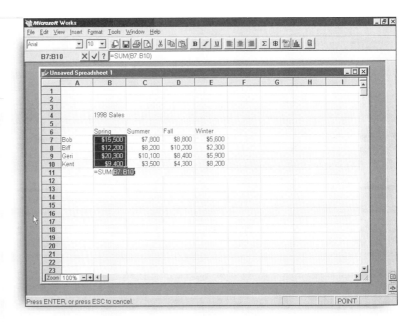

After you press Enter, you'll see a formula in the formula bar: =SUM(B7:B10). You have just created your first formula that uses a function! A function, as you'll learn a bit later in this chapter, is a special keyword that applies a certain bit of math to the selected cells. In this case, the function is SUM and the math it applies is addition. Don't worry too much about this now; just keep it in mind for later use.

Modifying Formulas

You can edit formulas in basically the same way you edit text and numbers in cells. Just click in the cell and then do your editing on the formula bar. Use the arrow keys to position the cursor within the formula bar, and use Backspace or Delete to remove unwanted characters.

Moving and Copying Formulas

You can move and copy formulas the same way you move and copy regular text: either with the drag-and-drop or cut-and-paste techniques described earlier. (The result is slightly different when you move formulas than when you move regular text, but we'll get into that momentarily.)

Copying with Fill

You can copy a formula cell as you would any data cell. Point at the cell's handle (small black box) in the lower-right corner of the cell border. The word FILL appears beneath the mouse pointer. Drag to the right to fill a row or down to fill a column, highlighting the number of cells to which you want to copy the formula, and then release the mouse button.

You can also copy with the **Fill** command on the menu. Highlight the formula cell, and then drag across the cells you want to fill to highlight them. Open the **Edit** menu and choose **Fill Right** from the menu for a row or choose **Fill Down** for a column.

Understanding Relative and Absolute References

Your formula may contain cell addresses. When you move or copy a formula, you probably don't want those addresses to stay the same. For example in Figure 4.8, cell B11 has an AutoSum formula that totals the values in that column. I want to copy that formula to cell C11, but I want the formula to refer to column C, rather than B, so the result in C11 is =SUM(C7:C10) rather than =SUM(B7:B10). Works handles this change automatically.

When you move or copy a formula, the new version refers to the cells in similar positions relative to its new home rather than to the original positions. This is called *relative addressing*.

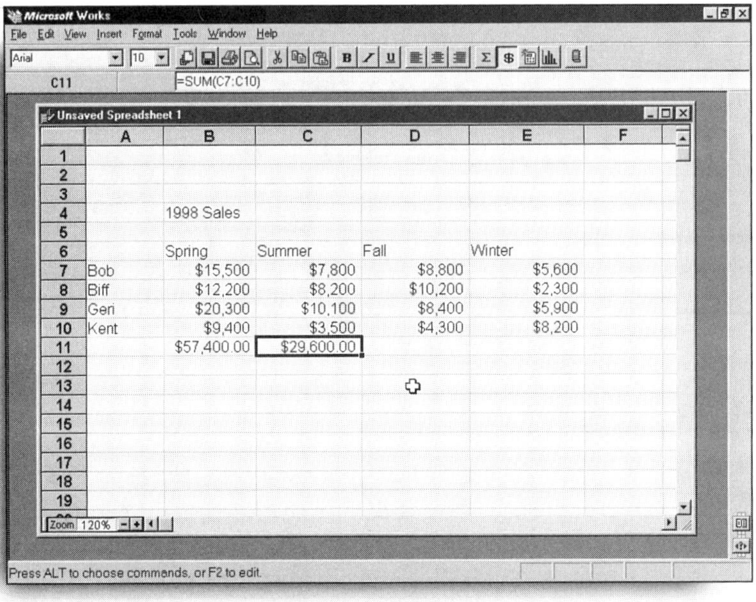

FIGURE 4.8

The formula in B11 was copied to C11, and when it got there, it changed its references automatically to refer to column C.

Relative addressing changes the cell addresses relative to the position of the formula. This is true if you copy the formula from one row or column to the next, or from one side of your worksheet to the other.

All this works beautifully until you want every copied formula to refer to the same exact cell. For example, take a look at Figure 4.9. You have the current sales commission rate in cell F3. In rows F7 through F10 you have values for the total sales for each salesperson. To calculate the amount of commission due each salesperson, you want to multiply the total sales amount by the rate of commission so you enter the formula =F7*F3 in cell G7. However, if you copy that formula down the column, the commission due amounts will be obviously incorrect for the remaining salespeople.

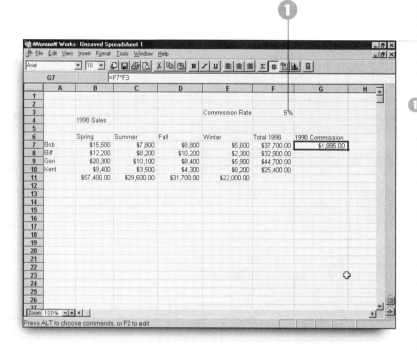

FIGURE 4.9

In this case, copying the formula would not give the desired result.

1 F3 needs to stay static in all copies.

The solution to this problem is to use *absolute addressing*. Absolute addressing marks the exact, original location of a cell in a spreadsheet. To reference such a location in a formula, use dollar signs before the column letter and row number (F3).

For example in Figure 4.9, the formula entered in cell G7 should have been =F7*F3. The F7 cell address could change as the formula was copied to another cell (it's relative), but the F3 cell address, which is absolute, should remain the same in every copied formula.

Refer to Table 4.5 to learn where to put the dollar signs in your cell address and how it affects the copied formula.

Making the reference absolute

You can type the dollar signs in manually, but there's an easier way. Highlight the cell reference in the worksheet to place the cell address in your formula in the formula bar. Then press F4, which cycles you through absolute, relative, and mixed reference types each time you press it. Mixed references keep row references absolute while the column references are relative, or row references relative while column references are absolute (dollar signs mark which references are absolute).

TABLE 4.5   **Where does the dollar sign go?**

Type of Reference	Example	How It Acts in a Copied Formula
Absolute column, absolute row	F3	Refers to an exact cell. The cell address doesn't change in the copied formula.
Absolute column, relative row	$F3	The column of the address always remains the same, but the row can change.
Relative column, absolute row	F$3	The row of the address always remains the same, but the column can change.
Relative column, relative row	F3	The row and the column can change.

SEE ALSO

➤ *To learn more about functions, see page 92.*

➤ *To recall how to move cell contents with drag and drop, see page 83.*

➤ *For more information about cut and paste and the Clipboard, see page 28.*

Working with Functions

Functions are built-in formulas that can save you time when you need to do complicated calculations. The amount of time they save you is proportional to the complexity of the math that the function performs. You have already seen one function at work: SUM. Recall that entering =SUM(B7:B10) is the same as entering =B7+B8+B9+B10. Let's look at another example that saves even more time.

Suppose you need to find the average of five cells of values. To do it with a formula, you would add all the values and divide by the number of cells. This could result in a formula like this: =(C1+C2+C3+C4+C5)/5. Works has a function (AVG) that will average for you and write the formula using a function name (=AVG(C1:C5)). Much simpler, isn't it?

Types of Functions

Functions fall into eight categories:

- *Financial.* Functions that deal with monetary matters, such as calculating interest on a loan or the term of a loan.
- *Date and Time.* Functions that perform operations to put the current date and time on your spreadsheet or pull out the serial number for the date or time for calculation purposes.
- *Math and Trig.* Functions that help you calculate logarithms, absolute numbers, rounded numbers, integers, exponents, and trigonometric functions (cosine, sine, tangent, cotangent, and so forth).
- *Statistical.* These functions do many of the everyday calculations such as sums, averages, and counting.
- *Lookup and Ref.* These functions work with lookup tables that you create within your spreadsheet. They also pull information from those tables into your formulas.
- *Text.* Functions that help you manipulate text strings by pulling out portions or by converting some portions of text for other use.
- *Logical.* These functions enable you to work with conditional statements (if this, then that).
- *Informational.* Functions used to notify you of errors in formulas and values.

Function Syntax

Several rules apply when writing formulas, and these rules are referred to as the *syntax rules*. You must follow syntax rules or your formulas will not work. Those rules that apply specifically to functions are

- Precede the function formula with an equal sign.
- Function names must be capitalized (such as SUM).
- If functions use *arguments*, the argument must follow the function (see the next section). These arguments must be enclosed in parentheses.

Using text strings in arguments

If text in a formula consists of single characters that aren't part of a cell address or one or more words, it is considered a text string. For example, in an inventory spreadsheet you might want the words "out of stock" to appear if the inventory of an item is 0. Such a formula might be written =IF(C7=0,"out of stock",C7). The phrase "out of stock" is a text string.

- Arguments must be separated by commas.
- If you use a *text string* as an argument, the text must be in quotes (" ").

Using Arguments

An *argument* in a function is the information you provide in order for the function to perform properly. An argument can be a number, a formula, a cell address, a range reference, a text string, or another function.

For example, in the function =IF(`condition,action,else-action`), "condition," "action," and "else-action" are the arguments.

Arguments are always enclosed in parentheses and separated by commas.

Entering Functions in Cells

You can insert a function into a cell in several ways, ranging from quickest to most foolproof:

- You can enter the function manually by typing it directly into the cell. This is fast, but it requires that you know exactly what the function name is and what arguments to enter.
- You can insert the function by opening the **Insert** menu and choosing **Function,** then replacing the placeholders with real arguments, as explained in the steps that follow this list.
- You can use Easy Calc to choose and insert a formula, which takes the most time but requires the least knowledge about functions.

Inserting the function in the cell

1. Click the cell where you want to use the function.
2. Open the **Insert** menu and choose **Function**. The Insert Function dialog box appears (see Figure 4.10).

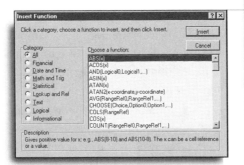

3. Under **Category**, choose the type of function you want. If you aren't sure, leave it set to **All**.

4. Click the function you want to use from the **Choose a function** list box.

5. Click **Insert**. The function appears in the cell with the first argument highlighted.

6. (Optional) Click the **Help** 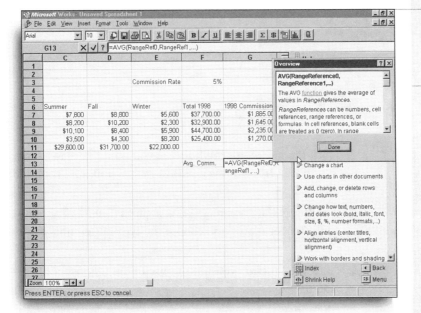 button in the bottom-right corner of the screen. A Help window appears with an overview of the function (see Figure 4.11).

7. Click the cells or type in the argument information required by the function. For example, if you want to average some cells, this is the time to drag across those cells to select them. Follow the instructions in the Help window if you're not sure what to do.

8. Delete any extraneous argument placeholders in the function. For example, if there were multiple placeholders for arguments but you only entered one argument, remove the rest with the Backspace or Delete key.

9. Press Enter to complete the function.

Using Easy Calc to enter a function

1. Click in the cell where you want the results of the formula to appear.

2. Open the **Tools** menu and choose **Easy Calc** or click the **Easy Calc** button ▦ on the toolbar. The Easy Calc dialog box appears (see Figure 4.12).

FIGURE 4.12

Use Easy Calc to choose a function and enter its arguments.

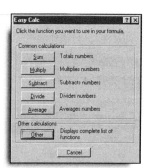

3. Click the button for the function you want and skip to step 7, or click **Other** to see a full list of functions and continue on to step 4.

4. The Insert Function dialog box appears (refer to Figure 4.10). Under **Category**, choose the type of function you want.

5. Click the function you want to use in the **Choose a function** list box.

6. Click **Insert**. A dialog box specific to the selected function appears (see Figure 4.13).

FIGURE 4.13
Easy Calc shows controls specific to the function you chose.

7. Enter whatever values or cell addresses you need to complete your formula (or click the appropriate cells to enter the addresses).

8. Click **Next**.

9. Easy Calc asks you to confirm the cell address where the formula will go. Enter the correct cell address if it isn't already showing in the **Result at** box.

10. Click **Finish**. The result of the function appears in the cell (you can see the function in the formula bar).

Moving Data Around in a Spreadsheet

Even after you get all your data entered and all your formulas and functions set, you still may not be satisfied with your work. Sometimes rows and columns need to be moved around, or sorted in a different order. The following sections offer some advice aimed toward organizing your spreadsheet in the most pleasing way.

Sorting Data

Another use for a spreadsheet besides raw calculations is keeping track of lists of things. The Database tool also does this, but if the list contains one or more columns of numbers that need to be totaled, it is sometimes easier to use the spreadsheet. Figure 4.14 shows how I have entered my tax-deductible medical expenses on a spreadsheet and entered a =SUM function to give me a total.

FIGURE 4.14

Keeping a list on a spreadsheet can sometimes make sense.

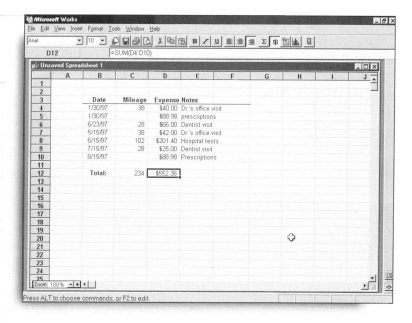

When you keep such records on a spreadsheet, you may find that you need to sort the rows differently than you had originally entered them. You can sort rows of data by any column, and all the items in that row stay together. For example, you could re-sort the lines in Figure 4.14 by the Expense column, either from least to most or most to least, and the appropriate dates, descriptions, and notes would stay with each expense.

Sorting data

1. Select the data you want to sort. Make sure you select the entire range, including all the columns that you want to stay together. For example, in Figure 4.14 you would select B4:E10. Do not select column or row labels or lines containing totals.

2. Open the **Tools** menu and choose **Sort**. (The first time you do this, an extra dialog box appears; click **OK** to clear it.) The Sort dialog box appears (see Figure 4.15).

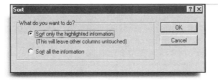

FIGURE 14.15

Specify what kind of sorting you want.

3. Leave **Sort only the highlighted information** marked, and click **OK.**

4. When the dialog box changes (see Figure 4.16) choose the column you want to use for sorting from the **Sort By** drop-down list.

FIGURE 4.16

Select the column you want to sort by and the sort order.

5. Choose your sort order: Select **Ascending** to sort the column A-Z, 1-100, **Descending** to sort Z-A, 100-1.

6. If the first row of your highlighted sort range has column headings, select **Header row** under **My list has** so Works will ignore that row when it sorts. Otherwise, select **No header row**.

7. Click **Sort**. The dialog box goes away and your data is sorted.

If you want to sort by more than one column, click the **Advanced** button in the Sort dialog box. As you can see in Figure 4.17, you can then specify a second and third column to sort by. (This is useful if the first column contains last names and the second column holds first names. You might want to sort first by last names and then by first names in case you have more than one person with the same last name.) To start the sort from the Advanced options box, click **Sort**.

Header row or **No header row**

If you followed my advice in step 1 when selecting, you will choose **No header row** in step 6 because the column labels are not included in your selected range. After you become familiar with this process, you may sometimes want to include the column labels in your selected range and then choose **Header row** in step 6; this has the advantage of putting the labels from that row in the Sort by drop-down list instead of generic names like Column B.

FIGURE 4.17

Click **Advanced** to sort by more than one column.

Inserting and Deleting Rows and Columns

As you build your spreadsheet, you may find that you need to make some changes. Perhaps you need to add a column to accommodate another type of data, remove an extraneous row, or widen a column. Let's take a look at the changes you can make.

Inserting columns

1. Click the column header to the right of where you want to add the column. This action highlights that column.
2. Open the **Insert** menu and choose **Insert Column**. The columns move over to make room for the new column.

Inserting rows

1. Click the row heading *below* where you want to add the row. That row will be highlighted.
2. Open the **Insert** menu and choose **Insert Row**. The rows move down to make room for the new row.

To delete a column or row, just click its row or column header to highlight it, and then open the **Insert** menu and choose either **Delete Column** or **Delete Row**.

Moving Columns and Rows

Moving columns and rows is actually more common than deleting them. You may need to move a column or row to reorganize your spreadsheet. (Your idea of the perfect layout may change as you enter your data. Mine often does.)

As I mentioned earlier in the chapter, when moving or copying cell data, you have to be careful about pasting data over the top of—and thereby overwriting—existing data. If you select a range of cells and drag them onto the top of another range that already contains data, the old data is replaced.

When moving and copying entire rows and columns in Works, you don't have this problem. That's because the existing rows and columns automatically move over to make room for the incoming stuff. That's good because you don't have to create new rows and columns to hold the moved or copied material, so it saves you a step.

You can use the cut-and-paste method to move or copy rows and columns, as you learned earlier in this chapter. But the easiest way to move or copy rows and columns is with drag and drop.

Moving or copying rows or columns

1. Click the gray column header to highlight the column you want to move, or click the gray row header to highlight the row you want to move.

2. Position the mouse pointer on the edge of the row or column, so the mouse pointer reads "DRAG."

3. If you are copying (rather than moving), press and hold the Ctrl key.

4. Hold down the mouse button and move the mouse until a dark line appears where you want the row or column to go. The mouse pointer reads "MOVE" as shown in Figure 4.18.

5. Release the mouse button (and the Ctrl key if needed).

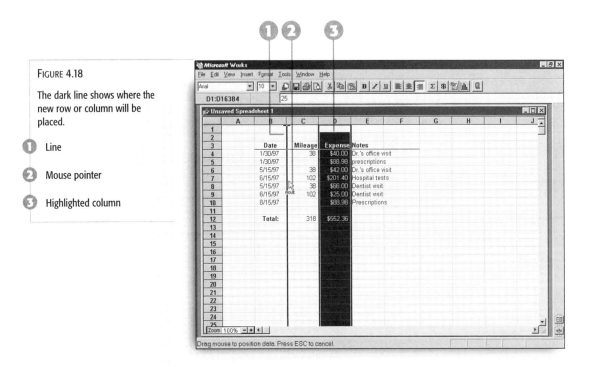

FIGURE 4.18

The dark line shows where the new row or column will be placed.

1 Line

2 Mouse pointer

3 Highlighted column

SEE ALSO

➤ *To learn how to rearrange rows through sorting, see page 97.*

➤ *To move or copy data in cells, see page 83.*

Formatting Your Spreadsheet

In some ways, formatting a spreadsheet is the same as formatting a word processing document. You have text that you can apply different fonts and sizes to, margins to set, and a paper size and orientation to specify. I won't bore you by repeating the steps for the procedures that are the same, but I do want to introduce you to some new formatting procedures that are unique to spreadsheets.

SEE ALSO

➤ *To format text in cells, refer to page 44.*

➤ *To set page margins, see page 59.*

➤ *To set the paper size and orientation, see page 60.*

➤ *To enter page breaks, see page 57.*

Changing Number Formats

Number "helpers" like dollar signs and percentages are not considered real characters in a number within a cell. Instead, they are *formats*, somewhat like bold and italic. When you apply the Currency format to a cell, and a dollar sign is placed in front of whatever number it contains. When you change the number in the cell, the dollar sign remains associated with the cell, as long as the cell is formatted as Currency.

If you type a dollar sign (or some other sign) as you are entering a number, Works interprets it as a message to format that cell with the specified number format. That's one way to apply a number format, but there's an easier way. You can enter the numbers "plain" and then apply the number formatting to an entire range of cells at once. For example, you could enter an entire column of sales figures, and then highlight the column and apply the Currency format to the entire column at once.

The number formats you can choose from are

- *General format.* Displays numbers as precisely as possible. The number of decimal places appears as it is typed. Trailing zeros, however, disappear (if you type 12.30 it appears as 12.3. Larger numbers are shown in exponential format (1.23E+03).

- *Fixed format.* Displays the numbers with the specified number of decimal places (if you specify 3 decimal places and you enter 12.3, it appears as 12.300).

- *Currency format.* Automatically adds a dollar sign to the beginning of the number and includes a comma separator if the number is 1,000 or over. You may specify the number of decimal places you want to see, but 2 is the default setting.

- *Comma format.* Automatically includes a comma separator if the number is 1,000 or over.

- *Percent format.* Automatically shows the number as if it had been multiplied by 100 and adds the percentage sign at the end of the number.

- *Exponential format.* Shows larger numbers as a base number with an exponent. For example, the number 1,000,000 shows as 1.00E+06.

Quick cash

You can quickly apply the Currency number format by clicking the **Currency** button $ on the toolbar.

Planning for percentages

If you're entering numbers that you intend to later format as percentages, make sure you write them in the correct decimal format (0.15 becomes 15%).

- *Leading Zeros format.* Adds zeros to show the specified number of places (if you enter 1, it appears as 00001 if you specify 5 places).

- *Fraction format.* Changes a fraction entered in decimals to a standard fraction preceded by a zero (0.03125 becomes 0 1/32). If you enter a number in fraction format, this format is automatically applied to that cell. However, the decimal equivalent of the number appears on the formula bar.

- *True/False format.* Displays all zeros as FALSE and all non-zero values as TRUE.

- *Date/Time format.* Displays the number as a date or time.

- *Text format.* Enables you to specify a numerical entry as text. For example, if you enter a phone number, you want to format it as text.

Formatting affects only the appearance of the number. Works still uses the unformatted number when calculating. Therefore, if you have formatted a cell to display the number 0.751 with 1 decimal place, it appears as .7, but when you refer to that cell in a formula, it uses the actual value of 0.751.

Changing a cell's number format

1. Select the cell or cells you want to format. You can format entire rows and columns at a time, or even the entire worksheet.

2. Open the **Format** menu and choose **Number**. The Format Cells dialog box appears (see Figure 4.19).

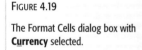

FIGURE 4.19

The Format Cells dialog box with **Currency** selected.

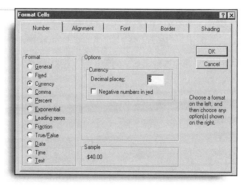

3. Under **Format**, select the type of format you want to use.

4. Under **Options**, specify any options you want for that format such as number of decimal places. Check the **Sample** area to see how your choice affects the number.

5. Click **OK**. Any formatting you chose is applied to the cell.

Changing Date and Time Formats

Dates and times are considered numbers in Works, so you can perform calculations on them. For a cell to properly display a date or time, it must be formatted with the Date or Time format. Otherwise, the cell's contents will appear as a meaningless string of numbers or characters.

Times are actually decimals of whole numbers. For example, 3:00 a.m. is 0.125 because that's the percentage of 24 hours that 3 hours represents. (24 hours represents a whole day, or 1.)

You can choose from many different date and time formats. To look at the formats, enter a date or time into a cell, and then follow these steps.

Changing the date or time format

1. Select the cell or cells you want to format with a date or time format (or a different one).

2. Open the **Format** menu and choose **Number**. The Format Cells dialog box appears.

3. Under **Format**, select **Time** or **Date**.

4. Under **Options**, choose the format you want from the list (see Figure 4.20). You'll find lots of different ways to express the date or time here, from simple ones like 2/98 to fancy ones like February 23, 1998.

5. Click **OK**. The formatting you selected is applied to the cell.

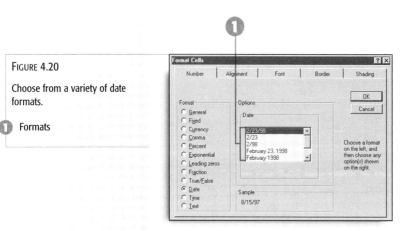

FIGURE 4.20

Choose from a variety of date
formats.

1 Formats

SEE ALSO

➤ *To learn more about entering dates and times, see page 79.*

Changing Column Width and Row Height

By default, the columns in your spreadsheet are set to a width of
10 characters. If you type more into a cell than it can hold, the
extra spills over into the next cell to the right. If that cell isn't
empty, the content is truncated, so you see only a portion of it.
(Even though you may not be able to see a cell's full content, the
content is still there, and is still applicable to any calculations
you perform on that cell's content.)

Row heights are somewhat different; they adjust automatically to
accommodate whatever is in the cell. For example, if you have
26-point type in a cell, the cell's height increases so you can see
the text. If you then reformat that text to 12-point, the cell's
height decreases.

The easiest way to change the column width or row height is to
drag it with the mouse. Point to the line to the right of the column, or below the row you want to adjust. The mouse pointer
reads ADJUST. Then drag in the direction you need to increase
or decrease the width or height (see Figure 4.21).

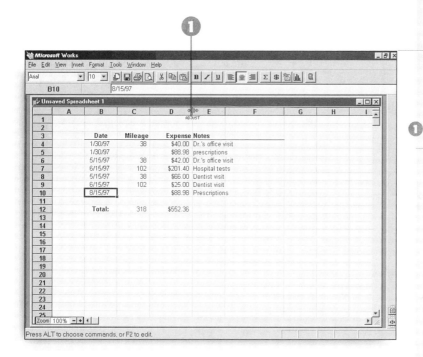

FIGURE 4.21

Position the mouse pointer between columns and drag to change the width.

① Mouse pointer

If you need more precise changes (for example, if you need all the columns to be exactly the same width), you must open a dialog box and make your changes there.

Changing column width

1. Click one of the cells in the column. If you want to change several columns at once, select them.

2. Open the **Format** menu and choose **Column Width**. The Column Width dialog box appears (see Figure 4.22).

FIGURE 4.22

Use the Column Width dialog box to precisely set the column width.

3. To specify the exact column width in number of characters, enter a figure in the **Column width** box. Then click **OK**. You can also do one of the following:

Click **Standard** to immediately return the column width to 10 characters wide and close the dialog box.

Click **Best Fit** to have Works automatically select a column width that best fits the text in the column and immediately resize the column. This also closes the dialog box.

The row height works the same way, except you use the **Row Height** command on the **Format** menu instead of the **Column Width** command.

SEE ALSO

➤ *Cell height can also be affected by wrapping, which lets the text in a cell wrap to multiple lines. To learn more about wrapping, see page 109.*

Aligning Text

You already know something about aligning text from reading the word processing chapters in this book: text can align to the left, center, or right. In the case of a spreadsheet, text aligns within its cell rather than within the entire printed page.

When you enter text in a spreadsheet, Works automatically aligns that text to the left within each cell, and numbers to the right. This may or may not be the most attractive placement for your spreadsheet; you can decide this for yourself and make a change to one or more cells as needed. For example, you may want to center labels you enter at the head of columns, or make the word "Total" appear on the right side of a cell.

The quickest way to change the text alignment is to use the buttons on the toolbar. They work the same as in the word processor.

Other special alignment options are available that pertain only to spreadsheets, but you can't access them from the toolbar; you must open the Format Cells dialog box.

Changing the cell alignment

1. Select the cell or cells whose alignment you want to change.

2. Open the **Format** menu and choose **Alignment**. The Format Cells dialog box appears with the **Alignment** tab selected (see Figure 4.23).

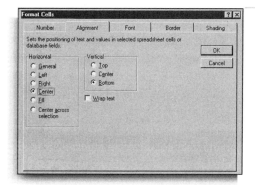

FIGURE 4.23
The Format Cells dialog box is shown with the **Alignment** tab selected.

3. Under **Horizontal**, choose one of the following:

- **General** to align text to the left, numbers to the right, and errors and logical values in the center

- **Left** to align the text on the left side of the cell

- **Right** to align the text on the right side of the cell

- **Center** to center the text between the left and right sides of the cell

- **Fill** to have the characters repeated until they fill the cell from left to right (such as to put asterisks across the cell)

- **Center across selection** to center the text across the cells you've selected

4. If your row is taller than the normal height of your text, select an option under **Vertical** to align your text with the **Top** of the cell, the **Center** of the cell from top to bottom, or the **Bottom** of the cell.

5. Click **OK**.

SEE ALSO

➤ *To learn more about text alignment options, see page 51.*

Using Word Wrap

As you've already learned, when your text overflows the size of a cell, it flows into the cell to the right only if that next cell is blank. If the cell to the right isn't empty, Works displays only the portion of the text that fits inside the left and right borders of your current cell.

However, the *Word Wrap option* in Works allows the text to wrap within the cell, making multiple lines of text within one cell. When you choose this option, you should be aware that the height of the cell increases, affecting the height of the entire row. This works especially well for cells that contain a lot of data, such as whole sentences. You won't want to widen such columns enough to accommodate the entire sentence, but you also won't want the sentence to be unreadable (see Figure 4.24).

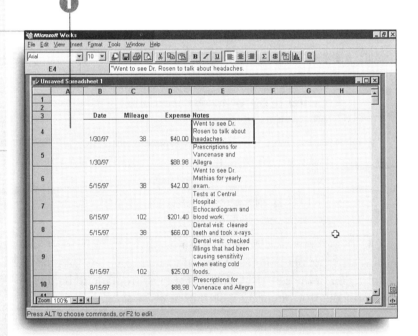

FIGURE 4.24

Word Wrap can be the answer to a tough formatting problem like this.

1 Row heights increase to accommodate extra lines.

Using Word Wrap

1. Enter the text in the cell.

2. Highlight the cell (or cells).

3. Open the **Format** menu and choose **Alignment**. The Format Cells dialog box appears with the Alignment tab selected (refer to Figure 4.23).

4. Click the **W**rap text check box.

5. Click **OK**.

Applying Borders and Shading

Using borders and shading organizes your spreadsheet into definite areas and makes a professional-looking printout. For example, you might want to shade the column headings to distinguish them from the data underneath them, or apply a bottom border to them to "draw a line" between heading and data.

A border can be applied to any or all sides of a cell individually. By applying a four-sided border around a group of cells, you "box them in." By applying a bottom border to a row, you draw a horizontal line under that row. Figure 4.25 shows some examples of what borders can do.

Borders versus gridlines

Don't confuse *borders* with *gridlines*. Those fine gray lines you see on the screen that separate each row and column are gridlines. They do not print unless you specifically set them to do so (by opening the **File** menu and choosing **Page Setup**). Borders are lines around cells that you manually apply yourself. They always print.

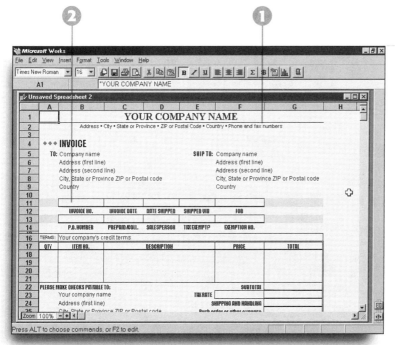

FIGURE 4.25

Borders can separate your work into meaningful groupings or create divisions.

1 This "line" is actually a bottom border applied to cells B1:G1.

2 This box is actually a four-sided border applied to B11.

Adding cell borders

1. Highlight the cells to which you want to apply a border.

2. Open the **Format** menu and choose **Border**. The Format Cells dialog box appears with the **Border** tab selected (see Figure 4.26).

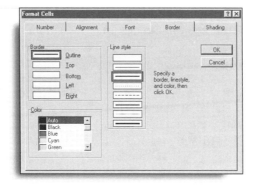

3. Under **Border**, select whether you want to apply the border to the **Outline** of the selection, or just the **Top, Bottom, Left**, or **Right** side. The **Outline** choice puts an outside border around the group of selected cells; the other choices refer to each of the individual cells in the selected range.

4. Under **Line style**, select the style of line you want to use.

5. From the **Color** list box, select a color to apply to the line.

6. If you want other kinds of borders around other sides of the selected range, go back to step 3 and choose another area, then work through steps 4 and 5 again to set a different style and color for it.

7. Click **OK**.

Shading works much the same way in a spreadsheet, calling attention to certain areas that you want the user to pay attention to. You can shade a cell that contains a total, for example, to draw the readers' eye there.

Applying cell shading

1. Highlight the cells to which you want to apply shading.

2. Open the **Format** menu and choose **Shading**. The Format Cells dialog box opens with the **Shading** tab selected (see Figure 4.27).

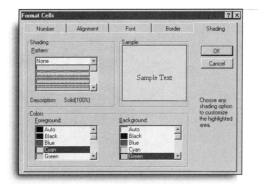

FIGURE 4.27
The Format Cells dialog box appears
with the **Shading** tab selected.

3. Under **Colors**, select a **Foreground** color and a
   Background color (for example, you could have blue checks
   on a yellow background). To use only one color, set the
   background color to white.

4. Under **Shading** make a selection from the **Pattern** list box.

5. Preview your selections in the **Sample** area. Click **OK** to
   accept your choices and close the dialog box.

Working with Charts

Works uses the word *chart* and *graph* interchangeably, and for the
most part, you can too. A chart is a pictorial representation of
the numerical information on the spreadsheet. A chart makes it
easier to understand a series of numbers, to interpret numbers as
trends, or to compare groups of numbers.

One of the most basic kinds of charts is a pie chart. A *pie chart* is
a circle divided into sections that represent percentages of a
whole (see Figure 4.28). It's a good way to illustrate how one
segment fits into the whole picture, or how a whole is being
divided (such as how your tax dollar is being used).

Another kind of chart plots numbers on an X and Y axis.
(Professionals call this kind of chart a *graph*, but Works doesn't
make the distinction.) The X axis is the horizontal line at the
bottom of the chart and the labels are categories. The Y axis is
the vertical line at the left of the chart and displays the values
(see Figure 4.29).

FIGURE 4.28

A pie chart shows how parts comprise the whole.

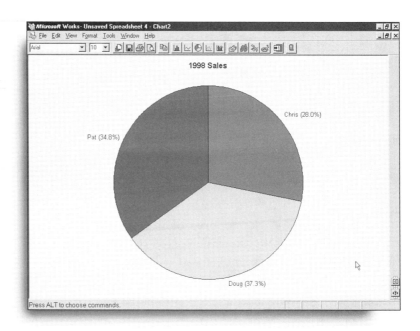

FIGURE 4.29

A bar chart compares values based on at least one variable. Here, the chart shows sales in 1997 compared to 1998.

1 Y axis

2 X axis

3 Legend

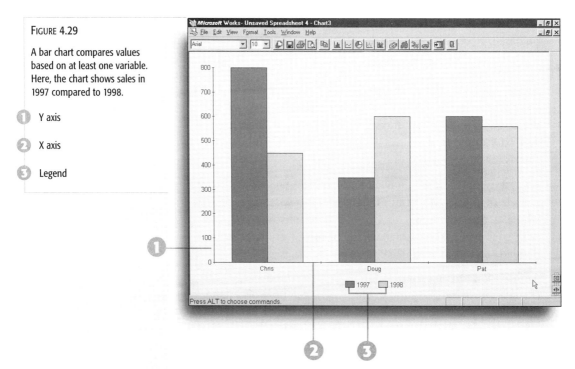

Works has several types of charts available:

- The *bar* chart is useful for comparing information.

- The *line* chart is useful for showing trends.

- Use the *area* chart to show trends versus a quota amount (as in actual sales versus planned sales) over a time period.

- *Scatter* charts are a favorite tool of statisticians who are plotting populations versus figures by showing just the data points.

- *Radar* charts are plotted around a center point and are used more by mathematicians.

- Works also has a *combined bar-line* chart.

After you've opened a spreadsheet and entered the data, the first step in creating a chart is to select the data to chart. If the chart is a pie chart, this involves only two sets of data: the slice labels and the values each slice represents. If the chart is some other kind, the data may involve several columns and rows.

To select the data, highlight the range. If you have rows that end in totals or columns that end in totals, don't include the totals in the chart range (unless you just want to chart the totals). If you have rows or columns that contain labels, however, you *should* include them, because they will become labels on the chart.

Using the general information provided in the preceding section, you should know what type of chart you want to make.

Creating a chart

1. Highlight the data you want to chart.

2. Open the **Tools** menu and choose **Create New Chart** or click the **New Chart** button [icon] on the toolbar. The New Chart dialog box opens (see Figure 4.30).

Chart smart

Don't use a chart just because it's pretty. If it doesn't have a point, don't bother with it. Don't spend a lot of time picking colors and line styles either. First of all, customizing a chart takes time. Secondly, a blue bar next to a red bar is just as readable as a blue bar next to a green bar, so if the chart gets the point across, changing the appearance isn't really necessary. Play with the colors only if you have a lot of time.

My data isn't all in one place

A chart requires *contiguous* data (all in one place on the spreadsheet). If yours isn't that way, use a nonprinting area of the spreadsheet and copy the data to that area. For example, to create a pie chart of the total sales for the year by salesperson, you only need the names of the salespeople and their totals. Copy just the names of the salespeople and their totals to another area of the spreadsheet and highlight that range to create the chart.

FIGURE 4.30

Select the chart type from the New Chart dialog box.

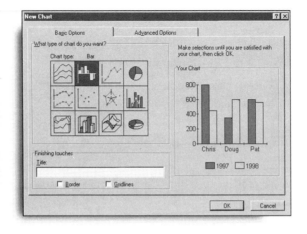

Gridlines and border

Gridlines are lines that run behind a chart (such as a bar or line chart) that help your eye follow the Y axis measurement across the screen. A *border* is a box around the entire chart.

3. Under **What type of chart do you want?** Works displays 12 chart types. Click one of the pictures to select that chart type. The **Your Chart** area displays the name of the chart and a sample of how your data will look using this chart type.

4. (Optional) Type a chart title in the **Title** text box, and mark the **Gridlines** and **Border** check boxes if you want either of those items.

5. Click **OK** to create the chart. The chart appears on your screen and a Chart toolbar is now available to use in modifying your chart.

From here, you can dress up and customize your chart with the tools on the toolbar and with the commands on the **Format** menu. (All the menus have special commands for modifying a chart whenever a chart is displayed.) Here's a sampling of what you can do:

- You can change the chart type or subtype by opening the **Format** menu and choosing **Chart Type**. Click a different chart type to change it. You can also click the **Variations** tab in the dialog box that appears and choose a different subtype. For example, with a pie chart, you can choose a subtype that displays the percentages next to each slice.

- On the **E**dit menu, you'll find commands that let you modify the data series, the title, and other text and data on the chart. For example, open the **E**dit menu and choose **T**itles to add a title to your chart.

- The **Fo**rmat menu contains many commands that fine-tune the chart appearance. For example, opening the **Fo**rmat menu and choosing **H**orizontal Axis lets you specify at what number that axis begins. Choosing the **F**ont and **St**yle command lets you choose the fonts in use on the chart.

- You can use the **T**ools menu commands to duplicate the chart, delete the chart, or start a new one.

If you would like more information about Works charts, consider picking up a book specifically about Works, such as *Using Microsoft Works, Special Edition*, also published by Que Corporation.

CHAPTER

5

Using the Works Database

What Is a Database?

A *database program* automates the process of creating, collecting, sharing, and managing almost any kind of information. That information might be a list of names and addresses used for club membership and for tracking dues. Like a spreadsheet, a database program keeps track of little bits of information in a well-organized format, but a database is designed specifically for organizing data rather than for making calculations. As such, a database can organize and present information even more efficiently than a spreadsheet.

Typical database applications include these:

- *An address book.* This is a list of names and addresses that can be sorted by name, address, zip code, or phone number. You can also extract a list of people in a particular area code or zip code.

- *An inventory.* This is a list of personal or business items that can be sorted by status (on hand, on order), location (dining room, warehouse), ordering information, vendor, value, or price of an item.

- *A customer list.* This is a list of customers that can be sorted by location, salesperson, status (active or inactive), or contact name.

As you build a database, you are building a table of information. As with a spreadsheet, a table has rows and columns. The primary components of any database are *fields* and *records*. Fields are the smallest pieces of data in the database. Fields represent such information as first name, last name, address, city, and so forth. A record is a set of fields. In a customer database, each customer is a record.

Fields are displayed in columns in the database table, and the field name appears at the top of the column. Records are displayed in rows in the database table. In the example of a club membership database, each person in the club would be a record. Figure 5.1 shows a database table with records and fields.

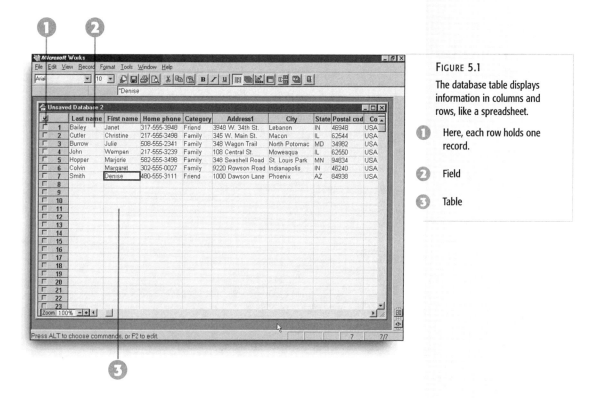

FIGURE 5.1

The database table displays information in columns and rows, like a spreadsheet.

① Here, each row holds one record.

② Field

③ Table

You can add information to the database by typing directly into the table, or you can create forms for entering data. *Input forms* are easier to read than tables. Figure 5.2 represents an input form for an address database.

You create reports when you want to print information from your database. With a report, you can print all or some of your data, and you can sort, extract, and format the appearance of that data. Figure 5.3 is a report from an address book in which the data is sorted alphabetically by last name. The records are *filtered* to show only people who had the word "Family" in the Category field.

FIGURE 5.2

You can use forms for inputting data.

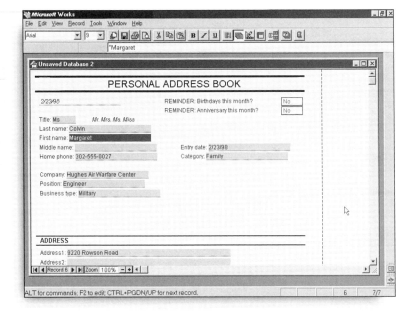

FIGURE 5.3

Create reports and print your data. Data can be sorted, manipulated, or extracted using reports.

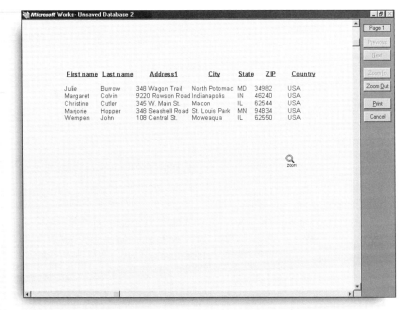

Creating a Database File

You can create the database file using a TaskWizard, or you can create it from scratch. A TaskWizard defines the fields for you and creates an attractive form—and perhaps a report, too. This is a very fast and easy way to get a professional-looking database, and I recommend it in most situations. The only time you would not want to use a TaskWizard would be if you needed a database that was radically different than those offered by a TaskWizard.

SEE ALSO

➤ *For more information on TaskWizards, see page 13.*

Creating a Database with a TaskWizard

Many people use a database to create and maintain an address book, whether for business or for personal use. The Works Address Book TaskWizard can help you create a number of different address books quickly and easily.

Creating a Personal Address Book

1. From the **Task Launcher** window, click the **Ta<u>s</u>kWizards** tab.

2. In the **Common Tasks** category, double-click **Address Book**.

3. A dialog box appears asking whether you want to run the TaskWizard. Click **<u>Y</u>es, run the TaskWizard**.

4. The TaskWizard asks what kind of address book you want (see Figure 5.4). For this example, click **Personal** and then click **Next**.

5. Works lists the fields that will be included. If these look right to you, click **Next**. If they don't, click **Back** and return to step 4 to select a different type.

6. Click any of these buttons to open additional dialog boxes; make selections from them and click **OK** to return.

FIGURE 5.4

Works customizes the fields depending on the type of address book you want.

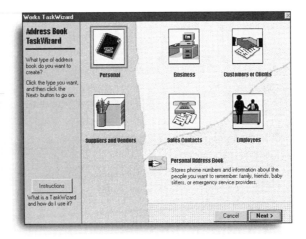

- If you want to use any of the fields Extended Phone, Personal Information, or Notes, click the **Additional Fields** button. Place a check mark next to each that you want.

- If you want to design some additional fields of your own, click the **Your Own Fields** button and enter the additional field information.

- If you want two pre-designed reports (Alphabetized Directory and Categorized Directory) to be included in your database, click the **Reports** button and place check marks next to the ones you want.

Default address book

Works has an Address Book button on its toolbar that you can use to pull in addresses for word-processing documents and other applications. If you set this database as your default address book, this will be the address book from which Works pulls those addresses when-ever you click the Address Book but-ton on the toolbar.

7. Click **Create It!** to create the database. A checklist appears showing what will be created.

8. If you want this address book to be your default address book in Works, click the **Yes, I want this to be my default address book** button.

9. Click **Create Document**. The Wizard creates the database, and a blank form appears on your screen. Enter your first record in this form (see Figure 5.5).

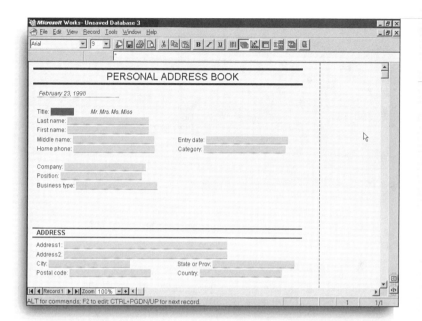

Creating a Database from Scratch

When you create a database from scratch, you must define each field that you are going to use. You must tell Works the name of the field, its size, its data type, and so on. This can be time-consuming, but it results in a database that's tailor-made just for you. For example, suppose you want to create a database that keeps track of the purebred dogs in a kennel. You will need many fields that none of the TaskWizards offer, such as AKC Registration Number, Call Name, Registered Name, Coat Color, and so on. For such a database, you have to start from scratch.

Creating a database from scratch

1. From the Works Task Launcher, click the **Works Tools** tab, and then click the **Database** button. A **Create Database** dialog box appears, prompting you for your first field name, as shown in Figure 5.6.

2. Enter the first field name in the **Field name** field. Each field name must be unique.

FIGURE 5.6

Works prompts you to describe the fields you'll need.

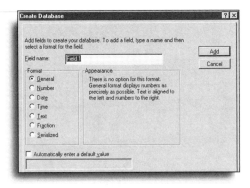

3. Choose a data type from the **Format** list (they're explained in Table 5.1).

4. If applicable, choose an appearance from the **Appearance** area. Not all data types have appearance options.

5. (Optional) If you want the field to have a default value (a value that appears unless you change it), click the **Automatically enter a default value** check box and enter the default value in the text box below it.

6. Click **Add** to add the field. The settings clear, so you can enter another field.

7. Continue entering fields until you are done, and then click **Done** to close the dialog box.

When you create a database from scratch, you do not have a predesigned data entry form to work with. You will need to create one from scratch if you want one. (That's one disadvantage of going it alone, without the TaskWizard.) You'll learn how to create a form later in this chapter.

Why use default values?

Default values can save you some data entry time if you have certain fields that are almost always the same. For example, if almost everyone in your database lives in the United States, you could create a Country field and set its default value to USA. Then when entering new records, you could skip that field unless it needed a non-USA value.

TABLE 5.1   **Field formatting options**

Type of Field	Used For
General	No formatting at all, and no restrictions on entry.
Number	Numbers that have numeric value and on which you might want to perform calculations. You cannot enter any text in these fields.
Date	For dates only. You cannot enter anything except valid dates.

Type of Field	Used For
Time	For time only. You cannot enter anything except valid times.
Text	For text and for numbers that have no value (such as ZIP codes and phone numbers). No restrictions on entry.
Fraction	For numbers that need to be expressed as fractions rather than decimal places (such as stock prices).
Serialized	For record numbers or fields in which you want to increment the value every time you add a record.

As with the other Works tools, it's a good idea to save your database early and often. To save your database, open the **File** menu and choose **Save**, or press Ctrl+S. You can also save by clicking the **Save** icon on the toolbar.

Understanding the Database Views

The database window opens when you have finished creating and entering new fields into a new database, or when you finish creating with the TaskWizard. This window has a menu bar and toolbar just like the other Works tools, so things should look at least a little bit familiar.

The main thing to know about the database window is that your database is always displayed in one of four *views*. To switch views, you can open the **View** menu and choose the view you want, or you can click the appropriate button on the toolbar:

- *List view*. This view looks like a spreadsheet, with field names as columns and records as rows. You saw this view in Figure 5.1.
- *Form view*. A list of your fields appears with a blank next to each one; you can enter data by filling in the blanks. This view appeared in Figure 5.2.
- *Form Design view*. Here's where you can customize your form.
- *Report view*. You can change the layout of an existing report here or create new reports. When you get the report the way you want it, you can preview it in Print Preview (refer to Figure 5.3) and/or print it.

Why serialize?

The *Serialized* data type can be very useful. Suppose, for example, that if you assign an account number to each new record, you can set up the Account Number field to automatically increment to the next available account number each time you enter a new record.

If you used a TaskWizard to create your database, it puts you in Form view so you can do your data entry. If you created the database from scratch, you're left in List view when it's all done. Whatever view you're starting in, go ahead and try some of the other views right now. If you used the TaskWizard, you will have fully designed reports and forms at your disposal in those views; if not, you will have a plain list of fields in Form view, and you'll be prompted to create a report when you enter Report view. (Click **Cancel** to avoid that for now.)

Editing Your Database Structure

The best time to modify a database's structure (that is, change its fields) is before you start entering data into it. If you add fields after you have some records in your database, you will have to go back through all your data and "clean up" by making entries in the new fields. And if you delete fields after entering data, you will have wasted the time it took you to populate that field originally. What a pain! Think about your database now, and try to make the changes upfront.

Adding and Deleting Fields

After you have created your initial database fields (either manually or with the TaskWizard), you may want to make some changes. Perhaps you forgot about a field or have decided that one of the fields is unnecessary.

Adding a field

1. Open the **View** menu and choose **List**.

2. Click on a field name that is adjacent to the spot where the new field should go.

3. Open the **Record** menu and point to **Insert Field**. A submenu appears with Before and After on it. Click **1 Before** if you want the new field to be placed to the left of the selected one, or **2 After** if you want it placed to the right.

4. The Insert Field dialog box appears. This dialog box looks almost exactly like the Create Database dialog box shown in Figure 5.6.

5. Follow the steps in the procedure "Creating a Database from Scratch," on page 125, to fill in the needed information for the new field.

To delete a field, select the field in List view. Open the **Record** menu and choose **Delete Field**. A dialog box appears asking you if you are sure; click **OK**.

SEE ALSO

➤ *You can also rearrange fields in the database. This works just like moving columns in a spreadsheet. Refer to page 100.*

Editing the Field Name or Type

It's not unusual to want to change a field name after you have completed the initial design of your database. For example, you might find that you want to shorten the Area Code field to AC. You might also want to change the field's type. For example, perhaps you formatted the Area Code field as Number, but you realize now that those numbers will never be used for calculations. You think you might want to set the field type to Text instead.

Changing a field

1. Switch to List view if you're not there already.

2. Select the field you want to edit by clicking its name.

3. Open the **F̲ormat** menu and choose **Fie̲ld**. The Format dialog box appears with the Field tab in front, as shown in Figure 5.7.

4. In the **F̲ield name** text box, change your field name by typing your new field name. The new text will replace the old field name.

5. If you need to change the field type, choose a different one from the **Format** area.

6. Click **OK** to save your changes and close the dialog box.

FIGURE 5.7

Change the field's properties from
the Format menu.

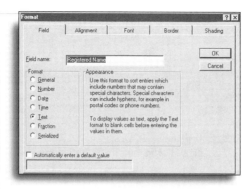

Moving Fields

Fields appear in your database in List view in the order in which
you entered them when you first created the database. You can
change these at any time.

Moving a field

1. In List view, click once on the field name to select that
   column.
2. Position the mouse pointer at the edge of the field. The
   pointer changes to say **Drag**.
3. Hold down the mouse button, and drag the field to the position you desire. Then release the mouse button.

Deleting Fields

You can delete a field in one of several ways. Remember that
when you delete a field, you delete all the data that is contained
in that field for every record. When you cut or delete a field,
Works displays a dialog box asking if you want to permanently
delete this information. This is a safety measure designed to
make you pause and think before you delete. When you see the
dialog box and are certain you want to delete the field, click **OK**
to close the box and delete the field.

To delete a field, do one of the following:

- Select the field, open the **Edit** menu, and choose **Cut**.
- Select the field and press Ctrl+X.

I didn't mean to delete this field!

If you accidentally delete a field, or if
you delete the wrong field, you can
undo the delete as long as it is the
very next step you take. To undelete,
press Ctrl+Z, or open the **Edit** menu
and choose **Undo Delete field**.

- Right-click the field and choose **Delete Field** from the pop-up menu.

Changing the Way a Field Appears Onscreen

In a database, the appearance of the fields in List view is not your primary concern. You should be more interested in how the data will look when printed in reports, which are designed especially for printing. The List view is designed to be rough and unformatted.

However, if this roughness bothers you, you can easily make some small changes that will enhance its readability onscreen. These changes are the same as the changes you learned to make to spreadsheets and word-processing documents. Refer back to these sections:

SEE ALSO
➢ *To format text in fields, refer to page 44.*
➢ *To widen the columns, see page 106.*

SEE ALSO
➢ *To text align differently in the field, see page 108.*
➢ *To use borders and shading in some fields, see page 111.*

Entering and Editing Data

The most cumbersome part of creating a database is *populating*, or adding records to the database. When you do your initial data entry, the upkeep of your database will seem like a piece of cake because all you'll need to do is make a few additions and deletions occasionally to keep everything updated.

Adding Records

When you add records, you don't need to be concerned about the order in which you add them. The very purpose of a database program is that it enables you to *sort*, *filter*, and *manipulate* data when you need to rearrange or find information. The only

Quick column widening

If a column in List view displays #### marks, it means the column is too narrow to display the data. To quickly widen a column just enough so that it can display the data in it, double-click on the divider between that column and the one to the right, next to the field name.

exception to this is if you are using a Serialized field and need the serial numbers to be in a particular order.

Most people find it easier to enter records in Form view, so you will want to switch to that view before you begin. To add records, simply position your cursor in the field of the database in which you want to add information. Click in the field where you want to start, enter the information for that field, and then press Tab to move to the next field (press Shift+Tab to move back to the previous field). When you press Tab at the last field, Works starts a new record, and your cursor moves to the first field of a new record. If you make a mistake and must return to a previous record, you can do so by clicking the left-pointing arrow button at the bottom of the screen (you learn more about moving between records in the next section of this chapter).

In List view, the database is displayed as a table. You can enter records by filling out each field in the database, then moving down the table to the next record. Use the Tab key to move from field to field and from record to record if you have reached the last field in a record. People who are experienced with spreadsheets may prefer List view for data entry because it is familiar, but most people prefer Form view for data entry.

Moving Among Records

In List view, you can move among records exactly as you would in the Spreadsheet tool. Just click the cells you want and type into them, using the scroll bars as needed to move around.

SEE ALSO

➤ *For more detailed instructions on how to navigate within a spreadsheet, see page 77.*

In Form view, you can click in the field in which you want to type and use the scroll bars to see any fields that may not fit on the screen. (Some data entry forms are larger than a single screen.) To move from record to record, use the navigation buttons in the bottom left corner of the screen:

- ▎◀▏ Go to first record
- ◀▏ Go to preceding record

Column widening?

If you are entering data in List view, the columns may be too narrow for you to see your entire entry in some fields.

You can widen the column to bring the data fully into view. Just position the cursor field column header on the separator line between columns. The cursor changes, displaying two arrows and the word ADJUST. Holding down the mouse button, click and drag the column header to expand or shorten the column width. You can also double-click between the field names (column headings) to automatically widen the column.

- ▶ Go to next record
- ▶| Go to the last record

If you click the **Go to next record** button when you are already on the last record in the database, Works displays a blank data entry screen in which you can enter another record.

Editing Data

You can edit data just like you entered it: Simply move the cursor to the field and type your changes. It's just like making edits in a spreadsheet.

When you move the cursor into a field that contains data, you can edit it with two methods: by deleting the characters you don't want and typing new ones, or by clearing out the whole field and starting afresh. To clear a field, press the Delete key on the keyboard.

To delete an entire record, you must select it. In List view, select its row by clicking the row number, and then press Delete. In Form view, open the **Edit** menu and choose **Cut Record**, or press Ctrl+Shift+X.

Adding More Records

When inserting a new record, you don't have to pay too much attention to its position in the database. If you are trying to enter your records alphabetically, for example, and you later find you missed one in the "A's," you don't need to insert the new entry in any particular spot. Just add it to the end of the database, and then sort the records alphabetically.

In List view, click on the first empty row in the table, and type the new entry there. In Form view, click the **Go to Last Record** button ▶|, and then click the **Go to Next Record** ▶ button to display a blank form.

However, if it is important to you to place a new record in a certain position in the database, you can do so from List view.

Inserting a new record between other records

1. Switch to List view if it is not already displayed.

2. Place your pointer on the record below where you want to insert the new record (row).

3. Right-click with your mouse and select **Insert Record** from the pop-up menu, or open the **Record** menu and choose **Insert Record** (see Figure 5.8). The new, blank record appears above your current cursor position.

FIGURE 5.8

Right-click the record below which the new one should go.

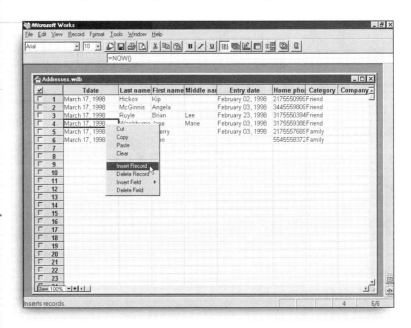

Inserting multiple records

If you need to insert several records in the same spot, select a number of rows in step 2 equal to the number of rows you want to insert. For example, to insert three records, select three rows. Then continue with the steps.

4. Using the Tab key to move between fields, enter the field information in the new record.

Modifying the Form

When you create a database, Works automatically creates a form from your database fields. If you use a TaskWizard, the form may be more attractive and graphical than that of a database you create from scratch.

You can modify the form by switching to Form Design view. Open the **View** menu and choose **Form Design**. In Form Design view, your form appears, but each part of it is movable, so you can rearrange, reposition, and add fields and descriptive text.

The form shown in Form Design view in Figure 5.9 was created when I created a database with a TaskWizard; if you did not use a TaskWizard, yours may look more like the plainer form in Figure 5.10.

Repositioning Fields

You can move fields in Form Design view by dragging a field to its new location. As you design your form, you may find you want to change the order of fields, perhaps to list first all the fields into which you generally input data, followed by all the default and calculated fields.

You can also move fields around the screen for aesthetic purposes. Perhaps you want to move the fields higher on the screen so they are clustered more tightly together and so you don't have to scroll down to see them all. Or perhaps you want to create space between certain fields to group the fields into logical units. Moving fields is a simple drag-and-drop operation in Form Design view.

Form or form design?

If you are ever unsure about which of the two views you are in, a quick look at the fields will tell you. In Form view, if you have any records, the first one appears in the fields. In Form Design view, there are no records; fields are empty. In addition, a dotted outline surrounds all movable objects in Form Design view; there are no such lines in Form view.

FIGURE 5.10

This plainer form is ready to be graphically enhanced.

Move several fields at once

To move several fields at a time, select them by holding down the Ctrl key as you click on each one; then drag them as a group. You can also select a group of fields by drawing a selection box around them. To draw a *selection box*, press and hold down the mouse button and drag over the group of fields. You can see a selection box surround the fields. Release the mouse button. The selection box disappears, but the group of items remains highlighted, ready for you to move.

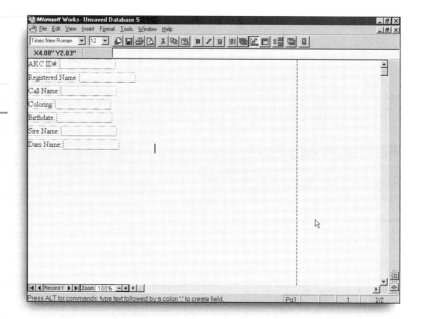

Moving a field on the form

1. Click on the field to select it.

2. Position the mouse pointer over the field. The mouse pointer changes to a **Drag** pointer.

3. Holding down the mouse button, drag the field to its new position. As you drag, you will see the pointer change to a **Move** pointer (see Figure 5.11). When you have positioned the field where you want it, release the mouse button.

Changing the Tab Order of Fields

The tab order is the path that the cursor takes when you press Tab to move from field to field as you enter records. In Works, the default order of the tab is left to right, top to bottom on your form. If you move a field, the tab order changes. Figure 5.12 shows the tab order on a sample form. If you reordered any of these fields, their tab order would automatically change.

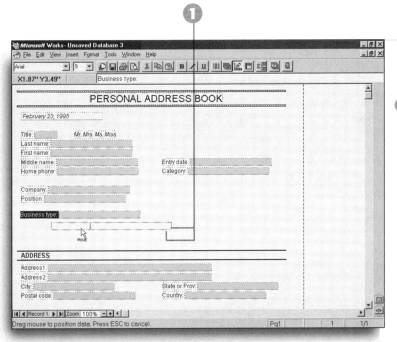

FIGURE 5.11

Drag fields around on the form to reposition them.

1 Outline shows where the field is moving.

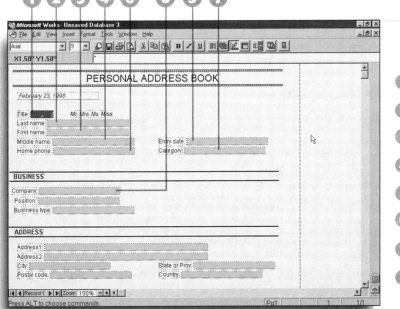

FIGURE 5.12

The Works default tab order is from left to right, top to bottom.

1 1

2 2

3 3

4 4

5 5

6 6

7 7

8 8

You can override the tab default order. You might want to do this if your database has a field that is rarely populated and often skipped over. You can make that field last in the tab order but keep it in its original location on the form.

Changing the tab order

1. From Form Design view, open the **Format** menu and choose **Tab Order**. The Format Tab Order dialog box appears, as shown in Figure 5.13.

2. Select the field you want to move in the tab order. Use the **Up** or **Down** buttons to reorder the field. To return to the default order, click the **Reset** button.

3. When you have the order you want, click **OK** to save your changes and close the dialog box.

4. To test the new tab order, press the Tab key to move through your fields in Form View or Form Design view.

FIGURE 5.13

You can modify the default Tab order from this dialog box.

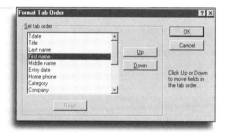

Adding Labels to the Form

You might want to add labels to your database to assist others when they are working in it. For example, descriptive text such as "Enter Mr. or Mrs. or Miss" next to a field called Title helps others to understand that the field is for common prefixes rather than for royalty. You can also use labels to divide one section of the form from another. If you refer back to Figure 5.12, for example, you'll notice that there are Business and Address labels that mark sections with certain fields. Labels are just like any other text on the form, and they print normally when you print the Form view. (Labels don't appear on reports, though, and they don't show up in List view.)

Adding a label to a form

1. In Form Design view, position the cursor where you want to place the label. Be certain that your cursor is not on an existing field but in a blank area of the form. If there is no room where you want to place the label, move the fields.

2. Type the text and press Enter.

Edit labels as you would edit any text; click one to select the label, and then type. Delete by selecting the label and pressing the Del key.

Finding Records

If you don't have many records, you might find it easy to browse through each of them. In List view, it is easy to skim the page and locate a record you want if the list is not too long. You can use the arrow keys on the status bar to move from record to record in Form View.

Works provides another tool that you can use if the list is long enough to be unwieldy: the Find command. This command works much like the Find command in other applications; in the database, Find looks for data in any field.

Finding a record containing specific data

1. Open the **Edit** menu and choose **Find**.

2. The Find dialog box appears, as shown in Figure 5.14.

3. Fill in the information you wish to find, such as the name **Jones**, in the **Find what** box.

4. Click **OK**.

FIGURE 5.14
Use the Find dialog box to locate a record.

Works will display the next Jones it finds in the database. If you want to see *all* Jones entries in the database, click on the **All**

Records option in the Find dialog box (see Figure 5.14). When you select this option, Works will display all occurrences of Jones, one record (form) at a time. Click the next record indicator to move through the records.

Sorting Records

A key feature of any database program is the capability of sorting records. Sorting records enables you to populate the database without concern for alphabetical or numeric order. When you have populated the database, you can sort any of your fields. To refine your sort order, you can sort up to three fields, giving you the ability to sort a database by committee, last name, and first name, for example.

Although you can sort while in Form Design or List views, it is easier to see the effects of sorting if you work in List view, which shows multiple records. Form Design view displays only one record at a time.

Sorting a database

1. In List view, open the **Record** menu and choose **Sort Records.** (If you see an extra dialog box asking whether you want a quick tour, click **OK** to bypass it.) The Sort Records dialog box appears (see Figure 5.15).

2. Using the drop-down lists, select the fields you want to sort, in the order you want them sorted.

3. Choose **Ascending** or **Descending** for each field as the order to sort.

4. Click **OK** to save your sort preferences and close the dialog box. Your database now appears in the order you indicated in the Sort Records dialog box.

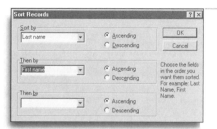

FIGURE 5.15
Sort up to three fields using the Sort Records dialog box.

Working with Filters

A *filter* is a search that gives you greater capabilities to locate information than a simple search performed with the Find command. You use the Find command when you want to search for John Jones, but you use a filter when you want to search for members in your database who have joined your organization after December 31, 1996, and before December 31, 1997, for example.

Works has two kinds of filters, the *Easy Filter* and the *Filter Using Formula*. This book focuses on the Easy Filter. An Easy Filter uses a comparison when searching for records.

At a minimum, you must supply three pieces of information for the easy filter:

- *Field Name*. The name of the field whose contents you are searching.

- *Comparison*. Comparison phrases are selected from a drop-down list. They contain phrases representing *operators*, such as *is less than*, *is equal to*, and *does not contain*.

- *Compare to*. The search criteria.

For example, you could find everyone with Indianapolis as their city by entering City for the Field name, Equals as the comparison, and Indianapolis as the Compare To.

When you apply the filter, you will see only those records that match the filter criteria. The other records in your database are not deleted; they are simply filtered from the view.

Filter or query?

In Access and some other more powerful database programs, you can create powerful filters called *queries*. Filters are Works' version of queries.

Creating a filter

1. From List view, open the **Tools** menu and select **Filters**. You can also click the Filters button  on the toolbar.

2. If this is the first time you have created a filter in Works, the First-Time Help dialog box will appear. Click **To Create and apply a new filter** to close this dialog box. The Filter Name dialog box appears, as shown in Figure 5.16.

3. A default name of Filter 1 is supplied. If you do not want this name, type a descriptive name for your filter. Click **OK** to save your filter name and close that dialog box.

FIGURE 5.16

Name your Filter in the Filter Name dialog box.

4. Use the drop-down menus to select a **Field name** and **Comparison**.

5. In the **Compare to** text box, type the value for your filter criteria. Figure 5.17 shows a completed filter comparison that finds all records where the Category field has "Friend" in it.

FIGURE 5.17

This filter finds everyone I have categorized as friends.

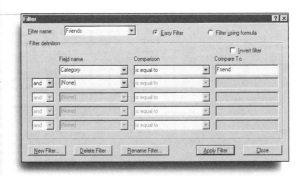

6. If you need to add a second filter, you must choose **and** or **or** from the drop-down list on the left of the second line. Use *or* to search for records that match any of your

comparisons; use *and* for records that match all your comparison criteria.

7. Click the **Apply Filter** button to close the dialog box and finish your filter. Works will display the search results. If no match was found for your filter, you see a message to that effect, and the Filter dialog box remains open.

To redisplay all records in the database, effectively removing the filter, choose **Record**, **Sh**o**w**, **1 All Records** from the menu.

To re-apply the filter, choose **Record**, **Apply** **F**ilter from the menu, and choose a filter from the list.

Creating Additional Filters

You can create multiple filters in a database, and each is saved. (In other words, when you create a second filter, the first one doesn't go away; it's still accessible.) To create additional filters, you must click the **New Filter** button in the Filters dialog box (*see* Figure 5.17). The New Filter dialog box reappears, and you can type a new name.

Deleting Filters

You may find yourself with filters that you don't want or need. It's good to clear them out so that they don't unnecessarily muck up your list of filters (which you see when you choose **Record**, **Apply** **F**ilter).

Deleting a filter

1. Open the **T**ools menu and choose **F**ilters. The Filter dialog box appears.

2. In the Filter Name drop-down box, select the filter you want to delete.

3. Click the **D**elete Filter button.

4. A message appears confirming that you want to delete the filter and display the filter name. Click **Yes.**

Creating Reports

Reports are designed to be printed. You can create a report using any or all fields in your database, and you can arrange and format them on the report in whatever way you like.

For example, suppose that Barbara is your club member responsible for recruiting other club members into committees, such as the Spring Dance committee or the Fund-Raising committee. Supplying Barbara with a list of club members who are not active committee members and their phone numbers would help Barbara recruit new committee members. Other member information contained in your database, such as dues and addresses, would not be contained in your report to Barbara, as this is information she doesn't need.

Report View changes

Due to space limitations, this book does not cover changing a report in Report View, but you can easily figure it out. Just use the same controls you have already become accustomed to in Works to change fonts, font sizes, alignments, and so on. Move items around by dragging them, just as you do when you edit forms.

When you create a report, you can apply filters or create new filters during the report creation process. After the report is created, you can edit or fine-tune it in the Report View.

You can create up to eight reports per database. To create a report, you use a Wizard called ReportCreator.

Creating a Report with ReportCreator

1. Open the **Tools** menu and choose **ReportCreator**. The Report Name dialog box appears.

2. Type a descriptive name in the Report Name dialog box. For example, if you are creating a report that lists everyone's phone numbers, you might call it Phone Numbers.

3. Click **OK**. The ReportCreator dialog box appears, as shown in Figure 5.18. Your report name appears in the title bar of the dialog box, and the Title tab is displayed.

4. You can shorten the name of the report by deleting the database name. (By default, the title is the name of the database plus the title you typed in step 2.)

5. Select an orientation for your report (**Portrait** or **Landscape**) and a **Font**. Then click **Next**.

SEE ALSO
➤ *For information about font controls, see page 44.*

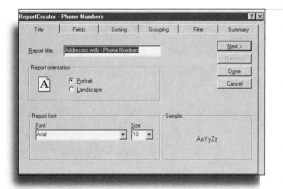

FIGURE 5.18
On the starting page of
ReportCreator, you specify a title,
a font, and orientation.

6. Works displays the **Fields** tab. Here, you indicate which
fields appear on your report and specify the order in which
they appear. Highlight the field in the **Fields available** list
and click on the **Add** button. Repeat for each field you want
to use. Figure 5.19 shows a report with the fields for a
phone number list.

Quick field add

To add all the fields in the data-
base at one time, click the **Add
All** button. If you add a field by
mistake, highlight the field in the
Field Order box and click on the
Remove button.

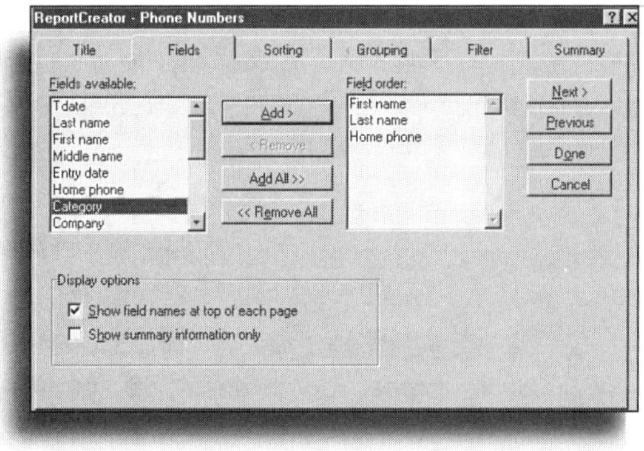

FIGURE 5.19
Add fields to the report by selecting
them and clicking **Add**.

7. Select or deselect either of the two Display options check
boxes as appropriate:

- **Show field names at top of each page**. Mark this if
  you want the field names to print. For example, next to
  each first name, you might want to say "First Name."

- **Show summary information only**. Mark this if the
  individual records are not important, but the summary

Plan for grouping

Do not add a field to the report
if you intend to group by that
field. For example, if you are
grouping by the Committee
field, you don't need to see the
Committee field in each record.

of them is. For example, if it is not important who is on the list but only that there are eight people on it, use this.

When you have finished, click the **Next** button to continue.

8. The **Sorting** tab appears next. Select the order in which you want your records to appear in the report. This works just like the sorting you did earlier in this chapter. Click **Next** when finished.

9. Next, the **Grouping** tab appears. Any fields that you selected in the Sorting tab appear here (for example, Committee), but in a turned-off state. Click the **When contents change** check box to enable a grouping (see Figure 5.20). This inserts a blank line in the report whenever a group of records that have a different value for the chosen field appear.

10. After you enable a grouping, choose from the following options for each field:

   • **Use first letter only**. Inserts a blank line in the report whenever the first letter of the field changes. This is appropriate when you are grouping by a field for which there are few or no duplicates, such as last name. This option groups by the first letter of the chosen field rather than by the entire content of it.

   • **Show group heading**. Prints the group header on the report. When sorting by committee, for example, each committee type (such as "Public Relations") appears as a group heading.

   • **Start each group on a new page**. Forces a page break each time this group changes, resulting in one group type per page. This is handy if you need to give the different lists to different people.

Sort by the Grouping field

If you intend to group your report, choose the field you are grouping by in the Sort by box on the Sorting tab. This places your groups in order. For example, if you are going to group by committee, choose **Committee** as the first Sort by field, and choose **Ascending** as the order. This results in a report grouped by committee, and the committees will be in alphabetical order.

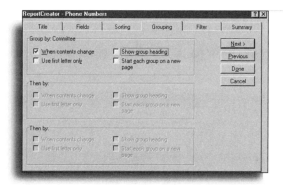

FIGURE 5.20
Select the grouping options for sorted records.

11. The **Filter** tab appears, as shown in Figure 5.21. Choose any existing filter, or click **Create new filter** to create a new one, as you learned to do earlier in this chapter. Then click **Next** to continue.

SEE ALSO
➤ *To learn more about filters, see page 141.*

Why can't I group?

The Grouping tab will be grayed out if you have not selected any fields on the Sorting tab. If you want to change or add the sorting information, click the **Sorting** tab, make your changes, and click on the **Grouping** tab to return to step 10.

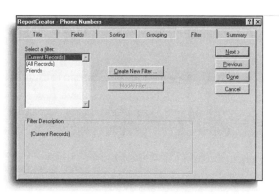

FIGURE 5.21
Apply filters to your report on the **Filter** tab.

12. The **Summary** tab appears next, as shown in Figure 5.22. Summaries generally apply to number fields, not text fields. For example, you should not elect to sum the contents of a field called First Name because there is no number to sum in that field. You can, however, elect to count the number of items in a field. Choose the field you want to calculate (or count) in the **Select a field** box, and check off your options in the **Summaries** box.

FIGURE 5.22

Use the Summary options to
perform calculations on your
report, if appropriate.

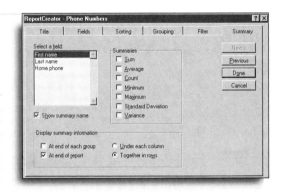

13. Select any of the summary options from the Display
Summary Information section, as appropriate. (These are all
fairly self-explanatory.) When you have completed your
summary options, click **D̲one**.

14. A message indicates that the ReportCreator is finished. Click
Preview to see your report in Print Preview.

When you have finished previewing your report in Print Preview
mode, click **Print** to print it or **Cancel** to return to your database.

There is a lot more you can do with a database report, but this
book is too short to cover it all. For more information about
working with Works databases, see *Using Microsoft Works 98,
Special Edition*, also published by Que Corporation.

Modify or preview?

You can select **Modify** in step 14 to
modify the report, but you will see
the report without data. It is much
more useful to see the report with
data in Print Preview mode.

Integrating the Works Programs

Copying material from one document to another

Creating dynamic links between documents

Using and customizing the Address Book feature

Performing a mail merge

Integrated Tools for Easy Sharing

With Home Essentials, you have two word processors from which to choose—Works and Word. Some folks might think that because Word is the more powerful of the two, there's no reason to ever use the Works word processor. But those folks would be wrong.

The main advantage of using the Works word processor is its tight integration with the other tools. Works makes it very easy to share data among the tools to create good-looking results. For example, with the Works word processor, you can easily integrate data from a Works spreadsheet or create mailing labels that pull the names from a Works database. In this chapter, you'll see some ways to make the integration advantage work for you.

Moving and Copying Between Documents

The simplest way of sharing data between two Windows-based programs is to use the Clipboard, as you learned in Chapter 2, "Introducing the Works Word Processor." You cut or copy to the clipboard and then switch to the program into which you want to paste. Then you issue the Paste command from that program. This works with all Windows programs, not just the tools in Works.

For example, suppose you want to include a few cells from a Works spreadsheet in a report you are creating in the Works word processor (as shown in Figure 6.1). The following steps can help.

SEE ALSO

➤ For more information about the Clipboard, see page 26.

➤ To learn about drag-and-drop moving and copying, see page 28.

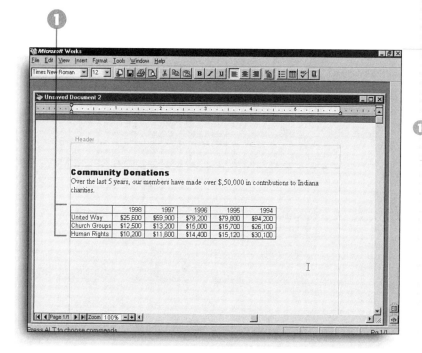

FIGURE 6.1

This report in the word processor has some cells pasted in from a spreadsheet.

1 Pasted spreadsheet cells resemble a table.

Copying between documents

1. In the Works tool of your choice, select what you want to copy. (To select, simply drag the mouse across your selection with the left button held down.) For example, to copy part of a spreadsheet, select all the cells you want to copy.

2. To copy, click the Copy button 🖻 or open the **Edit** menu and choose **Copy**. To move, click the Cut button ✂ or open the **Edit** menu and choose **Cut**.

3. If the document where you want to paste is not open, open it (you can do so by opening the **File** menu and choosing **Open**). If it is already open, open the **Window** menu and select it to jump to it.

4. Position the insertion point where you want the Clipboard content to be placed. (You might need to type some introductory text to explain the pasted item's presence, such as "Here are the sales figures for 1998.")

5. Click the Paste button 📋, or open the **Edit** menu and choose **Paste**.

Use the Task Launcher

In step 3, you can click the Task Launcher button 🔲 to return to the Task Launcher; you can start or open a document from there.

If you paste data into a tool that is not its native format (for example, spreadsheet data in a word-processor document), you will not be able to edit the data directly. The table in Figure 6.1, for example, may look like a regular table created in the word processor, but you cannot click inside it to make changes.

To change a pasted object, double-click on it. This opens the pasted data's native controls, as shown in Figure 6.2. From there, you can do your editing. When you are finished, click anywhere away from the object to return to your normal controls.

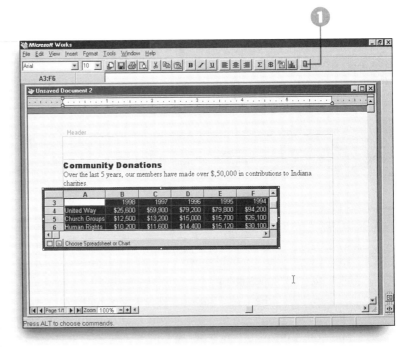

FIGURE 6.2

Double-click a pasted object to open its native tool's controls.

1 Notice that the toolbar buttons are those of the Spreadsheet tool.

Creating Dynamic Links Between Documents

When you copy or paste something, it is a *static* copy. That means there is no tie to the original. If you change the original, the copy does not change. You can also paste *dynamic* copies from one tool to another. With a dynamic copy, if the original changes, the copy changes too.

Suppose that you have a chart in your spreadsheet tool that changes every month when you input the latest financial data into the spreadsheet on which it is based. You want that chart to appear each month in a word-processor report that is always up-to-date. To do this, you insert an object. *Object* is a generic term that means any bit of data (usually in a format other than the native one to the program in which you're working). When you dynamically link an object to a spot in another program, you do not paste a copy of the object. Instead, you paste a *link* to the original. Every time the document containing the link is opened, the link is updated with a copy of the very latest version.

Creating a dynamic link

1. Make sure you have saved your work in the tool that contains the object you are copying.

2. Select the object (or range, or text, or whatever), and then copy it to the Clipboard. If you are pasting a chart from the Spreadsheet tool, you don't select it; you merely display it and issue the **Copy** command.

3. Switch to the document where you want to paste the dynamic link.

4. Open the **Edit** menu and choose **Paste Special**. The Paste Special dialog box appears (see Figure 6.3).

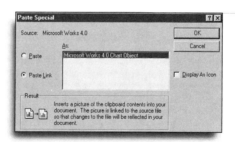

FIGURE 6.3

Use the Paste Special dialog box to paste a dynamic link.

5. Click the **Paste Link** option button. The **As** list changes to show only the valid formats for a pasted link. (There will probably be only one item on the list.)

6. If there is more than one item on the As list, make sure the one that ends in the word "object" is selected—for example,

OLE

The process of pasting dynamic copies is sometimes referred to as *object linking and embedding,* or OLE.

> **Microsoft Works 4.5 Chart Object** if you are pasting a chart.

7. Click **OK**. The object is pasted into the document with a dynamic link.

To test this link, close both documents. Then open the one containing the original of the object and make a change to it. Save your work, and then open the document containing the link. The document should display the updated version of the object.

Using the Address Book

You may have noticed the Address Book button on the Works toolbar. As you learned in Chapter 5, "Using the Works Database," when you create an address book database file with a TaskWizard, Works asks you whether you want to set that address book as your default. If you do so, that address book opens whenever you click the Address Book button 🔲 on the toolbar. This can come in handy when you are creating a letter in the word processor, for example. You may want to look up the recipient's address, and you can do so easily with the Address Book button.

SEE ALSO
> *For more information about the Database tool, see page 119.*

Strictly speaking, the Address Book button does not have to refer to an address book at all. It can refer to any database to which you need frequent access. For example, if you keep your dog kennel records in a database and you frequently need to look up the dogs' AKC registration numbers as you are typing contracts in the word processor, you might make that database file your default "Address Book."

Changing the default Address Book

1. Open any Works tool.

2. Open the **Tools** menu and choose **Options**. The Options dialog box appears.

3. Click the **Address Book** tab (see Figure 6.4).

4. In the Works Databases list, click on the database that you want to associate with the Address Book button.

5. Click **OK**.

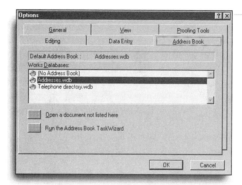

FIGURE 6.4
Choose which database pops up when you click the Address Book button on the toolbar.

Preparing a Form Letter

Many people shudder when they hear the words "mail merge" because mass mailings have traditionally been difficult to set up in word-processing programs. With Works, however, it's quite easy to create a mass mailing.

Mail merge refers to the fact that you create a generic letter in a word processor and then "merge" it with a list of addresses. These addresses can be taken directly from any Works database.

Creating a mass mailing form letter

1. Prepare the names and addresses by creating a Works database that includes them, as you learned in Chapter 5.

2. Start a new, blank word processing document. Type the date and your return address on the letter, up to the point where you are ready to enter the recipient's name and address.

3. Open the **Tools** menu and choose **Form Letters**. The Form Letters dialog box opens. The first page shows directions. Read them, and then click **Next**.

What are mass mailings?

A *mass mailing* can be any form letter in which you want a personalized copy of the same text to go to multiple recipients. You probably get sweepstakes entries in the mail all the time with your name on them; these are mass mailings, just like the ones you can create yourself in Works.

SEE ALSO
➤ *To review how to add names and addresses to a database, see page 123.*

4. On the **Database** tab that appears, choose which of your Works databases you will use for the mail merge (see Figure 6.5). Then click the **Recipients** tab.

FIGURE 6.5

Pick a database from which to pull the records.

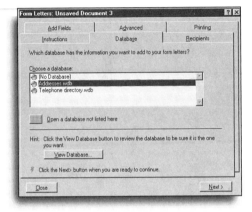

Which database?

If you didn't give your databases adequately descriptive names, you might be in a quandary determining which is the right file in step 4. If you can't tell by the names which database you want, choose one and then click the **View Database** button to see it. That way, you can tell which one is correct.

5. On the **Recipients** tab, you must choose which records from the database you want to use. The default is **All records in the database**, but you can apply any of the filters you've set up in that database by clicking the **Filtered records in the database** option button and then choosing the filter from the drop-down list.

6. Click the **Add Fields** tab. This is where you add fields to your document.

7. Click the name of the first field you want to add. For example, if you are creating the return address, click on **First Name**. Then click the **Insert Field** button.

8. Continue inserting the fields for the Last Name, Address1, Address2, City, State, and Postal Code. Don't worry that the fields are appearing all bunched up on the document behind the dialog box.

9. Click the **Advanced** tab and then click **Edit**. The dialog box shrinks so you can work on your document (see Figure 6.6).

10. Place hard returns after the Last Name, Address1, and Address2 fields so the return address is in proper mailing format. You might also want to insert a comma between the City and State fields.

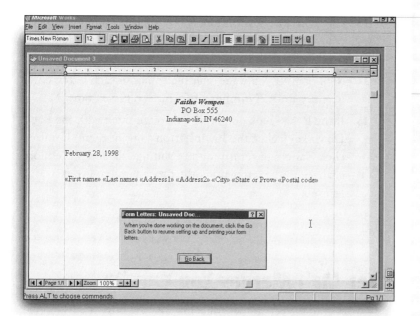

FIGURE 6.6
Whip your document into shape by editing and adding text around the inserted fields.

11. Begin typing the body of the letter. When you need to insert another field, click the **Go Back** button and return to the Form Letters dialog box to add another field. (For example, you might add the person's name in the body of the letter for emphasis.)

12. When you are finished building the letter, click the **Printing** tab in the Form Letters dialog box (see Figure 6.7).

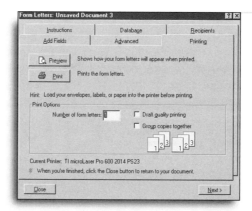

FIGURE 6.7
Now it's time to see what your letters will look like!

13. Click the **Preview** button. A box appears asking whether you want to preview all records. Click **OK**, and the letters open in Print Preview.

14. (Optional) If you want multiple copies of each letter, enter a quantity in the **Number of form letters** text box.

15. If the letters look good (page through them with the Page Down key), click the **Print** button to print them. If not, click **Cancel** to return to the Printing tab, and make more changes to the letter using the procedures you've just learned.

SEE ALSO

➤ *For more information about Print Preview, see page 40.*

Other Mail Merges You Can Do

Works offers very similar tools for creating other kinds of merged documents, such as envelopes and labels. When you catch on to the multi-tabbed dialog box approach, as in the preceding steps, it's pretty easy. Just follow the instructions onscreen.

- To create envelopes, open the **Tools** menu and choose **Envelopes**.

- To create mailing labels, open the **Tools** menu and choose **Labels**.

Using Word

Getting Started with Word

Build Word documents from scratch

Use templates to jump-start a document

Convert files from other formats

Change your view to edit more easily

Zoom in for a closer view and zoom out for
the big picture

Moving around in a document

Entering, editing, and selecting text

Previewing and printing your work

Word: What's It All About?

Word is a high-powered word processor. It does everything that the Works word processor does, and much more. The Works word processor is a great start for beginners, and I recommend that you master it first (see Chapters 2, "Introducing the Works Word Processor," and 3, "Creating Fancier Documents in Works") before you tackle Word. But after you get up to speed on your word-processing basics, you'll appreciate Word's power and flexibility. In this chapter, I'll introduce you to Word's basic features, and you'll pick up the skills you need to succeed in the upcoming chapters that detail Word's capabilities.

Creating a New Document

When you start Word by clicking its shortcut on the **Programs** menu, it automatically creates a new, blank document with the generic name Document1 (see Figure 7.1). At that point, you can simply start typing. You can also choose to create a new document based on a *wizard* or *template*, if the right one is available.

SEE ALSO

➢ *To learn all about templates, including how to create your own, see page 230.*

➢ *To quickly use a template to create a new document, see page 164.*

Starting with a Blank Page

When you start Word, it automatically starts a blank page for you. Go ahead and use it. If you later want another blank page, use one of the following techniques:

- Click the New button ▢.
- Press Ctrl+N.
- Open the **File** menu and choose **New**. Select **Blank Document** from the **General** tab and click **OK**.

Templates and wizards

Wizards and templates are shortcuts to creating professional-looking documents. Wizards are like the TaskWizards in Works. Templates are lesser full-service versions that start you out with certain margins and styles, and in some cases boilerplate text.

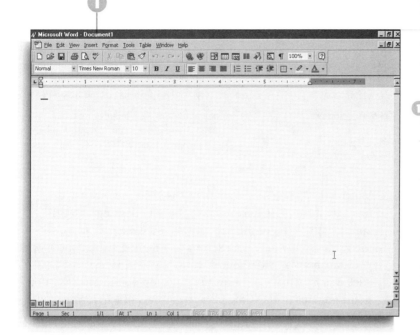

FIGURE 7.1

Word creates a blank document based on the Normal template every time you start the program.

1   The generic name of Document1 is a placeholder.

When you use any of these techniques, the new document you create looks like a blank sheet of paper. Although no text appears on the page, your new document is actually based on the *Normal document template*, which is contained in a file called Normal.dot.

The Normal document template is a tremendously important part of Word. Settings stored here define the basic look of every new document you create. Table 7.1 lists the basic settings for Normal.dot.

TABLE 7.1   **Document options saved in the Normal document template**

Document Option	Default Setting
Default margins	1 inch at top and bottom of page, 1.25 inches on each side
Default paper size and *orientation*	In the United States, Word uses 8.5×11-inch (Letter) paper in portrait orientation

continues…

TABLE 7.1   Continued

Document Option	Default Setting
Default font and font size	10-point Times New Roman
Styles	More than 90 built-in paragraph and character styles for specifying the look of text, lists, headings, and so on
Customization	Layouts for default menu bar, Standard and Formatting toolbars, plus 14 more toolbars and all shortcut menus

When you open a new document based on the Normal document template, just start typing. The thin flashing line that appears at the top of the page is called the *insertion point*, and it marks the spot where your letters and numbers will appear when you start typing. After your document contains text, you can click in a new place to move the insertion point. The insertion point remains in the same place regardless of where you aim the mouse pointer; to move the insertion point, you must click in a new location where you can enter text.

SEE ALSO
➤ *To find out how to modify the settings listed in Table 7.1, see page 231.*

Using Ready-Made Templates

Word's templates offer great head starts for creating common document types like reports, letters, faxes, resumes, and much more. If a template exists for the kind of document you want, you can really save some time by using it. (The downside is that the template has a lot of the decisions made already, like font and spacing, so you have less creative freedom.)

Starting a new document from a template

1. Open the **File** menu and choose **New**. The New dialog box appears with tabs for the various kinds of templates available.

2. Click a tab to look at the templates available in each category. Then click a template icon to see a preview in the **Preview** box (see Figure 7.2).

FIGURE 7.2

Pick a template from this dialog box.

3. When you find the one you want, click **OK** to open it.

In some templates, generic text is formatted using Word fields, which enables you to simply click to select the entire block of text and then type to replace it. In other cases, like the company name at the top of the Contemporary Letter template (see Figure 7.3), you have to use the mouse to select the sample text and then replace it before you can use the document.

Templates or wizards?

The wizards have magic wands on their icons; the templates don't. You'll learn about wizards in the following section. If you are following along now, choose one of the templates, such as **Contemporary Letter** on the **Letters & Faxes** tab, to try out.

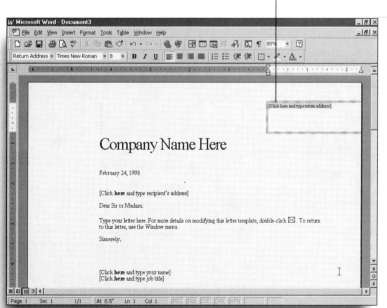

FIGURE 7.3

Select the "generic" text in a document template; it disappears as soon as you start typing.

❶ Generic text

Proofread templates carefully

Whenever you use a document template for the first time, check the results carefully. Nothing is more embarrassing than sending a fax cover sheet that identifies you as an employee of *Company Name Here*.

Installing more wizards and templates

By default, not all the wizards and templates are installed. To install some more from the Home Essentials CD, re-run the setup program (see Appendix A, "Installing Home Essentials") and choose a Custom installation. Then choose the additional templates from the list of options to install.

SEE ALSO

> *If you use a particular template regularly, and you want instructions on customizing it for your own use, see page 231.*

Using a Wizard to Create a New Document

If you install every available template, Word 97 offers a total of 10 wizards. These choices appear in the New dialog box mixed in with the regular document templates; you can tell a wizard at a glance by its name (which invariably includes the word wizard) and its distinctive icon (which includes a magic wand).

The wizards can be a great help, especially if you are unfamiliar with the type of conventions for the document that you need to create. For example, the Letter Wizard produces and formats a letter in your choice of three styles. The Fax Wizard creates a cover sheet that you can fax through a fax-modem or print out to use with a regular fax machine.

To use a wizard, double-click it in the New dialog box and then follow the prompts. Most Word Wizards include easy-to-follow online help. Choose options or fill in information on each of the wizard's dialog boxes, as in the Fax Wizard shown in Figure 7.4. Use the **Next** button as you complete each step and click **Finish** when you're done.

FIGURE 7.4

Wizards, like this one for making instant faxes and cover sheets, let you build a document by checking boxes and filling in blanks.

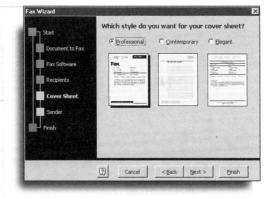

Saving Your Work

Each document you create in Word has a generic name like Document1, Document2, and so on. Word assigns these names to keep you from getting confused when there is more than one unsaved document open at once. When you save a document, give it a descriptive name that will help you remember its purpose.

Names can be up to 255 characters long and can include spaces. For practical purposes, however, you should keep the names reasonably short. You don't have to type .doc at the end of the filename because Word adds that automatically. After you save your document, a copy exists on your hard disk that you can open later. It stays there until you delete it. Each time you make changes to the document, you must save it again to include the changes in the copy on your hard disk.

There are two procedures for saving: Save and Save As. If you have never saved the document before, they are the same: they ask for a name and location for the file. After you save once, Save resaves the document with the same name and location that you initially entered, whereas Save As gives you the opportunity to save the document with a different name and location.

Saving a document for the first time

1. Click the Save button 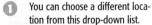 on the toolbar, or press Ctrl+S.
2. In the Save As dialog box (see Figure 7.5), enter a name in the **File name** text box. (Just type over what's there.)

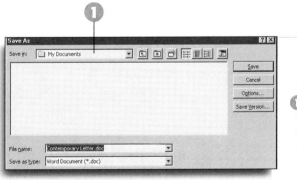

FIGURE 7.5

Save your work in the Save As dialog box.

1 You can choose a different location from this drop-down list.

3. (Optional) If you want to save your file in a different location, use the navigation buttons in the dialog box to change the folder or drive. The default folder is **My Documents**; leave the location as is unless you have a good reason for changing it.

4. Click the **Save** button in the dialog box. The document is saved, and the new name appears in the title bar.

Changing the folder and drive

You'll find the same folder and drive navigation system in the Save As dialog box and the Open dialog box in most Windows 95 programs. To change to a different drive, open the **Save in** drop-down list. Choose the drive on which you want to save the file. Next, choose the folder where you want to save the file. When you select the drive, a list of folders on that drive appears. Double-click the folder you want to select.

After you have saved the document once, clicking the **Save** button on the toolbar or pressing Ctrl+S saves the file again under the same name. If you want to reopen the Save As dialog box, as shown in Figure 7.5, open the **File** menu and choose **Save As** instead.

To force Word to save all open documents immediately, including the Normal document template, hold down the Shift key as you open the **File** menu and then choose **Save All**. This alternative pull-down menu also gives you a **Close All** option, which closes every open document window, prompting you to save any changes first.

Opening a Saved Document

To open a saved document in any Office program, open the **File** menu and choose **Open**. In the Open dialog box (see Figure 7.6), double-click the filename to open it. You can change the drive and folder if needed to locate the file, as explained in the "Changing the folder and drive" sidebar above.

FIGURE 7.6

Just locate the file you want to open and double-click it.

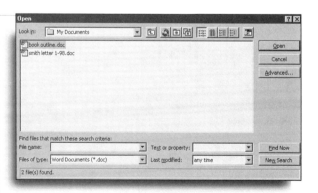

Converting Files from Previous Versions of Word

If you have used an earlier version of Word, you may have some files already saved that you want to open in Word 97. No sweat. Word 97 can recognize and open files from Word for Windows version 2.0 and higher seamlessly, just as if it were a native Word 97 file. When you save the files again, Word asks whether you want to retain the old format or update it to Word 97. In most cases it's best to update it, unless you need to share the file with someone who doesn't have Word 97.

Converting Files from Other Document Formats

When opening files that come from word processors other than Word, you may need to tell Word what program's files to look for. Just open the **Files of type** drop-down list (shown previously in Figure 7.6) and choose the file format desired. By default, Word can open plain text files, as well as files saved in Rich Text or WordPerfect 5.x and 6.x formats, or as Excel workbooks. You need to install additional converters to open files created using Lotus Notes, Microsoft Works, or versions of Word other than Word 97 or Word 6.0/95.

SEE ALSO

➤ *To install additional converters, re-run the Word setup program and use Custom setup to choose the converters; see page 521.*

Choosing the Right Document View

Word lets you choose one of four distinct views when you're creating or editing a document. Which view should you choose? The answer depends on what you're trying to do. Are you concentrating on writing? Trying to make your document look great? Organizing your thoughts? Word has a special view for each step in the writing process, as described in the following sections.

Entering and Editing Text in Normal View

Normal view is perfect for those times when you just want to get the words out of your head and you aren't concerned about

Switch views with one click

Word's five viewing options are all available on the **View** menu. You can also switch between **Normal**, **Online Layout**, **Page Layout**, and **Outline** views using the four buttons in the lower-left corner of the document window, to the left of the horizontal scrollbar and just above the status bar. Hover the mouse pointer over each button to identify it. No button is available for the rarely used Master Document view.

exactly how they'll look when printed. Normal view shows you all text formatting, graphics, and other objects on the page; you see placeholders where page breaks, margins, columns, and other page layout options should appear. Figure 7.7 shows this simplified view of a document.

FIGURE 7.7

Normal view uses the entire window to display your document. It's perfect for quickly typing a first draft.

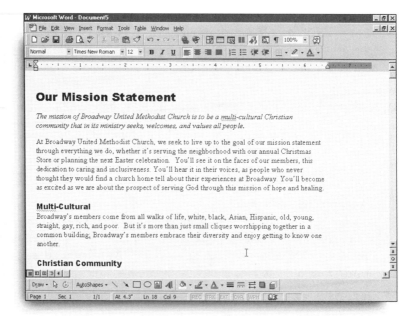

Previewing the Printed Page

When you select *Page Layout view*, you can see how much space is available in the margins on each side of the page. As you scroll through your document, you can see the bottom and top margins of each page as well. If you've put page numbers or a title on the page, those pieces will be visible, although they'll be grayed out. Page Layout view is particularly appropriate for tasks that involve fine formatting and precise placement of headers, footers, and other screen elements. Figure 7.8 shows what you see when you choose this view.

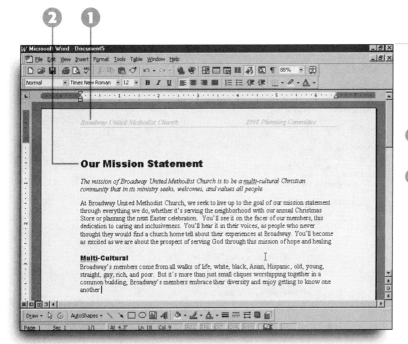

Organizing Your Thoughts with Outline View

Outline view is ideal for making sure your thoughts are well organized. When you use Word's built-in heading styles, you can switch to Outline view and collapse your document to see just its main points. The Outlining toolbar helps you collapse and expand each section (see Figure 7.9).

Optimizing Your Document for Online Reading

The *Online Layout view* is new in Office 97, and as the name implies, it's the proper selection when you want to read documents onscreen. As you can see from the example in Figure 7.10, the text in each paragraph is larger (for easy reading) and it wraps to fit the window instead of running off the edge of the screen. The Document Map at the left of the screen lets you see the headings in your document and click a heading to move through the document a section at a time.

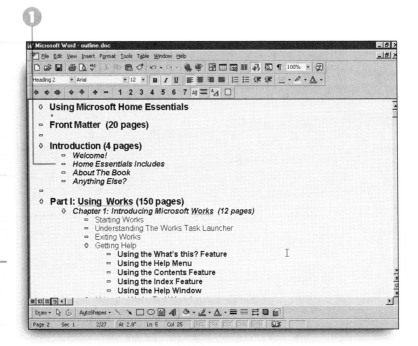

FIGURE 7.9

The Outlining toolbar appears automatically when you switch to Outline view. Use it to collapse and expand the document.

❶ Outline levels are shown with indents.

How do you get back to Normal view?

When you switch to Online Layout view, the **View** buttons at the lower-left corner of the screen disappear. Use the **View** menu to switch to a different view.

Using Full Screen View to Clear Away Clutter

If toolbars, rulers, and other screen elements are too distracting, open the **View** menu and choose **Full Screen**. In this view, all you typically see is the document itself and a simple toolbar with one button; all other toolbars, menus, and other screen elements, including the Windows taskbar, disappear. This is great for WordPerfect users who may be accustomed to a pristine working area onscreen. Click the **Close Full Screen** button to switch back to the regular program window.

Zooming In for a Closer Look

Regardless of which view you've selected, you can increase or decrease the size of the document displayed on the screen. Zooming in makes it easier to read or edit text when the words on the screen are too small to read easily. Zooming out lets you see the overall design of the page.

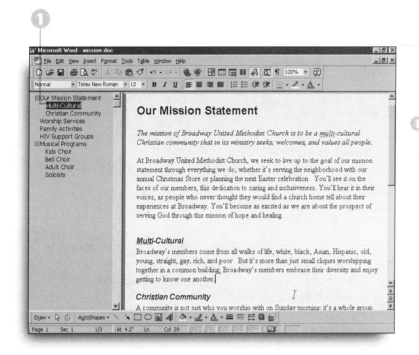

FIGURE 7.10

Use the Document Map (left) to see all the headings in your document in Online Layout view.

① Click a heading in the document map to jump there.

Use the Zoom 🔍 button on the Standard toolbar to choose a predefined magnification from 10 to 500 percent of normal size. Choose **Page Width** to expand the text so it's as large as possible without running off the edge of the screen. Try **Whole Page** to fit the entire page on the screen, or **Two Pages** for a side-by-side view. To see more Zoom options, open the **View** menu and choose **Zoom**.

Different zooms for different views

Your choices on the **Zoom** menu depend on what view you are using. For example, in Normal view, you don't have **Whole Page** and **Two Pages** as options.

Moving Around in a Word Document

Knowing the right navigation shortcuts can dramatically increase your productivity as you edit in Word. Instead of using arrow keys to move at a snail's pace through your document, mouse and keyboard shortcuts can help you move to the precise point where you want to be.

When you're editing text, the fastest way to move through the document is with the help of the keyboard shortcuts shown in Table 7.2.

TABLE 7.2   **Moving through a document using the keyboard**

To Do This…	Press This Key Combination
Move to the beginning or end of the current line	Home and End
Move one word to the right or left, respectively	Ctrl+Right arrow or Ctrl+Left arrow
Move to the previous or next paragraph, respectively	Ctrl+Up arrow or Ctrl+Down arrow
Move up or down one window	PgUp or PgDn
Jump to the top or bottom of the document	Ctrl+Home or Ctrl+End

Two additional keyboard shortcuts are worth noting. Shift+F5 is one of my all-time favorites. When you press this key combination, Word cycles the insertion point through the last three places where you entered or edited text. Use this cool shortcut if you've scrolled through a long document and you want to jump back quickly to the place where you started.

You can also move with the mouse using the scrollbars, of course, just like in any other Windows program. You can click above or below the scrollbox to move one screenful in that direction. Click the arrows at the ends of the scrollbar to move slightly in one direction or the other, or drag the scrollbox to move quickly. As you drag the scrollbox, a note appears telling you what page you're on, and in some views, even what heading you'll find there (see Figure 7.11).

Selecting Text in Word

Before you can move, copy, delete, or reformat text, you first have to *select* it. (You can tell when text has been selected because it appears in a dark bar, with white letters on a black background.) Selecting text using the mouse is easiest, but if you prefer to keep your hands on the keyboard, you can find plenty of shortcuts.

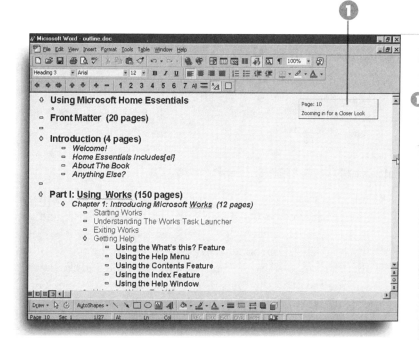

FIGURE 7.11
As you drag the scrollbox, Word tells you what page you're on.

1 If I were to release the mouse button now, I would be on this page.

Selecting Text Using the Mouse

Word enables you to use an assortment of mouse techniques to select chunks of text, as shown in Table 7.3.

TABLE 7.3   **Mouse techniques for selecting text**

To Select...	Do This
A word	Point to the word and double-click.
A sentence	Point to the sentence and triple-click or hold down the Ctrl key, point to the sentence, and click.
A paragraph	Point in the margin to the left of the paragraph; when the mouse pointer turns into an arrow, double-click.
A whole document	Move the mouse pointer to the left margin until it turns into an arrow and then triple-click.

You don't have to be precise to select an entire word using the mouse. Aim the mouse pointer anywhere within a word; as you drag the pointer left or right, the selection changes to include each new word. Most of the time, that's the correct action because you typically want to move, copy, or format an entire word rather than a few characters within a word.

What if you really want to select the end of one word and the beginning of another? To override automatic word selection temporarily, hold down the Ctrl and Shift keys as you drag the selection.

Selecting Text Using the Keyboard

If you're a speedy typist, nothing slows down your productivity more than having to take your fingers off the keyboard, find the mouse, click to select a block, and then move back to the keys. Every touch typist should learn to select text using the keyboard shortcuts; in most cases, you can hold down the Shift key while you use the same shortcuts that you use to move through a document. Table 7.4 lists these techniques.

Turning off automatic word selection

If automatic word selection bugs you, you can easily disable this feature. Open the **Tools** menu, choose **Options**, click the **Edit** tab, and remove the check mark next to the box labeled **When selecting, automatically select entire word**.

TABLE 7.4   **Keyboard selection techniques**

To Select...	Do This
One or more characters	Hold down the Shift key as you press the left or right arrow keys one or more times.
A word	Move the insertion point to the beginning of the word; then press Ctrl+Shift+Right arrow.
The beginning or end of the line	Press Shift+Home or Shift+End.
The beginning or end of the paragraph	Press Ctrl+Shift+Up arrow or Ctrl+Shift+Down arrow.
The beginning or end of the document	Press Ctrl+Shift+Home or Ctrl+Shift+End.
The whole document	Press Ctrl+A.

My favorite keyboard shortcut lets you quickly select a word, a sentence, a paragraph, or the whole document. Just move the insertion point where you want to begin selecting and then press the F8 key to turn on *Extend Selection mode*. (To see an onscreen reminder that you've turned on this feature, look in the center of the status bar at the bottom of the document window. If you see the letters EXT, Extend Selection mode is on.)

After you've pressed F8, you can press any key to extend the selection. If you press the period key, for example, Word extends the selection to the next period, which is usually the end of the sentence. Press the period key again to select the end of the next sentence.

After pressing F8 the first time, you can extend the selection further. Press F8 a second time to select a whole word, a third time to select the entire sentence, a fourth time for the current paragraph, and a fifth time to select your entire document. To exit Extend Selection mode, press the Esc key. To deselect your selection, move any arrow key.

Entering and Deleting Text

When you start a new document, all you have to do is type. Don't press Enter to start a new line; Word does that for you automatically. Press Enter only when you are ready to start a new paragraph. If you make a mistake, back up using the Backspace key. (If you make a big mistake, or need to back up a long way, see the editing suggestions later in this section.)

Replacing Text as You Type

Normally, Word lets you enter text in *Insert mode*—whatever you enter pushes any existing text out of the way to make room. Pressing the Insert key, deliberately or inadvertently, toggles into *Overtype* mode, in which each new character you type replaces the character immediately to its right. Be careful! When you press the Insert key by accident, you can wipe out massive amounts of work before you even realize anything is wrong.

Word offers a subtle clue that tells you when you've shifted from Insert to Overtype mode. In the center of the status bar at the bottom of the document window are five small indicator boxes.

Careful with that selection!

If you inadvertently press any character on the keyboard, including the Spacebar, whatever you type replaces whatever is currently selected. To bring back the original selection, click the Undo button or press Ctrl+Z.

nO mORE cAPS lOCK mISTAKES

How many times has your finger slipped as you struck the Shift or Tab key, accidentally hitting the Caps Lock key and producing text like the preceding headline? Touch typists can go for a paragraph or even a full page before they notice that all the text has been entered incorrectly. Word 97 is smart enough to detect when Caps Lock comes on inappropriately, automatically undoing the scrambled text and restoring Caps Lock to its correct setting.

Averting Insert key accidents

If you regularly find yourself accidentally shifting into Overtype mode, you can disable the Insert key's capability to switch into it by opening the **Tools** menu and choosing **Options**, then clicking the Edit tab. Click the **Use the INS key for paste** check box. This reassigns the mission of the Insert key, so it no longer toggles between overtype and insert mode.

If the letters OVR are visible, you've switched into Overtype mode. Press the Insert key to switch back to Insert mode.

Deleting Text

Keyboard shortcuts offer the fastest way to get rid of text. Touch typists should memorize the key combinations shown in Table 7.5.

TABLE 7.5   Keyboard shortcuts

To Perform This Action…	Use This Key or Combination
Delete the current selection; if no text is selected, delete the character to the left of the insertion point	Backspace
Delete the current selection; if no text is selected, delete the character to the right of the insertion point	Del
Delete the word to the left of the insertion point or selection	Ctrl+Backspace
Delete the word to the right of the insertion point or selection	Ctrl+Del
Cut the currently selected text and put it on the Clipboard	Ctrl+X

Adding Symbols and Special Characters to Your Documents

If you use the standard U.S. keyboard layout, you can find all the letters of the alphabet, the numbers 0 through 9, and most punctuation marks on the keyboard. Often, however, you may want to enter characters that aren't available on the keyboard: accented characters from foreign alphabets, for example, currency symbols other than the dollar sign, or copyright and trademark indicators.

If a character is not on the standard keyboard, Word considers it a *symbol* or a *special character*. The easiest way to insert any such character into the current document is to use the menus.

Adding special characters to a document

1. Position the insertion point where you want the special character to appear.

2. Open the **Insert** menu and choose **Symbol** to open the Symbols dialog box.

3. Click the **Special Characters** tab in the dialog box and choose from some commonly used special characters (like copyright symbols and foreign currency symbols) as shown in Figure 7.12. If you see the symbol you want to insert there, double-click it. You're done. If not, go on to the next step.

4. Click the **Symbols** tab to display the full list of characters in the currently displayed font. These include not only the characters available from the keyboard but also some special ones, like vowels with accent marks over them for foreign spellings.

Instant symbols

Word's AutoCorrect feature lets you enter some special symbols directly from the keyboard. If you type (tm) or (r), for example, Word automatically changes the entry to the trademark (™) or registered trademark (®) symbols. To see other such AutoText characters, open the **Tools** menu, choose **AutoCorrect**, and click the **AutoCorrect** tab. There, you can find smileys, "frownies," and "who cares" faces, as well as some lines and arrows. You'll learn more about this feature in Chapter 10, "Correcting and Polishing Your Document."

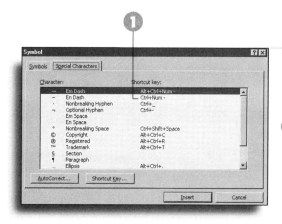

FIGURE 7.12

The Special Characters tab contains many of the most popular symbols that users need to insert.

❶ Some characters have shortcut keys.

5. If needed, click a character to enlarge it so you can see it better. If you do not see the character you want, try choosing a different font from the **Font** drop-down list.

6. When you find the character you want to insert, double-click it to place it in your document.

7. Click the **Close** button to close the dialog box.

Special character shortcuts

If you regularly use any of these special characters, memorize the keyboard shortcut listed to its right.

Undoing (and Redoing) What You've Done

What happens when you inadvertently delete an important part of your document? Relax. You can put everything back the way it was by using Word's Undo button . Click once to undo your last action. Keep clicking, and the Undo button rolls back as many as your last 100 actions. If you know you want to undo a lengthy sequence of actions, click the arrow at the right of the Undo button and then scroll through the drop-down list of steps Word can undo for you (see Figure 7.13). If you click the fourth step in the list, for example, Word automatically undoes the last four actions in a single motion.

FIGURE 7.13

Word's **Undo** key can reverse the effects of 1, 50, or even 100 recent keystrokes and mouse clicks.

Use the matching Redo button and its keyboard shortcut Ctrl+Y when you change your mind after using the Undo button. In combination, the two buttons can let you restore a chunk of text you deleted earlier in the current session, without losing other changes you've made since then. Use the Undo button to roll back your changes until the deleted text is visible again. Select the text, copy it to the Clipboard, and then use the Redo button to return to the most recent version of the document.

Finding and Replacing

The longer and more complex a document is, the more likely you'll need Word's help to find a specific section of the document. Have you used the same phrase too many times in the current document? Have you misspelled the name of a person or company? Where is the section that talks about second-quarter budget results?

To answer any of these questions, use Word's Find and Replace feature. Day in and day out, it is probably the most valuable Word editing tool you can master.

Finding Text

You can easily find a word or phrase anywhere in your document by using Word's Find feature.

Finding text in a document

1. Press Ctrl+F (or open the **Edit** menu and choose **Find**). You then see the dialog box shown in Figure 7.14.

2. Click in the **Find what** box and type the text for which you want to search—a word, a name, a phrase, or a complete sentence.

3. Click the **Find Next** button to jump to the first occurrence of the text you entered.

4. Keep clicking the **Find Next** button to jump to each successive location in the document where the selected text appears.

5. Press Esc or click the **Cancel** button to close the Find and Replace dialog box.

Normally, Word ignores the case of the text you enter in the **Find what** box. If you want to restrict the search further, click the **More** button and select one or more of the check boxes in the bottom of the dialog box. Turning on the **Match case** option, for example, forces Word to distinguish between

Spelling doesn't count

If you're not sure of the correct spelling of the word you're looking for, enter your best guess. Click the **More** button, if necessary, and check the **Sounds Like** box in the bottom of the dialog box.

upper- and lowercase letters. Right-click and choose **What's This?** for a brief description of how you can use these options.

Replacing Text

If you can find a piece of text, you can change it. That capability comes in handy if you've written a lengthy pitch for Acme Corporation and then discover the company's legal name is actually Acme Industries, Inc. Instead of searching through your document and painstakingly retyping the name each time it appears, let Word replace the existing text with the new text you specify.

Replacing text in a document

1. If the Find and Replace dialog box is visible, click the **Replace** tab. If this dialog box is not visible, press Ctrl+H or open the **Edit** menu and choose **Replace**.

2. Type the text you want to search for in the **Find what** box; type the replacement text in the box labeled **Replace with**. The dialog box should look like the one in Figure 7.15.

FIGURE 7.15

Use the Find and Replace dialog box to substitute one word or phrase for another automatically.

3. Click the **Find Next** button to jump to the first occurrence of the text you specified.

4. To replace the text in that location, click the **Replace** button. Word makes the substitution and moves on to the next spot where the search text appears.

5. To find the next occurrence of the search text without changing the current selection, click the **Find Next** button.

6. To change every occurrence of the selected text automatically, click **Replace All**.

7. Press Esc or click **Cancel** to close the Find and Replace dialog box.

Finding and Replacing Formatting and Special Characters

Sometimes you may want to search for (and replace) more than just text. For example, I might want to open a document, find every place where I've used Bold Italic, and change that formatting to Bold Underline. Or, if I've received a document that someone else formatted, I might want to remove all manual page breaks that were inserted.

Two buttons at the bottom of the Find and Replace dialog box let you expand the scope of a Word search. Use these buttons to search for formatting (including fonts and styles) or special characters (such as tabs and paragraph marks). You can combine these attributes, searching for a specific word or phrase that matches the formatting you specify.

Look just underneath the **Find what** and **Replace with** text boxes to see whether you've selected any formatting to accompany the current selection in either box. To remove formatting, click in the appropriate box and click the **No Formatting** button.

Preparing Your Document for the Printer

In every Office program, the Standard toolbar includes a Print button 🖨 that sends the entire current document to the default printer. When you click this button, you get one copy, using the default settings. That's fine for simple memos, but if you're planning to print a long document, do your readers a favor and add a few finishing touches first.

Page numbers, chapter titles, and section names help readers understand how a document is organized. You can add these and other milestones to long Word documents, enabling readers to find their way more easily around the printed page.

Don't close that box!

With the Find and Replace dialog box, you don't need to close it to resume editing your document. Leave the dialog box open if you want, and click in the document editing window to add a new sentence or make another change. Click in the dialog box to resume working with it.

When this sort of information is at the top of the page, it's called a *header*; at the bottom of the page, it's a *footer*. You can put just about anything in a header or footer, but most often you use these spaces for information such as titles, page numbers, dates, and labels (like "Confidential" or "Draft"). Usually, you don't need to add these details to short documents such as letters and memos or to documents that you expect will be read online.

Adding Information at the Top and Bottom of Each Page

Word's default document includes space for a header and footer 1/2 inch from the top and bottom of each page. Before you can add text or graphics to a header or footer, you first have to make these editing boxes visible. Open the **View** menu and choose **Header and Footer** (see Figure 7.16). Word switches to Page Layout view, if necessary.

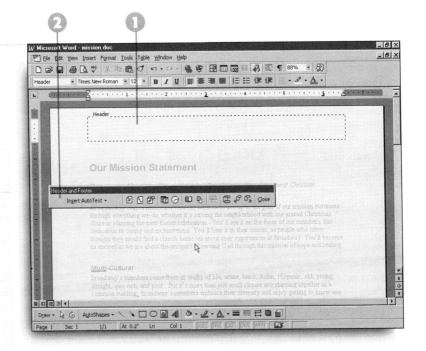

FIGURE 7.16

When you make the header and footer visible, Word switches to Page Layout view, and the text of your document appears in gray.

1 Header area

2 Header and Footer toolbar

You can enter any type of data in a header or footer box, including text, text boxes, drawings, pictures, tables, and *hyperlinks*. You can also change typefaces and sizes, realign text, and adjust the space between the header or footer and the body of your document.

While you work, the Header and Footer toolbar floats nearby with buttons you can use to navigate through your document or to insert page numbers, dates, and other information. Table 7.6 shows the buttons that are useful for working with headers and footers.

TABLE 7.6 **Buttons on the Header and Footer toolbar**

Button	What It Does
Insert AutoText	Adds an AutoText entry, such as your name or company name, at the insertion point
	Inserts the page number
	Inserts the number of pages
	Formats the page number
	Inserts the date
	Inserts the time
	Opens the Layout tab of the Page Setup dialog box
	Shows or hides document text
	Uses the header/footer from a previous section in the document, if you have used multiple sections
	Jumps from header to footer and vice versa
	Jumps to the header or footer in the previous section of the document, if applicable
	Jumps to the header or footer in the next section
Close	Hides the Header and Footer boxes and toolbar; returns to the previously selected view

One of the most popular uses for a document footer is to keep a running total of pages in the current document, automatically updating this information as you make a document longer or shorter.

Sections?

You can create section breaks in a document and have different headers, footers, margins, and so on for each section. To create a section break, open the **Insert** menu and choose **Break**. Choose one of the section breaks from the dialog box and click **OK**.

Adding page numbers to a document

1. Open the **V**iew menu and choose **Header and Footer**.

2. Click in the **Footer** box.

3. Type Page and press the Spacebar.

4. Click the Insert Page Number button ⊞ .

5. Press the Spacebar, type of, and press the Spacebar again.

6. Click the Insert Number of Pages button ⊡ .

7. Select and format the text you entered, if you want. Click the **Close** button to return to the main body of the document.

Customizing Header and Footer Use

Do you want the exact same header and footer on every page? Maybe not. If you've created a custom title page, the header and footer would mess up its careful design. Likewise, if you're planning to print on both sides of the paper and bind your work in book format, you might want to set up different headers and footers on left and right pages, with the title of your report on the right page header only, for example. (Look at this book to see an example of different headers for left and right pages.)

Word lets you handle both instances with ease. To open the Page Setup dialog box (shown in Figure 7.17), just click the Page Setup button ⊡ on the Header and Footer toolbar.

If you've created separate *sections* in a long document, you can use different headers for each section. By default, each section uses the same header information as the previous section. Click the Same as Previous button ⊞ to toggle this setting on and off.

Use the navigation buttons on the Header and Footer toolbar to jump back and forth between different headers and footers, like the ones you've created for left and right pages. In Page Layout view, double-click the header or footer area to activate it at any time and double-click anywhere on the page (outside the header or footer area) to return to the text of your document.

Field codes keep page numbers accurate

When you click the Insert Page Number or Insert Number of Pages button, Word actually inserts a *field code* in the header or footer. As you edit a document and it gets longer or shorter, Word keeps track of the total page count. When you view or print a document, Word updates the numbers on each page as needed. Date and time fields work the same way.

Which header is which?

Look at the top of the header or footer box to see at a glance which header you're currently working with. A simple Header or Footer label means you have only one of each. If you've set up additional headers or footers, you see different labels for each one—First Page Header or Even Page Footer, for example.

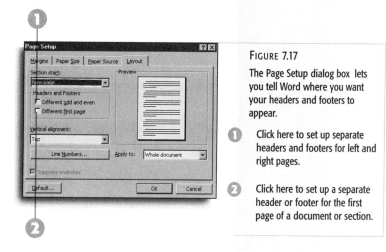

FIGURE 7.17
The Page Setup dialog box lets you tell Word where you want your headers and footers to appear.

❶ Click here to set up separate headers and footers for left and right pages.

❷ Click here to set up a separate header or footer for the first page of a document or section.

Adding Page Numbers Only

If all you want to do is number the pages in your document, you don't have to hassle with headers or footers. When you open the **Insert** menu and choose **Page Numbers**, Word creates a footer (or a header, if you prefer) in your document and then adds a page number to it. You can control the process by using the dialog box shown in Figure 7.18.

Before You Print, Preview!

I don't like surprises. I especially hate that surprised feeling I get when I pull a 48-page report out of the printer and discover that I forgot to add headers and footers to the document.

Before I send a document to the printer, I *always* click the Print Preview button 🔍. You should, too. With a single click, you get to see *exactly* what your printed output will look like—no surprises.

You can't add numbers in Outline view

The **Page Numbers** command is grayed out and unavailable when you're working in Outline or Online Layout view. Switch to Normal or Page Layout View and try again.

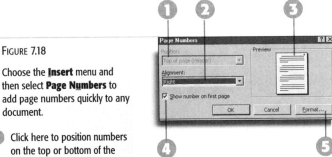

FIGURE 7.18

Choose the **Insert** menu and then select **Page Numbers** to add page numbers quickly to any document.

1 Click here to position numbers on the top or bottom of the page.

2 Tell Word how to align the page numbers: left, right, or centered.

3 This box shows you where the numbers will appear on the printed page.

4 Clear the check mark here to hide the first page number.

5 Click to display the Page Number Format dialog box, and pick a numeric format. If you're happy with a simple 1, 2, 3, skip this step.

The Big Picture: Seeing Your Entire Document at Once

The Print Preview screen (see Figure 7.19) is dramatically different from the normal document editing window. The Standard and Formatting toolbars vanish, and only the Print Preview toolbar is visible. Using this view, you can look at the pages in your document just the way they'll appear when printed, complete with graphics, headers, footers, and page numbers.

You can *preview* one page or an entire document. Zoom in for a quick look at the details; then step back to see a bunch of pages at once. If you find a mistake, or you just don't like the way one of your pages looks, you can fix it right there. The Print Preview toolbar lets you choose a view, zoom in, even edit your document in Print Preview mode.

- Click the One Page button to fill the window, from top to bottom, with just the page you're looking at right now.
- Click the Multiple Pages button to view two or more pages side by side in the preview window.
- Use the Zoom Control to choose a specific magnification; choices on this drop-down list let you select one or two pages, or zoom the current page to full width.
- Click the Full Screen View button to hide the title bar, menu bar, and taskbar, leaving only the Print Preview toolbar and the document you're previewing. (Click the **Close Full Screen** button to return to the normal view.)

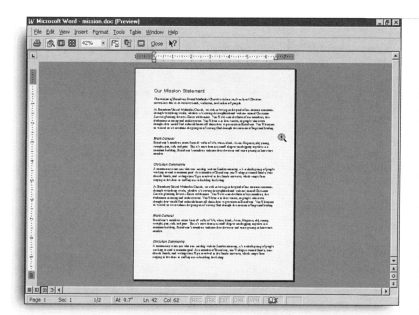

Selecting Multiple Pages view is a great way to see the overall
layout of a document—where graphics are placed and where
headlines fall, for example.

Previewing an entire document

1. Click the Print Preview button to switch to Print
   Preview mode.

2. Click the Multiple Pages button and hold down the left
   mouse button. Drag the mouse pointer down and to the
   right to select the number of rows and the number of pages
   in each row, as in Figure 7.20.

3. Release the mouse button to display the number of pages
   you selected.

4. If your document contains more pages than the view you
   selected, use the scrollbars or the Page Up and Page Down
   keys to move through the document.

5. Click the **Close** button to return to the normal document
   editing window.

**How many pages can you preview
at once?**

The answer depends on the
video resolution you've selected.
At 1024x768, for example, you
can see up to 50 pages at once,
in 5 rows of 10 pages each. At
800x600 resolution, you can
see only 24 pages at a time, in 3
rows of 8 pages each.

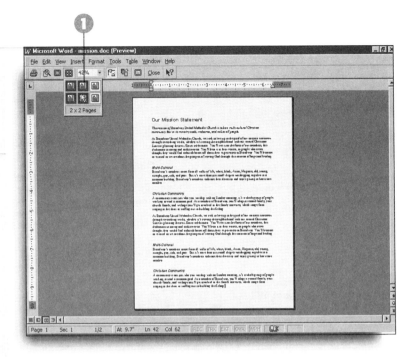

FIGURE 7.20

Click the **Multiple Pages** button and drag to select the number of pages you want to preview at once.

① Drag here.

Switching to Close-up View

In Multiple Pages view, you can quickly tell where a headline falls on a page. When you use this view of a document, you can also zoom in for a close-up look at any text, graphic, or other part of the document.

If you see an I-beam insertion point when you pass the mouse pointer over any page, click the Magnifier button. You then see a dark border around the current page. Click to select another page.

When you point to the selected page, the pointer changes to a magnifying glass with a plus sign in the center. Click any part of the page to *zoom* to 100 percent magnification. The mouse pointer changes to a magnifying glass with a minus sign in the center. Click again to return to Multiple Pages view.

Sending Your Document to the Printer

After you're satisfied that your document will print correctly, you can click the Print button ⎙. Whether you use the button on the Print Preview toolbar or click its twin on the Standard toolbar, the effect is the same: You get one copy of your entire document, and the job goes to your default printer.

If you want to print more than one copy, use a different printer or paper tray, or select just a few pages, don't click the Print button. Instead, open the **File** menu and choose **Print**, or use the Ctrl+P keyboard shortcut. In either case, you see the Print dialog box, shown in Figure 7.21.

FIGURE 7.21

To specify printing options, enter your choices in the Print dialog box.

① Enter the number of copies.

② Choose what to print, if not everything.

③ Adjust printing options, including which paper tray to use.

④ Configure Windows printer options.

⑤ Send the job to the printer.

CHAPTER

8

Formatting Documents in Word

Changing margins and page orientation

Choosing a different font and text style

Changing the space between lines and paragraphs

Working with indents and tabs

Creating bulleted and numbered lists

Using AutoFormat

Understanding Your Formatting Options

The goal of page design is to make documents easier to read. When you carefully select fonts, vary the use of bold text and other attributes, and arrange blocks of text and graphics on the page, you create natural "entry points" that guide the reader through your document quickly and effectively.

With Word, you can exercise pinpoint control over every part of a document's design, from the white space around pages to the placement of objects on the screen, to the size and shapes of text. In general, you can use three formatting options to turn plain text into well-designed documents: page setup options, character formatting, and paragraph formatting.

Page Setup Options

Open the **File** menu and choose **Page Setup** (see Figure 8.1) to adjust formats that affect the entire document. These settings define the margins at the top, bottom, left, and right of the page. They also enable you to specify what type of paper you plan to use for each document, how you want text oriented on the page, and whether you want headers or footers on each page.

Page settings can apply to your entire document, or you can divide a document into sections and set different margins, paper sizes, headers, and other page settings for each section.

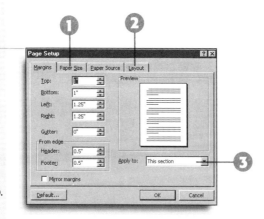

FIGURE 8.1

Use the Page Setup dialog box to change margins, paper sizes, and so on for the entire document or a single section.

 Choose between Portrait and Landscape on the Paper Size tab.

② Set up separate headers/footers for each section on the Layout tab.

③ Choose **This section** to apply special formatting to a single section of the document.

Character Formats

You can use font formatting to control the precise look of all the text in your document. You can choose separate fonts, adjust the size and style of the text, and use special effects such as underlining and strikethrough to accentuate words and paragraphs. Word also enables you to choose colors and animated effects for text; these formatting options are most useful for Web pages and other documents designed for online viewing.

Once, the distinction between the terms *typeface* and *font* was clear. Today, that line has blurred somewhat, although the basic principles are still the same.

When you choose an entry from Word's drop-down Font list, you're providing only one piece of the information needed to describe the look of the selected text. Old-time typesetters and printers would insist that each item on that list is a *typeface*—the catchall term that describes the general shape and weight of the letters, numbers, and punctuation marks in that family. The *font*, they would argue, includes much more detail—not just the typeface, but also its *size*, *weight* (bold or demibold, for example), and *style* (such as italic). In this strict definition, Arial is the name of a typeface, and 12-point Arial Bold Italic describes a specific font.

Paragraph Formats

As the name implies, paragraph formats control the alignment, spacing, and arrangement of entire paragraphs. You can use indents to adjust margins for individual paragraphs, and tab stops enable you to align text or numbers into columns.

Direct Formatting Versus Styles

When you create a document from scratch, Word starts with the basic formatting options defined in the Normal document template. If you use other styles to adjust character and paragraph formatting, those options affect the look of your document as well.

Serif versus sans serif

Typefaces come in all levels of complexity, but they can generally be divided into two broad categories: serif and sans serif. Serifs are the small decorative flourishes at the ends of some characters in some typefaces. Sans means "without," so a sans serif face has none of these decorations. Look at the tips of the capital T in the following type samples to see the difference clearly:

- This is a SERIF typeface.

- This is a SANS SERIF typeface.

Most designers agree that serif typefaces are the best choice for big blocks of text because they're easier to read, whereas sans serif typefaces are better for headlines and short paragraphs.

Even if you've used document styles to apply formatting, however, you can override these choices by selecting text and choosing options from Word's **Format** menu. Font choices and other formatting options that you make in this fashion override character and paragraph styles. To see all the formatting options for a given block of text (including direct settings and named styles), choose the **Help** menu and select **What's This.** Aim the question-mark-and-arrow pointer at a character, and click to see a window like the one in Figure 8.2.

SEE ALSO

➤ *To learn more about styles and templates, see page 219.*

FIGURE 8.2

Use **What's** **This** Help to inspect all the formatting for a given part of your document. Direct formatting always overrides formatting applied by a named style.

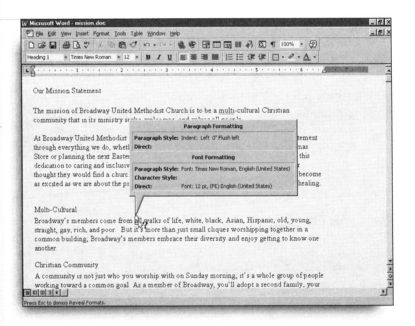

If you've mixed styles and direct formatting, trying to sort out which formatting is which can get hopelessly confusing. If you can no longer make heads or tails of the formatting in your document, you might want to reset formats to their defaults. To reset all paragraph format settings to those defined in the current style, position the insertion point within the paragraph and press **Ctrl+Q**. To reset any character formatting to the settings defined in the paragraph style, select the text and press Ctrl+Spacebar. (This method also removes any character styles applied within the selected text.) To remove all formatting and reset the paragraph to the Normal style, press Ctrl+Shift+N.

SEE ALSO

➤ *For more details about Word's Normal document template, see page 162.*

➤ *To find general information on saving and reusing formats, see page 220.*

Changing the Look of a Page

If you use the default settings in the Normal document template, Word assumes you want all your documents on $8\frac{1}{2}\times11$-inch letter paper, with roughly an inch of white space on all four sides. You can adjust any of these settings, however, and your changes can apply to the entire document or to individual pages or sections.

Working with Sections

You can divide up your sections by inserting *section breaks*. Each section can then have its own margins, columns, and headers/footers. For example, you might format the first page of a letter for printing on your company's letterhead, with remaining pages on ordinary letter stock. In this example, each section gets its own page setup settings.

Another example would be a newsletter with a masthead across the top that runs the entire width of the page. Beneath it is an article in three columns. Because each section can have only one number-of-columns setting, a section break separates the one-column text from the three-column text (see Figure 8.3).

SEE ALSO

➤ *To learn how to create multiple columns, see page 263.*

FIGURE 8.3

Use Continuous section breaks when you need to change the margins or number of columns on the same page.

Section break here (not visible onscreen)

Open the **Insert** menu and choose the **Break** command to create a dividing line between sections. Select **Continuous** if you want text to continue on the same page, with different margins and other page settings, as with the newsletter example. Choose the **Next page** option when you want to insert a section break and start a new page, as you would when changing paper types. The **Even page** and **Odd page** options are most useful if you're creating a bound booklet.

After you insert a section break, it is invisible in Page Layout view, but you can see it just like a page break in Normal view. To delete it, just select the break in Normal view and press the Delete key.

To apply a page layout change to a section, position the insertion point anywhere in that section and then make the change, as described in the sections that follow.

Adjusting the Margins

You can leave extra room on either or both sides, on the top, or on the bottom of your page. For example, when distributing a report to reviewers, you might leave room for comments in the right or left margin. You can also trim the margins to pack more words on the page, although that might make the document harder to read.

To adjust the margins, pull down the **File** menu and choose **Page Setup**; then click the **Margins** tab (see Figure 8.4). You can set margins for all four edges as well as the *gutter*, which is the inside of each page (the right side of a left-hand page and the left side of a right-hand page) when you're printing a book or other bound document. Click the box labeled **Mirror margins** to change the **Left** and **Right** boxes to **Inside** and **Outside** when printing documents you plan to bind book-style.

Zero is not an option

With most printers, you cannot set the margins to zero because standard laser and inkjet printers have an unprintable area that Windows doesn't let you use. If you try to set a margin to a value that is within the unprintable area, Word offers to change it to the minimum setting.

Type directly or spin

As with many Office dialog boxes, you can set the page margins by typing them directly into the boxes, or you can click the spinner buttons to nudge the value up or down in small increments—in this case, 0.1 inch at a time.

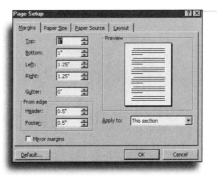

FIGURE 8.4

Click the **Margins** tab in the Page Setup dialog box to adjust the amount of white space around your pages.

Changing Paper Size and Orientation

You'll print most business documents on plain letter paper. But what do you do when you want to use legal-size paper or odd-sized stationery? Or when you want to print a table in landscape mode, with the wide edge of the paper at the top and bottom of the page?

Changing paper sizes

1. Pull down the **File** menu and choose **Page Setup** to open Word's Page Setup dialog box.

Mix and match margins

You can easily change margins and even paper size in the middle of a document. To do so, position your cursor where you want the new settings to begin. Then, just pick **This Point Forward** from the drop-down list labeled **Apply to**. This creates a section break in the spot where your cursor lies and applies the changes to the new section.

2. Click the **Paper Size** tab to display the dialog box shown in Figure 8.5.

3. The exact choices available in the **Paper size** list depend on the printer you've selected. Click the arrow to the right of the list to choose a predefined paper size.

4. If the paper size you want to use is not listed, choose **Custom size** from the bottom of the list and enter the dimensions of the paper in the boxes labeled **Width** and **Height**.

5. To use the selected paper size for all documents, click the button labeled **Default**.

6. Click **OK** to close the dialog box.

Is your paper compatible?

Before you specify a custom paper size, make sure that your printer can handle it. Some printers require that you use a manual feed for nonstandard sizes, and thick papers (such as the stock used for postcards or placards) can jam your printer. Read the printer's documentation if you're not certain.

FIGURE 8.5

Use these options to change paper sizes and switch from Portrait (tall) to Landscape (wide) orientation.

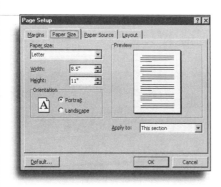

Starting a New Page

Sometimes you want to end the current page and force Word to start a new one—for example, to put a table on its own separate page. Press **Ctrl+Enter** to add a manual page break, or pull down the **Insert** menu, choose **Break**, and then select **Page Break** from the Break dialog box and click **OK**. In Normal and Outline views, you see a dotted line with the words **Page Break** where you added the break.

Pick the right paper for each page

Does your laser printer use letterhead in one tray and plain paper in another? Use the Page Setup dialog box to tell Word which tray to use. You can find the specific options for your printer under the **Paper Source** tab. The exact choices vary by printer; on Hewlett-Packard LaserJets, for example, you can specify an upper or lower tray, a manual tray, or an envelope feeder. Alternatively, you can let the printer automatically select the correct paper source.

Adding Emphasis to Text

By changing the appearance of words, numbers, symbols, and other text, you can dramatically enhance the readability of a doc-

ument. (Of course, if you make lousy design decisions, you'll
only make things harder on your readers. Check out a copy of
Wired magazine if you don't believe me.) Fonts and font effects
such as underlining can help the reader distinguish between
headings and body text, or help draw the reader's eye to individual words or phrases within a paragraph.

Choosing the Right Font

When you know exactly which font you want to use for a given
chunk of text, the easy way is to select the text and then choose
a font from the Font list on the Formatting toolbar. The fonts
you've used most recently appear at the top of the list so they're
easy to find; the rest of the fonts appear in alphabetical order.
Use the Font Size list (just to the right of the font list) to make
the font bigger or smaller.

Other buttons on the Formatting toolbar enable you to add
specific character formatting—**bold**, **underlined**, or **italic**, for
example.

Windows uses several kinds of *fonts*, but the most popular variety
is called *TrueType*. TrueType fonts are *scalable*, which means that
Windows can stretch (scale) them into the exact size you specify,
in virtually any size. They also look identical on the printer and
onscreen. *Printer fonts* and *screen fonts*, on the other hand, usually
come in a limited number of sizes and may cause problems when
displaying or printing documents. If you choose a printer font
that doesn't have a matching screen font, for example, Windows
has to substitute an installed screen font when displaying the
document, which means what you see onscreen will not look the
same as what you get from the printer.

When you want to add new fonts for ordinary documents, be
sure to choose the TrueType variety. They're guaranteed to work
with Word and other Office programs. TrueType fonts are preceded by a double T icon in the Fonts text box on the Formatting toolbar; a printer icon appears in front of fonts available
with the current printer.

Changing the current font

If you select no text at all, the
font selection applies to anything you type at the insertion
point. When you create a new
document and immediately
change fonts, for example, the
change applies to all text until
you change it again.

Windows gives you only five TrueType fonts for starters, and Internet Explorer adds a handful. The Typical Office 97 setup throws in five more, but you can find 150 extra fonts in the MSWord/ValuPack/Msfonts folder on Disc #1 of the Home Essentials CDs. Other programs come with fonts as well, and you can get more fonts for free or for a few dollars apiece. You can also search the Web for a nearly infinite assortment of free and inexpensive fonts. If you want to increase your document design options, adding fonts is one of the best investments you can make.

The easiest way to change a font is to select the text and then choose a different font from the Font drop-down list on the Formatting toolbar. There's one drawback to that, however: You can't see what the font will look like before you select it. If you aren't familiar with the font names, it can be a real chore applying first one font and then another, looking for the perfect one.

An alternate method of changing the font involves the Font dialog box. With this method, you can see a preview of the font before you apply it.

Changing fonts with the Font dialog box

1. Select the text you want to change; then right-click on the selection and choose **Font** from the shortcut menu. You then see the Font dialog box shown in Figure 8.6.

2. Choose a typeface from the **Font** list. For a preview of what your text will look like, see the panel at the bottom of the dialog box.

3. Pick a font style: Bold? Italic? Both? Neither? The exact choices available depend on the font you selected.

4. Specify the font size (measured in points). You must enter a number between 1 and 1,638 here. For most business documents, use 10 or 12 points for text.

5. Choose a text color from the drop-down list of 16 available colors, and specify any additional font effects, if you want.

6. Click **OK** to change the look of the selected text.

Installing fonts

To install fonts in Windows 95, choose **Start**, **Settings**, **Control Panel**, and double-click the **Fonts** icon. A window with all the installed fonts appears. From that window, open the **File** menu and choose **Install New Font**. An Add Fonts dialog box appears. In that dialog box, open the Drives drop-down list and choose the drive containing the additional fonts (for example, your CD drive). Then use the Folders list to navigate to the folder containing the fonts. When you do so, a list of the fonts appears. Click the ones you want to install (hold down Ctrl to click on more than one), and click **OK** to install them.

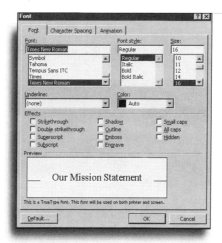

FIGURE 8.6
When you're not sure which font you want, use this Preview panel to see what your text will look like before you actually change it.

When you open a document created by a friend or coworker, it might not look the way that person intended. If the author used fonts that aren't installed on your computer, Word substitutes an available font for the one specified in the document. If the substitution is close enough, you may not notice the difference, but in other cases (especially with highly decorative fonts), the change can be downright ugly. To see details about substituted fonts, pull down the **Tools** menu, choose **Options**, click the **Compatibility** tab, and click the button labeled **Font Substitution**. The surest way to see the document with its proper formatting is to install the font on your computer. Otherwise, change the text formatting to a font that your PC can recognize. See the online Help topic "Specify fonts to use when converting files" for more advice.

Changing the Look of a Word or Character

Besides choosing the font, which dictates the shape and general appearance of characters, you can specify effects to be applied to that font. These options are independent of font selections; when you choose to underline the selected text, for example, underlining remains even if you change fonts. Click the **Bold** B , **Italic** *I* , or **Underline** u buttons to apply these common effects.

72 points = 1 inch

For more than 500 years, printers have used the point as a standard unit to measure the size of letters on a typeset page. There are approximately 72 points to an inch, so a six-line paragraph set in 12-point type fills an inch, and a 72-point character is one inch tall.

Figure 8.7 illustrates the effects you can apply with these and additional font effects in the Font dialog box. Hidden text, another available option, is discussed in the following section.

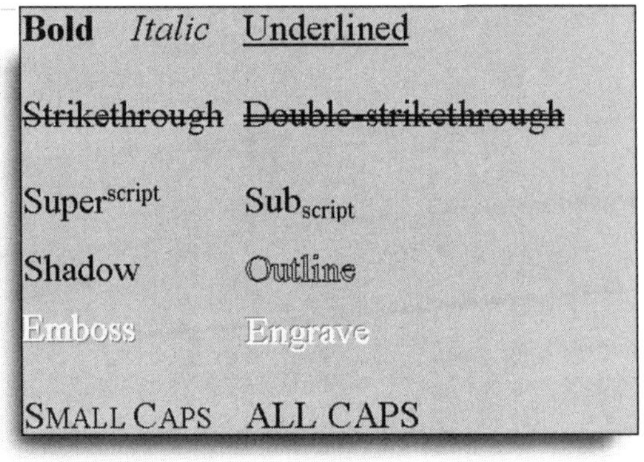

FIGURE 8.7

Word can apply these character effects.

Bold   *Italic*   <u>Underlined</u>

~~Strikethrough~~   ~~Double-strikethrough~~

Super^{script}   Sub_{script}

Shadow   Outline

Emboss   Engrave

SMALL CAPS   ALL CAPS

SEE ALSO

➤ *To learn which of these character effects will work with Web pages, see page 294.*

Hiding Text

One of the effects available in the Font dialog box is <u>**H**</u>**idden**. Select this font effect when you want the option to see text on the screen without seeing it on the printed page. Text formatted as hidden never prints out, and under most circumstances it's not visible on the screen either. To reveal hidden text, pull down the **<u>T</u>ools** menu, choose **<u>O</u>ptions**, click the **View** tab, and check the box labeled **H<u>i</u>dden text**.

Hidden text can be used for comments or notes to yourself as you work, or for directives to a layout person or proofreader. However, Word also provides another feature (not covered in this book) that you can use to add nonprinting notes: Comments. Look up "**Tracking Changes**" in Word's Help system index for more information.

Changing the Case of Selected Text

Two options in the Font dialog box enable you to specify **S<u>m</u>all caps** or **<u>A</u>ll caps** for the current selection. These formats work especially well with named styles. For example, you might create a Title style where the titles are all caps or small caps, and store it in a document template; when you apply that template to a document, text formatted with that style automatically displays correctly.

SEE ALSO

➤ *To learn how to create styles, see page 224.*

One of my favorite keyboard shortcuts helps me quickly change a word from uppercase to lowercase and back, without deleting and retyping. If you select text first, this shortcut affects the selected text; otherwise, it applies to the word in which the insertion point appears. Press **Shift+F3** to toggle from lowercase to mixed case (initial caps only) to all caps.

Arranging Text on the Page

By choosing the right fonts and applying other text formatting options, you can make words and sentences stand out on the page. When you design a document, arranging the words so that they fall in the right place on the page is equally important. Large headlines, for example, look better when centered between the left and right sides of the page, with ample white space above and below. Summary information stands out on the page when it's indented slightly. If you want to leave room for changes in a draft of a document, you can add extra space between lines.

With Word's paragraph formatting options, you can set off text with extra spacing, stack your words neatly on top of each other, center words on the page, and control precisely when Word ends one page and begins a new one.

Adjusting Space Between Lines

For most documents, most of the time, you'll use the default single spacing. Some kinds of documents, though, are more readable when extra space appears between each line. (Double-spacing is especially useful if you expect someone to add

Some fonts are all caps already

Certain fonts include only capital letters in their character set. If you format text using the Algerian font, for example, the lowercase and uppercase letters are identical. Whatever you type appears in caps, regardless of other formatting options.

Line spacing is for body text

Line spacing is most important in running text, when you have paragraphs that wrap around to multiple lines. To control space above and below headings, captions, and other one-liners, use paragraph spacing options instead.

comments and corrections to your work. Sometimes school papers need to be double-spaced, too, as part of the assignment.) You can allow Word to adjust the spacing automatically, based on each line's font size and any graphics or other embedded objects. Or, to maintain precise control over the look of a page, you can specify an exact amount of space between lines.

Changing spacing between lines

1. Position the insertion point in the paragraph. Then pull down the **Format** menu and choose **Paragraph,** or right-click anywhere within the paragraph and select **Paragraph** from the shortcut menu.

2. In the Paragraph dialog box, click the **Indents and Spacing** tab (see Figure 8.8).

FIGURE 8.8

Change the vertical spacing for a paragraph from here.

Can't adjust paragraph settings?

Paragraph formatting options are not available in Outline view. To adjust these options, switch to another view.

3. To adjust line spacing, choose one of the following options:

   - Select **Single**, **1.5 lines**, or **Double** from the drop-down list labeled **Line Spacing**.

   - Select **Multiple** from the drop-down list labeled **Line Spacing;** then choose the number of lines in the box labeled **At**. You can enter a fraction, such as 1.25; to use triple spacing, enter 3 here.

   - Choose **Exactly** from the **Line Spacing** list and enter the spacing you want (in points) in the **At** box. When you choose this option, Word maintains the precise line spacing you selected, even if you increase or decrease the font size or insert graphics.

- If you have large type or graphics mixed with small type, select **At Least** from the **Line Spacing** list. Enter the minimum spacing in the **At** box; make sure that this number is at least as big as the biggest type size you're using.

4. Click **OK** to close the dialog box.

Adjusting Space Before and After Paragraphs

Some people prefer to add space after each paragraph by pressing the Enter key twice. Don't! There's a better way to separate one paragraph from the next. To add space before or after a paragraph, right-click and choose **Paragraph** from the shortcut menu; then click the **Indents and Spacing** tab (refer to Figure 8.8). The default setting in the **Before** and **After** boxes is 0 points; add space here to provide extra separation between paragraphs. For example, if you're using a 12-point font and you want to add half a line at the end of each paragraph, enter 6 points in the box labeled **After**.

Note that this setting is separate from the line spacing settings I described previously. Line spacing affects the lines *within* a paragraph; Before and After set the spacing *outside* of it.

All these settings build on each other, so if you've selected double spacing with 12-point text, and you add 6 points after each paragraph, the effect is to add 2½ lines between paragraphs. The 2 comes from the double-spacing chosen from the **Line Spacing** list, and the ½ comes from the half-line (6 is half of 12) specified in the **After** field.

Indenting Paragraphs for Emphasis

The final controls to talk about in the Paragraph dialog box (refer to Figure 8.8) are the **Indentations**. When you set the margins for a document, they apply to every paragraph in that document (or in a section, if you've created multiple sections). Sometimes, though, you want to vary the relation between the text in one or more paragraphs and the white space in the document margins.

You might indent the first line to help make the beginning of a paragraph more noticeable. Indenting an important paragraph on both sides adds white space on the left and right so that it stands out from the rest of the page. Adding *negative indents*, which extend into the left margin, is a useful way to set off headings and lists. Finally, you might use a *hanging indent* to set off paragraphs in a list. Figure 8.9 shows examples of these three indent styles.

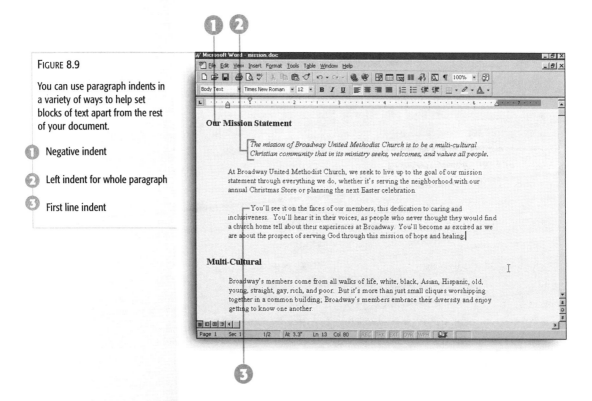

FIGURE 8.9

You can use paragraph indents in a variety of ways to help set blocks of text apart from the rest of your document.

1 Negative indent

2 Left indent for whole paragraph

3 First line indent

To set the indentation for a paragraph, just select it and then open the **Format** menu and choose **Paragraph** to display the Paragraph dialog box, as you did earlier. Then enter a positive or negative number in the **Left** or **Right** text box in the Indentation section. For a hanging or first line-indent, open the **Special** drop-down list and choose either of those, and then enter the amount in the **By** text box next to it.

Aligning Text to Make It Easier to Read

For every paragraph, you can also choose how it lines up on the page. You have four distinct alignment choices. When should you use each one?

- *Left* ▤. Because most Western languages read from left to right, this alignment is the most popular choice for text. Every line starts at the same place on the left edge and ends at a different place on the right, depending on how many characters are in each line.

- *Centered* ▤. Use centered text for headlines and very short blocks of text. Do not center lengthy passages.

- *Right* ▤. As you type, the text begins at the right edge, and each new letter pushes its neighbors to the left so that everything lines up perfectly on the right edge. Use this choice only for short captions alongside pictures or boxes, or when you want a distinctive look for a headline on a flyer or newsletter. Right alignment is also appropriate when numbering pages.

- *Justified* ▤. When you choose this option, Word distributes extra space between words so that each line begins and ends at the same place on the right and left. Justified text works best with formatted columns, as in a newsletter. Don't use it in memos because it makes them harder to read.

Positioning Text with Tabs

When you create a new tab stop, you define a point on the horizontal ruler. Each time you press the Tab key, the insertion point moves to the next tab stop. Of the five distinct types of tab stops, each is defined by the text alignment at that location. The most common use for tab stops is to mix and match different text alignments on the same line. For example, in a document footer you might set a center tab in the middle of the page and a right tab at the right margin; then you could enter a chapter number, press **Tab** to enter the chapter name and center it on the page, and then press **Tab** again to add a page number at the right margin.

One click handles a whole paragraph

The four alignment buttons on the Formatting toolbar enable you to change a paragraph's alignment with a single click. Because this setting applies to the entire paragraph, all you have to do is click anywhere in the paragraph and then click whichever button you prefer.

Table 8.1 describes how each type of tab stop works and shows what each one looks like when placed on the ruler in Word.

TABLE 8.1   **Tab stop types**

Symbol	Tab Alignment	How It Works
⌞	Left	Moves the insertion point to the tab stop; when you enter text, it extends to the right.
⊥	Center	Moves the insertion point and centers text you enter at the tab stop.
⌟	Right	Moves the insertion point to the tab stop; when you enter text, it extends to the left.
⊥.	Decimal	Text or numbers align at the decimal point, with all other text extending to the left; this type is used most often to align columns of numbers in currency format.
⎸	Bar	Draws a vertical rule at the tab stop; pressing the Tab key does not move the insertion point.

SEE ALSO

➤ *To learn more about using Word tables, see page 249.*

What's the best way to add tabs to your paragraphs? All the options are available in the dialog boxes that appear when you pull down the **Format** menu and choose **Tabs**. (We'll look at that dialog box shortly.) However, adjusting tab stops, indents, and even page margins is far easier with the help of Word's *ruler,* which sits just above the document editing window. Each of the small widgets on the ruler handles a specific alignment task. Because you can see the results instantly, this direct approach takes all the guesswork—and most of the dialog boxes—out of the process.

Figure 8.10 identifies each of the controls on Word's horizontal ruler. See Table 8.2 for instructions on how to use these controls to set tabs and adjust indents.

Alternatives to tabs

You might be tempted to just press the Tab key and keep pressing, but for most documents you should consider two alternative formatting options. For lining up columns of text and numbers, tables (with hidden borders) are easier to work with than tabs. Constructing a block-style résumé, for example, is a nightmare using tabs, but it's simple with tables. Likewise, simple paragraph alignment is easier, and the results are more predictable when you use indents (described later in this chapter) instead of tabs.

Hide the ruler

If your video display is set to a relatively low resolution (800 × 600 or less), Word's ruler takes up a significant chunk of the document editing window. To give yourself more room for editing, keep the ruler hidden until you need it. In Normal or Page Layout view, pull down the **View** menu and choose **Ruler** to show or hide the ruler.

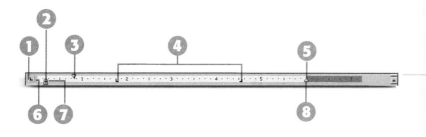

FIGURE 8.10

You don't need to memorize the names of these controls; let the mouse pointer rest over each one to see a descriptive ScreenTip.

TABLE 8.2 **Controls on the Word ruler**

Ruler Control	How You Use It
Left margin, Right margin	To adjust page margins, aim the mouse pointer at the border between the dark and light areas of the ruler; when the pointer turns to a two-headed arrow, click and drag.
Left indent	To indent the left side of the entire paragraph, drag this box. Both markers above it go along for the ride.
First line indent	To indent only the first line of the selected paragraph, drag the top triangle.
Hanging indent	To indent the second and subsequent lines in the current paragraph, drag the bottom triangle.
Tab button, Tab stops	Click the button at the far left of the ruler to cycle through left, center, right, and decimal tab types (use ScreenTips to tell which is which). Select the type of tab you want to add and then click on the ruler to add the new tab stop. Drag a tab stop to move it; drag it off the ruler to remove it.
Right indent	To indent the right side of the entire paragraph, drag this triangle.

1. Tab button
2. Left indent
3. First line indent
4. Tab stops
5. Right margin
6. Left margin
7. Indent for all lines except first
8. Right indent

When you press a Tab key, the insertion point usually simply moves to the next tab stop. However, you can also tell Word to add a *leader* character, such as a row of periods, between the text and the tab stop. These characters are commonly used with tables of contents and invoices, where you want the reader's eye to clearly see the relationship between the entry at the left and the matching entry to its right.

Which paragraph is which?

Remember, tab and indent settings apply to the entire paragraph where the insertion point is located. To adjust indents for more than one paragraph, you must select the appropriate text. When you press the Enter key to start a new paragraph, Word uses the ruler settings from the previous paragraph.

To set tabs with leaders, or to use the Bar tab stop, you must use the Tabs dialog box, shown in Figure 8.11. Open the **Format** menu and choose **Tabs**.

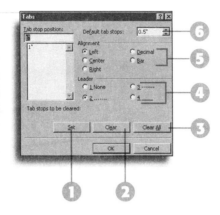

FIGURE **8.11**

You can use this dialog box to set precise tabs and configure them with leaders, if desired.

1 Click here to apply changes to the selected tab stop.

2 Click to clear the selected tab stop.

3 Click to clear all tab stops and start over.

4 Choose one of these leader characters to add a line between text and a tab stop.

5 Choose an alignment style for the selected tab stop.

6 Use this spinner to adjust the distance between default tab stops.

Using Large Initial Caps for Emphasis

Professional designers often enlarge the first letter of a paragraph to make it easier for readers to find the beginning of a section. Because the larger initial letter drops below the base of the first line, designers call this feature a *drop cap*. Word enables you to create drop caps easily in documents you create. Click in the paragraph where you want to add a larger first letter, pull down the **Format** menu, and choose **Drop Cap**. You then see a dialog box like the one in Figure 8.12.

FIGURE **8.12**

A drop cap should never be larger than the headline above it. In 12-point body text, a three-line drop cap goes with a 36-point headline.

Choose a font, pick the number of lines you want the first letter to extend downward, and specify how much of a gap you want between the drop cap and the text. Click **OK** to add the drop cap.

Formatting Simple Lists with Bullets and Numbers

When you need to communicate with other people, lists are among your most powerful tools. Whether the list items are single words or full paragraphs, bullet characters and numbers help set them apart from normal body text. Turning plain text into a list is one of the easiest things you can do using Word. After you've created a list, Word uses the same bullet character when you add new items, and if you rearrange items in a numbered list, Word renumbers the entire list automatically.

Creating a Bulleted List

To create a bulleted list on the fly as you type, just click the Bullets button ▦ on the Formatting toolbar. Type the first item in your list, and then press Enter to add another bulleted item. The items in a list can be anything—numbers, words, phrases, whole paragraphs, even graphics. To stop adding bullets and return to normal paragraph style, click the **Bullets** button again.

To add bullets to a list you've already typed, first select the items in the list; then click the **Bullets** button. The default bullet is a simple black dot in front of each item.

Changing the Default Bullet Character

When you first create a bulleted list, Word sets off each item with a big, bold, boring dot. If you would prefer a more visually interesting bullet, you're in luck. With Word, you can choose from seven predefined bullet types, or you can replace the bullet character with practically any symbol.

Changing the look of a bulleted list

1. Select the entire list. Then right-click and choose **Bullets and Numbering** from the shortcut menu.

Automatic bullets

Unless you've turned off the **AutoFormat As You Type** option, Word automatically converts items to bulleted list format whenever you begin a paragraph with an asterisk (*) or a hyphen and press Enter.

2. To use one of the seven predefined bullet characters, click the bullet style you want from the list shown in Figure 8.13.

3. To choose your own bullet character, click the **Cus<u>t</u>omize** button. In the Customize Bulleted List dialog box (see Figure 8.14), choose the bullet type you want to replace; then click the button labeled **Bullet**.

4. Pick a character from the Symbol dialog box. (Choose a new font from the drop-down **<u>F</u>ont** list, if necessary; the Wingdings font, for example, is full of good candidates.)

5. Adjust the size, color, and position of the bullet, if necessary. The Preview window shows you how each change will affect the look of your list.

6. When you're satisfied, click **OK** to change the bullets in your list.

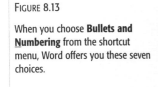

FIGURE 8.13

When you choose **Bullets and Numbering** from the shortcut menu, Word offers you these seven choices.

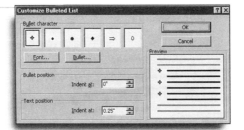

FIGURE 8.14

Choose any symbol you want to use as a bullet; you can even modify the size, color, and position.

Creating Numbered Lists

Bullets signify that the items on the list are of equal importance. If the order of items in a list is important, as when you're writing step-by-step instructions, you should use a numbered list instead.

When you choose to number the items in your list, Word doesn't simply plop a number in front of each paragraph; instead, it adds a hidden numbering code. If you add a new item or move items around, Word automatically renumbers the list to keep each item in the proper order.

To start a numbered list, click the **Numbering** button ▦ on the Formatting toolbar and then begin typing. Word adds the numeral 1, followed by a period and an indent. Type whatever you want—a word, a sentence, or a whole paragraph. When you press Enter, Word begins the next paragraph with the next number in the sequence.

Changing Numbering Options

The basic format of a numbered list is a simple 1, 2, 3, but Word enables you to choose another format if you want. You can switch to Roman numerals or capital letters, or you can add descriptive text to the bare numbers. If you're writing a list of instructions, for example, you might add the word Step before each number and a colon afterward, so your readers see Step 1:, Step 2:, and so on, in front of each item.

Changing the format in a numbered list

1. Select the entire numbered list, right-click, and choose **Bullets and <u>N</u>umbering** from the shortcut menu.

2. On the **<u>N</u>umbered** tab, click the **Cus<u>t</u>omize** button to display the dialog box shown in Figure 8.15.

3. To choose a predefined number format, choose an entry from the drop-down list labeled **Number style**. Choose a new font, position, or starting number, if you want.

Pick a number (or a letter, for that matter)

Although they're called numbered lists, the label is a bit misleading because Word also recognizes Roman numerals and letters as appropriate ways to order a list. You can begin a numbered list by typing 1, I), a., or whatever style you want to use. Press the Spacebar or the Tab key; then enter the text you want for that item. When you press Enter, Word automatically converts the paragraph you just typed into numbered format and continues the list in the paragraph you're about to type.

4. To create a custom format that includes text, click in the box labeled **Number format** and add the text before the number field. Be sure to add a space after the text.

5. Click **OK** to save your new numbering format.

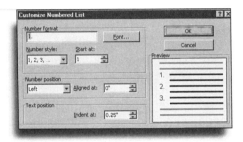

FIGURE 8.15

Replace Word's default numbering scheme with your own formats. Word takes care of the naming and numbering automatically.

FIGURE 8.15

Replace Word's default numbering scheme with your own formats. Word takes care of the naming and numbering automatically.

Rearranging and Editing Lists

Because bullet and number codes are contained in Word fields, you can easily rearrange, reorder, or expand items in a list. Here's how:

Don't forget the paragraph mark!

To move a bulleted or numbered item properly, you must make sure that you've selected the paragraph mark (¶) at the end of the item. (Click the **Show/Hide** button ¶ on the Standard toolbar to make it easier to see paragraph marks.) If you don't select the entire paragraph, the bullet or numbering formatting stays where it is, and only the text moves.

- *To move a list item to a new position,* first select the entire item, including the paragraph mark (¶). Then use the **Cut** and **Paste** shortcut menus, or simply drag the item to its new spot.

- *To add a new item to the end of the list,* move the insertion point to the end of the last paragraph in the list and press Enter.

- *To insert a new item,* click to position the insertion point at the beginning of the paragraph where you want to add the new item, and then press Enter.

- *To skip or stop numbering,* right-click on the paragraph where you want to skip an entry, and choose **Paragraph** from the shortcut menu. (Switch to Page Layout view if necessary.) Click the **Line and Page Breaks** tab; then check the box labeled **Suppress line numbers**. This technique is especially useful when you want to add a comment in the middle of a long list.

- *To restore a list to plain text format,* select the entire list and click the **Numbering** button 🔢 or the **Bullets** button 📋.

Let Word Do the Formatting

Word's AutoFormat feature is a great idea that doesn't always work as promised. It's supposed to make your documents look great, effortlessly and automatically. The bigger the document, however, the more likely AutoFormat is to make some mistakes. The most common one is to apply the wrong style tag, turning body text into lists, for example. AutoFormat works best on short documents. It also works well on blocks of text, such as numbered lists and addresses.

Don't confuse AutoFormat with the AutoFormat As You Type feature. Although the two features share some of the same settings, they're completely independent of one another.

When you use AutoFormat, Word works its way through your document from top to bottom, replacing standard quotes with smart quotes, taking out extra spaces and unnecessary paragraph marks, and so on. AutoFormat also tries to guess which style is best for each block of text. You can tell Word to skip one or more of these steps: Pull down the **Tools** menu, choose **AutoCorrect**, click the **AutoFormat** tab, and add or remove check marks as necessary.

To format the current document automatically, open the **Format** menu and choose **AutoFormat**. You then see a dialog box like the one in Figure 8.16. If you're feeling lucky, choose the **AutoFormat now** option. Word whizzes through your document, makes all its changes, and displays the newly formatted document in the editing window.

FIGURE 8.16

Use AutoFormat the fast way or the thorough way. Try the fast way first; if you don't like the results, click the Undo button and start over.

If you choose the second option, **AutoFormat and review each change**, Word formats the document and then asks if you want to **A**ccept, **R**eject, or Review **C**hanges. Click **Review Changes** and then click **F**ind to find the first change, as in Figure 8.17. To accept a change, simply skip over it by clicking **F**ind again to find the next change. To reject it, click the **R**eject button. When you are finished, click Cancel to return to the AutoFormat dialog box, and then click **Accept All** to accept all the changes (minus those that you rejected individually).

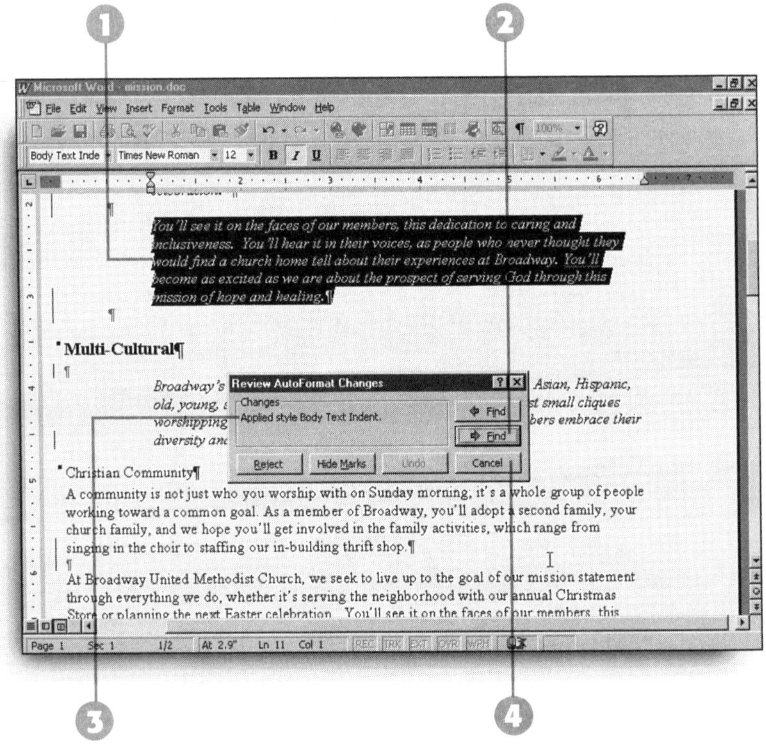

FIGURE 8.17

When you choose **Review Changes**, you can say yes or no to every step of the process.

1 Changed text

2 Click Find to move on to the next change.

3 This box explains the change that was made.

4 Click Cancel when finished looking at changes.

Using Templates and Styles

Save and reuse formats with Word styles

Choose between character and paragraph styles

Enable Word to format paragraphs automatically

Create new styles from existing text

Use templates to change a document's design

Customize Word templates

Copy styles and settings to a new document or template

How Styles Work

Styles and style sheets

Early versions of Word used *style sheets* to keep track of groups of styles. Word 97 doesn't use style sheets; instead it organizes the styles in template files, which you'll learn about later in this chapter.

The letters, memos, reports, and faxes you create every day use many of the same elements—body text, headings, signatures, address blocks, and so on. Instead of *formatting* each of these elements from scratch when you start a new document, you can save format specifications, called *styles*, and reuse them any time. When you attach a saved style to a word or paragraph, the effect is the same as if you had applied formatting directly—fonts, colors, line spacing, tab stops, you name it.

Using styles offers two significant advantages over direct formatting. First, it makes even complex formatting tasks easy, bypassing all the check boxes, lists, and dialog boxes that you would otherwise have to use. Second, it lets you create and share consistent formatting for all documents you create; that's especially important if you're using Word for a small business, where *typefaces* and other design elements can be as important as a company's logo in creating a visual identity.

Paragraph Versus Character Styles

Word enables you to create and use two types of named styles—*paragraph styles* and *character styles*.

As the name implies, a *paragraph style* applies to an entire paragraph. A named paragraph style can include alignments, line spacing, tab settings, and other paragraph formatting options. It also contains character formatting, such as a default *font* and font size. When you create a document using the Normal document template, the default paragraph style is also called Normal. It uses 10-point Times New Roman, with single spacing and left alignment. When you apply the built-in Heading 1 style, the selected paragraph changes to 14-point Arial Bold, with 12 points of extra spacing before the heading and 3 points of extra spacing in addition to the single line spacing.

Character styles, on the other hand, apply font, border, and language information to selected text or characters. When you use a character style, it overrides the font information contained in the paragraph style. When you enter a Web address in a Word document, for example, Word's AutoFormat As You Type feature applies the Hyperlink character style, which uses the Default Paragraph Font but displays the selection in blue, with a single underline.

You might want to create and use a custom character style for your company's name so it always appears in the proper typeface and size. When writing this book, I used a custom character style to define words and terms that I planned to add to the Glossary. By redefining the Glossary style (a 60-second job), I was able to change the appearance of every Glossary entry when the book designer decided to use a different format.

SEE ALSO

➤ *To find detailed explanations of all your paragraph formatting options, see page 205.*

➤ *To learn how to add emphasis to text, see page 200.*

Understanding Paragraph Marks

Word's Standard toolbar includes a button you won't find anywhere else in Home Essentials. It's called the **Show/Hide ¶** button, and the **¶** symbol is a paragraph mark. Click this button, and you'll see that symbol in your document everywhere you've pressed the Enter key. You'll also see placeholders for tabs, spaces, and other normally invisible formatting characters.

After clicking the **Show/Hide ¶** button for the first time, you may wonder how this extra clutter could possibly be useful. In fact, it's key to making sure formatting options remain as you intended when you move text from one place to another.

You must pay attention to paragraph marks for one important reason: Word stores all your paragraph formatting and styles in the paragraph marks. If you choose a paragraph style that instructs Word to display text in the Arial font with triple-line spacing, Word dutifully saves your instructions (along with any direct formatting) inside that paragraph mark.

Why does this information matter? Because if you copy or move that paragraph mark, you also move the styles that go with it. On the other hand, if you don't include the paragraph mark in your selection, the text you paste changes to the style of the paragraph you paste it into.

Viewing Available Styles

Show paragraph marks when moving blocks of text

Some Word experts recommend that you leave paragraph marks visible all the time when working with Word. I consider that advice extreme, but I do recommend that you click the **Show/Hide ¶** button to see all your paragraph marks whenever you plan to move one or more paragraphs. Make sure that you move a paragraph mark only if you also want to move the formatting that goes with it.

Every document contains the styles stored in the *template* on which the document is based. When you create a new style or edit an existing one, you can choose to save the style only in the current document, or you can revise the template's style collection. To see which style is currently in use, look in the Style box at the left of the Formatting toolbar.

To see a list of available styles, click the drop-down arrow to the right of the Style box on the Formatting toolbar. The default list shows only the styles in use for the current document, plus a few standard styles. To see every style choice available in the current document template, including those not currently in use, hold down the Shift key when you click the drop-down arrow at the right of the Style list. The full list resembles the one shown in Figure 9.1.

FIGURE 9.1

Hold down the Shift key to see a list of every available style; the icon at the right of each entry identifies the type of style and its size.

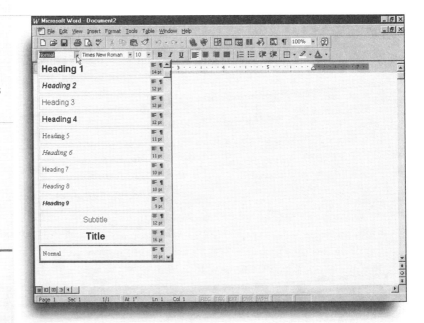

Identifying the current style

If you position the insertion point within a word that is formatted with a character style, the Style box displays that style's name. If no character style appears at the insertion point, or if you select two or more words that are formatted with different character styles, the Style box displays the name of the current paragraph style. When you select text from two or more paragraphs formatted with different paragraph styles, the Style box is empty.

For complete details about each style, open the **F̲ormat** menu and choose **S̲tyle**. By default you see only the styles currently in use in the document; open the **L̲ist** drop-down list and choose **All styles** to see them all. Figure 9.2 shows how to decipher the entries in this dialog box.

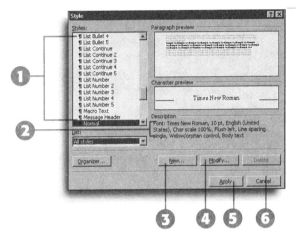

FIGURE 9.2

Use this dialog box to see and edit details about styles in the current document and template.

1 Select one of the styles here.

2 All settings for the selected style.

3 Click to define a new style from scratch.

4 Open a list of options that let you modify the selected style.

5 Apply the style to the current selection or paragraph.

6 Delete the selected style.

SEE ALSO

➤ *To find details on how styles and templates work together, see page 228.*

➤ *To find details on how to use the templates included with Word, see page 164.*

Applying Styles to Word Documents

The simplest way to apply a style to a document is with the help of the drop-down Style list on the Formatting toolbar. You can change the style for a text selection or a paragraph.

Using styles to format a Word document

1. Position the insertion point where you want to change the style. If you want the style to apply to only certain characters, or to more than one paragraph or word, select the text to be affected.

Selections affect styles

If you position the insertion point in a word without making a selection and then choose a character style, Word applies that style to the entire word. If you apply a paragraph style without selecting, the style applies to the current paragraph.

If you make a text selection, Word applies the style only to the selected words or characters. Paragraph styles always apply to the entire paragraph, regardless of whether you make a selection, except if they contain character formatting too; if they do, the character aspects of the style apply to only the selected text.

The quick Repeat key

One of my favorite Word keyboard shortcuts is the Repeat key. After you choose any Word command, you can repeat the command by pressing the F4 key. This shortcut is especially useful when you want to format a few widely separated paragraphs using the same style. Format the first paragraph using the steps shown here; then position the insertion point in the next paragraph you want to reformat and press F4.

2. To choose a style that is already in use in the current document, click the arrow to the right of the Style list on the toolbar. To choose a new style that is available in the current document template but is not yet in use, hold down the Shift key as you open the drop-down Style list.

3. Click a style on the list. Word applies the new formatting immediately.

You can also apply a style from the Styles dialog box (refer to Figure 9.2). Just open that dialog box (open the **Format** menu and choose **Style**), click the style you want, and then click **Apply** to apply it.

Saving Your Favorite Formats as Named Styles

Although the predefined styles in standard Word templates are a useful starting point, sooner or later you'll want to create and edit styles for documents you've designed. Word lets you define a style by example, or you can modify the styles included with Word templates, including the Normal document template.

Defining a Style by Example

If you've formatted an existing document, you can easily save some or all of your settings as named paragraph styles so you can reuse them later. (You cannot use these steps to create a character style; for that task, you have to open the Style dialog box, as explained in the next section.)

Creating a new paragraph style from a formatted document

1. Position the insertion point in the paragraph that contains the formatting you want to save.

2. Click in the Style box on the toolbar and type a name for the new style.

3. Press Enter. If the style name you entered is not currently in use, Word creates the new style using the formatting of the current selection.

4. If you enter the name of a style that already exists in the current document or template, Word displays the dialog box shown in Figure 9.3 asking what to do about it. To redefine the existing style, choose the option labeled **Update the style to reflect recent changes**. Click **OK** to save the change.

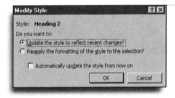

FIGURE 9.3

When you apply manual formatting and then enter the name of an existing style in the Style box, Word offers you these choices.

Creating a New Style Based on Another Style

If you want to create a character style, or create a style that is not based on some text you have already formatted, you must use the Style dialog box. The general procedure is this: Define a new style by naming it, and specify which existing style it is based on. Then enter formatting specifications that differentiate it from the original. For example, you might create a style called Normal Indent that is just like the Normal style (based on it) except each paragraph is indented one-half inch on the first line. If you later change the Normal style to use a different font, for example, Normal Indent's font changes also because it is based on Normal and follows its lead.

Creating a new style based on another style

1. Open the **Format** menu and choose **Style**. The Style dialog box opens (refer to Figure 9.2).

2. Click the **New** button. A New Style dialog box opens as shown in Figure 9.4.

3. Type a name for the new style in the **Name** box.

4. Open the **Style type** drop-down list and choose **Character** or **Paragraph** as appropriate.

5. Open the **Based on** drop-down list and choose the style on which the new style should be based. (If in doubt, choose **Normal**.)

Automatic style updates

When you update an existing style, Word offers to apply further format changes automatically. (Notice the check box in Figure 9.3.) Think carefully before you decide to allow automatic style updates. When you enable this feature, every manual formatting change you make applies instantly to other paragraphs formatted using that style. The results can be unwelcome.

FIGURE 9.4

Define the new style and choose which existing style it is based on.

Next style?

The **Style for following paragraph** setting can be useful if you use it correctly. If you are creating a new style that will primarily be used for single, sporadic lines in the document (like a heading, for example), set the Style for following paragraph to the style that you use for normal text. That way, when you press Enter at the end of a paragraph formatted with this style, the style resets itself back to your normal paragraph style.

6. Open the **Style for following paragraph** drop-down list and choose the style for paragraphs that follow this one. This specifies what the default style of the next paragraph should be following a paragraph formatted with this one.

7. Click the **Add to template** check box to make sure the style is added to the template, if you want that. If this style is for use only in the current document, you can skip that step.

8. Skip down to step 4 in the following section to modify the style's definition.

Modifying a Named Style

You can modify any character or paragraph style, including the Normal paragraph style. You can then choose precise formatting options for a style after you've created it.

Changing an existing style

1. Open the **Format** menu and choose **Style.** The Style dialog box opens.

2. Select an entry from the **Styles** list. Check the preview and description boxes at the right to confirm that you've selected the correct style.

3. Click the **Modify** button. The Modify Style dialog box appears. (It looks virtually identical to the Create Style dialog box shown previously in Figure 9.4.)

4. Click the **Format** button and choose one of the following entries from the drop-down menu (see Figure 9.5). For paragraph styles, all choices are available; for character styles, some of the seven choices are grayed out.

- **Font.** Adjust the current font, font size, color, effects, and other options for character and paragraph styles.

- **Paragraph.** Set line spacing, paragraph spacing, indents, and other paragraph options (not available for character styles).

- **Tabs.** Set and edit tab stops (not available for character styles).

- **Border.** Use rules and shading around the selected text or paragraph.

- **Language.** Select a language for the selected text or paragraph; this setting tells Word which dictionary to use when spell-checking documents.

- **Frame.** Choose size, text wrapping, and position options for text that appears in a *frame* (not available for character styles).

- **Numbering.** Define bullet and numbering options (not available for character styles).

FIGURE 9.5

Choose the type of modification you want to make to the style.

5. Each choice leads to a different dialog box. Adjust formatting options as you like and click **OK**. Repeat step 4 to set other formatting options, as needed.

6. Check the **Add to template** box if you want to save your changes in the current template and have them automatically applied to other documents based on that template. Leave this box blank if you want the style changes to apply only to text in the current document.

7. Click **OK** to save your changes and return to the Style dialog box. Click **Apply** to return to the editing window.

Collecting Styles (and More) in Document Templates

New document versus attaching a template

Document templates can contain boilerplate text that automatically becomes part of any new document you create using that template. You can open a new file by opening the **File** menu and choosing the **New** command.

When you attach a template to an existing document, however, Word ignores boilerplate text in the document and gives you access to styles and other document elements stored in the template.

Using templates is a handy way to start new documents, but they also play an important role as a storage place for styles, macros, AutoText entries, and custom Word commands and toolbar settings. When you attach a template to a document originally created using a different template, Word can automatically update document styles whose names match those in the new template.

SEE ALSO

➤ *To start a new document based on a template, see page 164.*

Changing the Template for the Current Document

Document templates are powerful tools for maintaining a set of standards. For example, if you create a template that contains a lot of the styles you use frequently, you can attach that template to other documents and thereby gain access to those styles in the other documents. This is done a lot in publishing; for example, a publisher provides a template to an author, and the author attaches that template to each chapter file he or she creates. You may find many home uses for it too.

Changing the template for the current document

1. Open the **Tools** menu and choose **Templates and Add-Ins.** The Templates and Add-ins dialog box shows which template is currently associated with the document (see Figure 9.6).

2. Click the **Attach** button to browse through a list of all available templates.

3. Select the template you want to use with the document and click the **Open** button.

4. If you want to open the attached template and update formatting every time you open the current document, check the box labeled **Automatically update document styles**. Leave this box blank if you want to base the document on the current version of the template only.

5. Click **OK** to save your changes. The formatting of your document changes immediately.

Choosing a Style from the Style Gallery

Word includes a built-in collection of templates. Each template is full of predefined styles. You may also receive templates from coworkers. How can you tell what styles are contained in each template? Use Word's *Style Gallery* for a quick snapshot. Open the **Format** menu and choose **Style Gallery** to see a close-up view of every template on your system. The three different views in the Style Gallery's **Preview** window enable you to do the following:

- See examples of how the styles within each template work so you can modify them to meet your own needs. (Figure 9.7 shows one such example.)

- See each style in a single, alphabetical list.

- Preview what *your* document would look like if you used that style.

Updating existing text

If you have some text in the document that is already formatted with a style that has the same name as a style in the incoming template, you must make sure that the **Automatically update document styles** check box is marked if you want the text to be reformatted with the new version of the style being attached. Otherwise, you will have to re-select the text and reapply the style manually after attaching the new template.

Missing template? No problem!

What happens when you open a document that was created by someone else using a template that you don't have? Word stores all the formatting information for the styles used in that document within the document itself, which means you see the formatting as the author intended it. If the author updates the template, however, your copy won't reflect those updates.

FIGURE 9.7

For a quick snapshot of each Word document template, preview it in the Style Gallery.

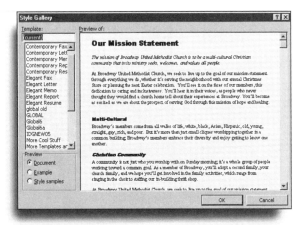

Using global templates

When you store a style in a custom template, it's available only to documents that are based on that template. When you store styles and other items in the Normal document template, however, they're available to all Word documents. You can designate any template as a global template that works the same way. In the Templates and Add-Ins dialog box, click the button labeled **Add** and choose the template you want to designate for use by all documents.

Managing Styles and Templates

Although you can save a template in any folder, you should make it a habit to store document templates in one of two locations. For personal templates, use the C:\Program Files\Microsoft Office\Templates folder. Word also lets you specify a secondary location where you store templates that you share with other members of your workgroup. (You can find this setting on the **File Locations** tab when you click the **Tools** menu and choose **Options**.)

Creating a New Template

To create a new document template, start with a document. Although you can edit the template file later, most people find it easier to create styles, AutoText entries, and other document elements first and then save the file as a document template.

Saving a Word document as a template

1. Create the Word document you want to use as a template. Do not include any text unless you want that text to appear when you create a new document based on the template.

2. Open the **File** menu and choose **Save As**.

3. In the list labeled **Save as type**, choose **Document Template (*.dot)**. Word switches to the Templates folder (see Figure 9.8).

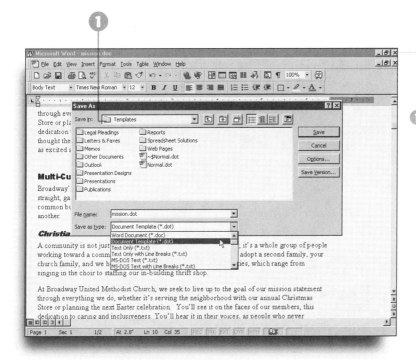

FIGURE 9.8

Make sure you set the document type to **Document Template**.

❶ The location changes automatically to the Templates folder.

4. If you want to, choose a subfolder within this folder to classify the new template.

5. Give the template a descriptive name in the **File name** text box.

6. Click **Save** to save the template.

Customizing Word Templates

Most of the built-in Word templates are made to be customized. You can remove sample text and graphics, replacing them with names, logos, and other details appropriate for you or your company and adding text and graphics of your own. You can also adjust styles, change or delete AutoText entries, edit macros, and rearrange toolbars and menus for use with documents you create using the template.

The most straightforward way to customize a document template is to click Word's **File** menu, choose **Open,** and then select **Document Templates** from the **Files of type** list.

Once a template, always a template

After you save a file in Document Template format, you cannot save it in any other format. When you open the template file for editing and make changes, Word grays out the **Save as type** list to prevent you from inadvertently damaging a template. To save the document using another format, first create a new document based on the template, and then save that document.

Make a copy first

Because templates are stored as files, you can easily copy a template, just as you would copy any file. In fact, before customizing a template, creating a backup copy that you can restore in case you want to start over is always a good idea.

After you've opened it, make any changes that you want to have on every document that you create with the template. For example, if you want documents based on the Elegant Letter template to use 12-point type instead of 10, select all the text areas (drag across them) and then change the font size to 12.

You might also want to type some boilerplate text that you'll use every time you use the template, so you don't have to type it each time. For example, for a letter you might pre-enter your return address and your signature block.

After making your changes, don't forget to save your work.

SEE ALSO

> *For more information about AutoText, see page 244.*

Copying Styles and Settings Between Templates

If you design lots of documents, eventually you'll wind up with a large collection of templates. If you've saved a style in a special-purpose template, you may want to make it available to all your documents. Or, you may want to consolidate styles, AutoText entries, macros, and other document elements from several templates. To manage styles and templates, Word includes an all-purpose tool called the Organizer.

Although you can open the Organizer in several ways, the easiest way is through the Style dialog box.

Copying a style from one template to another

1. Open a document that contains the style you want to copy to another document or template.

2. Open the **Format** menu and choose **Style**.

3. In the Style dialog box, click the **Organizer** button. The two-paned Organizer appears as shown in Figure 9.9. Click the **Styles** tab, if it's not currently visible.

4. The left pane displays styles from the current document. If

---

Save location is important

If you want to use a template to start new documents, you must save it in the designated Templates folder (by default it's C:\Program Files\Microsoft Office\Templates). If you save a template anywhere else, the template won't appear in the New dialog box so you can choose it.

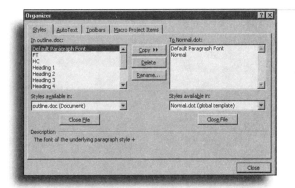

FIGURE 9.9

Use Word's Organizer to copy styles between documents and templates.

you prefer to see styles in the current template, select the template from the **Styles available in** drop-down list. (Be sure to use the left pane.)

5. By default, the right pane displays styles in the Normal document template. If you want to copy files to another template, click the **Close File** button beneath the right pane; when that button changes to **Open File**, click and open the template or document you want to use instead.

6. To copy a style, select its entry in the left pane and click the **Copy** button.

7. To manage styles in either pane, select the style and click the **Delete** or **Rename** button.

8. Use the other tabs to manage other document and template items. Click the **Close** button to save your changes.

Choose a document for one-shot jobs

Remember, you can stores styles in documents or in templates. If you want to reuse a style from another document, and you don't expect to reuse the style in other documents, just copy it to the document rather than store it in a template.

10

Correcting and Polishing Your Document

Checking your spelling

Checking for grammar problems

Customizing grammar rules

Automatically correcting typos

Saving time with AutoText entries

Helping Word AutoFormat as you type

Looking up synonyms with the Thesaurus

Using Word to Check Your Spelling

As you create or edit a document, Word automatically flags words it can't find in its built-in dictionary. When you click the Spelling and Grammar button ⟨ABC⟩, Word zips through the current selection or your entire document, stopping at each suspected misspelling and grammatical error. You can accept its suggestions, make your own corrections, or ignore the advice.

SEE ALSO

➤ *To create and edit a document in Word, see "Entering and Deleting Text," on page 177.*

What the Spelling Checker Can and Can't Do

Word comes with its own dictionary of words, plus a Custom dictionary in which you can add your own terms (such as proper names and technical jargon). When Word checks the spelling of words in your document, it compares them with the contents of its built-in dictionary and your custom dictionary, and reports any words that do not appear in either place.

The spelling checker also flags doubled words, which is good news if you sometimes type `the the end`.

You're already in the dictionary

When you first run Word, it adds your last name and your company's name to the custom dictionary file.

Word's spelling checker alerts you only when you use a word that isn't in its dictionary. If you've chosen the wrong word—typing **profit and less** instead of **profit and loss**, for example—Word does not flag the error. The moral? Spelling checkers are useful for catching obvious typos, but you should still proofread important documents carefully.

How to Check Your Spelling

Those red marks don't print

The red marks that flag possible misspelled words are visible only on the screen. They don't show when you print.

Word gives you two options for correcting spelling and typing mistakes. You can fix typos as you work, or you can type the words on the screen as fast as you can and clean up the misspellings later. Either way, as you go, Word marks words that it cannot identify with wavy red underlines, as you can see in the example in Figure 10.1. (If you see any green wavy lines, those are grammar problems.)

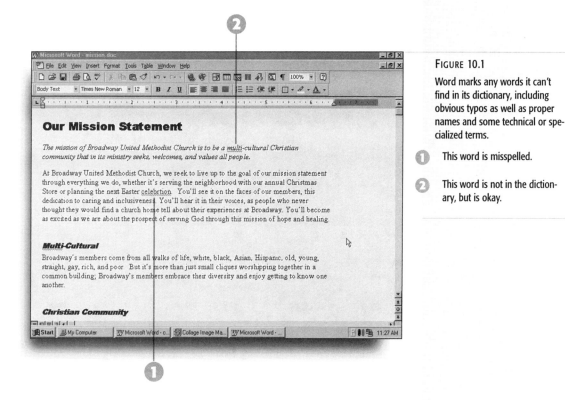

FIGURE 10.1

Word marks any words it can't find in its dictionary, including obvious typos as well as proper names and some technical or specialized terms.

❶ This word is misspelled.

❷ This word is not in the dictionary, but is okay.

To correct a typo right away, right-click the marked word and then make a selection from the pop-up menu you see in Figure 10.2.

Your choices are as follows:

- *Use one of the suggestions.* Word usually takes its best shot at guessing what you tried to type, offering one or more options. If the correct spelling is in this boldfaced list, select it.

- *Tell Word the spelling is correct.* The word in question may be a foreign word or a proper name, or it just may not be in Word's dictionary. In either case, click the **Ignore All** choice, and Word stops flagging all future occurrences of that word in the current document.

- *Add the word to your custom dictionary.* Select **Add**, and Word will never again mark the selected word as misspelled.

238

FIGURE 10.2

Choose the correct spelling from the list of suggestions, or select one of the other commands.

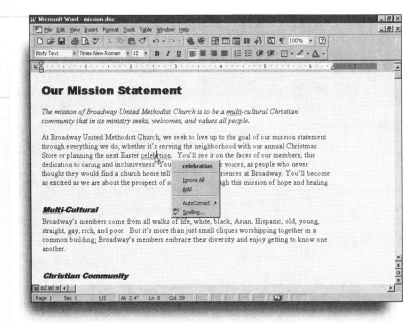

- *Add the word to your AutoCorrect list.* If you regularly misspell the word in question, and the correct spelling is listed as a boldfaced entry at the top of the shortcut menu, add the word to your AutoCorrect list. Click **AutoCorrect** and choose the proper spelling from the cascading menu that appears at the right; from now on, Word will automatically substitute the word you chose for the one you mistyped.

Checking the Spelling and Grammar in the Entire Document

Even when automatic spell-checking is turned off, you can still use the spelling checker to look up a word, check a paragraph, or go through your entire document.

Checking the spelling of your document

1. Select the text to check. If you don't make a selection, Word checks the entire document.

2. Click the Spelling and Grammar button ![icon] on the Standard toolbar.

3. If any misspellings or grammatical mistakes appear in the selection, Word highlights the possible error and pops up a list of suggested alternatives, as shown in Figure 10.3. (Figure 10.3 shows a spelling mistake; the controls may be slightly different for a grammar mistake.) Do whatever is appropriate to resolve the problem:

- Click the **AutoCorrect** button to add this typo and its correction to the AutoCorrect list.

- Select the correct spelling and then click **Change** to fix the typo instantly.

- Click **Change All** to fix every instance of this misspelling in the current document.

- Click **Add** to add the word to your custom dictionary so Word stops flagging it as misspelled.

- Click **Ignore** to tell Word to ignore this instance of this word.

- Click **Ignore All** to tell Word to ignore all instances of this word in the current document.

- Click in the **Not in Dictionary** box and type the correction yourself if Word's suggestions aren't correct.

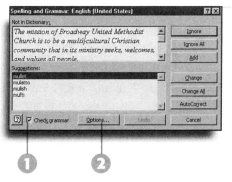

FIGURE 10.3

When Word identifies a word it doesn't recognize, you can ignore it, change it, or mark it as okay.

1 Uncheck this box to check only spelling, not grammar.

2 Click here for spelling options.

4. If no errors appear in the selected text, Word offers to check the rest of your document (without mentioning that the highlighted text is spelled correctly). Click **Cancel** to return to the document.

5. After Word has finished checking the entire document, it pops up a dialog box telling you the spell check is complete. Click **OK** to return to the editing window.

More About the Grammar Check

Grammar-checking works basically the same as spell-checking. Possible mistakes are wavy-underlined, but in green rather than red. You can right-click a green-underlined word or phrase to see what Word thinks is the appropriate correction. If you agree, accept the correction by clicking it on that menu. You can also check all the grammar at the same time that you check the spelling.

The main difference between the Spelling and the Grammar check is that the Spelling and Grammar dialog box has fewer options when it finds a grammar error. You can either **Ignore**, **Ignore All**, **Change**, or go to the **Next Sentence**. You can't change all at once because every instance is unique.

Beware the Grammar Checker

Word's grammar checker can sometimes steer you wrong. It may suggest a correction for a perfectly good sentence, and the correction, if made, causes the sentence to lose its meaning or become incorrect. For example, it may incorrectly suggest *whom* when *who* is appropriate, or it may recommend that you lowercase the words in a heading that should be all uppercase. Take its advice with a grain of salt.

Changing Your Spelling and Grammar Options

You can set a number of options to make the spelling and grammar checks go more according to your plans. You can set up special dictionaries, for example, and ignore certain types of false alarms.

From the Spelling and Grammar dialog box (refer to Figure 10.3), click the **Options** button to see your spelling and grammar choices (see Figure 10.4).

For example, you can turn off the red and/or green wavy lines on the onscreen display. To some people, those wavy lines are a distraction. You can still run the regular spelling and grammar check with the Spelling and Grammar button 🔤 , even with the word-by-word check off.

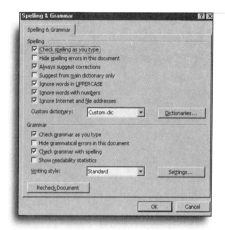

FIGURE 10.4

Customize how the spelling and grammar check works.

To turn off Word's on-the-fly spell-checking, remove the check mark from the box labeled **Check spelling as you type** at the top of the list. To hide the green marks (grammar errors), deselect the **Check grammar as you type** check box.

These changes affect not only the current document but all future documents you work on. You can also hide the red and/or green marks only in the current document. To hide the marks only in the current document, select the **Hide spelling errors in this document** and/or **Hide grammatical errors in this document** check boxes.

The grammar checker has several writing styles to choose from. **Formal** is the most picky, and identifies the most problems. **Casual** is the least picky, and allows the most leeway. The default is **Standard**. You can change the writing style by choosing a new one in the **Writing style** drop-down list.

If you are experienced with grammar, you may have your own opinions about some of these rules. To set the grammar checking rules, start in the Spelling and Grammar Options dialog box (refer to Figure 10.4).

Customizing grammar rules

1. Click the **Settings** button. The Grammar Settings dialog box opens (see Figure 10.5).

FIGURE 10.5

You can make your own decisions about various grammar rules from here.

2. Choose the writing style you want to modify from the **Writing style** drop-down list. Choose **Custom** if you want to leave the existing styles undisturbed.

3. Scroll through the **Grammar and style options** list and select or deselect check boxes for each rule.

4. In the **Require** section, open any of the drop-down lists and make your selection for these special grammar and punctuation rules.

5. Click **OK** to return to the Spelling and Grammar Options dialog box.

6. Click **OK** again to return to the spelling and grammar checker.

Saving Time with Automatic Changes

Does Word 97 have more Autos than a Ford factory, or what? That's the way it seems sometimes. Word alone has *AutoText*, *AutoComplete*, and *AutoFormat As You Type*, which all fall under the general heading of *AutoCorrect*. The names may be confusingly similar, but each one of these AutoSomethings has a specific purpose: To fix obvious mistakes automatically and eliminate unnecessary keystrokes as you work.

AutoCorrect helps you with your spelling. Word watches as you type, waiting for combinations of keys that it finds on the AutoCorrect list. In some cases, Word automatically replaces what you typed, usually so quickly that you don't even notice (if you type teh, for example, AutoCorrect changes it to the immediately). With AutoText entries, on the other hand, you have to press Enter or F3 after typing a shorthand name, at which point Word inserts whatever text you've assigned to that entry.

To see and adjust all the Auto- options that are available, open the **Tools** menu and choose **AutoCorrect**. Each of the tabs in this dialog box serves a slightly different purpose.

AutoCorrect: Fixing Typos On-the-Fly

When you add an entry to the AutoCorrect list, Word makes the substitution without asking your permission. For this reason, AutoCorrect entries are generally limited to replacements for words that you know are incorrectly spelled.

You can add AutoCorrect entries through the Spelling and Grammar dialog box; that's the easiest way. You can also add them through the AutoCorrect dialog box (see Figure 10.6). Open it by opening the **Tools** menu and choosing **AutoCorrect**. Then enter a new error-and-correction pair in the **Replace text as you type** list and click **Add**.

Use Undo to reverse AutoCorrect

Any time Word makes an AutoCorrect change, you can cancel the change by clicking the **Undo** button. When Word turns your (C) into a copyright symbol, for example, press Ctrl+Z or click the **Undo** button to change it right back, and then continue typing.

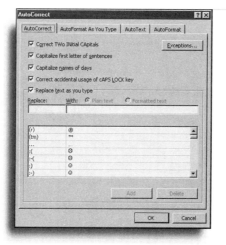

FIGURE 10.6

AutoCorrect lists all the "errors" and replacements it currently has on file.

If you find yourself getting annoyed with certain AutoCorrect corrections that you don't want, you can remove them from the list.

Removing an AutoCorrect entry

1. Open the <u>T</u>ools menu and choose **AutoCorrect**. The AutoCorrect dialog box opens (refer to Figure 10.6).

2. Turn off any of the check boxes in the dialog box that are applying rules you don't want.

3. Locate any AutoCorrect entry on the **Replace <u>t</u>ext as you type** list, and click it to highlight it. Then click the **<u>D</u>elete** button to delete it.

4. Click **OK**.

AutoText: Inserting Boilerplate Text with a Click

If you create business documents, you probably find yourself using the same sentences and paragraphs over and over again. Word lets you automatically insert this kind of *boilerplate* text by defining a shorthand name for it and then using pull-down menus or a shortcut key to expand the shorthand name into the full text.

In a press release, for example, the last paragraph is usually a standard description of the company issuing the release. You could define an AutoText entry for that paragraph and assign the shorthand name *pr-close* to it. Now, all you have to do is type that shorthand name and press Enter or F3 to stuff the entire paragraph into your document at the insertion point.

Adding an AutoText entry

1. In the current document, select the text and/or graphics you want to insert into future documents. (If your entry is a paragraph, make sure you include the entire paragraph in the selection.)

2. Open the <u>T</u>ools menu and choose **AutoCorrect;** then click the **AutoText** tab.

3. Check the **Preview** window at the bottom of the dialog box shown in Figure 10.7. If that entry is correct, type the shorthand name for your boilerplate text (in this case, `pr-close`) in the box labeled **Enter A<u>u</u>toText entries here**.

Entering days and months automatically

When you first install Word, the AutoText list includes more than 40 entries, most of them elements in common business letters. It also recognizes the days of the week and the months of the year, so if you type `febr` and press F3, `February` appears in your document.

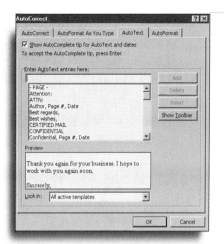

FIGURE 10.7
AutoText entries can be entire docu-
ments or simple words and phrases.
Word includes a list of predefined
AutoText entries that include dates
and common business phrases.

4. If you want the AutoText entry to be available to all documents, choose **NORMAL (global template)** from the list
labeled **Look in**. To assign the entry to another template,
choose its name from the same list.

5. Click **Add** to save the new AutoText entry.

6. Click **OK** to close the AutoCorrect dialog box.

After you've added an AutoText entry, you can use it in any document based on that template. When you store the AutoText
entry in the Normal document template, it's available to all documents.

Entering boilerplate text automatically

1. Position the insertion point in the document where you
want to add the AutoText entry.

2. Type the name of the AutoText entry (you don't need to follow the name with a space).

3. If you've turned on the AutoComplete option, Word pops
up a ScreenTip as soon as it recognizes what you've typed.
Press Enter to insert the AutoText item.

4. If AutoComplete is turned off, enter the shorthand name for
your boilerplate text (pr-close, in this example) and press
the F3 key.

Turning off AutoComplete

When you type the first four
letters of some (but not all)
AutoText items, such as months,
Word displays a pop-up tip that
suggests the complete word or
phrase. When you see this
ScreenTip, you can press Enter
or F3 to accept the suggestion
and insert the AutoText entry.
Just continue typing if you want
to ignore the AutoText suggestion. To prevent these
AutoComplete tips from pop-
ping up at all, clear the check
box labeled **Show
AutoComplete tip for
AutoText and dates** at the top
of the AutoCorrect dialog box.

5. Word inserts the boilerplate text at the insertion point.

To change an AutoText entry, follow the preceding steps to create a new AutoText entry with the same name as the old one. Answer **Yes** when Word asks whether you want to redefine the entry.

To delete an AutoText entry, just highlight its name and click the **Delete** button.

AutoFormat as You Type

By default, Word changes some characters you type into a different format. For example, when you enter a fraction like 1/2, Word replaces those three characters with a single, neat publishing character-½. Any time you find Word changing what you've typed for no apparent reason, this feature is probably the reason.

To see all the formatting changes that Word can make automatically, open the **Tools** menu and choose **AutoCorrect**. Click the tab labeled **AutoFormat As You Type**, and you see the dialog box shown in Figure 10.8.

FIGURE 10.8

Adjust the six AutoFormat options in the center of this dialog box to match your preferences.

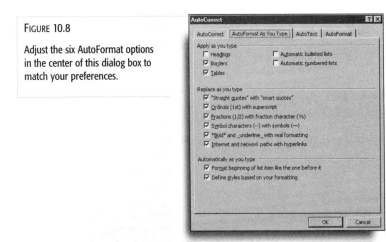

I like the way Word changes my straight quotes to the curly variety and changes a pair of hyphens to a dash, so I routinely leave these items turned on. I prefer seeing fractions as I type them, however, so I clear that check box. Also, because I usually create documents destined for paper rather than the Web, I turn off Word's option to convert Internet paths to clickable hyperlinks.

SEE ALSO

➤ *To learn how to format text within your Word documents, see page 193.*

➤ *To learn how to format entire documents, see page 223.*

Finding the Right Word

Sooner or later, every writer needs help finding the right word. When you're stuck, use Word's built-in thesaurus to look up other words that might work in your current document.

Looking up synonyms in the Word Thesaurus

1. Click to move the insertion point into the word you want to replace (you don't need to select the entire word).

2. Open the **Tools** menu, choose **Language**, and click **Thesaurus**. You then see a dialog box like the one in Figure 10.9, with the word you chose in the **Looked Up** drop-down list box.

FIGURE 10.9

Use Word's Thesaurus to search for a more appropriate word.

3. Select the appropriate meaning for the context in which you are using the word from the **Meanings** list. This list may also allow you to select related words or antonyms—words that are opposite in meaning to the one you selected.

4. If you find a suitable word in the **Replace with Synonym** list, select it and click the **Replace** button.

5. If one of the suggested synonyms is close, but not quite right, select that word and click the **Look Up** button.

6. To exit without making a change, just click the **Cancel** button or press Esc.

Working with Tables and Columns

Use tables to organize information into rows and columns

Draw a table using Word's pen and eraser tools

Convert text to a table with a few clicks

Move and copy rows, columns, and cells

Use Table AutoFormat to format a table quickly

Format text in multiple columns

Using Tables to Organize Information

How do you handle complex lists in which each item consists of two or more details? Word tables are the perfect tool to organize this kind of information into neat rows and columns. When you give each item its own row and break the details into separate columns, you wind up with an easy-to-read, information-packed table. With the help of tables, you can perform the following tasks:

- Align words and numbers into precise columns (with or without borders)
- Put text and graphics together with a minimum of fuss
- Arrange paragraphs of text side-by-side, as in a résumé
- Create professional-looking forms

Word tables include faint gridlines that help you see the outlines of the rows and columns when you're entering text. If you want, you can add borders, shading, and custom cell formats to give your tables a professional look. And if you've ever tried to line up columns using tabs, you'll appreciate how much easier you can work with tables.

Avoid using formulas in tables

Word tables enable you to perform basic mathematical calculations, including totals, averages, and counts. The procedures for adding formulas are daunting, however, and you have to update the results manually if you change the numbers that go into a formula. If you need to perform calculations on data in a table, use an embedded Works spreadsheet instead (see Chapter 4, "Using the Works Spreadsheet").

How Word Tables Work

As with spreadsheets, Word *tables* organize information into *rows* and *columns*. You add text (or numbers or graphics) inside *cells*; if you enter text that's wider than the cell, it wraps to a new line, increasing the height of the cell automatically. You can insert and delete rows and columns, or move entire columns by dragging from one location to another. You can also change column width and row height, or you can merge cells to form headings and labels. Figure 11.1 shows the parts of a typical Word table.

SEE ALSO

➤ *To learn more about merged cells, see page 259.*

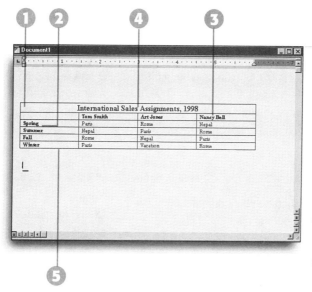

FIGURE 11.1

Use Word tables to organize detailed information in easy-to-follow rows and columns.

1. *Cell.* The basic unit of a table. Each cell is formed by the intersection of a row and a column.

2. *Row.* A table can have up to 32,767 rows.

3. *Column.* Each table can have up to 63 columns.

4. *Heading.* Designate one or more rows to serve as labels for the columns below.

5. *Border.* Unlike the nonprinting gridlines, these lines show up when you print. You can adjust their thickness and location.

By default, Word tables include *borders*—lines that separate cells and define the boundaries of the table itself on the printed page. Using tables with borders is a good way to insert feature comparisons, price lists, and other tabular material in documents. Remove the borders to use tables as a way to arrange blocks of text and other objects on the page without having to fuss with columns and tabs stops.

SEE ALSO

➤ *To find details on how to set tab stops, see page 209.*

➤ *To perform calculations on data in a table by using an embedded Works spreadsheet, see page 150.*

Adding a Table to a Document

If you've struggled to create and adjust tables using previous versions of Word, you're in for a pleasant surprise when you tackle the same task with Word 97. You can still put together a table from scratch, but using one of Word's many wizards to do the job is much easier.

Turn off gridlines

If you want to hide all traces of a table, turn off gridlines after you've entered data. Pull down the **Table** menu and choose **Hide Gridlines** from the end of the menu. If gridlines are hidden, choose **Show Gridlines** to reveal them again. This command affects all tables in the current document.

Creating Tables Quickly with a Few Clicks

Watch the toolbars

When you click within a table, the buttons on the Standard toolbar change slightly. The **Insert Table** button disappears, replaced by the Insert Rows ⬚ or Insert Columns ⬚ buttons.

Click the Insert Table button ⬚ on the Standard toolbar to add an unformatted table to your document quickly. When you click the button, a table grid (like the one in Figure 11.2) drops down from the toolbar. Drag the pointer down and to the right to select the number of rows and columns for your table.

FIGURE 11.2

Click and drag to insert an unformatted table. The caption tells you this table will include five rows of four columns each.

❶ Click the Insert Table button.

When you use the **Insert Table** button, the resulting table is completely unformatted. It fills the entire width of the current page, with columns of equal size and rows that match the height of the font defined in the Normal paragraph style. If you're willing to go through the extra formatting steps, using this button is an acceptable way to add a few rows and columns to a document. But there's a much faster and easier way to create the exact table you want.

Drawing a Complex Table

For anything more complex than a few simple rows and columns, you can use Word's extremely effective Table Drawing tool. Instead of dropping a simple rectangle in your document and forcing you to rearrange the cells to fit your data, this feature turns the mouse pointer into a pen, which you can use to draw the table exactly as you would like it to appear on the page.

Drawing a table within a Word document

  1. Click the Tables and Borders button ⬚ on the Standard toolbar. Word switches into Page Layout view if necessary, displays the floating Tables and Borders toolbar, and changes the shape of the pointer to a pen.

2. Point to the place in your document where you want the upper-left corner of the table to appear.

3. Click and drag down and to the right until you've drawn a rectangle that's roughly the size you want your final table to be.

4. Use the pen to draw lines for the rows and columns inside the table. You don't need to draw full lines; as you draw, you'll see the lines "snap" to connect with those you've already drawn, as in Figure 11.3.

5. If you make a mistake, click the Eraser button ⟨⟩. Drag the eraser-shaped pointer along the line you want to remove until the line appears bold; then release the mouse button to remove the line.

6. After you're finished, click the **Close** button to hide the Tables and Borders toolbar.

Don't worry about spacing

As you draw, rows and columns may appear in varying sizes, with uneven spacing between them. Don't worry. Just draw the proper number of rows and columns; then select some or all of them and click the Distribute Rows Evenly ⊞ and/or Distribute Columns Evenly ⊞ buttons to resize them all in one smooth motion.

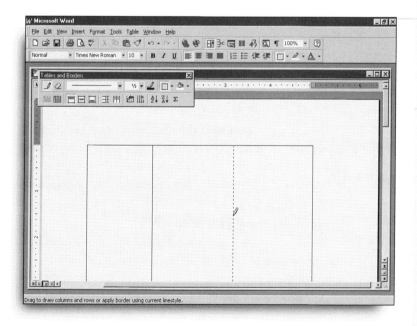

FIGURE 11.3

Use this pen-shaped pointer to draw the table you want. Use lines of varying lengths to create merged cells for titles and group headings.

Don't worry about neatness when you're using the Table Drawing tool. After you have the basic outline of your table in place, you can use the Tables and Borders toolbar to give it a slick, professional appearance.

SEE ALSO

➤ *To save a table with **AutoText**, see page 244.*

Converting Text to a Table

What do you do when you've already entered text in a document and you know it would work better in a table? You don't need to cut and paste. Instead, you can convert the block of text to a table.

Converting a block of text to a Word table

1. Select the entire block of text you want to convert. Make sure to include the paragraph mark for each row you plan to convert (see Figure 11.4).

2. Click the Insert Table button 🔲 on the Standard toolbar to surround the selected text with a table instantly.

3. If the one-button approach doesn't work (if the columns are too wide, or the table doesn't have enough rows, for example), click the **Undo** button on the Standard toolbar and try again. This time, pull down the **T**able menu and choose **Con**v**ert Text to Table**.

4. In the **Con**v**ert Text to Table** dialog box (see Figure 11.5), choose the separator character your text uses. Look in the **Number of **c**olumns** box; if the number displayed here doesn't match the number of columns you expect to see in the new table, click **Cancel** and make sure that the selected text contains no stray paragraph marks.

5. If you want to apply automatic formatting options during the conversion process, click the **A**u**toFormat** button and adjust options as needed.

6. Click **OK** to complete the conversion.

Save your favorite table formats

If you regularly use the same type of table in documents, create a blank table and save it as an AutoText entry, complete with formatting and headings. To reuse the table, insert that AutoText entry into your documents whenever you need it.

See the hidden codes

Click the Show/Hide button ¶ on the Standard toolbar to see tabs and paragraph marks when you're getting ready to convert text to a table. This step enables you to see easily whether you need to add another tab character to a row.

Separate items properly

If you want to split data into two or more columns per row, the data must include separator characters that define the end of each row and each item within the row. Word can use tabs, commas, or other characters as separators. If the text-to-table conversion doesn't give the expected results, you may need to edit your raw data to add separator characters in one or more places.

Convert a table back to text

To convert the contents of a table to text, reverse the process: Select the entire table, pull down the **T**able menu, and choose **Con**v**ert Table to Text**. Word enables you to choose tab characters or paragraph marks to separate items in each row.

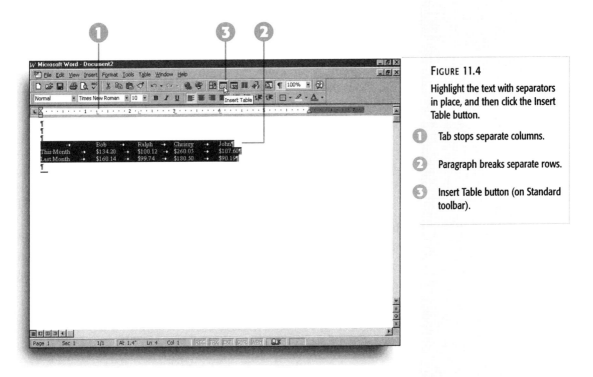

FIGURE 11.4

Highlight the text with separators in place, and then click the Insert Table button.

1 Tab stops separate columns.

2 Paragraph breaks separate rows.

3 Insert Table button (on Standard toolbar).

FIGURE 11.5

Before you convert text to a table, specify which character separates items in each row. Make sure that the number of columns matches the number you expect.

Working with Tables

Anything you can put in a Word document can also go into a table—text, numbers, symbols, or graphics, for example. You can even add automatic numbering to the items in a row or column of a table; as you move items around, they stay in the right sequence.

After you have your information neatly stashed in a table, you can rearrange it to your heart's content. You can move cells, rows, or columns; change the height of a row or the width of a column; even instruct Word to reformat your entire table automatically—all with a few mouse clicks.

SEE ALSO

➤ *To learn how to format simple lists with bullets and numbers, see page 213.*

Selecting Cells, Rows, and Columns

Before you can rearrange, resize, or reformat a part of a table, you must select it. Table 11.1 lists the specific techniques required to select parts of a table.

TABLE 11.1   **Selecting parts of a table**

To Select This Part of a Table	Do This
Cell contents	Drag the mouse pointer over the text you want to select.
Cell	Point to the inside left edge of the cell, and click.
Entire row	Point and click just outside the left edge of the first cell in the row.
Entire column	Point to the gridline or border at the top of the column; click when you see a small arrow pointing downward.
Multiple cells, rows, or columns	Select a cell, row, or column; then click and drag to select additional cells, rows, or columns.
Whole table	Pull down the **Table** menu and choose **Select Table**.

Entering and Editing Table Data

How to add a Tab character within a table

Pressing the Tab key moves from cell to cell within a table. If you want to insert a Tab character, hold down the Ctrl key and then press Tab.

To begin entering data into a table, just click to position the insertion point anywhere in the cell, and then start typing. Don't press Enter unless you want to start a new paragraph within the cell; if Word runs out of room, it wraps the text within the cell. To move to the next cell, press Tab. (If you're already at the end of a row, this action moves the selection to the first cell in the next row.) To move to the previous cell, press Shift+Tab. Use the arrow keys to move up or down, one row at a time.

Moving and Copying Parts of a Table

If you know how to move and copy text and objects in a Word document, you'll have no problem moving and copying parts of a table. You can use the Windows Clipboard, or drag cells, rows, and columns from one place to another.

Similar to the **Cut** or **Copy** menu commands (or their keyboard shortcuts) used to place one or more cells, rows, or columns on the Clipboard, Windows adds a **Paste Cells**, **Paste Rows**, or **Paste Columns** command on the **Edit** menu. You can also find the command on right-click shortcut menus. To use drag-and-drop techniques, select the object you want to copy or move first and then drag it to its new location.

When you move or copy cells, the contents of the Clipboard replace the cells in the new location. When you move or copy rows or columns, existing rows and columns slide out of the way to make room.

SEE ALSO
➤ *To learn more details about cutting and pasting in a Windows program, see page 28.*

Changing Column Widths and Row Heights

One way to make a table more readable is to adjust its column widths so that each column takes up just enough room to accommodate the information in it.

To adjust the width of a column, point to the right border of the column; when the mouse pointer turns to a two-headed arrow, click and drag to the left or right. Hold down the Alt key while dragging to see column and table measurements in the ruler, as in Figure 11.6.

The case of the missing menu choices

Using Word's **Table** menu can be a frustrating experience because the choices are context-sensitive. Before you can use the menus to delete a row or a column, for example, you must select a row or column; otherwise, you'll never see the menu choices you're seeking.

Don't use the ruler

When the insertion point is within a table, markers on the horizontal ruler define the margins and tab settings for each cell. Although you can adjust column and table widths using the rectangles, triangles, and other symbols, manipulating the table directly is far easier.

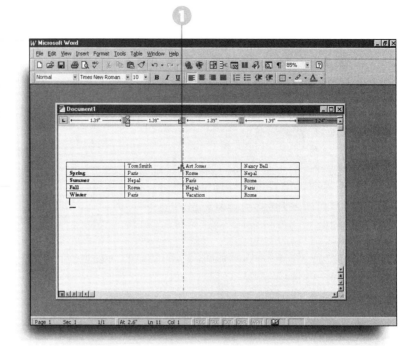

FIGURE 11.6

To change a column's width, point to the right border until the pointer changes to this shape and then drag. Hold down the Alt key as you click to see column and table measurements.

1   Mouse pointer

Make your text fit perfectly

Want to adjust the width of your columns automatically according to what you've already typed in them? If you want to use AutoFit for the entire table, make sure to select the entire table. Then pull down the **Table** menu, choose **Cell Height and Width,** and click the **AutoFit** button on the **Column** tab. Note that this choice may not work properly if your table contains any merged cells.

Quickly add a new row

After you insert a row or column, you can easily add another in the same location. Just press F4 (the Office-wide keyboard shortcut for Repeat Last Action).

When you use the mouse pointer to reduce the width of a column, Word automatically increases the width of the adjacent column, and vice versa. To maintain all other column widths, hold down the Shift key while you drag the ruler markers or the column boundaries; when you do so, the width of your table increases or decreases the same amount as the change you make in the selected column.

Adding and Deleting Rows and Columns

You can easily add or remove rows and columns in your table. If you're comfortable with Word's Table and Borders toolbar, use the **Draw Table** and **Eraser** tools to add and delete new rows within an existing table. You can also follow the mouse- and menu-based procedures listed in Table 11.2.

TABLE 11.2 **Table-editing techniques**

To Perform This Action	Do This
Add a new row at the bottom of the table	Click in the last cell of the last row; then press Tab.
Insert a row within the table	Click in the row just below the place where you want to insert a new row; then click the Insert Rows button [⊞], or right-click and choose **Insert Rows** from the shortcut menu.
Insert a column within the table	First, select the column to the right of the place where you want to add the new column; then click the Insert Columns button [⊞], or right-click and choose **Insert Columns** from the shortcut menu.
Add a new column to the right	Aim the mouse pointer of the last column just to the right of the top-right edge of the table until it turns to a down-pointing arrow. Click to select the column; then click the **Insert Columns** button, or right-click and choose **Insert Columns** from the shortcut menu.
Delete one or more rows or columns	Select the row(s) or column(s), right-click, and choose **Delete Rows** or **Delete Columns** from the shortcut menu.

Merging and Splitting Cells

For part of an effective table design, you may want to use a single large cell that spans several rows or columns. This technique is a great way to add a title to the first row of a table, as in the example in Figure 11.1 at the beginning of this chapter. It's also the best way to label subgroupings within a table.

If you know that your table needs to include this design element, you can add it when you create the table. Use the pen-shaped **Draw Table** tool to create rows or columns of the appropriate size and shape. On the other hand, if you've already created a table, you can merge two or more cells into a single larger cell.

Modifying tables that extend beyond the margin

When you add a new column, it may extend well beyond the right margin. In Page Layout view, you cannot see the right edge of the table to resize the column and bring the table back within the page margins. Switch to Normal view and then use the *horizontal scroll bar* to see and modify the entire table.

Don't just press Delete

If you want to remove rows or columns, don't use the Delete key. Pressing this key simply clears the contents of the selected cells, leaving the basic structure of the table intact. To remove rows or columns, you need to choose the appropriate command from the pull-down or shortcut menus.

Select the cells you want to merge, pull down the **T_a_ble** menu, and choose **Merge Cells**. Note that this action preserves the contents of the first cell in the selection but erases the contents of everything else. To reverse the process and split a merged cell back into the original cells, open the **T_a_ble** menu and choose **S_p_lit Cells**.

Making Great Looking Tables

Every table starts out as just a collection of cells, rows, and columns, with identical character formatting in each cell. To make a table easier to read, you need to resize rows and columns, reformat headings, add decorative borders, and use background colors and shading to set off individual sections. You can tackle each of these tasks individually, or you can use Word's Table Auto_F_ormat feature to jump-start the process.

Letting Word Do the Work with AutoFormat

Save your work!

Before you start using Table AutoFormat, save your work (select **File** and then **Save**). That way you can revert to the original if you are unhappy with the changes that Table AutoFormat makes.

Any time the insertion point is within a table, you can open the **T_a_ble** menu and choose **Table Auto_F_ormat**. Although I don't recommend that you use Word's AutoFormat feature for general documents, the **Table Auto_F_ormat** feature usually works quite well. Because information is contained in neat rows and columns, Word can more easily analyze and format rows, columns, and headings automatically—and you can control each part of the process.

Formatting a table automatically

Study the Preview pane

Different formats are appropriate for different types of data; for example some AutoFormats work perfectly with lists, and others give you your choice of grids. The Preview area in the **Table AutoFormat** dialog box shows you how each element of the table will look with the selected format. As you add and remove formatting options, the preview display changes.

1. Position the insertion point anywhere in the table.

2. Pull down the **T_a_ble** menu and choose **Table Auto_F_ormat**.

3. Choose one of the prebuilt designs (see Figure 11.7).

4. Adjust other format options in this dialog box:

   • AutoFormat can add borders, adjust colors and shading, and resize columns. To skip any of these steps, clear the associated check mark in the section labeled **Formats to apply**.

   • To preserve the fonts you've already defined for the table, deselect the **F_o_nt** box.

- AutoFormat assumes your table has labels in the first column and headings in the first row. If your table doesn't include these elements, remove one or both check marks in the section labeled **Apply special formats to**.

- In tables that contain numbers, AutoFormat assumes the last row or last column contains totals. If this is not the case in the current table, deselect these check boxes in the section labeled **Apply special formats to**.

- The **AutoFit** feature doesn't work properly if you've merged cells to form a single cell in one row. Deselect this option if you have trouble.

5. Click **OK** to apply the selected formats to the entire table.

FIGURE 11.7

The Table AutoFormat feature gives you more than 30 different looks for your table.

Don't be afraid to experiment!

If the **Table AutoFormat** feature doesn't work when you try it, pull down the **Edit** menu, choose **Undo AutoFormat** (or press Ctrl+Z), and start again, choosing different options this time.

Adding Emphasis to Rows and Columns

Use lines and shading to help your readers follow along as they read items in the same row or column. This formatting step is especially important when you have wide rows and long columns filled with details. Format column headings in bold, easy-to-read fonts so that they stand out clearly from the details in each row.

Adding borders to a table is simple. Use the Tables and Borders toolbar to specify thick or decorative lines around the outside of the table, thin lines between rows and columns, custom borders to separate headings and totals, or colored borders anywhere.

Adding custom borders to a Word table

1. Select the cells, rows or columns where you want to add borders. If you simply click in the table without making a selection, Word assumes that you want to add borders to the current cell only.

2. Click the Tables and Borders button ⊞ to display the Tables and Borders toolbar.

3. Open the **Line Style** drop-down list and choose the look you want for your borders.

4. Open the **Line Weight** drop-down list and choose a border thickness. The default setting is a relatively thin ½-point line.

5. Click the Border Color ▱ button. Choose the default setting (Automatic) for printed documents; select one of 16 available colors if you plan to use your table in a Web page or send it to a color printer.

6. Click the drop-down arrow to the right of the Borders button ▱▾ to display all 10 available combinations of borders; if you plan to set multiple borders, click the horizontal bar just above the two rows of buttons, and drag the Borders menu off the toolbar so that it floats.

7. Click the button that corresponds to the border you want to adjust. The **All Borders** button adds a line to all sides of all cells in the current selection, and the **Bottom Border** button is useful for putting a thin double line under headings or under the last row before totals.

8. If necessary, select another cell or cells and repeat steps 3 through 7.

To add a gray or colored background within one or more cells, first select the cells, rows, or columns; then click the arrow to

---

Use the dialog box

All the choices on the Tables and Borders toolbar are also available in a three-tabbed dialog box. If you prefer dialog boxes to toolbars, click the **Format** menu and choose **Borders and Shading**.

Remove borders with another click

To remove an individual border, choose **No Border** from the list of Line Style options; then click the **Borders** button that corresponds to the border you want to change. To remove all lines around and within the selected cell or cells, click the **Borders** button; then click the **No Border** option at the far right of the second row.

the right of the Shading Color button [icon] on the Tables and Borders toolbar. The palette includes 40 choices, most of them representing various shades of gray.

Working with Long Tables

Two special format settings can help make reading and following long tables easier. First, if your table includes column headings and you expect it to print on two or more pages, tell Word you want to repeat the headings on subsequent pages. Select the row or rows that you want to repeat; then pull down the **Table** menu and choose **Headings**.

Second, if your table includes some cells whose contents wrap to two or more lines, you can prevent those rows from splitting across page breaks. Select the cell or cells (or the entire table), pull down the **Table** menu, and choose **Cell Height and Width**. Click the **Row** tab and clear the check mark next to the box labeled **Allow row to break across pages**.

Working with Multiple Columns

There are several ways to create multiple columns of text in Word. One, as you have already seen, is to create a table and put text in each cell. This method is called *parallel columns* because you can make information of varying lengths align perfectly in parallel lines. Figure 11.8 shows an example. You can also create the same effect with tabs, but it is much more difficult to keep everything aligned if you edit the text later.

Identifying the right color

Let the mouse pointer hover over the squares in the color palette to see the name of each one in a ScreenTip. For the sake of readability, avoid using more than a 20% gray background behind ordinary text.

You must use the first row for headings

Word assumes that the first row of your table includes headings. If this assumption is correct, just click anywhere in that row before you define headings to repeat on subsequent pages. If you want to use multiple rows, select them before choosing the **Headings** command. You must include the first row in your selection; otherwise, the command is grayed out and unavailable.

FIGURE 11.8

Placing text in a table is one of the easiest ways to make parallel columns.

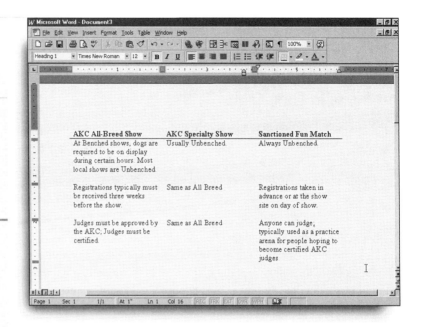

FIGURE 11.8

Placing text in a table is one of the easiest ways to make parallel columns.

Borders in parallel columns

If you create text in parallel columns (as in Figure 11.8) with a table, you will probably want to turn off the gridlines for the table.

You may want to selectively apply borders to certain sides of certain cells to create divider lines. For example, you might add borders to the bottom of the cells in a header row, or you might create vertical lines between parallel columns by applying borders to the sides of the cells.

Section breaks

When you select some text before changing the Columns setting, Word inserts section breaks before and after the text so that the formatting change is in its own section. You can create your own section breaks in documents, too, by opening the **Insert** menu and choosing **Break**.

The other kind of columns you can create are the snaking kind, like those in a newspaper, where an article runs down one column and then the next. You set up this kind of column with Word's Columns feature.

Formatting an article in multiple columns

1. If only a portion of your document should be formatted in multiple columns, select all the text that should be included. If you don't, the change will apply to the entire section (or the entire document, if you have not created any section breaks).

2. Click the Columns button 🔲 on the Standard toolbar.

3. Drag across the number of columns you want, much like you did with tables (see Figure 11.9).

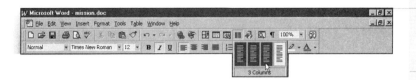

4. To change the number of columns at any time (for example, to go back to a single column layout), just repeat the steps.

5. To fine-tune your columns (for example, to change the spacing between them or to change the width of one or more), use the Columns dialog box (open the **Format** menu and choose **Columns**). In this dialog box, you'll find controls to set specific column widths, change the number of columns used, and add vertical gridlines between columns (see Figure 11.10).

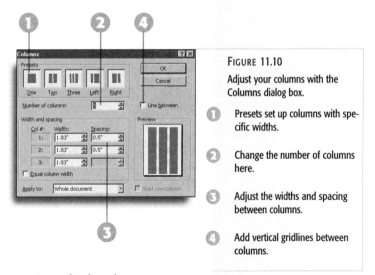

FIGURE 11.10

Adjust your columns with the Columns dialog box.

1 Presets set up columns with specific widths.

2 Change the number of columns here.

3 Adjust the widths and spacing between columns.

4 Add vertical gridlines between columns.

As you are typing and editing text in multiple columns, you may want to end a column early—for example, to force a heading to be at the top of the next column. To do so, insert a column break by pressing Ctrl+Shift+Enter. A column break is like a page break, except that it moves the text to the next column rather than to the next page. If you have only one column on the page, a column break and a page break have the same effect.

Working with Graphics

Add pictures to any document

Choose appropriate clip art

Get more clip art from the Microsoft Web site

Create stylized text with WordArt

Draw your own lines and shapes

Wrap text around objects for desktop publishing effects

Compatible graphics formats

Word recognizes and imports the following common graphics file formats: Windows Metafile (WMF) and Enhanced Metafile (EMF), JPEG File Interchange Format (JPG and JPEG), Windows Bitmap (BMP) , and PC Paintbrush (PCX) . If you have an image in another file format, such as those created by professional drawing and drafting programs, you may be able to import it directly into Word if you first install the correct *graphics filter*. For a detailed list of compatible file formats, search for the Help topic "Graphics file types Word can use."

Adding Pictures to Your Documents

Word's desktop publishing capabilities could easily fill a book. With the creative use of imported graphics, columns, sections, and text boxes, you can create sophisticated newsletters, brochures, flyers, and other complex documents.

To add a picture or a graphic image to any Word document, position the insertion point at the spot where you want the picture to appear, pull down the **Insert** menu, and then choose **Picture**.

Choices on this menu include the following:

- *Clip Art*. This selection opens the Microsoft Clip Gallery application. Your options include hundreds of drawings and a smaller number of high-quality scanned photos.

- *From File*. Import a file saved in any of several graphics formats. The Web is a good source of high-quality images.

- *From Scanner*. If you've installed a scanner, you can convert photographs, documents, magazine pages, and other hard copy to editable images. Choose this menu option to launch Microsoft Photo Editor and begin scanning the image.

- *AutoShapes*. Word includes drawing tools that enable you to create and edit basic shapes, such as squares, stars, and arrows. Use these building blocks to create logos, flowcharts, or simple illustrations.

- *WordArt*. Start with a word or two; then stretch the text and add background colors, shadows, and other effects. This tool is useful for creating logos and headlines.

- *Chart*. This menu option inserts a Microsoft Chart object into the current document. Use the spreadsheet-style data entry window to add numbers and quickly convert them to a chart.

The following sections take you through some of the most popular kinds of graphics that beginning and intermediate users need for their documents: clip art, WordArt, Word drawings, and AutoShapes.

Using Clip Art

Clip art is pre-drawn artwork that comes with Word. You access it from the Clip Gallery (see Figure 12.1). The Clip Gallery does more than just display clip art; notice in Figure 12.1 that there are four tabs, one for each type of clip that Word helps you organize. We'll be focusing mainly on the clip art, but keep in mind that you can also use the Clip Gallery for sounds, videos, and pictures (that is, bitmap images such as scans).

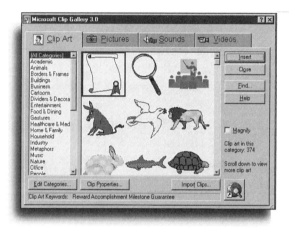

FIGURE 12.1

In the Clip Gallery, each of the various types of multimedia files has a separate tab.

To open the Clip Gallery, open the **Insert** menu, point to **Picture**, and choose **Clip Art**. If a dialog box appears telling you that there is additional clip art on the CD, and if your CD is handy, go ahead and put it in your CD-ROM drive. (If it's not handy, don't worry about it.) Then click **OK**. If you have a specific topic in mind, you might want to click on a clip category, as shown in Figure 12.1. Select the art you want, and then click **Insert**.

When the clip is in your document, you can move it and resize it as needed. Just drag the clip's center to move it around, or select it and then drag the handles in the corners to resize it. You can also right-click the clip and choose **Format Picture** to open a dialog box of controls for the image.

Importing Clips

If you use your own pictures frequently in Word, you might want to import them into the Clip Gallery so they'll be available for browsing on the Pictures tab. (If you don't want to bother with that, you can continue to insert the pictures with the **Pictures** tab of the **Insert** menu, as previously described.)

Importing art into the Clip Gallery

1. If the Clip Gallery isn't open, open the **Insert** menu, point to **Picture**, and choose **Clip Art**.

2. Click the **Pictures** tab.

3. Click the **Import Clips** button. The **Add pictures to Clip Gallery** dialog box appears.

4. Change the drive and folder to display the contents of the folder where the art is located (see Figure 12.2). You'll find some .BMP (bitmap) images to practice with in the Windows folder.

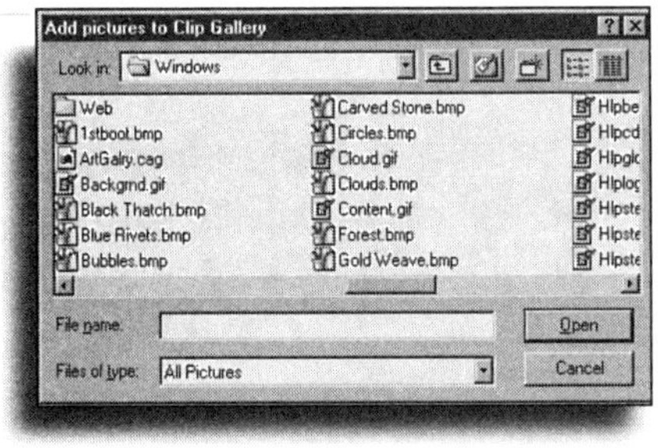

FIGURE 12.2

Choose the graphic file to link to the Clip Gallery.

5. Click the file that you want. To import more than one file, click on the first file and then hold down the **Shift** key while you click on the last one. This selects all the files between those two.

6. Click the **Open** button. A **Clip Properties** dialog box appears for the first clip, as shown in Figure 12.3.

7. Choose the categories into which to put the clip, or create a new category by clicking **New Category**.

8. (Optional) Type any keywords to help you find the clip later.

9. Click **OK**. The image appears on the Pictures tab of the Clip Gallery, as shown in Figure 12.4.

You can follow the same procedure to import any kind of file as a clip—video, sound, picture, or additional clip art.

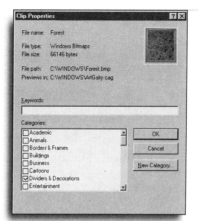

FIGURE 12.3
For each imported clip, you must give Clip Gallery some information.

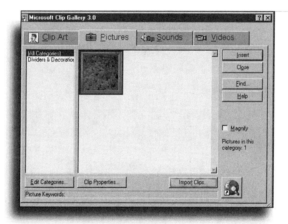

FIGURE 12.4
Now you can use any of these pictures in Word through the Clip Gallery.

Getting More Clips from the Internet

Microsoft has a Web site on the Internet that offers a number of clips you can download. These include sounds, videos, pictures, and clip art. To get them, you must have a way to connect to the Internet (an online service or a dial-up or network Internet connection). To see what's available, follow these steps.

Downloading additional clip art

1. Establish your Internet connection. This may involve starting your online service software and connecting, or using Windows 95's Dial-Up Networking to connect to your Internet service provider.

2. Start Word, or switch back to it if it was already open.

3. Open the Clip Gallery (open the **Insert** menu, choose **Picture**, then choose **Clip Art**).

4. Click the tab representing the type of clip you want to import (**Clip Art** or **Pictures**, for example).

5. Click the globe button in the bottom right corner of the Clip Gallery.

6. If you see a dialog box telling you that you should click **OK** to browse the Web, do so. (You may not see this dialog box at all, depending on your setup.) Internet Explorer opens and the Clip Gallery Live page loads.

7. Read the licensing agreement in the upper right pane, and then click the **Accept** button to move on. The upper right pane changes to show the controls in Figure 12.5.

8. Click the **Clip Art**, **Pictures**, **Sounds**, or **Motion** tab to choose which type of clip you want.

FIGURE 12.5

Microsoft's Clip Gallery Live page enables you to browse the available clips or search by keyword.

1 Click here to retrieve the selected clips.

2 Click here to download a single clip immediately.

3 Click here to select a clip.

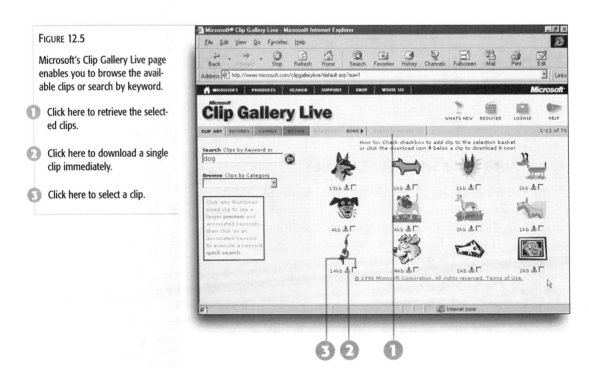

9. Type keywords in the **Search** box and then click **Go**, or choose a category from the **Browse** drop-down list. The clips appear.

10. Do any of the following to download clips:
    - To download a single clip immediately, click its **Download** button (refer to Figure 12.5).
    - To mark a clip for retrieval, click to place a check in its check box.
    - To retrieve all marked clips, click the **Selection Basket** link.

11. When the File Download dialog box appears, choose **Open this file from its current location**. This places the clip in your Clip Gallery.

12. Jump back to your browser and get more clips if you want. When you are finished, terminate your Internet connection and jump back to the Clip Gallery to use your new clips.

SEE ALSO

➤ *For information about connecting to the Internet and using Internet Explorer, see page* *399.*

Creating WordArt

Microsoft WordArt is a text-manipulation program within Word. This program enables you to type short bits of text and then mold, twist, and otherwise reshape the text to make it look more interesting and graphical. Figure 12.6 shows some examples of WordArt.

Creating WordArt

1. If it is not already displayed, display the Drawing toolbar at the bottom of the screen by clicking the **Drawing** button ![drawing icon] on the Standard toolbar.

2. On the Drawing toolbar, click the **WordArt** button ![wordart icon]. The **WordArt Gallery** dialog box appears.

3. Click on one of the samples that's similar to what you want (see Figure 12.7). (You can change later, so don't agonize over it.)

FIGURE 12.6

Here are some examples of the hundreds of effects you can create with WordArt.

1 Drawing toolbar

FIGURE 12.7

Choose a basic WordArt design.

4. Click **OK**. The Edit WordArt Text dialog box appears.

5. Type the text you want in the title, replacing the "Your Text Here" text (see Figure 12.8).

6. (Optional) If you want a different font, font size, or attributes, change them using the controls at the top of the **Edit WordArt Text** dialog box.

7. Click **OK**. Your text appears as WordArt in the document, and the WordArt toolbar appears, as shown in Figure 12.9.

Don't overdo

Try to keep it short; WordArt looks best when the text is not cluttered. If you use more than two or three words, it often ruins the effect.

FIGURE 12.9

The WordArt now appears in the document.

① WordArt

② White squares are handles.

③ WordArt toolbar

Now that you have some WordArt in a document, you can do any of the following:

- Drag the WordArt to a new position by dragging it from its center (when the mouse pointer is a four-headed arrow).
- Resize the WordArt by dragging one of the handles.

Notice that WordArt has its own toolbar, made especially to help you make changes to your WordArt objects. This toolbar appears automatically when you create a piece of WordArt. Table 12.1 explains the functions of these buttons.

TABLE 12.1 WordArt toolbar buttons

Button	Purpose
	Opens the WordArt Gallery dialog box for a new WordArt object
Edit Text...	Reopens the Edit WordArt Text dialog box
	Reopens the WordArt Gallery dialog box for the existing WordArt object
	Opens the Format WordArt dialog box, where you can change the lines and colors used
Abc	Opens a pop-up array of shapes to which you can conform your WordArt
	Enables you to rotate the WordArt (works the same way as the Free Rotate tool on the Drawing toolbar)
Aa	Makes all the letters the same height
Ab bↄ	Toggles between vertical and horizontal text orientation
	Opens a pop-up menu of text alignments (centered, left-aligned, and so on)
AV	Changes the spacing between letters

To edit a piece of WordArt, double-click it. This displays the WordArt toolbar (if it isn't visible already) and the Edit WordArt Text dialog box. When you are done making changes to the

WordArt, click outside it to deselect it. As with any other drawn object, you can drag the WordArt around the worksheet to reposition it, or you can resize it using the selection handles in the corners.

Drawing Your Own Shapes and Lines

You saw the Drawing toolbar in the preceding section; to display it, click the **Drawing** button 🔲 on the Standard toolbar.

Drawing Lines and Shapes

The Drawing toolbar contains two types of tools—tools that draw shapes, and tools that manipulate shapes. Because you can't manipulate a shape before you've drawn it, let's look at the drawing tools first:

⬛	Line
⬛	Line with arrow
⬛	Rectangle
⬛	Ellipse

The procedure is basically the same for all these tools, although it may take you a bit of practice to master them.

Drawing with the drawing tools

1. Click the drawing tool you want.
2. Point the mouse pointer where you want the line or shape to begin.
3. Hold down the mouse button and drag to where you want the line or shape to end.
4. Release the mouse button to view the finished line or shape.

Practice with the lines and shapes for a while until you get comfortable.

Multidrawing shortcut

If you double-click instead of click in step 2, you can repeat the procedure from step 3 to draw more of the same shape. Otherwise, you must go back to step 2 each time.

Drawing AutoShapes

AutoShapes are pre-drawn shapes that function just like the lines and boxes that you draw. They're great for people who want shapes such as arrows and starbursts but aren't coordinated enough to draw them (or simply don't have the time to do so). To use an AutoShape, follow these steps.

Adding an AutoShape to your document

1. Click the **AutoShapes** button on the Drawing toolbar. A menu pops up listing categories of shapes.
2. Point your mouse at the category you want (for example, Block Arrows). A menu of the available shapes in that category appears (see Figure 12.10).
3. Click on the shape you want. Your mouse pointer turns into a crosshair.
4. Drag on the document to draw a box where you want the shape to appear. When you release the mouse button, the shape appears on your document.

FIGURE 12.10

Choose the category of AutoShape you want, and then choose the shape itself.

Manipulating Lines and Shapes

Moving lines and shapes is the same as moving WordArt, which you learned earlier in this chapter. To move a line or shape, simply click on it to select it, and then position the mouse pointer over it so that your pointer becomes a four-headed arrow. Then drag the line or shape to its new position.

Resizing a line or shape is the same as resizing WordArt, too: Just point to one of the line or shape's selection handles and drag it to change the line or shape.

Copying and Deleting Lines and Shapes

You can copy lines and shapes the same way that you copy anything else in Word.

Copying lines and shapes

1. Select the line or shape.

2. Open the **Edit** menu and choose **Copy**, click the **Copy** button on the toolbar, or press **Ctrl+C.**

3. Click in your document to indicate where you want the copy of the line or shape to go.

4. Open the **Edit** menu and choose **Paste**, click the **Paste** button, or press **Ctrl+V**.

5. If needed, reposition the copy in the exact location where you want it.

Deleting is just what you'd expect, too: Select the object and then press the **Delete** key on the keyboard.

Rotating and Flipping Lines and Shapes

Suppose you've drawn an arrow that points up with the AutoShape feature, but you want it to point down. No problem—just flip it.

Flipping a drawing

1. Select the drawing.

2. Click the **Draw** button on the Drawing toolbar. A menu appears.

3. Point to **Rotate or Flip** on that menu. Another submenu appears.

4. Choose **Flip Vertical** or **Flip Horizontal**, depending on what you're after.

As you saw when you had the menu open, the **Rotate or Flip** submenu also has commands for **Rotate Right** and **Rotate Left**. You can use these to rotate your shape 90 degrees in either the left or right direction.

If you want to control the precise amount of rotation, use the **Free Rotate** feature.

Free-rotating a drawing

1. Click the **Free Rotate** button 🔄 on the Drawing toolbar. The selection handles around the shape turn into green circles.

2. Position the mouse pointer over one of those circles so that the mouse pointer turns into a circular arrow. Then drag that selection handle to rotate the shape to the exact position you want (see Figure 12.11).

3. Click anywhere away from the shape to finish.

FIGURE **12.11**

Drag the round green selection handles to rotate the shape.

1️⃣ Free Rotate tool

2️⃣ Selection handles change to circles.

3️⃣ Dotted lines show where the rotated shape will appear.

4️⃣ Mouse pointer becomes a circular arrow.

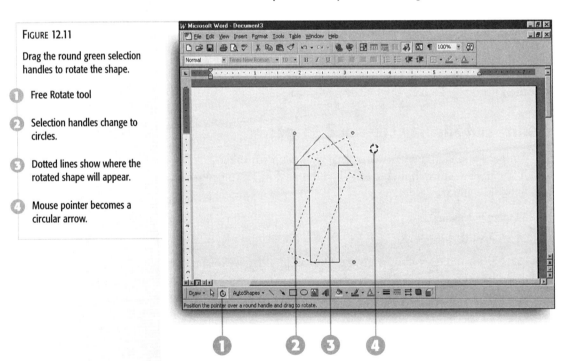

Changing a Line or Shape's Appearance

The Drawing toolbar contains several tools that control how a drawing appears.

Fill Color. Open the drop-down list to choose a fill color, and then click the button to apply the color to the selected shape. (This does not work with lines.)

 Line Color. Open the drop-down list to choose a line color, and then click the button to apply the color to the line or shape. (If you're working with a shape, this changes the outline color around the shape.)

 Line Thickness. Select the line or shape, and then open this drop-down list and select the line thickness to use. If applied to a shape, this changes the border around the shape.

 Line Style. Select the line or shape, and then open this drop-down list and select the line style (dotted, dashed, and so on). If applied to a shape, this changes the border.

 Arrow Style. Select the line, and then open this drop-down list and select the type of arrow to use (including None to remove an arrow). This doesn't work with shapes.

 Shadow. Select the shape, and then click this button to open a list of shadow types. Click on the one you want to apply. This doesn't work with lines.

 3D. Select the shape, and then click this button to open a list of 3D types. Click on the one you want to apply. This doesn't work with lines.

Positioning Text and Graphics Precisely

By default, pictures "float" on the page; that is, you can position them exactly where you want them, whether in front of or behind text or other objects. With this option, text wraps around the object without disturbing its position on the screen.

WordArt, too

The **Line Color** and **Fill Color** buttons, the **Shadow** button, and the **3D** button also work with WordArt.

Working with a dialog box

You can access all the controls from the Drawing toolbar in a more formal form, with more precise controls, by right-clicking on the shape or line and then choosing **Format AutoShape** from the shortcut menu. (It doesn't matter whether you actually created the shape or line with the AutoShape button or not; Word considers all shapes and lines AutoShapes after they're drawn.)

You can change a floating picture to an inline picture—one that is positioned directly in the text at the insertion point. When you choose this option, the picture or graphic attaches itself to a point within your text and moves as you add or delete text.

Anchoring a Graphic to a Fixed Spot

To change a floating picture to an inline picture, select the picture, then right-click and choose **Format Picture** from the shortcut menu. Click the **Position** tab and clear the **Float over text** check box.

Wrapping Text Around a Graphic or Other Object

You can choose how you want text to wrap around any graphic object or AutoShape. Within a report, for example, you can place graphics directly within a long block of text, or you can insert a graphic between columns and maintain the column format.

To set text-wrapping options, first select the graphic or AutoShape, then right-click and choose **Format Picture** or **Format AutoShape**. Click the **Wrapping** tab, as shown in Figure 12.12, and then select the wrapping options you want.

FIGURE 12.12

Use this dialog box to control how text wraps around a picture or other object.

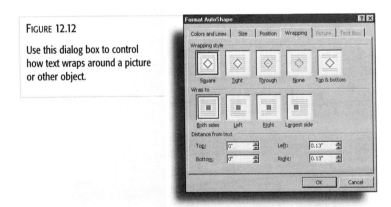

Creating Web Pages with Word

Learn about Word's Web tools

Create a Web page from a wizard

Create a Web page from scratch

Add and format text

Create text boxes on Web pages

Add graphics and lines

Publish your work to a server

Do you need to know HTML?

No! Web pages are created and saved in Hypertext Markup Language (HTML), but Word is designed to help you develop pages even if you have little or no HTML knowledge. Therefore, little HTML information is presented here. Later in the chapter, you'll learn how to insert your own HTML code if you like, but you don't need to be an HTML expert to create Web pages with Word. If you'd like to learn more about writing your own HTML code, see *Special Edition Using HTML 3.2,* published by Que.

Is Word the Right Web Tool for You?

Documents on the Web are called *Web pages* because they are designed in basically the same way as traditional ink-on-paper pages. Creating a Web document is analogous to creating a layout for a newspaper or magazine article.

Expert designers and advanced HTML programmers may find Word's World Wide Web authoring tools somewhat lacking—but they aren't designed for experts. They're designed for busy people, like you, who have other responsibilities besides creating Web sites.

Word provides easy-to-use tools and templates that help you create fairly sophisticated Web pages with most of the popular features, including text, images, hyperlinks, tables, sounds, and even videos.

Creating Web Pages in Word

You can use Word to create Web pages in several ways. You can use a special wizard, create a page from scratch, or convert content you've already created in other documents into Web pages. Let's take a look at each of these options right now.

Creating a Web Page with a Wizard

If you're creating a Web page for the first time, you may want to use Word's Web Page Wizard. This tool helps you get started because it creates a template with a layout designed for a specific type of Web document, such as a personal home page or a table of contents.

The wizard also enables you to choose a graphic theme (such as "festive," "community," or "elegant") and then adds a thematically appropriate background and other graphic elements.

After you use the wizard to select and open a sample page, you can change the text and delete or customize the graphics to meet your needs.

Using the Web Page Wizard

1. Choose the **File** menu and select **New**.

2. Select the **Web Pages** tab on the New dialog box, and double-click the Web Page Wizard (see Figure 13.1). A dialog box opens and asks whether you want to connect to the Internet to check for new Web authoring tools Microsoft has developed. If you do want to check, your system must be set up for Internet access.

SEE ALSO

➤ *If you don't see the Web Pages tab in the New dialog box, Word's Web page authoring tools aren't installed. Run Word Setup again (see page 521) and select the Web page authoring components.*

3. After you've looked for new authoring tools or closed the inquiring dialog box, the first step of the wizard opens in another box. This step asks you to decide what type of page you want to create, such as a two- or three-column layout, a form page, or another type of Web document. When you make a selection by clicking on the name of a layout in the list, you can see the effect it has on the Web page behind the dialog box (see Figure 13.2). After you've made a final decision, choose **Next**.

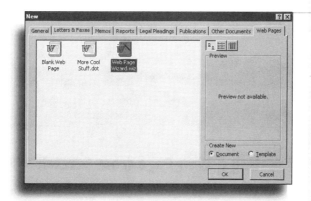

FIGURE 13.1
The Web Page Wizard creates a customizable template.

4. In the next dialog box that opens, you can select a style or graphic theme, such as "elegant," "festive," or "jazzy." As in step 3, when you select the name of a theme in the list, you can see the effect in the sample behind the dialog box.

When you decide on a theme, select it and choose **Finish**. The Web page template then opens in Word's document window (see Figure 13.3).

5. Highlight any text and type your own words to replace it. Select and delete any graphic elements you don't like. In other sections in this chapter, you'll learn how to add elements to the page.

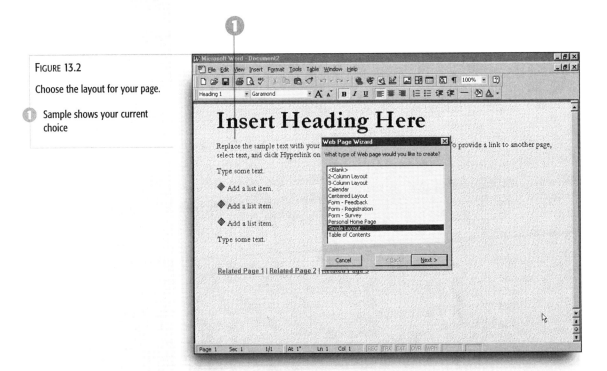

Creating a Web Page from Scratch

You can also work from a totally blank Web page and add your own text and graphics. This works well for experienced Web designers and people who want different results than any of the Wizard's options can provide.

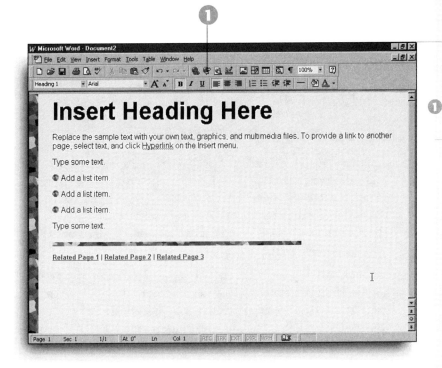

FIGURE 13.3

Highlight and type over the sample text to insert your own.

1 Toolbar contains special Web page tools.

Creating a Web page from scratch

1. Click the **File** menu and choose **New.**

2. Select the **Web Pages** tab on the New dialog box (refer to Figure 13.1).

3. Double-click the **Blank Web Page** template.

4. Type the text for your page.

5. See the sections on the rest of this chapter to continue formatting your Web page and to insert hyperlinks.

SEE ALSO

➤ *To apply styles to a word document, see page 223.*

➤ *To format a Web page, see page 289.*

➤ *To add hyperlinks, see page 296.*

Special Web tools

You can tell when the Web author-ing features are active in Word because the software interface changes to include toolbars and menus customized for working on Web pages. For example, the Web toolbar, which gives Word the func-tionality of a browser, appears (refer to Figure 13.3).

After you've made any changes to either a blank or a sample page, you should save your work. If you're creating several relat-ed pages, consider putting them in a separate folder. Having them all in one location may be helpful when you put them on the Web (see the section "Publishing to a Web Server" at the end of this chapter).

Saving Your Document in HTML Format

Another way to create a Web page is to create a regular docu-ment and then save it in HTML format. To save a pre-existing Word document in the HTML format, just open the document, select the **File** menu, and choose **Save As HTML**. Word closes the document, reopens it, and displays it similar to the way it will appear in a Web browser.

Though this may seem like an easy way to create a Web page, it's not quite that simple. Many items appear different in Web page format. Formatting not supported by HTML may be changed or removed, including margins, page borders, and head-ers and footers. Fonts may not be the same size anymore and may not have special attributes, such as embossing or shadows. Any special objects, such as AutoShapes, WordArt, and text boxes, are removed. Equations, charts, and other OLE objects are converted to GIF (a graphic format). The list goes on and on.

SEE ALSO

➤ *To find a complete list of the elements that are changed or removed when a document is converted to HTML, look up the article "Learn what happens when you save a Word 97 document as a Web page" in the Microsoft Word Help file.*

If you're creating a document you plan to use as both a standard Word document and a Web page, you can save yourself some work by using a simple layout and simple text formatting. If, for example, you're creating the original document as a standard Word file, don't create multiple columns or other elements that won't be retained when you convert the document to the HTML format. The simpler the document, the better the results when converting it to HTML.

Formatting a Web Page

Now that you have a Web page in front of you (by one method or another) in Word, what can you do to change it? Generally, you edit the page the same way as you edit any other document. The differences are explained in the following sections.

Adding Backgrounds and Textures

The Web Page Wizard creates a default background matching the theme for the page you've created. You can customize the background or add one (if one isn't chosen already) through the **Fo̲rmat** menu.

Changing the page background

1. Open the **Fo̲rmat** menu and choose **Background.**

2. Click the color you want on the pop-up palette (see Figure 13.4).

3. Click **M̲ore Colors** if you want additional choices, or click **F̲ill Effects** to select from a palette of woven, marble, and other background textures.

4. Word saves your background as a separate graphics file, such as Image.gif, in the folder in which your Web page was created. If you move your page to a different folder or other location (such as a Web server), be sure to move the image file, too.

You also can use a picture as a background for your Web page. The image is tiled (repeated) to fill the screen.

Using a picture as a background

1. Choose the **Fo̲rmat** menu and select **Background.**

2. Select **F̲ill Effects.**

3. Click the **Texture** tab.

4. Choose **O̲ther Texture**.

5. When the **Select Texture** dialog box appears, select the image file from the list, or enter the path and name in the **File N̲ame** box. Then click **OK**.

6. Click **OK** again to close the Fill Effects dialog box. The picture you selected is then tiled to fill the background of your page.

Assign a title to your Web page

If you assign a title to your page, it appears in the Web browser title bar when people visit the page. The title also appears in Web users' history and favorites or bookmark lists. To assign the title, choose the **File** menu, select **Properties**, and type the title in the **Title** box. If you don't assign a title, Word creates one based on the first few characters on your Web page.

What is a GIF file?

Word saves your background texture as a Graphics Interchange Format (GIF) file because it is a format compatible with the Web environment and because it will display in most browsers. Another type of image file you're likely to see on the Web is Joint Photographic Experts Group (JPEG), a popular format for photographs.

FIGURE 13.4

Unless you're using light-colored text, be careful you don't make your background so dark that you can't read the words.

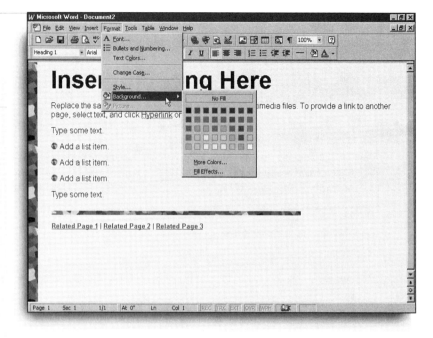

Get the latest Web tools

If you have Internet access, you can download recently developed software tools for creating Web pages (plus extra templates and art) from the Microsoft Web site. To access this site, choose the **Help** menu, select **Microsoft on the Web**, and choose **Free Stuff**.

Creating Text Boxes

A text box is a container for text that can be positioned and sized on your Web page. Adding a text box can help you accomplish two goals: It can add a bit of visual pizzazz, and it can shorten the length of lines of text (long text lines can be difficult to read). In a normal Word document, you can insert a text box with the Text Box button on the Drawing toolbar. But in a Web page, there is no access to the Drawing toolbar, so you must go about creating your text box in a round-about way. You must create a Word picture that contains text, as shown in the following steps.

Adding a text box to a Web page

1. Choose the **Insert** menu and select **Object**.

2. Select the **Create New** tab.

3. Click **Microsoft Word Picture** under **Object type** (see Figure 13.5).

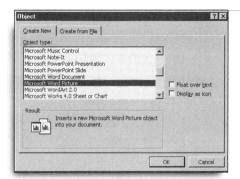

4. Click **Float over text** if you want to put the text box in a
drawing layer. You then can position it in front of or behind
other objects. Clear **Float over text** to place the text box
inline, which means it will behave like regular text.

5. Click **OK**. The Drawing and Edit Picture toolbars then
appear, along with a blank drawing box (see Figure 13.6).
(You can ignore the boundary lines on the page.)

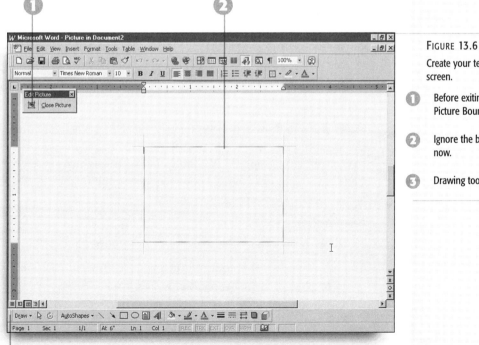

FIGURE **13.6**
Create your text box on this
screen.

1. Before exiting, click this Reset
Picture Boundary button.

2. Ignore the boundary lines for
now.

3. Drawing toolbar

Repositioning the box on the Web page

If you chose Float Over Text when creating the text box object, you can drag the box freely around on the page. If you didn't, it's not too late. Right-click on the box and choose **Picture Object**, **Convert** from the menu that appears. In the dialog box, click on the Float Over Text check box and click **OK**. If you still have trouble positioning it, click the Left Wrapping 📄 or Right Wrapping 📄 button on the floating Picture toolbar (which appears every time you select the object) to change the way text aligns with the object.

Caution: don't use transparency

If you apply transparency to a text box, for example, by selecting the **Semitransparent** check box for the background, the image is not saved correctly when the box is converted to the GIF format. If you want to use an image with a transparent area, create it in Microsoft Photo Editor or another graphics program and then insert it on your Web page as you would any other image (see the section "Using Graphics in Web Pages" later in this chapter).

6. On the Drawing toolbar, click the Text Box button 📄.

7. Drag to create a text box where you want it. The box need not correspond with the boundaries shown onscreen.

8. Click in the new text box and type your text.

9. Edit the appearance of the text as you normally would. Use the tools on the Drawing toolbar to change the box background and other box properties.

SEE ALSO

➤ *To learn how to format text, see page 200.*

➤ *To learn about formatting boxes and other drawn objects with the Drawing toolbar, see page 277.*

10. Click the **Reset Picture Boundary** button on the Edit Picture toolbar (refer to Figure 13.6).

11. Click **Close Picture** on the Edit Picture toolbar. The text box then appears on your Web page (see Figure 13.7). You can drag the text box to reposition it, or drag its handles to resize it.

When you save the page, Word converts the text box into a GIF image, so you cannot edit it in Word again. You can, however, double-click on it to return to the Drawing screen, where you can edit it.

Inserting Lines

Adding lines to your Web page can help you organize your information and make it more visually appealing. These are not the same black horizontal lines that you saw in Chapter 12, "Working with Graphics," when dealing with graphics; these lines are *actually* graphics. Check them out in the following steps.

Inserting lines

1. Click on the page where you want to insert the line.

2. Open the **Insert** menu, and then choose **Horizontal Line**. The **Style** box opens (see Figure 13.8).

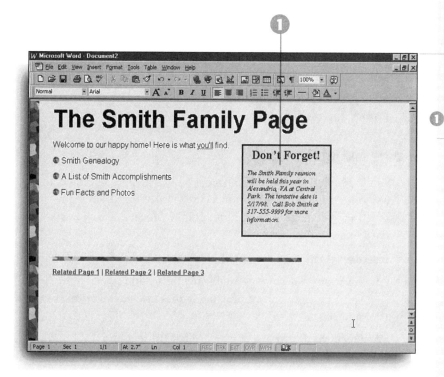

FIGURE 13.7

Your text box is converted to a static GIF image when you save your file.

① Text box

3. Double-click the type of line you want, or click **More** for additional choices.

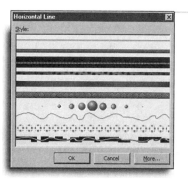

FIGURE 13.8

A line can help you organize the content on your Web page.

The first line in the **Style** box is a plain, generic line that doesn't require any special graphic file to display. The other lines are graphic images, so when you save a page on which they appear, they are saved as GIF files in the same folder. If you move the page to a different location (a Web server, for example), be sure to move the GIF files, too.

After you've inserted one line, you can easily insert another of the same style by clicking the Horizontal Line button [⊟] on Formatting toolbar.

Adding Bullets

Bullets on Web pages and other documents

You can't customize bullets on Web pages as much as you can in other types of documents. For example, you can't change the distance between bullets and text. Also note that the dialog box you use to insert bullets and numbers on a Web page is quite different from the dialog box you use in other documents.

Adding bullets to your Web page is similar to adding bullets to any other type of document in Word. However, when you're creating Web pages, you can use graphic images as well as standard bullet symbols.

Inserting bullets

1. Click on your page to establish an insertion point, or highlight the text in front of where you want the bullet to appear.
2. Open the **Format** menu and select **Bullets and Numbering.**
3. When you see the dialog box shown in Figure 13.9, double-click the type of bullet you want. This bullet is then inserted on your page.
4. If you don't see the type of bullet you want, or if you want to insert your own image file, choose **More.** By default, an image used as a bullet is saved as a GIF file, which is placed in the same folder as your Web page.

If you want to replace a bullet you've already inserted, select it, press the **Delete** key, and insert a new one.

Changing the Appearance of Text

You can't customize the text on your Web page as much as you can in other types of documents, but you can change the color, size, and font.

To change the color of an individual word or phrase, highlight it, click the Font Color drop-down palette button [A▾], and select the color you want to use.

FIGURE 13.9

The Bullets and Numbering dialog box enables you to select bullets supported by HTML. Click **More** to use your own images as bullets.

To change the default colors for all the text and hyperlinks on a page (except for text changed with the Font Color button), choose the **Format** menu, select **Text Colors**, and then select the colors you want in the **Body text color**, **Hyperlink**, and **Followed hyperlink** lists. If you select **Auto** in each list, the text and links appear in the default colors set in the individual Web browsers used to access your page.

To change the font of selected text, highlight it, choose the **Format** menu, **Font,** or right-click the text and select **Font** from the pop-up menu. Make changes in the Font dialog box (see Figure 13.10) as you would any text on a regular page. The dialog box is somewhat simpler than usual but contains all the same controls.

As you can see in Figure 13.10, you can change the size of the text as well as apply special formatting in the Font dialog box. (You also can increase or decrease the text size and apply bold, underline, and italics through buttons on the Formatting toolbar.)

FIGURE 13.10

You don't have as many options for formatting text on a Web page as you do in other types of Word documents.

Some text effects aren't available

When you're creating Web pages, you won't find some of the standard text effects in the Font dialog box (see Figure 13.10). For example, line spacing, margins, character spacing, kerning, text flow settings, and special effects such as emboss, shadow, and engrave aren't available because they aren't supported in the Web's HTML format.

Although you can't change the spacing before and after paragraphs, you can create paragraphs with no space between them by pressing **Ctrl+Enter**.

Tabs aren't available because many Web browsers display them as spaces. If you want to shift the first line of a paragraph to the right, use an indent.

Adding Hyperlinks

Hyperlinks are the primary navigation tools on the Web. You can use them to enable your readers to jump from one of your pages to another, from one section to another on the same page, or from one of your pages to a completely different Web site. You also can turn your email address into a hyperlink so that people can contact you easily. The following sections explain how to add the various types of hyperlinks.

Adding a Hyperlink to Another Page in Your Site

How do hyperlinks work?

Hyperlinks are embedded in an element (usually a word, phrase, or image) of an electronic document. When you click a hyperlink on a Web page, it instructs your browser to retrieve and display a different document or a different section of the same document. You can tell when an object on a Web page is a hyperlink: If you pass your mouse pointer over it, the pointer changes from an arrow to a pointing finger.

With Word, you can use both text and images as hyperlinks. You can link from a word, phrase, or image to another page in your Web site.

One of the first things you may want to do is replace the "dummy" hyperlinks (underlined words) at the bottom of a page created by the wizard with some real links to other Web pages you plan to create for your Web site (see Figure 13.11). (If you don't plan to have more than a single page, you can delete those bits of underlined text altogether.)

Inserting a hyperlink

1. Select the text or image you want to turn into a hyperlink. For example, you might want to start with the dummy hyperlink text on a wizard-created page. (Modify its wording first so it accurately reflects your link.)

2. Open the **Insert** menu and choose **Hyperlink,** or click the Insert Hyperlink button 🖳 on the toolbar.

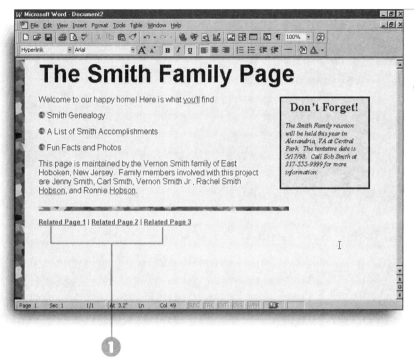

FIGURE 13.11

Replace these dummy links with real hyperlinks to other pages you'll create.

1 Dummy links

3. If you haven't already done so, Word prompts you to save your file. After you do, the Insert Hyperlink dialog box appears (see Figure 13.12). Type a filename and path in the **Link to file or URL** box, or click the **Browse** button and select the file you want to link.

4. Make sure that the **Use relative path for hyperlink** box is checked. Using a *relative path* ensures that the hyperlink won't be broken when you publish your pages by moving them to a Web server. A path relative to the new location of the pages will determine the link.

5. Click **OK**.

To display the destination of a hyperlink you've inserted, rest your mouse pointer over it.

Future links

If you haven't yet created the Web page to which you're going to be linking, use the planned name in step 3. For example, if you plan on creating a page called Genealogy, type **genealogy.htm**. Then make sure that when you create that page, you use the exact name and file location that you specified here.

FIGURE 13.12

You can insert a link to another page you've created, a different section of the same page, or a separate Web site through this dialog box.

Adding a Hyperlink to an External Page

If you're linking from your page to another Web site (as you would in a list of your favorite links), follow the steps in the "Inserting a hyperlink" step by step, with one exception: In step 3, type the address (or *URL*) of the Web page in the **Link to file or URL** box. For example, to link to my Home page, you would type **http://members.iquest.net/~fwempen**.

In step 5, make sure the **Use relative path for hyperlink** box is *not* selected. This means you're using *absolute addressing*, which creates a direct path from your page to a document in a fixed location. The path will not be affected when you publish your page on a Web server.

Besides using the Insert Hyperlink dialog box, you can use Word's automatic formatting feature to create links to other Web sites just by typing URLs on your page.

Autoformatting URLs as hyperlinks

Copying URLs

You can highlight the address of a Web page in Internet Explorer, choose **Edit**, **Copy**, and then switch to word and choose **Edit**, **Paste** to paste its address directly into your Web page.

1. Choose the **Tools** menu and select **AutoCorrect.**
2. Choose the **AutoFormat As You Type** tab.
3. Under **Replace as you type**, make sure the **Internet and network paths with hyperlinks** check box is selected.
4. Click **OK**. Now, when you type an URL and a space after it on your Web page, the URL automatically becomes a hyperlink.

5. If you want a word or phrase to appear on the page instead of the actual URL, just select the URL and type the new text. For example, after the URL **http://members.iquest. net/~fwempen** is blue-underlined, you might select it and type **Faithe Wempen's Home Page**.

If you are typing a document that contains URLs that you don't want to be formatted as real hyperlinks, you can turn off the AutoFormatting (follow the first three steps in the preceding procedure). If it happens only rarely that you don't want hyperlinks, you can just highlight the text and press Ctrl+Z whenever AutoFormatting is applied.

Turning an Email Address into a Hyperlink

When someone visiting your Web page clicks a hyperlinked email address, a message composition screen with the address already inserted in the To: line is created—if the visitor has an email program (also known as an *email client*) installed on his or her system.

You can turn email addresses into hyperlinks just by typing them on your page if Word's automatic formatting feature is active. (To check this, choose **Tools**, **AutoCorrect**, click the **AutoFormat As You Type** tab, and make sure the **Internet and network paths with hyperlinks** check box is active.)

Previewing a Web Page as You Work

If you have a Web browser installed on your system, you can click the Web Page Preview button on the Standard toolbar to see quickly and easily how the page you're working on will look in a Web browser. After you've viewed the page, you can go back to Word either by clicking the program's icon in the taskbar or by closing the browser.

Using Graphics in Web Pages

Get more free images

You can download free images for your Web page from a Microsoft site on the Web. To access it, choose the **Insert** menu, select **Picture**, and click **Browse Web Art Page**. You can also access the page through your Web browser with the URL http://www. microsoft.com/word/ artresources.htm. When you connect with the Web site, follow the instructions to find and download the images you want.

On your Web page, Word enables you to add images in many different file formats (TIF, for example), but they are converted to the GIF format when you save the page. The only type of image that isn't converted is a JPEG file, which remains in that format. (JPEG and GIF are the two image types supported on the Web.)

Inserting images

1. Click the page to establish an insertion point.

2. Choose the **Insert** menu, select **Picture**, and select the appropriate image source (see Figure 13.13).

3. The associated dialog box opens for the image source you selected. If you chose **Clip Art**, for example, the Microsoft Clip Gallery opens. Choose and insert the image you want in the dialog box as you normally would in a document.

SEE ALSO

➤ *To find more information about graphics in Word, see page 267.*

FIGURE 13.13

Choose the image source in the **Picture** submenu.

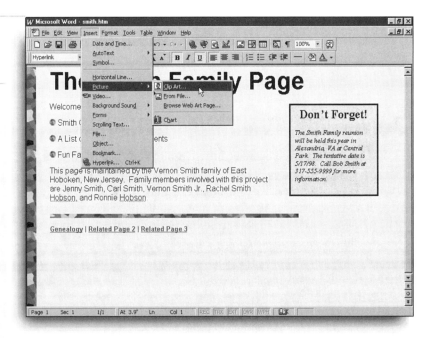

When you insert a graphic on a Web page, it is aligned by default with the left margin. If you need to resize or reposition the image, select it and drag it, or drag the resize handles.

As you drag, the surrounding text and objects move to accommodate the image, but by default, text doesn't flow around it. You can control how the picture interacts with text by clicking the Left Wrapping 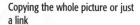 or Right Wrapping buttons on the Picture toolbar. Or, you can open the **Format** menu, select **Picture**, and use the positioning controls there, as shown in Figure 13.14.

Copying the whole picture or just a link

When you save your Web page, Word automatically copies the image into the same folder as the page. If you insert a graphic from a file (rather than clip art) and you want to link to an image at a fixed location, such as another Web server, click **Link to file** in the Insert Picture dialog box.

FIGURE 13.14

Use the Picture dialog box to determine how text flows around an image.

Publishing to a Web Server

To publish your pages to the Internet, you copy them to a server. The *server* is a computer that's connected to the Internet full-time. It's usually owned by the company where you get your Internet service (your ISP or an online service such as America Online). The monthly fee you pay for your Internet connection (in most cases) also entitles you to a small amount of space on their server to publish your own Web pages. All you need to know is the address of the server and the directory on it where you should copy your files.

Determining Your Save Location

Before you can publish your pages to the Internet, you need to contact your service provider and find out where on their server you need to put your pages. (If you are using an online service

Use images as hyperlinks

To turn an image into a hyperlink, select the image, choose the **Insert** menu, and select **Hyperlink,** or click the Hyperlink button on the Standard toolbar. Then enter the appropriate inform-ation in the Insert Hyperlink dialog box (see the section "Adding Hyperlinks" earlier in this chapter). On your Web page, you may want to add some explanatory text (`click here`, for example) in front of the image so that your readers know it is a hyperlink.

such as America Online, there is information available in the online help about it.) For example, your service provider might give you a path like this one:

ftp.*servername***.com/pub/web/homepage/members/***yourname*

This is the physical location on the server where you will send your files via File Transfer Protocol (FTP). FTP is an alternate way of transmitting information on the Internet and is used for file transfers from computer to computer. This is *not* the address you will give to other people who want to access your page, however. The Web address to your page will likely be much simpler, like this one:

http://www.*servername***.com/~***yourname*

These addresses are just made-up examples; your service provider must tell you what real addresses to use.

Installing the Web Publishing Wizard

Your Microsoft Home Essentials CD comes with a program called Web Publishing Wizard that can transfer both HTML files and graphic files to a server. It's the MSWord/ValuPack/ WebPost folder on CD #1. You can install it from there, or you can download a more recent version from Microsoft's Web site. I recommend the latter, even though it's more trouble, because it's a better program. But here are the steps for both.

Installing the CD version of Web Publishing Wizard

1. Use Windows Explorer to open the contents of the CD, and navigate to the MSWord/ValuPack folder.

2. Double-click the **WebPost** folder.

3. Double-click the **WebPost.exe** file to run the installation program.

4. Follow the onscreen prompts to install.

5. Restart your computer before you attempt to use the Web Publishing Wizard.

Downloading and installing a newer Web Publishing Wizard

1. Start your Internet connection if it is not already running, and open Internet Explorer.

SEE ALSO

➤ *To learn how to use Internet Explorer, see page 399.*

2. Go to the following site:

http://www.microsoft.com/windows/software/webpost/

3. Follow the downloading instructions and download the file to a temporary folder on your computer.
(C:\Windows\Temp will do.)

4. Navigate to the new file on your hard disk using Windows Explorer, and double-click on it to install the program.

5. Follow the onscreen prompts to install.

6. Restart your computer before you attempt to use the Web Publishing Wizard.

Using the Web Publishing Wizard

To start the Web Publishing Wizard, open the **Start** menu and choose **Programs**, **Accessories**, **Internet Tools**, **Web Publishing Wizard**. I won't give you specific steps for this because the steps are different depending on which version of the wizard you are using. The dialog boxes that appear are very clear in their instructions, though; you shouldn't have any problems.

You will upload either a single file or a single folder at a time. That means that you will have to run the wizard many times if you have many files to upload. The shortcut, of course, is to create a separate folder on your hard disk and put all the files into it that you want to upload. Then just run the wizard once and upload that one folder.

If you have any problem getting your pages on the Web, you can contact your Internet service provider for help.

PART

III

Using Money

Setting Up Your Money Accounts

What Is Money?

Different versions of Money

The basic version of Money comes with Home Essentials, but a more powerful version called the Microsoft Money 98 Financial Suite is also sold in stores. It contains some special features such as enhanced planning and budgeting tools and more sophisticated investment tracking.

Everyone knows what money is, of course, but how about *Microsoft Money*, the program? Microsoft Money is a financial management tool designed for home users. It can help you keep your checking account balanced, remind you to pay your bills, check the current stock prices, and more. Money is also tightly integrated with the *Internet*, so you can have the most recent financial information available to you at all times.

Starting Money

If you haven't installed Money yet, do so now. After it's installed, you're ready to roll.

Starting Money 98

1. Click the **Start** button, opening the **Start** menu.

2. Point to **Programs**. A submenu appears.

3. Click **Microsoft Money** and the program starts.

CD Required

You must have the Home Essentials Disc #1 in the Drive to view the Money 98 tutorial.

If you still have the Home Essentials CD in your CD-ROM drive the first time you start Money, a big red Tour window opens, as shown in Figure 14.1. (If you don't see it, reinsert Disc #1 of the Home Essentials CD set and then open the **Help** menu and choose **Product Tour**.) From here, you can run a quick tutorial that shows you how the program works. If you have the time and want to complete the tour, go ahead and click the appropriate button for your situation—**Tour for New Users**, **Tour for Money Upgraders**, or **Tour for Quicken Users**. When you're finished with the tour, click the **Use Money** button in the tour window to close it. You can view the tour again at any time by opening the **Help** menu and choosing **Product Tour**.

SEE ALSO

➤ *To install Money, see page 523.*

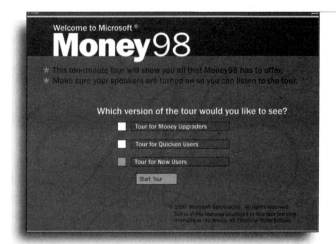

Exiting Money

If you need to leave Money for any reason, you can easily close the program and reopen it again later. Any changes you make to your accounts are automatically saved, so you don't have to worry about saving your work.

When you exit Money, you are asked whether you want to *back up* your file. Backing up is different from saving. Backing up creates or updates a spare copy of your data file, in case something happens to the original. For maximum data safety, you may want to set the *path* (in step 2 of the following steps) to a drive other than your hard disk, such as A:\.

Exiting Money

1. Open the **File** menu and choose **Exit,** or press **Alt+F4.** If you've left the default settings to **Backup on Exit**, a box appears asking whether you want to back up your data file, as shown in Figure 14.2.

2. Confirm that the path listed in the **Back up file to** text box is the correct path. (If in doubt, leave it as-is.)

3. Click the **Back Up** button. Your file is backed up and Money exits.

Setting backup preferences

If you don't want to back up your data file each time you exit from Money, and you want to skip the dialog box asking you about it, open the **Tools** menu and choose **Options**. Click the **General** tab if it's not already on top. Then open the drop-down list in the **Backup** section and change the setting to **Do Not Back Up**. You can also have your Money file backed up automatically without the dialog box displaying each time by setting that same drop-down list to **Back Up Without Reminding Me**.

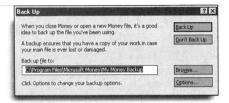

FIGURE 14.2

Money asks whether you want to back up each time you exit the program.

A Look at the Money Interface

When the tour window closes, you see the main Money window, shown in Figure 14.3. This window has two main parts: The top of the screen contains controls you can use to navigate the program; the large white area below those controls contains an assortment of tips, articles, and charts that change depending on the accounts and goals you enter.

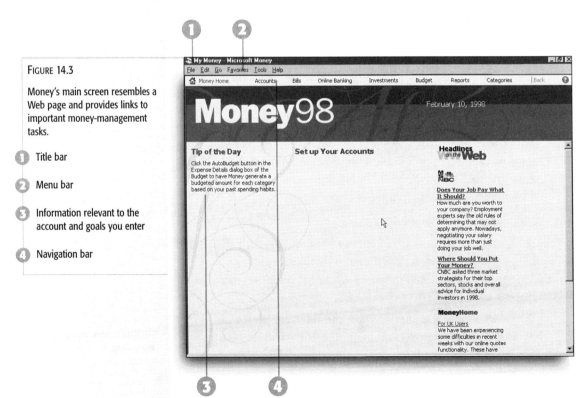

FIGURE 14.3

Money's main screen resembles a Web page and provides links to important money-management tasks.

1 Title bar

2 Menu bar

3 Information relevant to the account and goals you enter

4 Navigation bar

We'll look at the planning advice and charts later, but for now let's focus on the onscreen controls:

- *Menu bar.* Click a menu name to open a menu, then click the command you want to issue, just like in any other Windows-based program.

- *Navigation bar.* Below the menu bar are words representing the various parts of the Money program, like Accounts, Bills, and Online Banking. You can click any of these to jump quickly to the corresponding part of the program.

Notice in Figure 14.3 that one piece of advice appears in the middle of the page—**Set Up Your Accounts**. (You may have a second link here, **Take a Tour**, depending on whether you have the Home Essentials CD #1 still on your CD-ROM drive.) You can't do anything else until you have set up at least one bank account, so let's look at how to do that next.

Understanding Accounts and Data Files

First, let's talk about what we mean when we say "accounts." An *account* in Money is equivalent to an account at your bank or with your investment broker. One person might have many accounts (for example, a checking account, a savings account, several credit card accounts, an auto loan account, and so on).

All your accounts are tracked in a single data file in Money. The default data file, which is created when you install Money, is called My Money. You can tell that it's active because its name appears in the title bar: My Money – Microsoft Money. For most people, this one data file is sufficient. It's a good idea to keep all your accounts in a single data file so Money can report on all of them as a unified whole. For example, when computing your net worth, Money needs access to all your account balances to produce an accurate figure. Do not create a different data file for each of your bank accounts.

Why use more than one data file?

You might use a second data file in special cases, for example, if you need to keep the finances for two people, or for a family and a business, completely separate. For example, if two unrelated people share a computer, each could have their own Money data file. To create another data file, open the **File** menu and choose **New** (Ctrl+N) and follow the prompts. Then switch among available data files by opening the **File** menu and choosing **Open** (Ctrl+O).

Creating Accounts

Money offers many different account types, and the choices can be overwhelming to a beginner. By far the most common account types are Checking and Savings, but everyone's situation is different. You may find a use for at least one of the other account types, listed in Table 14.1.

TABLE 14.1   **Account types used in Money**

Account Type	Used For
Assets	Valuable things you own, such as an art collection.
Bank	A generic type of bank account to cover any account that does not fall under Checking, Savings, or Line of Credit.
Cash	Day-to-day money that is not associated with any financial institution (for example, the money you carry around in your wallet).
Checking	A checking account through a bank or other financial institution.
Credit Card	Any credit card you use. (It need not be associated with one of your other bank accounts.)
House	The equity you have in your home, and any changes in its market value.
Investment	Stocks, bonds, and mutual funds. Create one investment account for each brokerage statement you receive.
Liability	Money you owe that you don't pay interest on (for instance, money borrowed from a friend, short-term debt, taxes to be paid).
Line of Credit	Charge cards that directly debit (deduct from) an account.
Loan	Amortized loans, such as a car or house loan.
Other	Other expenses that do not fall into any other category.
Retirement	Any tax-deferred retirement plans such as IRA, SEP-IRA, 401(k), and so on.
Savings	Savings accounts (usually interest-earning). You can also keep track of checks and ATM transactions from such an account if you have those privileges.

Setting Up an Account

The procedure for setting up an account is basically the same for all account types. The details vary a little, and we'll look at those variations later in this chapter, but first let's take a look at account creation in general. We'll practice by setting up your checking or savings account, because almost everyone has one of those.

Other ways to display the Account Manager screen

You can press Ctrl+Shift+A or open the **Go** menu and choose **Accounts**.

Before you set up an account, you should locate the pertinent financial records for it (your checkbook or passbook and/or a recent statement). These records will provide the numbers that you will need to enter into the program.

Setting up a checking or savings account

1. Click the **Accounts** link on the Navigation bar. The Account Manager screen appears.
2. Click the **New Account** button at the bottom of the screen. A New Account dialog box appears (see Figure 14.4).

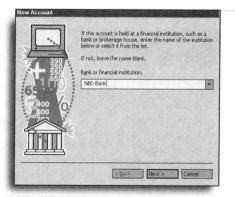

FIGURE 14.4

Start by identifying the bank or other financial institution that the account is with.

3. Type the bank's name in the **Bank or financial institution** text box, and then click **Next**. (This text box also has a drop-down list that you can choose already-used bank names from, but because this is your first account, you don't have anything on that list yet.)
4. The next box shows the list of account types from Table 14.1. Click **Checking** or **Savings** as appropriate, and then click **Next**.

5. Next you're asked what you want to call this account. Type a "friendly" name that you will remember, such as **Faithe's Checking**, but make sure the name is unique enough that you won't confuse it with any of your other accounts. Then click **Next**.

6. Money then asks the purpose of the account, as shown in Figure 14.5. Click the button next to the appropriate purpose (for example, **Spending Money** for a checking account or **Short-term Savings and Rainy-Day Fund** for a savings account), and click **Next**.

FIGURE 14.5

Identify the account's purpose, so Money can help you manage it later.

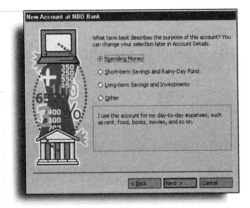

Opening balance

The figure for the *opening balance* can come either from your last bank statement or from your checkbook. If you enter it from your bank statement, it might be more accurate, but you will have to enter all the checks you have written since that statement. (Actually, that's not a bad thing to do, because then they will be recorded in Money when it's time to balance with the next statement.)

Other accounts?

Even if you do have other accounts at this same bank, you can answer **No** to the question in step 9 if you don't want to set up those other accounts right now.

7. When prompted for the account number, enter it. It should be at the bottom of your checks. If you don't have it, don't worry—just leave it blank for now. Click **Next** when finished.

8. In the **What is the balance for this account** text box, fill in your current account balance. Then click **Next**.

9. Money asks whether you have other accounts with this same bank. Click the appropriate option button, and then click **Next**.

10. Click **Finish**. You're done! You're ready to use the account to enter transactions.

SEE ALSO

➤ *To enter transactions in an account, see page 330.*

Setting Up a Credit Card Account

Credit card accounts are a little more trouble to set up than regular bank accounts because they charge you interest and may have regular payments associated with them. To set one up, locate your account number and your last statement so you'll know the amount of any outstanding balance.

When you choose **Credit Card** as the account type, you're asked some special questions in addition to those you saw with your checking or savings account. They include

- How much you owe on the credit card.
- Whether the card is a credit card or a charge card. A lot of people use these terms interchangeably, but a credit card is one where you don't have to pay the entire balance off each month (like a VISA), and a charge card is one that is due in full each month (like American Express).
- Whether you always pay the entire balance each month (if it's a credit card where you're not *required* to do so).
- The interest rate you pay on your outstanding balance.
- If an introductory interest rate is in effect, what it is, and how long it is in effect (see Figure 14.6).
- The credit limit on the card.

Introductory interest rate?

If you get an introductory interest rate that later becomes higher, you can click the **An introductory interest rate is in effect** check box and enter that information, and Money will automatically start calculating the interest at the different rate on the specified day.

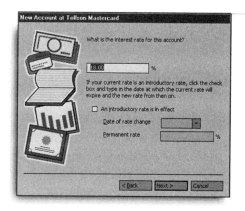

FIGURE 14.6

Enter the interest rate, and if applicable, indicate any special limited-time rate in effect.

- Whether you want Money to auto-balance the account for you each month. Your choices are

  Keep track of individual credit card charges. If you choose this option, Money will wait for you to balance the account each month, reconciling your paper copies against the statement.

  I will not keep track of individual credit card charges. By choosing this, you give Money permission to auto-balance the account each month, saving you time. Choose this if you do not plan to enter each charge into Money prior to the monthly statement arriving.

- Whether you want the monthly payment to be included in your list of recurring payments, so Money reminds you when the bill is due (see Figure 14.7).

FIGURE 14.7

Money can help you remember to pay your credit card bill each month.

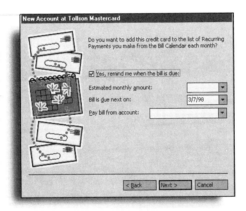

After filling in all the appropriate information, when asked if you have other accounts at this bank, click **No** and then click **Finish** to end the procedure.

After you set up your credit card account, turn to Chapter 15, "Managing Bank Accounts and Loans" to learn how to enter transactions into the account. You will want to record each item you charge and each payment you make, and then "balance" the account against your monthly credit card statement, just like a regular bank account.

SEE ALSO

➤ *To enter transactions into an account, see page 330.*

➤ *To balance an account, see page 348.*

Setting Up an Investment Account

If you have investments such as stocks, mutual funds, CDs, and so on, you will track them with one or more investment accounts. Here's an important point to remember: You should *not* set up a separate account for each individual stock you own. Instead, you should set up an investment account for each statement you receive.

For example, let's say I have three stock portfolios: a portfolio of individual stocks that I trade through DLJ Direct (an online brokerage), a non-retirement portfolio of mutual funds through Scudder, and a mutual fund SEP-IRA through Scudder. I receive three statements each month: one from DLJ and two from Scudder. Therefore, I would set up three separate accounts in Money. I would then enter transactions in the appropriate accounts to describe the contents of each portfolio.

In this chapter, I'll show you how to set up each of your accounts, but they will be empty shells until you add your stock, bond, and mutual fund portfolio to them.

When setting up an investment account, you have a choice of account types—investment and retirement.

An *investment account* generically handles both regular and tax-deferred investment accounts. Use this for non-retirement accounts, regardless of the account's tax status. When setting up an account of the Investment type, you are asked about the current estimated balances, and you can choose whether the account is tax-deferred and whether you have an associated cash account.

The *retirement account* type is especially for accounts that you will not be withdrawing from until you reach retirement age. For this account type, it is automatically designated tax-deferred, and an associated cash account is automatically created.

When entering an investment or retirement account, you need to decide how far back you want to go with it. Do you want to enter every buy and sell since you opened the account 10 years ago? Or would you rather enter your current holdings as of

Investment taxability

A tax-deferred account allows money to grow interest-free in the account until you withdraw it. For example, dividends on the stock might be used to purchase more stock, and you don't have to report the dividends as income on your taxes.

A tax-deductible account (usually a retirement account) allows you to deduct your contribution from your income on your taxes. For example, if you made $30,000 this year, and contributed $2,000 to your IRA, your adjusted income would be $28,000. Tax-deductible accounts are almost always tax-deferred, too.

today and go from there? It's your choice. Whatever starting date you choose, you will have to enter all the transactions between then and now.

Setting up an investment account

1. Click the **Accounts** link on the Navigation bar. The Account Manager screen appears.

2. Click the **New Account** button at the bottom of the screen. A New Account dialog box appears.

3. Type the bank or brokerage name in the **Bank or financial institution** text box, and then click **Next**.

4. The next box shows the list of account types from Table 14.1. Click **Investment,** and then click **Next**.

5. Next you're asked what you want to call this account. Type a "friendly" name that you will remember, such as **Fidelity Mutual Funds**. Then click **Next**.

6. Next you're asked whether the investments are tax-deferred or not. Click **No** or **Yes** as appropriate, and then click **Next**.

7. If you want to, enter the estimated value of the securities in the account (do not include any uninvested cash) as shown in Figure 14.8. You can just leave this blank for a zero balance if you want, and enter each of your securities later.

FIGURE 14.8

Enter the opening value of your holdings.

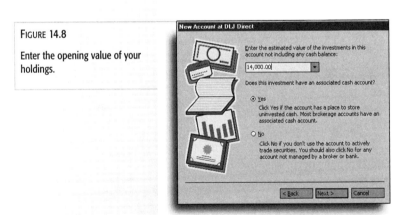

8. Under the question **Does this investment have an associated cash account?**, click **Yes** or **No** as appropriate. Then click **Next**.

9. If you chose **Yes** in step 8, an extra screen appears where you can enter the cash in the account. Enter it (in dollars) and then click **Next**.

10. Now you need to categorize the account, as you have done with other accounts. This one is probably Long-Term Savings and Investments, the option already selected for you. Click **Next**.

11. An explanation appears for the way the transactions should be entered for the account. Read it, and then click **Next**.

12. Money asks whether you have other accounts with this same bank or not. Click the appropriate option button, and then click **Next**. You're done!

When you're finished setting up your investment accounts, you'll want to add your stocks and other holdings by entering Buy and Sell transactions. See Chapter 16 to learn how to do so.

SEE ALSO

➤ To add your holdings to the account, see page 362.

➤ To enter stock sales, see page 369.

➤ To learn how to enter individual stocks and other investments into a portfolio, see page 362.

➤ To learn how to enter investment transactions, see page 362.

Setting Up a Loan

If you have ever applied for a mortgage, you know that it feels like the application is asking for your whole life story. There are so many questions! Money asks a ton of questions when you set up a loan, too, but there's a good reason. The more information you can provide about the loan, the better Money can help you manage it. Money can provide updated *amortization charts* that show you how many payments you have left at any given moment, tell you how much you've paid in interest on the loan this year (useful for tax time), and more.

You can set up to either borrow or lend money using the same account type—Loan. Because borrowing is more common than lending (unfortunately), let's look at how borrowing works. I'll use a home mortgage as an example here, because many of us are making monthly payments toward that "American dream."

Setting up a loan

1. If you aren't already at the Account Manager screen, click the **Accounts** link on the Navigation bar or press Ctrl+Shift+A. The Account Manager screen appears.

2. Click the **New Account** button at the bottom of the screen. A New Account dialog box appears.

3. Type the financial institution or individual that is loaning you money, and then click **Next**.

4. On the list of account types, click **Loan**. Then click **Next**.

5. Read the information that appears detailing this specific wizard, and then click **Next**. Then read some more information detailing the collection of general data, and click **Next** again.

6. Click **Borrowing Money** and then click **Next**. (If you are lending, the steps are only a little bit different from what's described here.)

7. In the **Loan Name** field, fill in a friendly name that you will easily associate with this loan, such as **Home Mortgage**.

8. In the **Make Payments To** field, enter the name you will write on the check each month. This may or may not be the same as what you entered in step 3. Click **Next** when finished.

9. Click the appropriate button to describe your interest rate— **Adjustable Rate Loan (ARM)** or **Fixed Rate Loan**. Then click **Next**.

10. The next several screens vary depending on your answer in step 9. Fill in the information as prompted regarding the loan terms and whether payments have been made. Click **Next** to move to the next screens until you get to the three-item list shown in Figure 14.9, with the second line (**Calculate Loan**) in bold lettering.

Payee already entered?

If you have already written a check to this payee (as explained in Chapter 15), you can open the drop-down list in step 8 and choose the payee from the list rather than typing the name from scratch. This is helpful if you know you have already made and recorded payments, but you don't remember the exact wording of the payee name.

FIGURE 14.9

Both ARM and Fixed Rate loans end up at this screen after you enter the details about them.

11. Click **Next** to continue.

12. Open the **Paid How Often** drop-down list and choose the payment frequen. (**Monthly** is most common.) Then click **Next**.

13. Next, you're asked how interest is calculated on the loan. Click the option button corresponding to the method (**Based on the date payment is due** is the most common), and click **Next**.

14. The next few fields work as a group: **Loan amount**, **Interest rate**, **Loan length**, **Principal + interest**, and **Balloon amount**. You can leave any one of these blank and Money will calculate it for you. On this first screen of the set, enter the loan amount in the **Loan amount** text box, as shown in Figure 14.10, or leave it blank if that's the one you want to calculate. Click **Next** to continue.

15. On each of the next screens, enter the value as prompted, skipping the one (if any) that you want Money to calculate. When all information is entered, Money calculates the field you left blank, and presents the calculation in a dialog box, as shown in Figure 14.11. Click **OK** to accept the calculated amount.

16. Click **Next** to continue. The three-item list reappears, this time with **Manage Payments** highlighted. Click **Next** again to move on.

Taxes and insurance are extra

When entering the **Principal + interest**, do not include any taxes and insurance that are included with your payment. You will have the opportunity to enter these amounts later in the setup procedure.

FIGURE 14.10

Enter the loan amount, and then click **Next** to enter the value for the next line.

FIGURE 14.11

Money has calculated the loan amount based on all the other values entered.

17. Choose the financial category and subcategory for the money spent on interest from the **Interest Category** and **Interest Subcategory** drop-down lists. (We'll talk more about categories in Chapter 15.) For example, for a mortgage you might use **Bills** as the category and **Mortgage Interest** as the subcategory, as shown in Figure 14.12.

18. To the question Is this a house mortgage?, click **Yes** or **No**.

19. To the question Is the interest on this loan tax-deductible? click **Yes** or **No**. Generally, interest on your primary home is deductible. Click **Next** to continue.

20. Next you're asked about the extra amounts that go into your loan payment. Click the **Other Fees** button to display the Other Fees dialog box, shown in Figure 14.13.

FIGURE 14.12

Tell Money how to categorize the monthly expense for the loan interest.

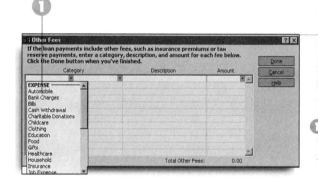

FIGURE 14.13

Choose the appropriate categories and enter descriptions for the other fees that you pay into your mortgage or other loan account.

1 This drop-down list opens automatically.

21. Choose the appropriate category and subcategory for your first line (for example, for homeowner's insurance, choose **Insurance** for the category and **Homeowner's/Renter's** for the subcategory).

22. Type a description in the **Description** field and an amount in the **Amount** field.

23. Repeat steps 21 and 22 for each additional amount that you pay in your loan payment (for example, other insurance payments or property taxes). Click **Done** when finished.

24. Click **Next** to go on to the scheduled payments screen.

25. If you want Money to remind you to make the payment each month, leave the **Yes** option button selected. Then enter the next due date and choose which account to pay from. Or, if you prefer, click the **No** option button to not be reminded. Click **Next** when finished.

26. Check out the summary of the loan that appears (see Figure 14.14) and then click **Next**.

FIGURE 14.14

Money displays all the information you entered about the loan.

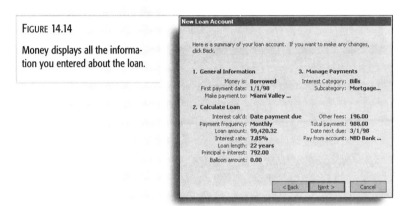

27. Next Money asks if there is an asset to be associated with the loan. For example, if your loan is a home mortgage, you might associate your house as an asset with the loan. If the loan is paying for a valuable asset (like a home or boat), choose **Yes**. Then click **Next**.

28. If you answered **Yes** in step 27, you're asked which asset to associate the loan with. Choose it from the drop-down list, or if you don't already have an asset account set up for the item, type a new name in the box (for example, the house's street address or the name of your boat). Then click **Finish**.

29. If the asset didn't exist already, additional boxes appear asking for details about the new asset account. Fill in the blanks as prompted.

30. When Money asks if you have other accounts with this institution, click **No**, and then click **Finish** to end the setup.

Why associate assets?

The value of your home is not necessarily just the amount you have paid on your mortgage loan. Home improvements you make can increase the value of the asset, as can changes in property values in your area. That's why it's useful to set up an asset account to track your home value.

After setting up a new loan, you need to enter any payments you have made on the loan since its inception (or since the beginning of the year if you chose not to set up old payments from prior years).

SEE ALSO

➤ *To learn how to enter loan payment transactions, see page 330.*

Setting Up Other Account Types

By now you can see that all account setups are basically the same, with a few variations specific to the account type. Just start a new account with the **New Account** button on the Account Manager screen, and follow the prompts presented to you.

Managing Bank Accounts and Loans

Enter checks and deposits

Enter ATM transactions

Find and edit transactions

Split a transaction among categories

Balance an account with a statement

Change account details

Track bills to be paid

Understanding the Account Register

In Money, *transactions* are entered into account registers, and a *register* (a "page") exists for each account you created in Chapter 14, "Setting Up Your Money Accounts." When entering a transaction, you have to make sure you put it into the right register.

You can get to an account register in two ways. You can go to the Account Manager, as you learned in Chapter 14 by pressing Ctrl+Shift+A or opening the **Go** menu and choosing **Accounts**. Then when all the icons for the accounts appear, double-click the icon for the account register you want to see.

Another way to go to an account register is to click the arrow button on the Home screen next to the account name, as shown in Figure 15.1. This is a quicker method that most people prefer, but you can use it only from the Home screen. (The former method works from anywhere.)

FIGURE 15.1

Your accounts appear on the Home page for easy selection.

❶ Click the arrow next to the account name.

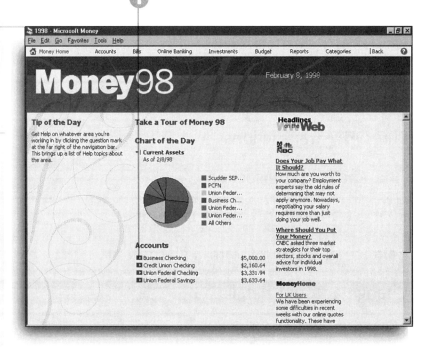

Account registers vary slightly by account type, but they all have lines for transactions and a running total. Figure 15.2 shows an empty checking account register, ready for transactions to be entered.

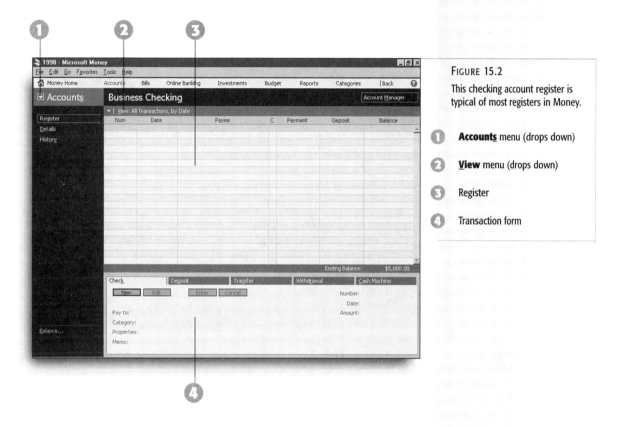

FIGURE 15.2

This checking account register is typical of most registers in Money.

1. **Accounts** menu (drops down)

2. **View** menu (drops down)

3. Register

4. Transaction form

Let's review the controls in the register before going on:

- *Accounts list.* **Accounts** opens into a drop-down list when you click it, so you can switch to a different account's register quickly. You can also click the name of the current account (Business Checking in Figure 15.1) to see the exact same list.

- *Register, Details, and History.* These words are actually buttons that you can click to change the view of the register. **Register**, obviously, shows the register. **Details** shows the account number, bank address, opening balance, and other pertinent facts. **History** shows a running balance since you opened the account.

- *Balance*. This button opens a wizard that helps you reconcile your account with your bank statement.

- *Account **Manager***. This button takes you back to the Account Manager screen.

- *View menu*. This menu and the name of the current view (**All Transactions, By Date**, shown earlier in Figure 15.1) are shown in the thin blue bar just above the transaction register. Click here to open the **View** menu, and choose which transactions are displayed and in what order.

- *The register*. These are the columns into which you enter the transaction information. They include **Num, Date, Payee**, and so on.

- *Transaction form*. The forms at the bottom of the register enable you to enter the transaction information in a more natural, friendlier format, as you'll see shortly. Tabs appear for each of the major transaction types: **Check, Deposit, Transfer**, and so on.

SEE ALSO

➤ *For more information on the Account Manager, see page 311.*

➤ *Learn how to balance an account, see page 348.*

➤ *For more about the choices in the **View** menu, see page 346.*

Entering Transactions

In Chapter 14, you created the empty "shells" for each account, and entered opening balances for each. Now you must enter all the transactions that have happened since that opening balance point. For example, if you entered the opening balance for your checking account as the balance from your last bank statement, you now need to enter all the checks you've written and deposits you've made since that time. So dig out your checkbook and any bank deposit receipts, and let's get started.

Toggle forms on/off

You can turn the display of transaction forms on or off with the **Transaction Forms** command on the **View** menu. You might, for example, turn off the forms so you could see more lines of the register onscreen at once.

Entering a transaction is basically the same in all account types, although the individual *fields* may change somewhat. For example, when entering checks, you're asked for a check number, but when entering investments you're asked for stock symbols and *commission fees*. If you just read carefully and enter what's requested, you should be fine.

Entering a check

1. Display the register for the checking account into which you want to record the check.

2. Click the **New** button on the **Check** tab in the transaction forms area. Fields appear so you can enter the check information, as shown in Figure 15.3. The cursor flashes in the **Number** field.

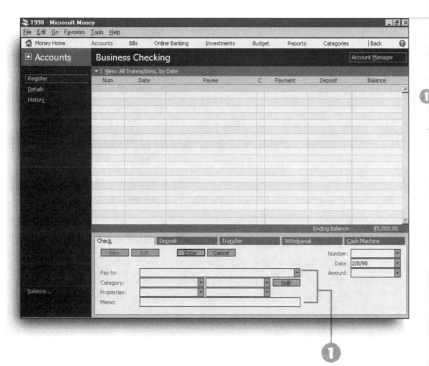

FIGURE 15.3

Money prompts you for the pertinent details about the check.

① Enter check information in the **Check** tab fields.

3. Do one of the following:

- If you are writing (or have already written) the check by hand, enter the check number. After you enter a check number, Money will increment that number for the next check you write. For example, if you enter 100 for this check, the next check you write will have 101 pre-entered in the **Number** field.

- If you plan on printing a check on your computer (using special check paper you have bought), open the drop-down list in the **Number** field and choose **Print this transaction**.

- If you plan to send the check using online bill paying, choose *Electronic Payment (E-Pay)*.

- If the check is an electronic transfer from one bank account to another, choose *Electronic Transfer (Xfer)*.

4. Today's date appears in the **Date** field. Change this value if needed (for example, if the check was written several days ago and you are catching up your Money register).

5. Click in the **Pay To** field and type the payee. If you've written a check to the payee before, Money auto-completes the name for you after you type the first few characters; if this happens just press Enter to accept it. If Money makes the wrong assumption about the payee, continue typing to enter the correct name. You can also choose payees from the drop-down list in this field.

6. Enter the check amount in the **Amount** field.

7. (Optional) Choose a *category* (and a *subcategory* if appropriate) from the **Category** drop-down lists. See the following section in this chapter for more information about categories.

8. (Optional) If you use *properties* (which are basically additional ways to categorize things), choose the properties from the **Properties** drop-down lists. Properties are also explained in the following section.

Moving around

As in any register, to move from field to field you can either press Tab or click in the field where you want the cursor to go. By default, pressing Enter completes the transaction. However, some people like to use the Enter key to move between fields instead of Tab. Such folks must set up Money to work that way. Open the **Tools** menu, choose **Options**, click the **Editing** tab, and then place a check mark in the **Use Enter Key to Move Between Fields** check box.

Pop-up calculator

Most down-arrows next to fields open drop-down lists, but the one next to the **Amount** field opens a calculator that you can use by clicking its buttons.

9. (Optional) Enter any notes to yourself in the **Memo** field (use this field as you do the Memo line on hand-written checks).

10. When you're finished with the transaction, press Enter to complete it.

Entering other types of transactions is similar to entering a check. Just click the appropriate tab for the form you need, and fill in the blanks:

- *Deposit*. Use this for all deposits into the account (except transfers from other accounts). The fields are basically the same as for a check.

- *Transfer*. This form has an additional field so you can indicate which account the money is coming from and which it is going to. Such a transaction makes entries in both registers automatically. You can initiate a transfer from whichever register is more convenient—the one gaining the money or the one giving it.

- *Withdrawal*. The fields are identical to those for a check. You might use this if you were withdrawing money directly from your account (for example, with a withdrawal slip at the teller window) instead of by writing a check.

- *Cash Machine*. This form omits the **Pay To** field because you are paying yourself. Otherwise it's the same as for a check. The category is automatically set to **Cash Withdrawal** for you, although you can change it easily if you want.

You may occasionally run into a situation where the correct transaction type is not apparent. For example, if you're making a payment on a loan, would that be a check (because you're writing a check) or a transfer (because you're moving money from one account to another)? Technically, it's both. You would enter it as a check, and then specify the loan account as the payee. The payment would then be added to the loan account's register.

Ending a transaction

If you have enabled the Enter key to move you between fields, as explained earlier, you can end the transaction by clicking the **Enter** button on the transaction form. If you don't do that, you must press Enter repeatedly until you have moved through the last field (**Memo**) to end the transaction.

ATM deposits

If you deposit money at a cash machine, it's considered a Deposit. The Cash Machine transaction type is only for cash machine withdrawals.

Categorizing Transactions

When you set up your Money account, it created a few categories automatically which are ready for your use. As you're entering a transaction, you can skip over the **Category** line completely, or you can open the drop-down list and choose one. You can also type a new category on-the-fly.

You can set up categories in a couple of ways. One is to do it on-the-fly as you enter transactions. I like this method because it ensures that you only create the categories you'll really use.

Other people may prefer to set up all their categories and subcategories before they enter transactions (or before they enter any more). With this method, you can carefully plan your categories by looking at the complete list of existing ones and filling in the gaps for your own situation. This method also enables you to enter more detailed tax and description information about a category than the quicker on-the-fly method allows.

Creating categories on-the-fly

1. Open the account register and begin a new transaction. Enter the payee, check number, date, and amount.

2. Move the cursor to the first **Category** field and type the name for the new category. Then press Tab to move to the next field. Before the cursor moves to the next field, a New Category dialog box appears.

3. Make sure the appropriate button is selected (**Income** or **Expense**) and that the name is spelled correctly in the **Name** field, and then click **Next**.

4. Next you're asked to map the new category to one of the preexisting tax and report *concepts*, as shown in Figure 15.4. Choose the item on the list that fits most closely, and then click **Finish**.

What are categories?

Categories are used to classify your income and expenses, so you can create reports and charts later that show how you are spending and receiving money. For instance, if you categorize each check you write to the grocery store as Groceries, you will be able to create a report that shows how much money you spend per month on groceries. *Subcategories* are further breakdowns of categories. For instance, if Food is the category, you might have Groceries and Dining Out as two subcategories. Categories are optional; you don't have to use them. However, many of Money's powerful features, like reports, can't be used unless you use categories.

Be descriptive

When inventing names for your categories, be as descriptive as possible. The more precisely you categorize your transactions, the more useful your reports and charts will be. For instance, "Pay" is not the greatest category name, especially if you have more than one job. "Salary XYZ Corp." is better.

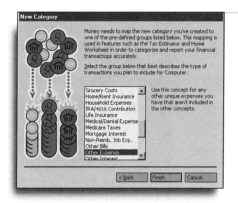

FIGURE 15.4
Choose the description that best fits your new category.

5. Now the cursor is in the **Subcategory** field. Type a new subcategory if you want, and repeat the procedure in steps 3 and 4 to define the new subcategory. Or, if you do not want a subcategory, complete the transaction normally, leaving that field blank.

The other way to create a category is by working with the Payees and Categories screen.

Creating a new category from the Categories list

1. Click the **Categories** link on the Navigation bar. The Categories screen appears, with the categories you have set up so far (see Figure 15.5).

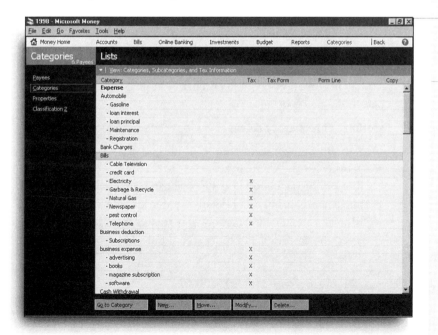

FIGURE 15.5
The categories list neatly displays all your categories at once.

2. If you want to create a subcategory, first click the category that it should be subordinate to. If you're creating a top-level category, it doesn't matter which category is selected when you start.

3. Click the **New** button. The New Category dialog box appears with two choices: **Create a new category**, or **Create a subcategory** to the category you selected in step 2. Click the option button you want, and then click **Next**.

4. In the **Name** field, type the name for the new category.

5. Click the **Income** or **Expense** option button to indicate what type of category it is. Then click **Next**.

6. Choose the concept to map the new category to, just as you did earlier in Figure 15.4. Then click **Finish**.

From the Categories screen (refer to Figure 15.5) you can also delete categories. Just select the category you want and click the **Delete** button. If the category has been used in one or more transactions, a dialog box appears asking you to choose a different category to assign to those transactions. Do so and click **OK**, and you're done.

To rename a category, right-click it and choose **Rename**, or select it and click the **Modify** button. A Modify Category (or Modify Subcategory) dialog box appears. Type the new name and click **OK**.

Notice the special columns for **Tax**, **Tax Form**, **Form Line**, and **Copy** on the Categories screen. These help you export your Money information into a tax preparation program, or to prepare tax-time reports for your accountant.

Working with category details

1. On the Categories screen, select the category you want to work with and then click the **Go to Category** button at the bottom of the dialog box. Or, you can double-click the category name. A screen of details for that category appears, showing the tax information, a history of transactions that used the category, and more (see Figure 15.6).

Right-click shortcut

You can right-click any category or subcategory to get a shortcut menu. On this menu, you'll find commands equivalent to the four buttons at the bottom of the Categories screen. It's just another way to issue the commands—entirely optional.

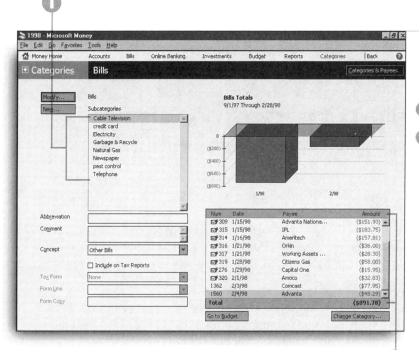

FIGURE 15.6

You can see all available information about the category at a glance on the Categories screen.

1   Subcategories of this category

2   Transactions using this category

2. Do any of the following as needed.

- To rename the category, click the **Modify** (Alt+I) button.

- To create additional subcategories, click the **New** (Alt+W) button.

- To set up the category for *tax reporting*, click the **Include on Tax Reports** check box and then choose the appropriate tax forms and lines from the drop-down lists beneath it.

- Click the **Go to Budget** button to see how the category fits within your budget.

- To recategorize a transaction on the list, click it and then click the **Change Category** button.

- To change the concept, choose a different one from the **Concept** drop-down list.

3. When you're finished working with the category, click the **Back** link on the Navigation bar to return to the list of categories.

SEE ALSO

➤ *To set up a budget, see page 374.*

Splitting a Transaction Among Categories

Have you ever written a single check for lots of different household items at one of those giant mega-superstores? It's oh-so-convenient to buy your groceries, hardware, lawn fertilizer, and home electronics at a single store. But then you get home and try to enter the check into Money. Uh oh. In the excitement of those discount prices, you loaded up your card with lots of items, including a gallon-size jug of ketchup, a Thighmaster, and a new VCR. How in the world can you stuff all that into a single category?

Of course you can't. That's where the **Split** button comes in. Click it as you're entering a transaction, and you'll open a *Split* Transaction window. (You can also select **Split** from the **Category** drop-down list to do the same thing.)

In the Split Transaction window, you can enter lots of line-items that all roll into a single check, and categorize each line separately. For instance, you can put that keg-o-ketchup under **Food:Groceries**, the VCR under **Furnishings:Electronics**, and the Thighmaster under **Leisure:Equipment**. Just fill in the category, subcategory, description, and amount of each item. Figure 15.7 shows how to apportion such purchases. Don't forget the sales tax! Click **Done** when you're finished.

Extra properties

When filling in your splits in the Split Transaction dialog box, be aware that there are four drop-down lists for each one: **Category**, **Subcategory**, **Property**, and **Sub-Property**. The latter two are on the second line of each split. For the most part you can ignore them unless you have chosen to use *properties* to additionally categorize transactions.

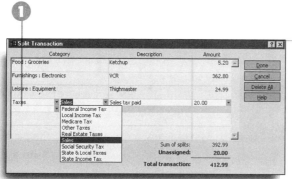

FIGURE 15.7

In the Split Transaction window, each line has its own drop-down list for category and subcategory.

① Ignore this second line; it's for properties.

Printing Checks

If you want, you can print checks directly from your printer rather than writing them with your actual checkbook. It requires special check paper, which can be rather expensive, but some people find it worth the expense.

If you want to print a check, you must indicate this by setting the **Number** field to **Print This Transaction**. You can do this for a whole batch of checks, and then print them all at once. When you have checks to print, a Print Checks reminder appears to the side of the register.

Testing Your Printer

Before you print checks for the first time, you should test your printer to determine how to feed in the paper. To do so, take a blank sheet of paper and draw an upward-pointing arrow on one side. Then feed the sheet of paper into your printer, arrow up, point first, and print any document from any program (not necessarily Money). If the document comes out with the arrow on top, right-side-up, you know that you should feed your checks in exactly as you fed the test paper. If not, the test sheet demonstrates how you need to feed the paper (and thus your page of blank checks) into the printer.

If you still aren't sure whether your checks are inserted properly into your printer, and you don't mind wasting a check, open the

Ordering checks for your printer

To get information about what kind of checks you can order and how much they will cost, open the **Help** menu and choose **Ordering Checks**.

File menu, choose **Print Checks**, and then click the **Print Test** button. One sheet of checks will feed through, with a voided check printed, and the Print Checks dialog box will reappear with **2** entered in the **For a Partial Sheet** text box, indicating that there are now two checks left on the sheet you just used. Tear off the voided check and insert the remaining two checks into your printer's manual feed.

If your printer consistently misaligns the printing on checks, you may need to "nudge" the lettering a bit in one direction. To do so, open the **Tools** menu, choose **Options**, and click the **Print Checks** tab. Then enter an offset in the appropriate direction in the **Printing Alignment** section.

Printing Checks

Money 98 is very good at making the check-printing process as friendly and foolproof as possible. It provides a helpful wizard that steps you through the check printing process. You just enter the requested information and go.

Printing checks

Printer ID

The first time you print checks, an extra dialog box may appear asking for your printer type or asking you to choose which printer you are going to use. If you see that, just make your selection and click **OK** to go on.

1. Either click the **Print Checks** button next to the reminder in the register or open the **File** menu and choose **Print Checks**. The Print Checks dialog box appears, shown in Figure 15.8.

2. Choose the appropriate options in the dialog box. The options include

    *   *Print*. Your choices are **All checks** or **Selected checks**. If you choose the latter, a box opens prompting you to choose which checks you want among those with the check number set to Print that have not yet been printed.

    *   *Number of first check in printer*. Enter the check number on the first check to be printed. Money automatically keeps track of the number of any others in the batch.

- *For a partial sheet....* A full sheet of checks contains three checks. If you have already used one or two of the checks, enter the number of checks remaining. Otherwise leave it set at **3**.

- *Paper fed*. Indicate how you will feed in the checks (applicable only if you're not using a full sheet).

- *Paper inserted*. Indicate which direction you are feeding in the checks. (If you are using less than a full sheet, you feed it in sideways, either left or right edge first.)

- **Options**. To change any of the other information in the dialog box, such as the printer being used, click the **Options** button to open the Print Options dialog box.

Print options

Many print options are available, too many to list here. You may want to click the **Options** button to check them out, just so you'll know what's there. For example, you can set Money to prompt when a check is post-dated, and you can set an offset in inches that the printing should be moved over (in case your printer consistently mis-aligns the printing on checks).

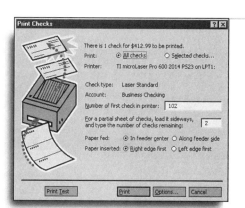

FIGURE 15.8

Use this dialog box to specify how you want the checks to print.

3. Click the **Print** button to print the checks. A dialog box appears immediately, letting you know the check(s) have been sent to the printer.

Wait for the checks to print, so you can check them. Some additional controls appear (notably a **Finish** and a **Reprint** button), but don't click either one until the checks have printed.

4. After examining the printed checks, if they are okay, click **Finish**. If they aren't okay, make any adjustments needed and then click **Reprint**.

Reprint later

If you don't discover a printing problem until after you've clicked **Finish**, return to the register, open the **Number** drop-down list, and select **Print this transaction** again. Then reprint the check as if you had not printed it yet.

Finding a Transaction

As you add more and more transactions to a register, it becomes increasingly hard to find a particular one that you might need to check on. Did you pay $500 to the I.R.S. last month, or was it $650? How much was your electric bill at this time last year? You can find answers like these by finding the transaction and looking it up.

To find a transaction, you specify criteria based on all the information you know about that transaction. For example, if you know the payee and the date, you find the transaction based on that information. If you know only the amount, you can find all transactions with that amount. You can find transactions based on any field. Enter all the information you know—finds based on multiple fields provide narrower results.

Finding transactions

1. Open the **Tools** menu, choose **Find**, and then choose **Transactions**. The Find Transactions dialog box appears as shown in Figure 15.9.

FIGURE 15.9

Enter the Find criteria you want on one or more of the displayed tabs.

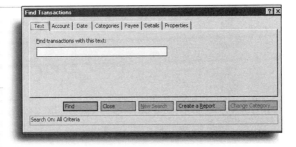

Finding loans and investments

The Find procedure shown here applies only to regular bank account transactions. If you are finding loan or investment transactions, there are separate commands for those Find activities. Open the **Tools** menu, choose **Find**, and then choose either **Loan Transactions** or **Investment Transactions**.

2. Narrow the search by entering the information you know about the transaction. Click the appropriate tab and then set the dialog box options.

3. When you have specified all the criteria, click **Find**. A window opens below the dialog box showing the found transactions. For example, in Figure 15.10, all transactions that had no payee appear.

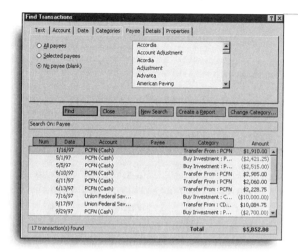

FIGURE 15.10
The results of the search show the date, account, category, and amount of each transaction that meets the search criteria.

After finding a group of transactions, you can do a variety of things with the information:

- To edit or take a closer look at one particular transaction, double-click it. This opens an Edit Transaction window.

- To go quickly to the register for the account that a particular transaction is in, right-click the transaction and choose **Go to Account**.

- To change the category of one or more transactions on the list, select them and then click the **Change Category** button.

- To create a *report* that you can print consisting of the found transactions, click the **Create a Report** button.

- To perform another search, click the **New Search** button.

- If you are finished with the Find window, click the **Close** button.

Besides the Find feature, Money offers several other ways to find transactions based on a particular criterion. For example, to find all transactions based on a certain category, you can view the category details for that transaction, as explained earlier in this chapter. At the bottom of that screen is a list of all transactions that have used that category. The same works for payees, discussed later in this chapter. When you display the details for a payee, you also get a list of all transactions involving the payee. Reports and charts are yet another way of pulling up information about certain transactions.

SEE ALSO

➤ *To learn more about reports, see page 379.*

Editing a Transaction

To edit a transaction, go to the register where it is entered and click it. The transaction reappears in the Forms area below the register, and you can make changes to it there. When you are finished making changes, just click the **Enter** button. (If you didn't choose to add the **Enter** button earlier in this chapter, you must press the Enter key repeatedly until you have moved through the last field to end the transaction.)

If you are looking at a list of found transactions (as in the preceding section), you can double-click any of the found transactions to open an Edit Transaction dialog box. This box is just like the transaction form in the register, as you can see in Figure 15.11; make your changes and click **OK**.

FIGURE 15.11

When editing transactions while not in a register, the transaction form appears in a dialog box.

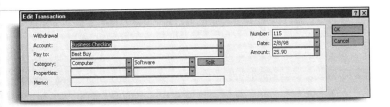

Canceling, deleting, and voiding

I try to stay away from the word "cancel" to mean deleting or voiding a transaction because cancel is often used in the financial world to refer to a check that has cleared the bank. A "canceled check" is not really canceled at all; it is cleared. *Deleting* and *voiding*, in contrast, both refer to methods of negating the effect of the transaction.

Voiding or Deleting a Transaction

You can get rid of a transaction in two ways, and each method is good for a certain circumstance. Unfortunately, most people don't understand the difference between the two.

Deleting is for transactions that were a mistake from the start—like data entry errors. If you enter a transaction into the wrong account, for example, and you didn't want to move it to the correct account right away, you could delete that transaction and then reenter it later in the correct account. Or let's say you entered a few bogus transactions just to practice, but they don't have any correlation to any real transactions you've ever made. Delete those and you'll never see any trace of them again.

Voiding is kind of like taking a big rubber stamp and red inkpad and stamping VOID (or UNDO or WRONG) on a contract or bill. With voiding, the transaction stays in your register, so you can be reminded that it exists, but its income or expense isn't reflected in your account balance, and the transaction won't affect any of your reports or charts. You might void a paper check that you started to write, then made a mistake and tore up. That way, if you ever wonder what happened to that check number, you will be able to look at your register and see that it was voided (rather than stolen).

Deleting a Transaction

To delete a transaction, just select it and press the **Delete** key on the keyboard. When asked if you want to delete the transaction, click **Yes**. It's gone immediately.

If you delete a transaction that has been reconciled (or voided), you'll get a warning message telling you this. Click **OK** to delete the transaction anyway. Be careful, however; deleting a reconciled transaction could mean an error in your account balance. (If your account balance matched your bank statement balance, and you delete a reconciled transaction, it will no longer match.)

Voiding a Transaction

Personally, I don't like voiding, because I don't like being reminded of my mistakes. I would rather be confused than depressed about my human fallibility. If your ego is less fragile, you will appreciate the ability to void a transaction.

To void a transaction, select it in the register, and then open the **Edit** menu, choose **Mark As**, and then choose **Void**. **VOID** appears in the **Balance** column, letting you know that this transaction doesn't affect the balance.

The nice thing about voiding is that, unlike deleting, it's reversible. Just repeat the procedure to unvoid the transaction. **Void** is a toggle that turns on or off each time you select it. When you're unvoiding a transaction, you'll get an error message telling you that this transaction has been reconciled (whether it actually has or not); click **OK** to get past that.

Controlling How Transactions Are Displayed

Each register has a **View** menu with commands that control how transactions appear. To open the **View** menu, just click the thin blue bar where it says "**View**" as shown in Figure 15.12.

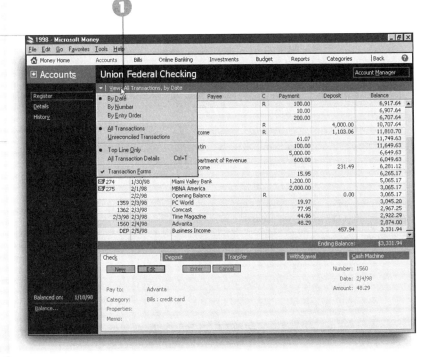

FIGURE 15.12

Use the **View** menu to control the register display.

1. Click here to open the **View** menu.

The **View** menu is divided into several sections, each with its own set of mutually exclusive options. (It's just like option buttons in a dialog box or buttons on your car stereo.) Here's what you're looking at:

- *By (Sort Order)*. The options in the first group control the order in which the transactions appear in the register. You choose between **By Date** (the entry in the **Date** field), **By Number** (the entry in the **Number** field), or **By Entry Order** (the actual order in which you inputted them).

- *Which Transactions*. The second group of options controls whether some transactions will be hidden or not. You choose between **All Transactions** and **Unreconciled Transactions** (which are the ones that have not yet been balanced with your bank statement).

- *Transaction Detail*. The options in the third group control how much detail you see about each transaction in the register. By default, you see **Top Line Only**, which makes for a nice, compact register. (If you want to see the details of a transaction, just select it, bringing its details into the **Forms** area.) Your other choice is **All Transaction Details**, which expands the register to show all detail lines (see Figure 15.13). This is useful primarily if you turn off the Transaction Forms (see next bulleted item).

- *Transaction Forms*. If you want to see more lines of the register onscreen, you can turn off **Transaction Forms** to do so. You won't be able to use the forms to enter new transactions; however, you'll have to enter data directly into the register, which is somewhat more awkward.

FIGURE 15.13

Transaction detail is set to **All Transaction Details**, and the **Transaction Forms** option is turned off.

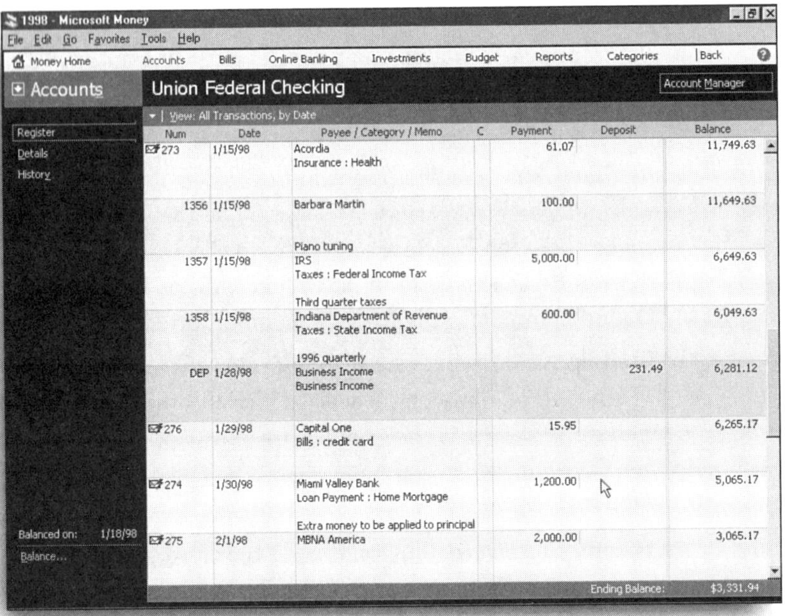

Balancing an Account

Balance versus reconcile

Money uses the term *balance*, but you may have heard the process called *reconciling*. It's the same thing. You compare your bank statement to your own records and identify and correct errors.

I used to dread getting a bank statement in the mail, because it meant an hour or more of frustration. I would find all the math errors I had made over the previous month. The bank statement would get littered with scribbles and check marks from trying over and over to compare my poor, sloppy records with the bank's printout. With Money, however, balancing is considerably easier, and takes only a few minutes.

Balancing an account

1. Display the register for the account you want to balance.
2. Click the **Balance** button (bottom-left corner of the screen). A dialog box appears explaining why you balance an account. Click **Next** to move on.
3. Next you get to fill in some numbers, as shown in Figure 15.14. Enter the following data in the appropriate fields:
   - *Statement date*. Enter the date from your bank statement.

- *Starting balance*. Don't change this; it's the ending balance from the last statement (or your opening balance you entered, if this is your first time). If your starting balance is wrong on your bank statement, call your bank.

- *Ending balance*. Fill this in with the ending balance from the bank statement.

- *Service <u>c</u>harge*. Scan your statement quickly; if you were charged any service charges, enter them. You can categorize them if you want to.

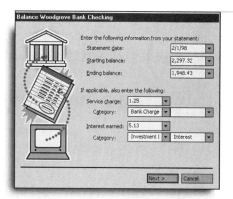

FIGURE 15.14
Enter all the pertinent details from the statement into this dialog box.

- *<u>I</u>nterest earned*. If your statement shows that you accrued any interest, enter it. You can categorize it too if you want. Although you can enter the interest as a separate transaction if you want to, and then mark it as cleared, it's much more efficient to just enter it here in the dialog box instead.

4. When you've entered all the requested information, click **Next** to move on to the next step; clearing individual transactions.

5. Compare your bank statement with the list of unreconciled transactions onscreen (see Figure 15.15) and click in the **C** column to place a C next to each one that matches up.

Watch for ATM fees

If you were charged fifty cents or a dollar each time you made an ATM withdrawal, these charges may not be neatly summarized in one spot on your statement. You may have to search for them and add them up in your head, and then enter that total in the **Service <u>c</u>harge** field.

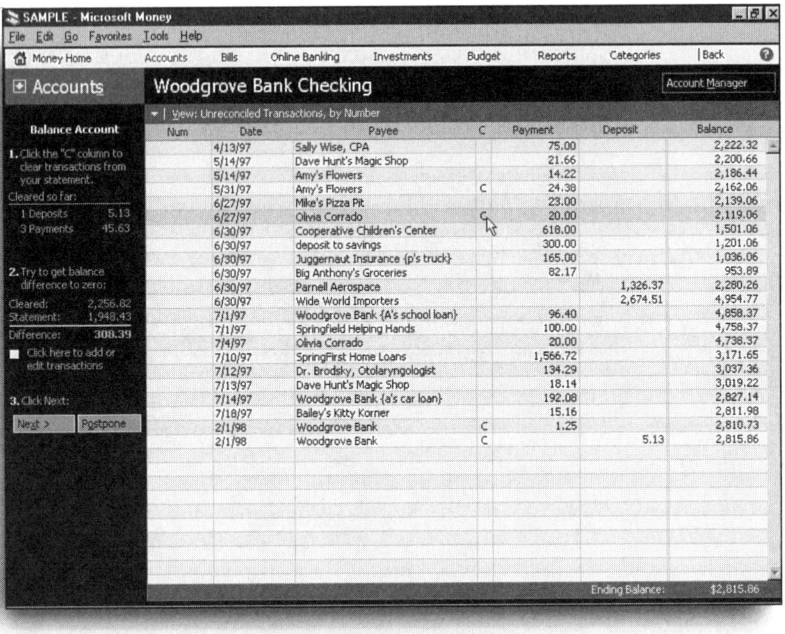

FIGURE 15.15

Click to place a C in the **C** column, meaning "cleared."

Missed one?

You can edit or add transactions as you balance. Just click a transaction to edit it. To add one, click the **Click here to add or edit transactions** check box under the **Difference** line to enable additions.

6. When all the transactions on the bank statement have been accounted for, look to the left of the register for the **Difference** line. It should read 0.00. If it does, congratulations! You balance! Click **Next**. (If you don't have 0.00, see the information that follows these steps.)

7. A congratulatory box appears; click **Finish**. You're done. The transactions you marked with C have now changed to R, indicating they are fully reconciled.

If you can't seem to make it balance, look into these factors for causes:

- *Does the ending balance you entered match the one on your bank statement?* Check the number next to **Statement** on the balancing screen. If it's not the same as your statement's ending balance, click **Postpone**, then click the **Balance** button again to return to balancing, but enter the correct ending balance this time.

- *Does the starting balance match that of your bank statement?* In general, you shouldn't change the entry in the **Starting**

Balance field. It comes from the ending balance of last
month's bank statement, or your starting balance for the
account if this is the first month. If a discrepancy exists, it
may be a bank error, but if you're sure it's your own error,
go ahead and change it.

- *Did you enter all the transactions?* Every transaction on your
  bank statement must match a transaction in Money. You
  may need to add transactions that don't appear in Money
  but should. Note that the reverse is not true, however—you
  may have transactions that appear in Money, but not on
  your bank statement. That just means that those transactions
  have not yet been sent to your bank from the payee.

- *Did you remember the service charges and interest?* Not all
  banks statements label these clearly. Look closely at your
  bank statement to see if these small additions or subtractions
  apply to your account.

- *How about ATM withdrawals?* ATM transactions are handy,
  but it's also easy to forget to record them in Money, because
  there's no check stub to help remind you. Go through your
  pockets and/or purse to see if you can find any unrecorded
  ATM receipts.

If you still can't find the problem, click the **Next** button anyway.
Money presents several solution options, as shown in Figure
15.16.

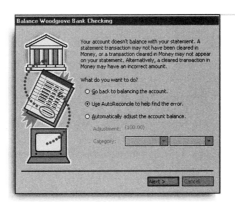

FIGURE 15.16

Money can sometimes help you
identify the error causing the
imbalance.

Your first line of defense should be to let Money's AutoReconcile feature try to find the problem. AutoReconcile looks for likely transactions that you may have marked incorrectly, and reports them to you. Click the middle option button in Figure 15.16 to try it out.

What happens next depends on what AutoReconcile finds. If it can't find any obvious errors, it lets you know. However, if it finds a problem, it reports it in a dialog box, as shown in Figure 15.17. In Figure 15.17, it shows how I forgot to clear a transaction. Because it was for exactly the same amount as my balance was off, AutoReconcile noticed it. To correct the problem, I can just click **Yes**. If AutoReconcile were mistaken, I could click **No** to tell it to keep looking, or click **Cancel** to give up.

If AutoReconcile is no help, you can adjust the balance using the controls shown previously in Figure 15.16. Click the **Automatically adjust the account balance** option button. (You can categorize the adjustment if you want. If you don't, you'll be asked whether you want to.) Then click **Finish**. Congratulations, you're done.

FIGURE 15.17

AutoReconcile alerts you to a possible problem.

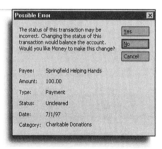

Changing Account Details

Changing the account name

Notice in Figure 15.18 that you can't change the account name. Actually, you can change it, but not from here. You must click the **Modify** (Alt+I) button next to the **Account name** field to open a special dialog box in which it is possible to make a name change.

Account details are little facts about the account that you don't need every day, but that come in handy occasionally. They include the original starting balance for the account, the bank's name and address, and so on.

To view (and change) the account details, start at the register. Then click the **Details** button (left side of the screen) to see the details. Figure 15.18 shows the details for a checking account. You can change any of the information in any of the editable fields.

When you're done, click the **Register** button (again, on the left side) to return to the Register.

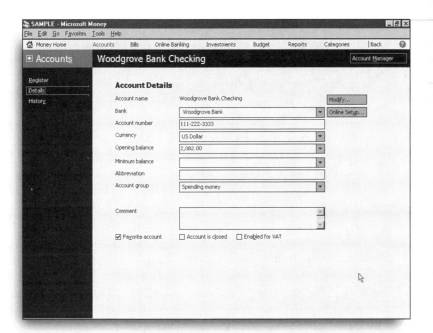

Managing Payees

Just as you can manage categories, you can also manage your list of payees. This isn't essential—you can get by just entering payees on an as-you-go basis. By working directly with the Payees list, however, you can enter extra information for each payee. Here are some perks:

- You can enter the payee's address, so it automatically prints on any checks that you print. This is great if you have to address an envelope for the payment, because the address is right there.

- You can record the payee's phone number, so it's handy in case you have a question. Also, in the case of credit card companies, if you ever lose the card, the phone number that you would call to cancel the card is right there.

- You can have Money remember your account number, if you have one, for that payee. This can be valuable for your own records, and also for printing on the check. (Some companies ask you to write your account number on each check.)

- By entering payees up front, you ensure that you don't have several variations of the same payee on your list. Because you can create some reports by payee, it's important that all payments to the same payee be recorded as such. You won't have separate entries for Amoco, Amoco Oil, and Amoco Credit Card, for example, when they all refer to the same bill that you pay every month.

Entering a New Payee

Every time you write a check, you are entering a payee. That's one way to enter one. Another, more formal way lets you enter payees that you have not written any checks to yet, for future use. That way you can enter names and addresses for all the payees you pay frequently, so you don't have to go back and enter their contact information individually later.

Entering a payee

1. Go to the **Categories** list by opening the **Go menu and choosing Categories** (or press Ctrl+Shift+C).

2. Click the **Payees** button (left side of the screen). A list of current payees appears.

3. Click the **New** button. A Create New Payee dialog box appears.

4. Type the name for the new payee, and then click **OK**. The new payee is added to the list.

Entering or Changing Payee Details

The real value of the **Payees** list comes in entering details for each one. This is where you can record important addresses, phone numbers, and account numbers.

Working with payee details

1. On the **Payees** list, double-click the payee you want to see details for, or click it once and then click the **Go to Payee** button. The details appear, as shown in Figure 15.19.

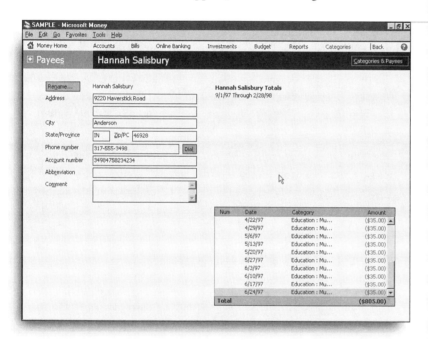

FIGURE 15.19

You can enter or edit extra information about a payee here.

2. Enter or change any information in any of the editable fields.

3. If you want to rename the payee, click the **Re_name** button to open a box where you can enter a new name. The new name will be applied to all future transactions with this payee, but the payment history under the old name will remain associated with it.

Payee payments

Notice also the list of payments made to that payee in the bottom right corner of the screen. You can also double-click any of the payments listed on the payee screen to have a closer look at a payment you have made to that payee. This is a great informal way to get a report of all payments made to a particular payee without fussing with the Reports section of Money.

4. When you are finished working with this payee's details, do one of the following:

- To work with a different payee, open the **Payees** drop-down list in the top-left corner of the screen and choose a different payee.

- To return to the list of payees, click the **Categories & Payees** button in the top-right corner of the screen.

Deleting a Payee

If you find that your list of payees is cluttered with people or organizations that you did business with once, but will never deal with again, go ahead and delete them. Deleting a payee will not affect any transactions you have already entered—that payee will still appear for that transaction. (This is *unlike* categories, where deleting a category wipes it out from all existing transactions too.)

To delete a payee, select it from the **Payees** list and then click the **Delete** button (bottom of the screen). A message appears asking if you really want to delete it. Click **Yes**, and it's outta there.

Tracking Bills to Be Paid

Changing the reminder interval

The ten-day warning is just a default. You're free to change it to be notified earlier or later, or not at all. Just open the **Tools** menu, choose **Options**, and click the **Bills** tab. In the **Bill Reminders** section change **10** to some other number, and click **OK**.

If you have a lot of payments that you make on a regular basis, like mortgage payments, car payments, or gym dues, you'll appreciate Money's Bill Calendar. If you set up a loan in Money (Chapter 14), you had the opportunity to create a scheduled payment at the end of that setup process. If you did so, you already have a scheduled payment.

Like a wake-up call in a hotel, a scheduled payment helps you meet your obligation. It reminds you ten days in advance of the due date, and will even print the check for you, or make the payment via modem. Believe me, it's a lot better than tacking up a Post-it note reminder on your refrigerator and hoping it doesn't fall off.

All scheduled transactions are created and modified in the *Bill Calendar*. To see it, click the **Bills** link on the Navigation bar, or open the **Go** menu and choose the **Bills** option. Figure 15.20 shows a sample Bill Calendar. Notice that it already has payments set up for the mortgage loan and the credit card that we created new accounts for in Chapter 14.

A scheduled transaction on the Bill Calendar need not be a check; it can be an automatic withdrawal from an account (for example, your gym membership) or a deposit (for example, the automatic Direct Deposit of your paycheck).

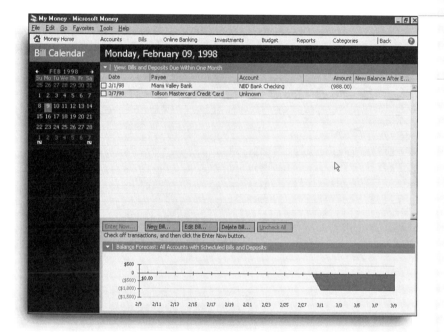

FIGURE 15.20
This Bill Calendar already has two payments set up.

Creating a new scheduled transaction

1. From the Bill Calendar, click the **New Bill** button. The Create New Recurring Payment dialog box appears.

2. Choose the option button for the type of transaction: **Bill**, **Deposit**, **Transfer**, or **Investment Purchase**. Then click **Next**.

3. An information screen appears explaining how the Bill Calendar works; read it and then click **Next**. A dialog box appears in which you can enter or edit the transaction. Its name depends on what type you chose in step 2—for example, for a scheduled deposit, it's called Edit Scheduled Deposit.

4. Fill in the fields to describe the recurring transaction (see Figure 15.21).

- *Account*. Choose which account should pay or receive the payment.

- *Pay to* (*or from*). Choose the payee (or the person or company from whom a deposit is coming).

- *Number, Date, Amount, Category*, *and Memo*. Use these fields as you would with any other transaction. For fields where the value will vary each time, such as **Date**, enter the appropriate value for the first time and Money will increment the others as appropriate.

FIGURE 15.21

Enter information about the recurring payment or deposit.

5. Open the **Frequency** drop-down list and choose the interval for the transaction (for example, **Monthly**, **Weekly**, and so on).

6. If the transaction happens without any action from you (such as a direct deposit), open the **Entry method** drop-down list and choose **Automatic Entry**. If you need to take action on it yourself (for example, sending a mortgage check), leave the **Entry method** set for **Manual Entry**.

7. Click **OK**. The new transaction now appears on the calendar.

To edit a recurring transaction, just double-click it on the list, or click it once and then click **Ed̲it Bill**.

To delete a recurring transaction, click it and click **De̲lete Bill**. A dialog box appears asking whether you want to delete one instance or all instances. Click the appropriate button for whichever you want to complete the deletion.

Managing Your Investments

A Quick Look at the Investing Game

Two kinds of investments exist—those that carry a risk, and those that tie up your money for a certain period of time. Investments in the first category may or may not pay off; as with gambling, the higher the risk, the larger the potential prize. If you buy the stock of a company that's doing poorly, you can get a great deal, but there's a bigger chance that the stock's value will drop even further than there is with a company that is doing well. *Certificates of Deposit*, or CDs, are an example of the latter category of investments. You buy a CD at a certain interest rate for a certain period of time. At the end of that time, you get your money back, plus the amount of interest that you agreed upon. (*Money Market funds* and *bonds* are other variations on this theme.) These investments don't risk your principal (your original money you put in).

You'll do your investing through your bank or investment broker, so why would you want to enter the information into Money? There are a couple of reasons. One is that your investments are part of your larger financial picture, and you can't really understand how much you're worth unless you take them into consideration. A second reason is convenience. If you buy stock, for example, and write a check for it, you can enter a single transaction in Money to show that the cash was moved from one account (your checking) to another (your brokerage account).

Money recognizes two types of investment accounts: retirement and investment. Actually, a retirement account is a type of investment account, so in this case "investment account" means a non–retirement account. Retirement accounts usually have some tax benefit associated with them. You may have, for example, a *401(k)*, an *IRA*, a *Keogh*, or a *SEP-IRA*. These retirement accounts can consist of any of the investments that a regular investment account can contain.

Money considers any *non-retirement* account that either ties up your money for a certain time or has a certain amount of risk to be an investment. Such investments can include *bonds, CDs, Money Market funds, mutual funds, stocks, treasury bills, treasury notes,* and *treasury bonds.*

SEE ALSO

➤ *To learn how to put together net worth reports, see page 379.*

Preparing Your Investment Accounts

You'll store your investments in investment accounts, one for each bank or brokerage that you deal with. You may have already created these accounts when you set up Money in Chapter 14, "Setting Up Your Money Accounts." If not, turn back to Chapter 14 now and create a new investment account.

It's important to remember the distinction between investment accounts and investments. An *investment account* summarizes all your holdings with a particular brokerage or bank. An *investment* is the individual stock or security that you buy or sell. For example, you might have 10 different investments that you bought through Fidelity Investments (a brokerage). They would all be contained in a single account in Money.

If you followed along in Chapter 14, you now have at least one investment account. Check out what's there by clicking the **Investments** link on the Navigation bar. The Investments screen appears (see Figure 16.1).

SEE ALSO

➤ *To set up investment accounts, see page 317.*

Another account?

If you need to set up another investment account, you can do so from here; just click the **New** button and then select the **Investment Account option** button. Then follow the prompts, which are the same as those described in Chapter 14.

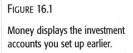

FIGURE 16.1

Money displays the investment accounts you set up earlier.

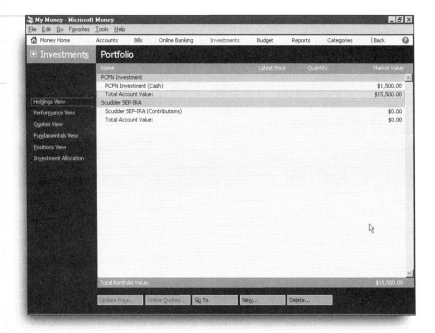

Entering Your Current Holdings

You can enter the holdings in your portfolio in one of two ways. You can start with a zero balance in your account and then enter "Buy" transactions to create the portfolio value, or you can enter your holdings with an "Add Shares" transaction. What's the difference?

When you enter a "Buy," you are making a recording of the actual transaction that acquired the shares for you. The price you paid for them is recorded, along with any commission you paid. This is useful information to have because when you sell the investment, you will have to pay taxes on the *capital gain*, which is the selling price minus the buying price and commissions. If it's important for Money to be able to calculate your taxable profits, you should build your portfolio this way.

In contrast, when you "Add Shares," you are recording the fact that you own certain investments, but you are not recording how much you paid for them or on what date you acquired them.

This is a much simpler way to enter your existing holdings into Money, but it does not provide the profit data, and can't help you prepare tax reports.

Entering Past Buys

When you created your investment account, you may have entered an estimated value for it that included all your current holdings. If you have decided to build up your portfolio by entering all your past buys, you will need to start with a zeroed-out account balance for the account.

Zeroing out an investment account balance

1. From the Investments screen (refer to Figure 16.1), double-click the account name. The register for the account appears.

2. Click the **Details** button (left side of screen) to see the details for the account.

3. Change the **Estimated value** number to **0.00** (see Figure 16.2).

4. Click the **Back** link on the Navigation bar to return to the Investments screen.

Stocks are not the only thing...

The step-by-step activities in this chapter focus mainly on stocks and mutual funds because these are the most common kinds of investments. But the procedures also work equally well for other investments, such as CDs and bonds. The only difference is that when you enter a fixed-value investment such as a CD, Money asks only for a total dollar amount invested, not a price per share and number of shares.

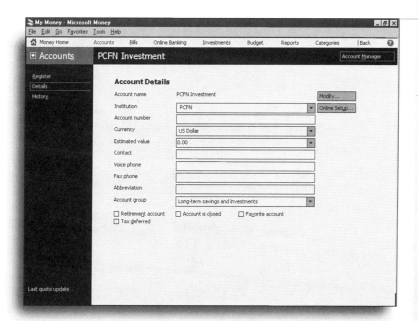

FIGURE 16.2

If you want to enter all your stocks from scratch, zero out the value of your investment account.

If there is an associated cash account for the investment account, you might want to increase its opening balance so the money to "pay for" the investments that you'll soon be recording can come from somewhere. To do this, repeat the preceding steps, double-clicking the cash account in step 1, and changing the **Estimated value** of that account.

To enter an investment, start from the register for the investment account. (You can get there by double-clicking the account name on the Investments screen or from the Account Manager screen.) Then enter the transaction as you would any other transaction in any account. There are minor differences in the fields, and you may be asked for more information about the particular stock or security you are buying, but it's really similar to what you've been doing with your regular accounts.

Entering a Buy transaction

1. Display the account register for the investment account where you want to enter the investment.

2. Click the **New** button. Fields appear to enter the new investment.

3. In the **Date** field, change the date to the date when the transaction occurred. If you are entering stocks that you have already bought, make sure you date the transaction accurately. (It will make a difference on your tax reports.)

4. In the **Investment** text box, carefully type the name of the stock or other investment.

5. Press Tab to move on. If this is the first time you have entered anything for this investment, a Create New Investment dialog box appears, as shown in Figure 16.3. (If not, skip to step 9 to fill in the **Activity**.)

6. Click the appropriate button, and then click the **Next** button.

7. Fill in additional details about the investment. The fields vary depending on the investment type; for stocks, for example, you are prompted for the stock symbol.

8. Click the **Finish** button. The dialog box closes and the cursor moves to the **Activity** field.

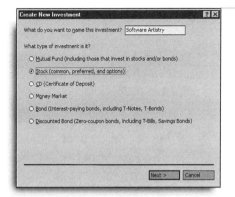

FIGURE 16.3

Use these option buttons to specify what type of investment it is.

9. Choose **Buy** from the drop-down list.

10. Enter the **Quantity**, **Price (per share)**, and **Commission** in the corresponding fields. Money calculates the amount in the **Total** field automatically.

11. If the money is coming from some other account (such as the associated cash account), select it from the **Transfer From** drop-down list. If you don't want to indicate where the money is coming from, leave this blank.

12. Repeat these steps until you have entered all your past buys, so all your current holdings are represented.

When you are finished entering, click the **Investments** link on the Navigation bar to see a summary of your current holdings. This is an easy way to see if you have missed anything. If you have, go back and add it.

If you have any sales to enter, or dividends or interest received, create new transactions for each action, changing the **Activity** type from **Buy** to the appropriate activity (**Sell**, **Reinvest Dividends**, and so on).

Adding Shares

When you use the Add Shares activity, Money makes a note that you have a certain quantity of a certain investment. You can use this activity to build up a list of your portfolio holdings without having to know what date you purchased them or what price you paid. This is useful, for example, for a retirement mutual fund, because it doesn't matter what you paid for the original shares.

The steps here are the same as for entering a Buy transaction, up until you choose the activity (in step 9). From that point, it's a different ballgame.

Adding shares

1. Display the account register for the investment account where you want to enter the investment.

2. Click the **Ne<u>w</u>** button. Fields appear to enter the new investment.

3. In the **Date** field, change the date to the date when the transaction occurred. If you are entering stocks that you have already bought, make sure you date the transaction accurately. (It will make a difference on your tax reports.)

4. In the **Investment** text box, carefully type the name of the stock or other investment.

5. Press Tab to move on. If this is the first time you have entered anything for this investment, a Create New Investment dialog box appears, as shown earlier in Figure 16.3. (If not, skip to step 9 to fill in the **Activity** text box.)

6. Click the appropriate button, and then click the **Next** button.

7. Fill in additional details about the investment. The fields vary depending on the investment type; for stocks, for example, you are prompted for the stock symbol.

8. Click the **Finish** button. The dialog box closes and the cursor moves to the **Activity** field.

9. Choose **Add Shares** from the **Activity** drop-down list.

10. Enter the quantity in the **Quantity** field, and press Enter. A box pops up asking you whether you have a recent price for the investment, as in Figure 16.4. Enter one if you have it, and an associated date, and click **OK**. Or, just click **Cancel** to bypass this for now if you have no idea what a current price might be.

There is also a Remove Shares activity, which you can use to take shares out of an investment account without entering a Sell transaction. The difference? When you sell, Money takes the current value of the investment and transfers that money over to the associated cash account. When you remove shares, it removes them and their value disappears from your Money account. You might remove shares that have become worthless from your account—for example, if the company went bankrupt.

Updating Prices

You can update prices manually by entering the most recent prices from your local newspaper's financial section. But if you have an Internet connection, a much easier way to update the prices is to use Online Quotes. Let's look at both ways.

Manually updating a price

1. Display the register for an investment account that includes a transaction involving the stock (or other investment).
2. Click the investment you want to update, and then click the **Update Price** button (bottom left corner of screen). The Update Price dialog box appears (see Figure 16.5).
3. Enter the price in the **Price** text box.
4. Click the **Update** button.
5. If you want to update another stock's price, open the **Investment** drop-down list and select it. Then return to step 3. Otherwise, click **Close**.

FIGURE 16.5

You can manually enter the
stock's new price here.

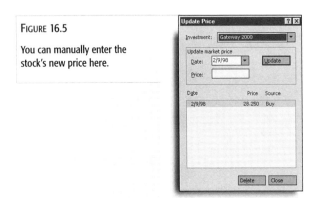

FIGURE 16.5

You can manually enter the
stock's new price here.

Updating prices online

1. Display the register for an investment account.

2. Click the **Online Quotes** button in the bottom left corner
   of the register screen. An Online Services dialog box appears
   with all the investments listed that you have entered in any
   of your investment accounts (see Figure 16.6).

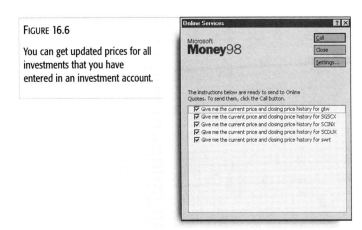

FIGURE 16.6

You can get updated prices for all
investments that you have
entered in an investment account.

3. If there are any investments listed for which you do not
   want an updated price, deselect the check boxes next to their
   names.

4. The first time you use Online Quotes, click **<u>S</u>ettings** and follow the prompts to set up Money to use your Internet connection. When you finish that setup, you return to the screen shown in Figure 16.6.

5. Click the **<u>C</u>all** button.

6. If you're not already connected to the Internet, a dialog box appears asking for your username and password so Money can sign on to your Internet account. Enter them and click **OK**.

7. Wait for Money to connect to the Internet and retrieve the latest prices. (Remember these prices are delayed by at least 20 minutes.)

When the dialog box showing the connection in progress goes away, you are done.

8. Click the **Investments** link on the Navigation bar to jump to the Investments screen, where you see the latest prices reflected for each investment.

> **Free Internet connection**
>
> If you don't have an Internet connection, check out the free two-month MCI offer that came with Home Essentials. Details are in the Home Essentials box.

> **Updating Internet information**
>
> Another way to update prices is to open the **Tools** menu and choose **Update Internet Information**. This command not only updates your stock prices but also updates the news items on your Money Home page.

Recording Sales and Other Adjustments

You record investment sales and other transactions in the same way you record the buys. Just choose a different activity from the **Activity** drop-down list. The activities include **Sell**, **Reinvest Dividend**, **Reinvest Interest**, **Short Sell**, **Cover Shares**— almost any type of transaction that you can accomplish through your bank or investment broker. The fields may be slightly different for different transaction types, but they're mostly self-explanatory.

Recording Stock Splits

Sometimes when a stock's price gets fairly high, the company decides to *split* the shares. For example, if you had 100 shares of the stock at $100 per share, you now have 200 shares at $50 per share. You still have the same amount of money ($1,000), but you have twice as many shares.

Sometimes stocks split at odd rates (such as 2 5/8 to 5) rather than the simple 2-for-1. Money can handle any split ratio.

Recording a stock split

1. In the investment account's register, click any transaction involving the stock you want to split. Or, from the Investments screen, click the stock name.

2. Click the **Split Shares** button. The Split Shares dialog box appears (see Figure 16.7).

FIGURE 16.7

Money handles stock splits through this dialog box.

3. Confirm that the stock name is correct; if it's not, choose it from the **Investment** drop-down list.

4. Change the date, if needed, to reflect the date of the split.

5. Enter the split ratio in the **Split the shares** box. For example, if the stock is splitting 2 for 1, enter 2 in the first box and 1 in the second.

6. Click **OK**. Money makes the change in your records.

Understanding the Investment Views

Investment views are like mini-reports: They show you your portfolio in different ways, so you can make different evaluations about it. The default investment view is Holdings, which is what you see when you click the **Investments** link on the Navigation bar. The other views are described as follows:

- *Performance View*. Shows the investments' latest prices, your profit since you bought them, the percentage of profit, and annualized rate of return (see Figure 16.8).

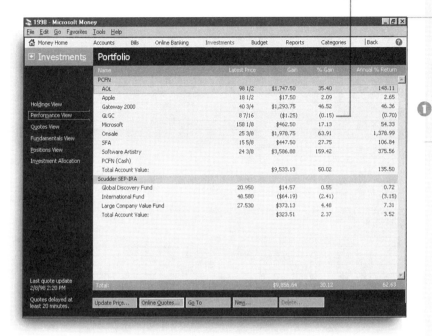

FIGURE 16.8

Performance view shows you how well your investments are performing on an annual percentage basis.

1 Note the percentage of gain or loss for each investment.

- *Quotes View*. Shows the latest prices, the change since the day before, the daily high, the daily low, and the volume.

- *Fundamentals View*. Shows the latest prices, the 52-week highs and lows, the P/E (a rating of how stable the company is), and the Volatility rating.

- *Positions View*. Shows the latest price, how much you own of each investment, and the current market value of your holdings (see Figure 16.9).

- *Investment Allocation*. A pie chart showing what percentages of your investment assets lie in certain asset types (stocks, mutual funds, bonds, and so on.)

SEE ALSO

➤ *To produce a variety of printed reports detailing your investment holdings, see page 385.*

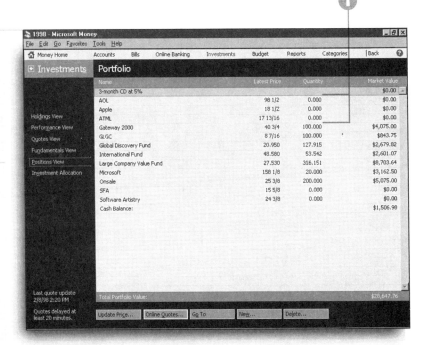

FIGURE 16.9

Positions view shows your holdings and how much they're worth today.

1 These investments with 0 quantity were bought and sold in the past.

CHAPTER

17

Planning and Reporting

Setting up a budget

Tracking your budget progress

Viewing reports and charts

Customizing reports and charts

Printing reports and charts

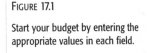

More budgeting tools

The deluxe version of Money (the Money Financial Suite) that you can buy in stores contains many more planning and budgeting tools; the budget planner in the standard version of Money is only a small part of the total offerings. If you need more planning and budgeting features, you might consider investing in an upgrade.

Setting Up a Budget

Two major tasks involved with a budget are: setting it up and sticking to it. Setting it up is the easy part, especially when you're working with an easy-to-use tool like Money.

Setting up a budget in Money

1. Click the **Budget** link on the Navigation bar to open the Budget and Savings Plan screen, shown in Figure 17.1.

2. The first field is for your gross income. It is already selected, as you can see in Figure 17.1. Type your monthly income in the **I earn a total of** field (to the right of the budget).

FIGURE 17.1

Start your budget by entering the appropriate values in each field.

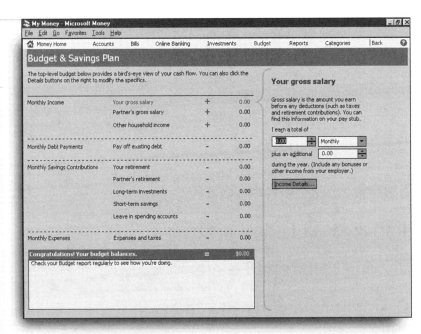

3. Now click the **Income Details** button directly below where you entered your number. A detail screen appears for specifying how you plan to earn that money (see Figure 17.2).

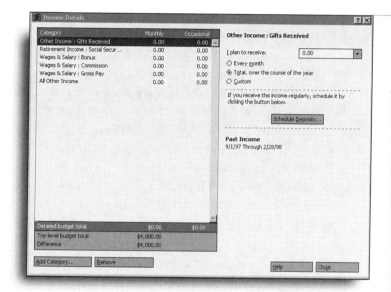

FIGURE 17.2

Now you need to break down the total amount into the appropriate categories.

4. Click one of the categories listed (for example, **Other Income: Gifts Received**), and then enter the estimated amount for that income source in the **I plan to receive** text box.

5. Click the next category for which you plan to have some income, and enter its estimated amount. To enter the estimate, do one of the following:

Click the **Every month** option button and then enter the regular amount you receive for that category each month. For example, if you receive a regular salary, enter it for the **Wages and Salary: Gross Pay** category as an **Every month** amount.

Click the **Total, over the course of the year** option button and then enter the amount you receive for the category for the entire year. Money will equally distribute the income over each month. For example, if you don't know your monthly salary but you do know that you make $40,000 a year, you would enter $40,000 for the **Wages and Salary: Gross Pay** category as a **Total, over the course of the year** amount.

Adding a category

The categories listed are the income categories you have already set up in Money. If you need to add a category, click the **Add Category** button and follow the prompts.

Changing the total amount

If you realize you have entered a wrong total amount, click **Close** to return to the Budget and Savings Plan screen and make the change; then click the **Income Details** button again to return to the details.

Occasional doesn't count

Notice in Figure 17.3 that the amounts in the **Occasional** column (placed there by entering custom numbers) don't count toward the monthly budgeted amount. That's because such income is sporadic and shouldn't be used to calculate the regular monthly plan.

Click the **Custom** option button to open a Custom dialog box with fields for each month. Then enter the amount you expect to receive for the category in each month. For example, if you receive $400 bonuses in January and July, you would enter them in the **January** and **July** boxes. Click **OK** when done, and Money enters this income in the **Occasional** column on the budget.

6. Repeat step 5 for all the income categories until the **Difference** line at the bottom of the budget window is $0.00, as shown in Figure 17.3. This means you have allocated the entire amount among the categories.

7. Click the **Close** button. The main Budget and Savings Plan screen appears.

8. Click the next line for which you have income (for example, **Partner's Gross Salary** or **Other Household Income**). Then repeat steps 2 through 7 to categorize the additional income.

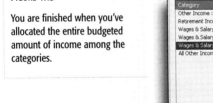

FIGURE 17.3

You are finished when you've allocated the entire budgeted amount of income among the categories.

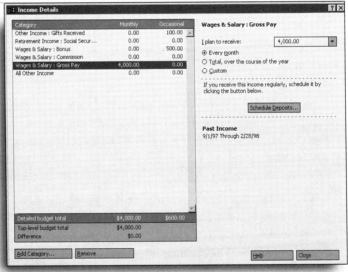

9. Now you're ready to enter your expenses. Click the **Monthly Debt Payments** line.

10. Enter your total monthly debt in the **Monthly Payments** field. This includes all mortgages, car payments, credit card payments, and so on. If you aren't sure of the amount, estimate.

11. Now let's work on your monthly expenses. Click the last line of the Budget & Savings Plan screen, **Expenses and Taxes**, and then click the **Expense Details** button that appears on the right side of the screen.

12. Enter budget amounts for each of the expense categories listed, just as you did for income categories. When you're finished, click **Close**. Money asks if it should transfer the new budgeted amount over to the budget window; click **Yes**.

13. Click the **Tax Tracking** button and then repeat step 12 for tax expenses.

14. Back at the main Budget and Savings Plan window, check out the blue line under the budget: **Your monthly income exceeds spending by (an amount)**. This amount is what you have left over to allocate to your savings accounts. (If you don't have any left over, or if you are in the hole, go back to your expenses and try to be a bit more austere in your estimates.)

15. In the **Monthly Savings Contributions** section, click a kind of savings you plan to do (for example, **Your Retirement**). Then enter the amount you plan to save each month in the **My Monthly Contribution Is** field.

16. Repeat step 15 for the other savings types you plan to employ, until you see the message Congratulations! Your budget balances. on the blue line beneath the budget (see Figure 17.4).

Employer contributions for retirement

In the **Your Retirement** and **Partner's Retirement** sections, you'll see a button for **Employer's Contribution**. You can click it to enter any contributions your employer makes for you. These contributions are not a part of your budget.

FIGURE 17.4

A balanced budget is your goal.

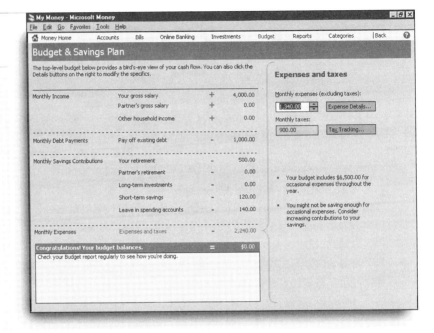

Checking Up on Your Budget

Categorize each transaction

If you are budgeting, it's essential that you categorize each income and expense transaction carefully to match the categories you have budgeted for. If you are sloppy about entering transactions with the wrong categories (or none at all), your budget won't do you any good.

The time-consuming part of budgeting in Money is over; now all you have to do is view the *My Budget report* to see how you're doing. You'll learn how to work with reports in the following section, but a quick preview is provided here.

Viewing your budget reports

1. Click the **Reports** link on the Navigation bar.

2. Click the **Spending Habits** button (left side of screen).

3. Double-click the **My Budget** report on the list of reports. The budget report appears. This shows your original budget.

4. Now click the **Back** link on the Navigation bar to return to the **Reports** list.

5. Double-click the **How I'm Doing on My Budget** report to see how your spending compares to the budget.

If neither report tells you what you need to know, you might try customizing it or changing the chart type. For example, personally, I don't get a lot out of the default **How I'm Doing on My Budget** chart. So instead I click the **Report** button (far bottom-left corner of the screen) while viewing it to change the picture to a text-based report, as shown in Figure 17.5.

SEE ALSO

➤ *To see more thorough coverage of customizing reports, see page 383.*

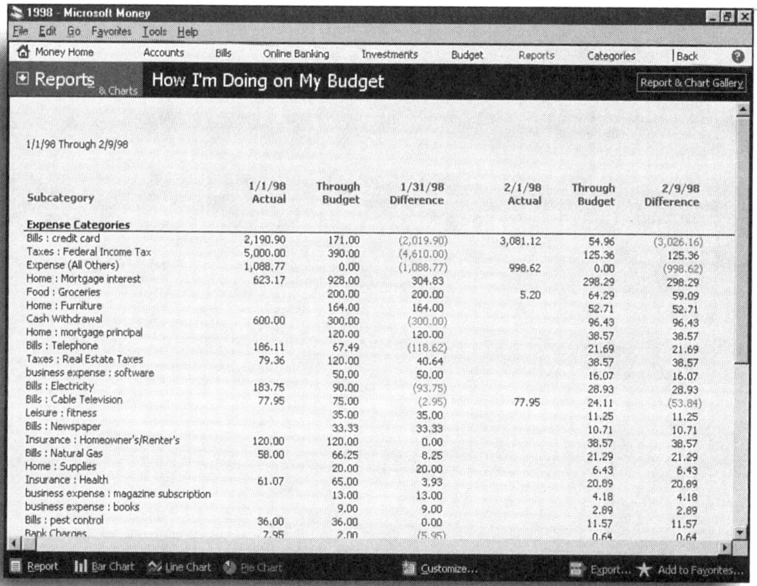

1/1/98 Through 2/9/98

Subcategory	1/1/98 Actual	Through Budget	1/31/98 Difference	2/1/98 Actual	Through Budget	2/9/98 Difference
Expense Categories						
Bills : credit card	2,190.90	171.00	(2,019.90)	3,081.12	54.96	(3,026.16)
Taxes : Federal Income Tax	5,000.00	390.00	(4,610.00)		125.36	125.36
Expense (All Others)	1,088.77	0.00	(1,088.77)	998.62	0.00	(998.62)
Home : Mortgage interest	623.17	928.00	304.83		298.29	298.29
Food : Groceries		200.00	200.00	5.20	64.29	59.09
Home : Furniture		164.00	164.00		52.71	52.71
Cash Withdrawal	600.00	300.00	(300.00)		96.43	96.43
Home : mortgage principal		120.00	120.00		38.57	38.57
Bills : Telephone	186.11	67.49	(118.62)		21.69	21.69
Taxes : Real Estate Taxes	79.36	120.00	40.64		38.57	38.57
business expense : software		50.00	50.00		16.07	16.07
Bills : Electricity	183.75	90.00	(93.75)		28.93	28.93
Bills : Cable Television	77.95	75.00	(2.95)	77.95	24.11	(53.84)
Leisure : fitness		35.00	35.00		11.25	11.25
Bills : Newspaper		33.33	33.33		10.71	10.71
Insurance : Homeowner's/Renter's	120.00	120.00	0.00		38.57	38.57
Bills : Natural Gas	58.00	66.25	8.25		21.29	21.29
Home : Supplies		20.00	20.00		6.43	6.43
Insurance : Health	61.07	65.00	3.93		20.89	20.89
business expense : magazine subscription		13.00	13.00		4.18	4.18
business expense : books		9.00	9.00		2.89	2.89
Bills : pest control	36.00	36.00	0.00		11.57	11.57
Bank Charges	7.95	2.00	(5.95)		0.64	0.64

FIGURE 17.5

I find that the How I'm Doing report is easier to understand in report form than as a chart.

Viewing Reports and Charts

Reports are text-based summaries of your data—for example, a report could add up all the transactions that were categorized as Food:Groceries and tell you how much you spent last month for groceries. Charts are graphical summaries of the same data. I'll tend to talk about reports and charts as a single entity in this chapter. That's because (at least in Money) they're just two different, interchangeable views of the same data. Every Money report can be viewed as a chart, and vice versa.

The procedure for viewing reports is the same for every report: Just pick the one you want and double-click it. It doesn't get much easier than that.

Customized report

The little clipboard and pencil icon next to a report's name means that it has been customized. In Figure 17.6, for example, the How I'm Doing on My Budget report has been customized.

Viewing a report

1. Click the **Reports** link on the Navigation bar, or open the **Go** menu and choose **Reports**, or press Ctrl+Shift+R. The list of reports appears (see Figure 17.6).

FIGURE 17.6

Money's list of reports is arranged into several types.

1 Report types.

2 A list of reports of the selected type.

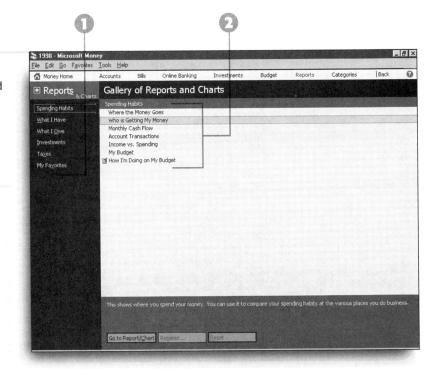

2. Choose a report type (**Spending Habits**, **What I Have**, and so on) from the list on the left side of the screen.

3. Double-click a report name to view that report.

4. To return to the list of reports, click the **Back** link on the Navigation bar or click the **Report & Chart Gallery** button (right below **Back**).

Want a closer look at a particular report or chart? Just move your mouse pointer over any report or chart element—for example, a number, pie slice, or bar. A pop-up box shows you its value. For example, in Figure 17.7, I have positioned the mouse pointer over the largest of the pie slices.

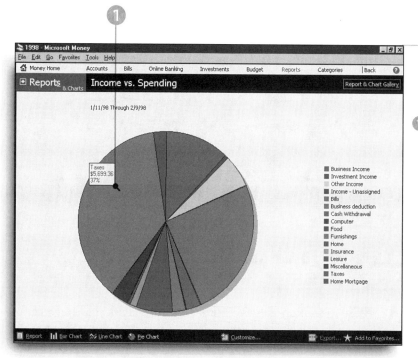

FIGURE 17.7

Just point at any part of a chart to see its value and find out what it represents.

❶ Mouse pointer.

Even more information is available by double-clicking the report or chart element to show a list of transactions it represents. For example, Figure 17.8 shows what happens when I double-click the same pie slice that I'm pointing to in Figure 17.7.

FIGURE 17.8

Double-click a chart element to see a list of the transactions that it represents.

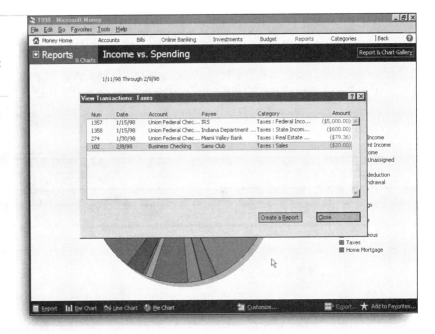

Changing a Chart into a Report (or Vice Versa)

Restoring a chart's native format

To put a report or chart back to its original format, select it from the Reports & Charts gallery and then click the **Reset** button. When asked to confirm, click **OK**.

Although almost all the reports/charts listed in the Reports & Charts gallery can be viewed either way, certain ones lend themselves naturally to one form or the other. The "natural" form of any item is what you see by default. For instance, Account Transactions is naturally suited to a report: It's highly detailed and text-oriented. Who Is Getting My Money, on the other hand, is more suited to a graphical format, because the whole point is to see a breakdown of where the money is going, not to read about individual transactions.

To change to the alternative form (report to chart or vice versa), or to change the chart type, click one of the format buttons at the bottom of the screen.

Money considers any format change to be a customization, and you'll see a customization icon next to the altered report or chart name in the report list.

Customizing a Report or Chart

Money's reports and charts are extremely versatile. You can change the report name, the time frame it encompasses, the chart type, the account(s) it accesses, and even the colors and patterns used, if you think any of those changes would make the report more useful to you.

To customize any chart or report, just click the **Customize** button at the bottom of the chart or report's display. A dialog box appears showing you your customization options.

The two sets of options are **Report** and **Chart**. The **Report** options control what data is included, and the **Chart** options control how a chart is formatted.

Customizing the Report Options

Let's start by looking at the **Report** options (the options that affect the data, not just the appearance) because you set these for both reports and charts. (Actually, when you get down to it, a chart is just a picture of a report.)

To customize your report, display the report or chart, and then click the **Customize** button. The Customize Report dialog box appears, as shown in Figure 17.9. If the Customize Chart dialog box opens instead, click the **More Options** button in that dialog box to switch to Customize Report.

I won't go into every detail of this dialog box, but some of the highlights include

- Enter a new title for the report in the **Title** text box.
- Change the date range that's included in the report by selecting one of the preset ranges from the **Dates** drop-down list. Or, if you prefer, type a range in the **From** and **To** text boxes.
- To use a different account, select it from the **From account** drop-down list. One of your choices is **Multiple Accounts**, which opens a box where you can choose several.

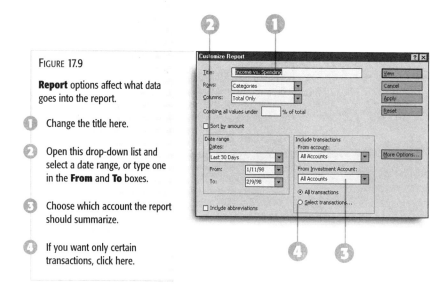

FIGURE 17.9

Report options affect what data goes into the report.

1 Change the title here.

2 Open this drop-down list and select a date range, or type one in the **From** and **To** boxes.

3 Choose which account the report should summarize.

4 If you want only certain transactions, click here.

- If you want to include investment accounts, select them from the **From Investment Account** drop-down list. You can select **No Investment Accounts** to exclude them all.

- If you don't want to include all transactions, click the Select transactions option button. A dialog box appears in which you can select which transactions to include.

Make your selections, and then click **View** to close the dialog box and apply your changes. If you change your mind and want to return to the default settings for the report or chart, click the **Reset** button in the Customize Report dialog box.

Changing Chart Options

In most cases, Money uses (by default) the most useful chart or report format. When you need to customize, however, you can change all the same things on a chart that you can change on a report—and more. For example, you can choose a different chart type, change the way labels are displayed, and add 3D effects. These changes can give you a different perspective on your data, helping you think about your situation in different ways. For example, if a chart of your expenses isn't meaningful because there are too many categories, you might limit the report's scope to a single account and look closely at one account at a time.

When you click the **Customize** button for a chart, the Customize Chart dialog box appears (see Figure 17.10). You can display or hide legends and gridlines, change the chart type, switch between colors and patterns, and more.

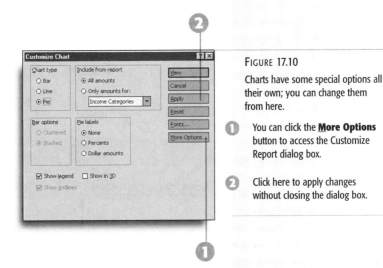

FIGURE 17.10

Charts have some special options all their own; you can change them from here.

1. You can click the **More Options** button to access the Customize Report dialog box.

2. Click here to apply changes without closing the dialog box.

You can also click the **Fonts** button (it works the same as it did from the Customize Report dialog box), or click **More Options** to view the Customize Report dialog box again. When you're finished, click the **View** button to close the dialog box and apply your changes.

Printing Charts and Reports

When your chart or report is exactly the way you want it, you may want to share it with others (unless you were just creating it for your own satisfaction, which is fine, too). At that point, you're ready to print your chart or document and then make copies of the printout to share.

Printing a chart or report

1. Display the report or chart onscreen.

2. Open the **File** menu and choose **Print**, or press Ctrl+P, or right-click the report or chart and choose **Print**. The Print dialog box appears. It will say either Print Report or Print Chart at the top, depending on which you're printing (see Figure 17.11).

Print quality

The lower the print quality, the faster the document will print. Use the highest quality for a final draft. Some printers have only one print quality available; in that case, you're stuck with whatever is offered.

3. Set any options desired in the dialog box. If you are printing a report, you'll have a field for the page range, in addition to the fields shown in Figure 17.11.

4. Click **OK** to print. The report or chart prints, and you've got a handsome printout to share with the world.

You can use the **Setup** button in the Print dialog box to set some additional options for your printer. The available options vary depending on what kind of printer you have. You may be able to choose between **Portrait** and **Landscape** orientation, change the paper size, and choose which paper tray to use. You can also select a different printer, if you have more than one, from the **Name** drop-down list in this dialog box. Check your Windows 95 documentation for more information about setting up a printer.

Investigating Online Banking and Bill Paying

Finding out what your bank offers

Setting up online services

Retrieving statements online

Transferring funds

Paying bills online

Banking You Can Do Online

Money offers two kinds of online service—Online Banking and Online Bill Payment.

Anyone can use Online Bill Payment, regardless of their bank. It works through a service called *Checkfree*, which is totally separate from Microsoft. You sign up for an account with Checkfree, and for your monthly fee, Checkfree processes up to a certain number of payments for you (something like 15, I think, is the limit).

You prepare your payments in Money by entering them in your register and setting the **Number to Electronic Payment (E-Pay)**. Then you click the **Connect** button in Money and dial the toll-free number with your modem. The payment information is sent to Checkfree, and they process your request and send a payment to the payee for you.

Online Banking is totally different. Online Banking works only with certain banks that have set up an online presence (usually through the Internet). You can pay bills through your bank's Online Banking, and send letters to the bank, retrieve electronic copies of your statements, check on a particular transaction, and maybe more, depending on your bank.

You set up your requests for transfers, statements, and so on in Money. Then when you click the **Connect** button to go online, Money sends all that information to the bank's computer. If you have requested anything to come back, such as a statement, Money retrieves it, then disconnects, and you can look at your statement offline at your leisure.

Where does Checkfree get the money?

Checkfree doesn't pay your payees with its own cash; it merely prints a computerized check with your own checking account number on it and mails the check for you. Or, in some cases, where Checkfree and a certain payee have made an agreement, Checkfree authorizes that payee to make an electronic withdrawal from your checking account.

What You Need

To use Money's online features, you need Microsoft Money (obviously!) and a modem. Almost any modem will do (14.4K or faster), although faster is better. You also need access to a telephone line.

Also, if you have Internet Explorer 4.0 (IE4) installed on your computer (as opposed to version 3.02, which you received free

No ISDN

ISDN modems, especially internal models, may not work correctly with Money; it's better to use a regular, Hayes-compatible modem.

with Home Essentials), you need to download a *128-bit security* patch to use Money's online services. Yes, I know, they are two totally separate programs, and it shouldn't make a bit of difference, but it does. If you try to use Money's online services with the regular 40-bit version of IE4 installed, Money will lock up every time. To download this patch, visit `http://www.microsoft.com/ie/download`.

Investigating Your Bank's Offerings

Now you'll use your existing Internet connection to go online and see what your bank offers. (If you don't have an Internet connection, consider the two-month free MCI offer included in your Home Essentials box.)

Finding out what the bank has to offer

1. Click the **Online Banking** link on the Navigation bar to reach the Online Banking & Investments screen (see Figure 18.1).

Taking a tour

If you want to know more about Money's online services, take a few moments to go through the interactive tour on the subject. Put Home Essentials Disc #1 in your CD-ROM drive, then click the **Online Banking** link on the Navigation bar. In the screen that appears, click **Take a Tour**. Click the **Close (X)** button when you've finished the tour.

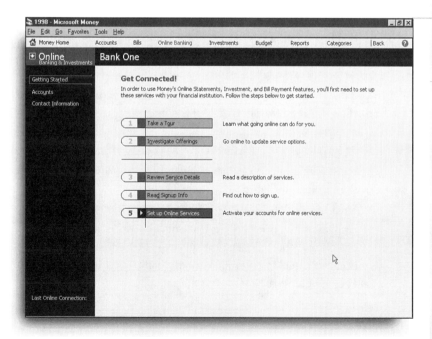

FIGURE 18.1

This screen is your home base for online transactions.

About those check boxes...

Some banks give you a setup file on a disk so you can set up their online services. That's the sort of thing that the first check box in step 2 is looking for.

The second check box should be marked if you have an Internet connection already. If you don't, Money will have to dial a special number with your modem.

2. Click the **I<u>n</u>vestigate Offerings** button. A dialog box appears with two check boxes—**<u>I</u>'ll be using an Online Services Setup File** and **<u>U</u>se my existing Internet connection**. Select or deselect these check boxes as appropriate for your situation. Then click **Next**.

3. Enter (or confirm) the name of the bank to check on. Try to be as specific as possible. For example, if you use National Bank of Detroit, write that rather than its abbreviation NBD. Then click **Next**.

4. What happens next depends on whether you marked the **<u>U</u>se my existing Internet connection** check box in step 2.

   If you did, a window appears prompting you for your Internet user ID and password. Enter them and click **OK** to connect.

   If you didn't, a dialog box appears with two buttons: **Change <u>D</u>ialing Options** and **Change <u>M</u>odem**. Click each of these in turn and examine and change the settings as needed, then click **Next** to connect.

5. Wait for Money to retrieve information about your bank.

6. Read whether services were found, click **Next**, and then click **Finish** to finish this exploratory portion of the setup. Now you are ready to read about the details of the offerings.

7. Back at the main Online Banking & Investments screen, click the **Review Ser<u>v</u>ice Details** button.

8. Click **Next** to see the first service available for your bank. The text explains what the service does and how much it costs. Repeat until you have read all the information for all the services available.

9. Next, you're prompted to select the provider. Even if your bank does not offer online banking, you will still see Checkfree (the bill payment service) as a provider here, because Checkfree works with any bank. Click the provider you want, and then click **Next**.

10. A confirmation message appears. Click **Finish** to accept your selection. The dialog box goes away, and you are ready for sign-up.

11. Click the **Read SignUp Info** button to open yet another dialog box. (Whew!) Information about the service you selected appears (for example, Checkfree).

12. Click the **Print** button to print the information shown. For some services (Checkfree, for example), this is especially important because they require you to fill out a hard-copy application and send it in by U.S. Mail.

13. Read the onscreen information carefully, and look for any special underlined text (hyperlinks) that you may need to check out (see Figure 18.2). For example, when enrolling with Checkfree, you should click the **Enrollment Form** link and then connect to the Internet to display and print the form from your browser.

14. When you are done reading, click **Finish**.

15. Review the printout you created, and follow the instructions to enroll in the services you chose.

Bank Online/Pay Online

Checkfree used to be called *Pay Online* or *Bank Online*, depending on which branch of the company you were dealing with. If you have used online bill paying or banking online with earlier versions of Money, you might have signed up for the service under one of those names.

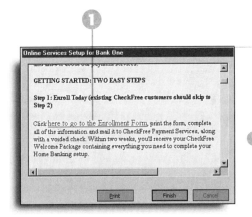

FIGURE 18.2
The text may contain hyperlinks (underlined phrases) that you can click to view more information through the Internet.

1 Hyperlink

Setting Up Your Online Services

After you have mailed off all your enrollment materials and received your confirmation letter, you are ready to set up your account in Money for online services. The exact procedure varies depending on the bank's services, so let's take a look at the one for Checkfree, which everyone can use. (The steps are similar for all services.)

Setting up online services

1. Click the **Online Banking** link on the Navigation bar to reach the Online Banking & Investments screen.

2. Click the **Set up Online Services** button. Then click **Next** to begin.

3. The first question Money asks is whether you have received your online password and access information. If you haven't, you won't be able to complete the setup, so click **Cancel**. If you have, click **Yes** and then **Next**.

4. Enter your name, address, and other personal information in the fields provided on the next screen as shown in Figure 18.3. Then click **Next**.

FIGURE 18.3

Money needs this information about you to identify you to the bank or bill payment service.

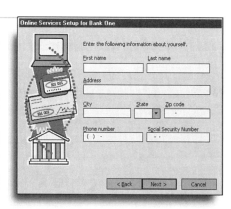

5. When prompted for the financial institution ID, enter the number from your setup materials. For Checkfree, this is always 1001. For online banking, it will be a unique number assigned to your bank. Then click **Next**.

6. A list of your Money accounts appears. Click the account you will be using with the online service, and then click **Next**.

7. Check boxes appear for each of the services offered by that bank. (If your bank offers none, you will have only one check box—**Online Bill Paying**.) Mark the check boxes for the services to use, and then click **Next**.

8. The next screen prompts for your account number and bank routing number, as shown in Figure 18.4. Enter these and click **Next**.

Account and routing numbers

Both numbers can be found on your checks; the *routing number* is the number in the bottom left corner of the check, and the *account number* is the number to the right of it.

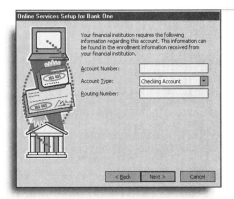

FIGURE 18.4
Enter the numbers that uniquely identify your account at your bank.

9. Next, you're asked whether you have other accounts at this same bank to set up. If you do, click **Yes** and then click **Finish** to set up the others. If not, click **No** and then **Finish** to end.

Banking Online

Online banking is considered a separate component from bill-paying online. Unlike the bill-paying, which works through an independent clearinghouse, online banking works intimately with your own bank. Your modem dials the regular Internet connection number, but the information it retrieves comes directly from your bank.

Online Banking has two basic features:

- *You can download a current bank statement at any time.* This is better than your monthly paper statement you receive in the mail because it is updated daily. If you have questions about whether a transaction has cleared, you can check the statement.

- *You can transfer funds between accounts (as long as they're both at the same bank).* Most banks normally require a trip to the local branch office to do this, but with Online Banking you can do it from the privacy of your home.

Retrieving a Bank Statement

When working with a downloaded bank statement, you must first retrieve the statement.

Retrieving a bank statement

1. Click **Online Banking** in the Navigation bar.

2. Click the down arrow at the upper-left of the screen, then choose the financial institution that has the account you want to update.

3. Click the **Connect** button (left side of screen) and review the list of transactions on the **Connect** tab. **Retrieve Statement** should be among them.

4. Click the **Connect** button (bottom of the screen) and follow the instructions on the screen.

5. After you have downloaded a bank or brokerage statement, click **Statements & Balances** in the left pane of the screen.

6. Click **Read Statement**, and follow the instructions on the screen.

Transferring Funds Online

You enter an electronic transfer the same way you enter a regular one in an account register. Then the transfer is sent the next time you connect.

Transferring funds from one account to another (at the same bank only)

1. Display the register for either of the accounts involved in the transfer.

2. Click the **Transfer** tab to display the Transfer transaction form. If the fields do not appear for data entry, click the **New** button.

3. Open the **Number** drop-down list and choose **Electronic Transfer (Xfer)**.

4. Complete the fields normally, choosing the appropriate **From** and **To** accounts from the same bank.

5. When you complete the transaction, a Things to Do: Online Banking indicator appears to the left of the register showing that you have online transactions to send. Click that indicator to jump to the Online Banking area.

6. Click the **Connect** button to connect to the Internet and send your transfer. A Call Your Financial Institution box appears.

7. Enter your PIN number (from your signup materials) in the **Online PIN** text box.

8. Click the **Connect** button. Your transactions are sent.

9. When you see the Call Summary box telling you your call was completed successfully, click the **Close** button to close the box.

Paying Bills Online

When you start paying your bills online with Checkfree, you'll never want to go back to writing checks by hand. It's very convenient. No stamps, no trips to the post office, and no writer's cramp in your hand.

To pay a bill online after you have signed up for Checkfree, just set the check number for the transaction to **Electronic Payment (E-Pay)**. Then connect using **Online Banking**, and the rest is gravy.

Go through Online Banking

Instead of clicking the indicator in the register to jump to online banking, you can click the **Online Banking** link on the Navigation bar and then click the **Connect** button on the left side of the screen.

Storing payee information

Money records the payee information you enter when paying bills electronically in the Payee Details dialog box. Whenever you pay that payee in the future, the details are automatically sent with your online transaction.

Checkfree also automatically updates address and/or account numbers of payees with which it has established a special direct account. If you later view the payee's details and the address or account number seem to have been changed, don't change it back to the original settings because it will mess up the direct account function.

Paying bills electronically

1. Display the register for the checking account from which you want to pay.

2. Start a new Check transaction, but instead of entering a check number, open the drop-down list and choose **Electronic Payment (E-Pay)**.

3. Complete the check normally. When you enter the payee, Money prompts you for the payee's address and telephone number, and for your account number as shown in Figure 18.5. Enter it and click **OK** to continue.

4. When you have completed the transaction, a Things to Do: Online Banking reminder appears to the left of the register telling you that you have transactions to send. Click it to jump to online banking.

5. On the Online Banking screen, click the **Connect** button at the bottom to connect. A Call Your Financial Institution box appears.

6. Enter your PIN number (from your signup materials) in the **Online PIN** text box.

7. Click the **Connect** button in the dialog box. Your transactions are sent.

8. When you see the Call Summary box telling you your call was completed successfully, click the **Close** button to close the box.

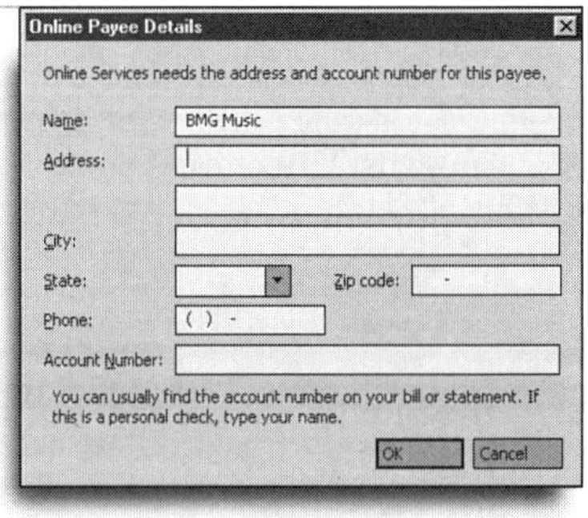

FIGURE 18.5

You enter this information only once for each payee; then Money remembers it.

Using Internet Explorer

Surfing the Internet with Internet Explorer

What Home Essentials Offers

Home Essentials comes with Internet Explorer (IE) 3.02 as well as two accessory programs—Internet News and Internet Mail. Internet Explorer is a *Web browser*, a program that enables you to explore the portion of the Internet known as the World Wide Web. Internet News grants you access to *newsgroups*, which are public Internet discussion groups. Internet Mail is an email program with which you can send and receive electronic mail.

How to Set Up an Internet Connection

You must have an Internet connection before you can use Internet Explorer, Internet Mail, or Internet News. Windows makes it easy for you to configure your Internet connection. First you'll need to get an *Internet service provider* (ISP). An ISP provides you with all the information—IP address, DNS address, host name, phone number to dial, and so on—you need to configure Windows 95 for the Internet.

After you set up your computer for using Internet Explorer, you can explore Web pages, send and receive email, and access news groups on the Internet. Windows makes it easy to set up and use the Internet by providing a wizard that guides you through the steps.

If you chose MCI as your ISP when you installed Internet Explorer, you do not have to go through these steps because the connection is already set up for you.

SEE ALSO

> *Home Essentials comes with two months of free Internet access from MCI. To learn how to set up MCI as your default service provider, reinstall Internet Explorer, as explained on page 525.*

Setting up your Internet connection

1. Click the **Start** button and point to **Programs**. Then point to **Accessories**, **Internet Tools**, and then click on **Get on the Internet**. The Internet Connection Wizard appears. Click the **Next** button to start the process.

2. Choose the **Manual** option if you have an account with an ISP and want to set up your computer with addresses and information your ISP has provided. Click the **Next** button to continue setup. If you chose Manual, an introductory screen appears; choose **Next**.

3. The **How to Connect** Wizard box appears. Select the method you'll use to connect to the Internet. You'll most likely use the phone line to connect; however, if you're a member of a network, choose the LAN option instead. These instructions assume you're using a phone line. Click **Next**.

4. The Wizard next asks if you want to use Windows Messaging to send and receive email; choose **Yes** and click the **Next** button. (If you choose **No** here, you won't be able to send or receive email messages over the Internet using Windows' Internet Mail application.)

5. The **Installing Files** dialog box appears. Click **Next** to continue the process.

6. If prompted to choose which modem to use, choose it from the **Select a modem to use to connect to the Internet** drop-down list and then click **Next**. You may not see this dialog box if you have only one modem installed.

7. Next you see the Service Provider Information Wizard dialog box. Enter the name of your ISP and choose **Next**. This name does not have to be exact; it is for your own reference only.

8. In the **Phone Number** Wizard dialog box, enter the area code (if applicable) and the phone number of your ISP (see Figure 19.1). (This is the phone number that your modem dials, not the phone number that you call for help.) Choose the country code, if different from the United States. Click the **Next** button.

SEE ALSO
➤ *If you do not see the Get on the Internet choice on the menu, make sure you have installed Internet Explorer. See page 525 for details.*

Need Windows files?

Windows may prompt you for your Windows CD-ROM at some point during the process of setting up your Internet connection. Have your Windows CD handy, and if you're prompted for it during setup, insert the disc and choose **OK** to continue.

Automatic

If you do not have an ISP and you want Windows to find an ISP for you, choose **Automatic** and follow the directions onscreen in the Wizard dialog boxes that follow.

Existing ISPs welcome

If someone has already set up a connection to your ISP on this computer, you can select it from the drop-down list in step 6 rather than re-entering it.

Area code required

You must enter an area code in step 7 even if the area code is the same as your own. Windows will not dial the area code unless it is different from yours.

FIGURE 19.1

Enter the phone number to use to connect to your ISP, including the area code.

Special characters for logon

Some ISPs require you to supplement your user ID with some special character when connecting. For example, my provider requires that I enter a "1" after my name, like this: username1. Check with your ISP to find out if you need to do something like this.

9. In the User Name and Password dialog box, enter the User name and password assigned to you by your ISP. Notice the password enters as asterisks instead of characters, to protect your privacy. Click **Next**.

10. In the IP Address dialog box, choose the appropriate response and click the **Next** button. Either your ISP assigns an address each time you log in, or you use the same IP address each time. If the latter, click **Always use the following** and enter the address to use (see Figure 19.2). Typically, this option will be set to have the ISP assign the address, but check your ISP's documentation to be sure.

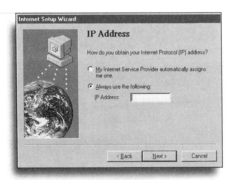

FIGURE 19.2

If appropriate, enter a specific IP address to use.

11. In the DNS Server Address dialog box, enter the IP number(s) or DNS name(s) for the DNS server(s) your ISP uses. This information, as well as all other you use in this wizard, should be obtained from your ISP. Click **Next**.

12. If you want to use the email program provided with Internet Explorer, leave the Use Internet Mail check box marked. If not, remove the check mark and skip to step 14.

13. Enter your email address and your ISP's Internet mail server in the Internet Mail dialog box. (This is usually something like pop@*yourisp*.com.) This information, as well as all other you use in this wizard, should be obtained from your ISP. Click **Next**.

14. When asked which **Windows Messaging profile you want to use**, choose the correct one from the drop-down list (if there is more than one on your system). Then click **Next**.

15. The **Complete Configuration** dialog box appears to let you know that the setup wizard is complete. Click the **Finish** button. When you click The **Internet** icon on the desktop, the connection you just created will appear.

> **No special characters for email address**
>
> If you entered a special character with your user name in step 8, you do not need it when entering your address in step 12. It is needed only for the initial login, not for checking email.

Accessing the Internet

After you have set up your Internet connection (in the preceding steps), that connection starts whenever you start Internet Explorer.

Using an initial Internet Explorer

1. Double-click the **The Internet** icon on your desktop. The **Connect To** dialog box appears (see Figure 19.3), with your connection information pre-entered.

> **FIGURE 19.3**
> Windows prompts you to establish your Internet connection.

Microsoft home page

The Microsoft home page is the first Web site you see after connecting to the Internet. This site tells you about Microsoft as well as other services you can access over the Internet.

2. If your password is not in the **Password** text box, enter it.

3. Click **Connect** to dial and connect to the Internet. The Explorer dials your ISP and then displays the Internet Explorer window and the Microsoft home page.

Using Internet Explorer

When you start Internet Explorer for the first time, a special Web page may appear prompting you to register your software and advertising Microsoft products. If you want to go through that, you can follow the directions onscreen. If not, click the Home button on the Internet Explorer (IE) toolbar to display the Microsoft Internet Start page. This is the page that will usually appear each time you start the program in the future.

The Internet Start page is updated daily, so yours will look different from the one in Figure 19.4. However, it will contain many of the same features.

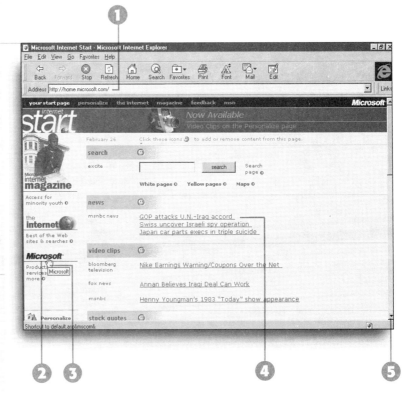

FIGURE 19.4

The Internet Start page appears by default each time you start IE.

 The page's address appears here.

2 Most pictures are hyperlinks, too.

3 Mouse pointer becomes a hand over a hyperlink.

4 Underlined text is a hyperlink.

5 Scroll down to see the rest of the page.

A Look at the IE Screen

Before we go any further, take a moment to examine the controls in IE (see Figure 19.5).

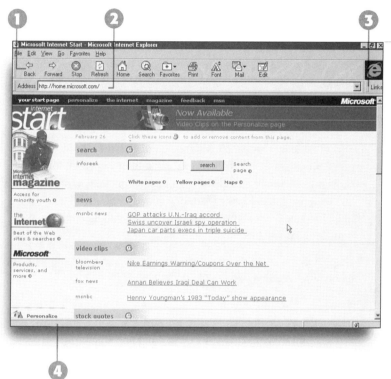

FIGURE 19.5

IE makes it easy for you to navigate Web pages on the Internet.

1 Toolbar

2 Address bar

3 Links bar

4 Status bar

Besides the normal menu system that all Windows programs have, IE has these items:

- *Toolbar*. As in Word and Works, IE employs a toolbar to provide shortcuts for the most common menu commands.

- *Address bar*. The address bar shows the address of the current page you're seeing. You can visit other pages by typing their addresses here and pressing Enter.

- *Links bar*. The links bar contains buttons that you can click on to visit some popular sites. You can't really see the Links bar by default; you can see only its name. To see the whole bar, click on it. The bar expands to replace the address bar. Click on its name again to reshrink it.

Hyperlinks

A *page* is an Internet document with a particular address all its own. Notice the address of the Internet Start page in Figure 19.4. A *hyperlink* is a pointer to another page's address. When you click a hyperlink, that page is displayed. Hyperlinks can be underlined text (the most common kind), or they can be graphics. To tell the difference between a plain graphic and one that is a hyperlink, position your mouse pointer over it. If the mouse pointer turns into a hand, as in Figure 19.4, the graphic is a hyperlink.

- *Status bar.* The status bar shows the status of the current page. As a page is loading, it will tell you what percent of the loading process is done.

You can turn off the display of the toolbar and status bar by opening the **View** menu and clicking on either of them to remove the check mark next to them. This frees up about an inch of extra space in the window where the pages appear. For best results as a beginner, however, you should leave both displays on.

Moving Between Pages

You have several ways to go from page to page. If you're in the mood to explore, you can simply click on a hyperlink on the current page to move to a different one. In this way, you can follow an endless chain of links from one place to another, something like that "free association" word game where one word makes you think of the next.

IE provides some important toolbar buttons for people who like to browse like this:

- *Back.* Each time you click Back, you return to the preceding page. You can click it as many times as you want, until you are finally back at your original default starting page.

- *Forward.* If you have clicked Back, you can go forward again by clicking this button. (Note that you can't go forward unless you have gone back.)

Getting Out of Trouble

Occasionally you may get "lost," or a page may not load correctly. Here are a few ways to get out of one of these messes:

- *Stop.* This button stops the loading of a page. You might use it, for example, to stop either a page that you really didn't intend to load or a page that you're not really that interested in that is taking a long time to load.

- *Refresh.* Sometimes there is a snafu in sending the data from the Internet to your browser, and a page may not look right.

Maybe some of the pictures are missing or the text is out of whack. You can sometimes correct this by refreshing the page. Refreshing also updates the page information from the server, so if you are looking at a page that updates frequently (for example, to show the current stock prices), the figures will be updated each time you click Refresh.

- *Home*. If you ever get lost and you aren't sure where to go, why not go home? Click the Home button to return to your default Internet start page.

Going to a Specific Address

These days it seems like everybody and his corporate sponsor has a *Web site* (a collection of pages), and they all want you to visit. Even TV commercials show Web site addresses. Chances are good that if you haven't already, you will soon find an address that you want to visit.

Going to a specific Web page

1. Click in the **Address bar**. The address that's currently there becomes highlighted.

2. Type the new address. The old one disappears immediately when you start typing.

3. Press Enter. IE takes you to that page.

If an error message appears, perhaps you typed something wrong. Check the address in the address bar. If you see an error, correct it. To correct an error, click once on the address to highlight it, and then click on it a second time to move a cursor into it. Use the arrow keys to move the cursor and the Backspace key to delete, just like in a word processor.

SEE ALSO

➤ *One of the sites you might want to visit is the Home Essentials Web site. See page 529 for details.*

Searching the Internet

Unfortunately, there is no complete yellow pages of the Internet. There are many so-called directories or indexes, but none lists every Web page.

Home is where you say it is

You can change which page appears when you start the program and when you click the Home button. Your home page doesn't have to be Microsoft's official Internet start page. To change it, open the **View** menu and choose **Options**. Click the **Navigation tab**, and enter the address for the page you want to use in the **Address** text box.

Address or URL?

Another term for a Web address is *Uniform Resource Locator* (URL).

That's the "cup is half empty" approach; the optimistic thought is that there are millions and millions of interesting sites that you can readily find with many of the hundreds of search engines available online.

The Internet start page offers a shortcut to the Infoseek search engine right there, so you don't even have to visit any other sites. Just type a subject of interest into the text box (see Figure 19.6) and click the Search button.

FIGURE 19.6

You can use the Infoseek search engine right from the Internet Start page.

Search engine

A *search engine* is a program that looks up keywords or other criteria you specify in a huge database collection of information about Web pages. To use a search engine, you first go to the page where it is located.

Each of the hundreds of search engines available on the Internet maintains its own database, and each produces different results. If you're doing serious research, you should work with several different search engines. If you're just using the Internet for fun, you can get by with one or two.

For example, suppose you are searching for Shetland Sheepdog, as in Figure 19.6. Figure 19.7 shows the results that might appear. As you can see, the search engine provides lists of pages that contain the words you entered; you just scroll through the list and pick the site(s) where you want to go. When you are finished working with a site, click Back to return to this results page and try a different site.

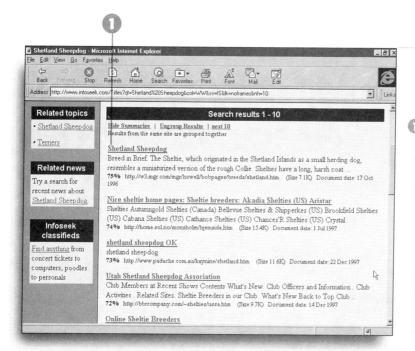

FIGURE 19.7

The Infoseek search engine produces these results from looking for "Shetland Sheepdog."

1 Click any underlined link to go there.

You can also visit a special page where many search engine links are collected. Follow these steps.

1. Click the Search button on the toolbar. A Search the Web page appears (see Figure 19.8).

2. If you have a preference among the various search engines, click the option button for the one you want to use. Otherwise, just accept whichever one appears (this selection changes daily).

3. Type the words you are searching for in the text box. (The exact label on the text box depends on which search engine you're using.)

4. Click the button next to the text box. (The exact name of this changes, too—it might be Find, Seek, Search, Go Get It, or some other such phrase.)

Which search engine?

Of all the major search engines, only Yahoo! limits its sites to those that the Yahoo! staff have checked and approved. Use Yahoo! if you want to see fewer—but better—sites. If you're looking for quantity, use one of the other search engines.

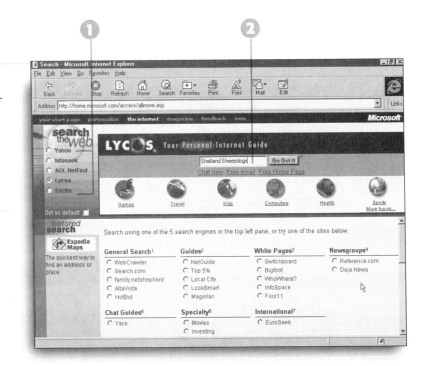

FIGURE 19.8

From here, you can try out a variety of different search engines.

1. Choose one of these search engines.

2. Type your words to search for here.

5. Examine the results (like the ones you saw in Figure 19.7), and visit whatever pages interest you. Click Back as needed to return to the results page after visiting a site.

6. If you want, click Back until you return to the Search the Web page again, and try your search again with a different search engine.

Notice that at the bottom of the Search page are listings of other search engines. If you are doing serious research, you should check out most or all of these to make sure you have found every Web page possible.

Using the Favorite Places Feature

Bookmarks

If you have worked with other Web browsers (such as Netscape) before, you may be more familiar with the term *Bookmarks* than with *Favorite Places*. They both mean the same thing: saved Web page addresses.

Sometimes you'll stumble on a site by accident that is really cool, and you'll want to remember to come back to it later. That's where the Favorite Places list comes in.

You can use Favorite Places to mark and record sites in a convenient listing; to revisit the site, you need only click its name in the list. You also can sort and edit the list to manage this time-saving feature.

Adding a Favorite Place

Adding a Web site to your Favorite Places list takes only a moment—and can save you lots of time later.

Saving an address as a Favorite Place

1. While viewing the site you want to save, click the Favorites button on the toolbar to display the Favorites menu.

2. Click the **Add to Favorites** command, opening the Add to Favorites dialog box (see Figure 19.9).

3. The name of the site is already included. Change it if you want the name to appear differently on your list, and then click **OK**.

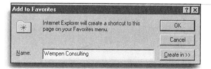

FIGURE 19.9

You can identify the site on your list with any title you want; just change the title here.

If you want, you can organize the Favorite Places into folders as you save them. To do so, click the **Create in** button (see Figure 19.9). An extra section of the dialog box opens, as shown in Figure 19.10. (Notice in Figure 19.10 that there are two folders I have already created; you may not have any yet on your own screen.)

If you want to put the new favorite in one of the existing folders, just click on its name and then click **OK**.

To create a new folder, click the **New Folder** button, enter a name, and click **OK** to accept the new folder name. Then choose that folder on the list and click **OK** to close the dialog box.

FIGURE 19.10

Favorites can be grouped into folders for tidier housekeeping.

Revisiting a Favorite Place

After you have saved a favorite place, you can jump to it quickly. Just click the Favorites button on the toolbar to open a menu of the favorite places you have saved. If you have created folders for them, the folders appear; point to a folder to swing out a submenu of the places it contains. Then click on the site you want to visit (see Figure 19.11).

FIGURE 19.11

To revisit a favorite place, select it from the Favorites menu.

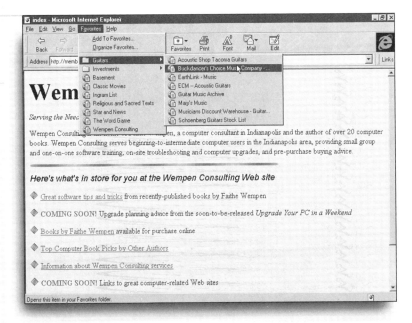

Managing the Favorites List

You aren't stuck with the initial names and folder locations you assign to your favorite places; you can change them at any time. For example, you might decide that you want to group all your favorites that deal with your job in a folder called "Job," or all the ones that you don't use very often in a folder called "Extras." You can also delete favorites that are…well, no longer your favorites.

Managing your favorites

1. Click the Favorites button, and choose **<u>O</u>rganize Favorites** from the menu that appears. The Organize Favorites dialog box appears (see Figure 19.12).

FIGURE 19.12

You can sort your favorites and group them into folders from here.

❶ Create New Folder button.

2. Click on the item that you want to move, rename, or delete.

3. Do one of the following:

   - To delete the item, click the **Delete** button.

   - To rename the item, click the **Rena<u>m</u>e** button. Then type the new name and press Enter. To move the favorite to a different folder, click the **Mo<u>v</u>e…** button. In the window that appears, click the folder to move it to, and then click **OK**.

   - To create a new folder, click the **Create New Folder** button. Type the name for the new folder and press Enter.

Reordering favorites within a folder

The favorites in a folder always appear in alphabetical order. You can't change that. You can, however, rename them to achieve the order that you want. For example, rename the item you want on top so that it begins with a number instead of letters; numbers come first on the list.

In keeping with that thought, you can order all your favorites in a folder precisely by renaming each one to start with the number that you want it to be on the list.

4. Repeat step 3 for each of the items you want to change, and then click **Close** to exit the dialog box.

Shutting Down Your Internet Connection

When you're done surfing the Web and you're ready to close Internet Explorer, you can either remain connected or disconnect from the Internet. If you remain connected, you can access Internet Mail or Internet News, as explained in Chapter 21, "Working with Internet News and Mail."

To exit Internet Explorer, choose **File**, **Exit**. If the Disconnect dialog box appears to confirm that you want to disconnect from the Internet, choose **Yes** to disconnect or **No** to continue working online. (Stay online if you are planning to work on Chapters 20, "Customizing Internet Explorer," and 21 right now.)

If the Disconnect dialog box doesn't appear, double-click the connection icon on the taskbar (down by the clock) to open the **Connected To** dialog box. Depending on your setup, the icon may look like two computers hooked together with a cable, or it may look like a modem with two flashing red and green lights. Click the **Disconnect** button to disconnect from the Internet.

That's about all you need to know to use Internet Explorer.

You can do a few special things with IE to customize how it works, though. You may or may not be interested in this; if you are, make sure you read the following chapter.

Customizing Internet Explorer

Changing the Way You Connect to the Internet

When you set up your Internet connection in Chapter 19, "Surfing the Internet with Internet Explorer," you specified which modem you were going to use, entered a phone number for the connection, and so on. If you later get a different modem or the phone number changes, you might have to make a switch.

Testing Your Modem

If you get a new modem, you must first install it in Windows 95. The modem must be recognized in Windows 95 before you can use it to connect to the Internet. Follow these steps to check which modems Windows 95 recognizes.

Checking your modem in Windows 95

1. In Windows 95, click the **Start** button and point to **Settings**. Then click **Control Panel** to open the Control Panel window.

2. Double-click the **Modems** icon to see a list of modems you have installed.

3. If the modem you want to use does not appear on the list, click the **Add** button and follow the onscreen instructions to install drivers for it.

4. To test an installed modem, click the **Diagnostics** tab. Click on the port for the modem you want to test (see Figure 20.1), and then click the **More Info** button. A window appears reporting some codes. You don't need to understand them—just look for the word **OK** next to some of ATI diagnostic codes. If at least a few of them say OK, the modem is working.

   If all codes are blank or say ERROR, your modem is not installed correctly or is defective. In that case, you will need to either reinstall the modem drivers or seek additional technical help from your modem's manufacturer.

5. If these tests are successful, close all the dialog boxes and rest assured that your modem is fine.

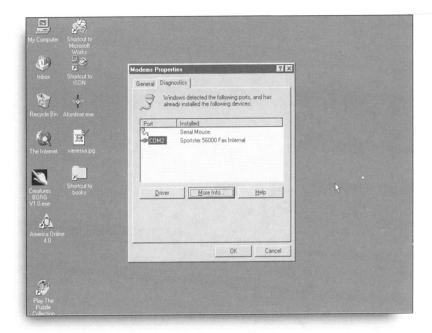

FIGURE 20.1

You can check out a modem's operation by clicking its port and then clicking **More Info**.

Changing the Dial-Up Connection Properties

After you have confirmed that the modem you want to use is working, you must change your Dial-Up Networking settings or create a new Dial-Up Networking connection.

You may not have realized it, but when you went through the setup procedure in Chapter 19, you created a Dial-Up Networking connection. To see it, open the My Computer window by double-clicking the **My Computer** icon on the desktop. Within that folder, double-click the **Dial-Up Networking** icon. A window appears showing all the dial-up networking connections on your system (see Figure 20.2).

To create a new dial-up connection (for example, if you have a second ISP that you sometimes use), click the **New Connection** icon and follow the instructions onscreen.

To modify an existing connection, right-click its icon and choose **Properties** from the menu that appears. This displays the properties dialog box for that icon (see Figure 20.3).

FIGURE 20.2

Locate the connection that you currently use to connect to the Internet.

FIGURE 20.3

Changing the properties changes the way the connection is established and maintained.

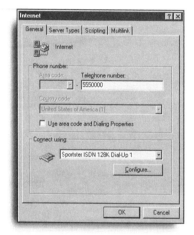

From this dialog box, you can perform the following functions:

- Change the phone number being dialed by entering a different number in the **Phone number** text box.

- Choose a different modem to use (if you have more than one) by selecting it from the **Connect Using** drop-down list.

- Change the IP address and DNS address by clicking the **Server Types** tab and then the **TCP/IP Settings** button.

Click **OK** when finished with any of these functions to direct the system to accept your changes.

Changing the Dial-Up Connection in Internet Explorer

If you made changes to an Internet connection in the above section, you do not need to change anything in Internet Explorer as long as the name of the connection stayed the same. However, if you created a new ISP connection or changed the name of your existing one, you must inform Internet Explorer. Follow these steps:

Choosing a different dial-up connection in Internet Explorer

1. Start Internet Explorer (IE) by double-clicking the **The Internet** button on your desktop.

2. If the **Internet AutoDial** dialog box appears (see Figure 20.4), open the drop-down list and choose the connection you wish to use. Then click **OK**.

FIGURE 20.4

This dialog box appears if the connection you formerly specified in IE no longer exists or has been renamed.

3. The **Connect To** dialog box appears. Connect to the Internet as usual.

SEE ALSO

➢ *For more information about the Connect To dialog box, see page 403.*

4. In IE, open the **V**iew menu and choose **Options.** The Options dialog box appears.

5. Click the **Connection** tab (see Figure 20.5).

6. If the connection listed is not the one you want to regularly use for IE, open the **U**se the following Dial-Up Networking connection drop-down list and choose the correct connection to use.

7. Click **OK**.

FIGURE 20.5
You can choose how Windows
95 connects to the Internet to
run Internet Explorer.

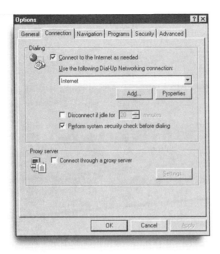

SEE ALSO

➤ *You may also need to change your Internet Mail and Internet News setup if you have*
changed ISPs. To learn how to change that configuration, see page 431.

Changing the Way Pages Appear Onscreen

Web pages send certain codes to your Web browser, but each
browser can interpret those codes in its own way. For example, a
page might send the code "Use a heading font for this heading,"
but the browser decides what constitutes a heading font.

Because of this difference, there are lots of settings you can
change in IE that control how Web pages display on your system. The following sections detail a few of the more popular
changes you can make.

Changing the Starting Page

If you want to start with a different Web page each time you
start IE, you can do so. The Microsoft Internet Start page is the
default, but you can point to any page that has a valid address.
Whatever page you choose will also be the page that you return
to when you click the **Home** button.

To change the starting page, follow these steps.

Changing the starting page

1. Open the **View** menu and choose **Options**. The Options dialog box appears.

2. Click the **Navigation** tab (see Figure 20.6).

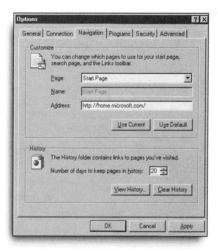

FIGURE 20.6
You can specify which Web page to open when IE starts.

3. Type a different address in the **Address** text box. Or, if you prefer, do one of the following:

   • If you want to start with a blank page each time, clear all text from that text box.

   • If you want to set the currently displayed page as the start page, click the **Use Current** button.

   • If you want to reset to the default home page address after you have set it for some other page, click the **Use Default** button.

4. Click **OK** to close the dialog box.

SEE ALSO

➤ *To learn about the Search Page, see page 407.*

Choosing a search page

If you want to start with the Search page that you worked with in Chapter 19, open the Page drop-down list and choose **Search Page**.

Changing the Display Font

As mentioned earlier, your Web browser settings determine the font and font size of text on displayed Web pages. If you are finding it hard to see the text on your browser window, you can make that text larger very easily. Just open the **View** menu and point to **Fonts**, and choose a larger size from the submenu that appears. The default is **Medium**, but you can choose **Large**, **Largest**, **Small**, or **Smallest**. The latter two can help fit more words on the screen at once so you don't have to scroll as much, if your vision can handle the smaller type.

Changing the Colors Used

If the font is chosen by the Web browser, not the Web page, what about the colors and background? These can go either way. IE has settings for text color and background, but they are used only for pages that do not provide their own font color and background information. The default background in IE is to use the same color scheme that you use in Windows 95. The Windows Standard scheme uses plain white with black text.

Visited and unvisited hyperlinks

IE uses a history list to keep track of which Web pages you have displayed. If a hyperlink refers to a page on that list, it's considered a visited hyperlink, and it displays in a different color. To clear this list, clear the History list. This process is explained in the section "Protecting Your Privacy" later in this chapter.

You can also change the color of the underlined hyperlink text in the pages you view. The default is blue for unvisited hyperlinks, and green for visited hyperlinks.

Changing colors in IE

1. Open the **View** menu and choose **Options**. The Options dialog box opens.

2. Click the **General** tab if it is not already displayed (see Figure 20.7).

3. If you want to override Windows colors, deselect the **Use Windows colors** check box. (If not, skip to step 6.)

4. Click the **Text** button to pop up the Color dialog box for text, and click on the color you want to use (see Figure 20.8). (Choose a color that contrasts well with the color you want for the backgrounds.) Then click **OK**.

5. Click the **Background** button and do the same as in step 4 to choose a new background color.

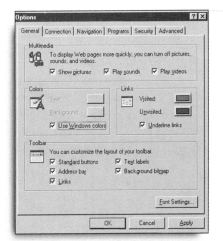

FIGURE 20.7
Make your color choices from
the **General** tab.

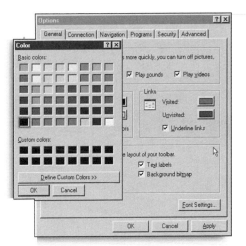

FIGURE 20.8
Click the color that you want to
use.

6. To change the color for visited hyperlinks, click on the
Visited button. In the Color dialog box, click on a new
color to use and click **OK**.

7. Click on the **Unvisited** button and do the same as in step 6,
choosing a new unvisited hyperlink color.

8. Click **OK**.

Enabling and Disabling Multimedia

At the top of the General tab, which you worked with in the
previous section, you may have noticed the Multimedia check

boxes (refer to Figure 20.7). These check boxes are labeled **Show pictures, Play sounds,** and **Play videos.**

By default, all these multimedia options are checked because they enhance your Web-browsing experience. You can turn them off, however, if they aren't appropriate for you or if you don't want to speed the page-loading process. For example, if you don't have a sound card, playing sounds does not do you any good, and loading the sounds into your computer's memory wastes time. You might deselect **Play sounds** and **Play videos,** too.

Most people want to leave **Show pictures** marked because today's Web pages are so graphically based that you can miss out on a lot of content by not showing pictures. However, if you have a very slow modem (slower than 28.9), each page may take a long time to load. Turning off the graphics can make each page load a lot faster. Figure 20.9 shows how a page loads when you turn off **Show pictures.** Notice the placeholders for the images. If you want to display a certain graphic, you can click its place-holder to display it.

FIGURE 20.9

This page does not show any pictures, so it loads in your browser very quickly, even with a slow modem.

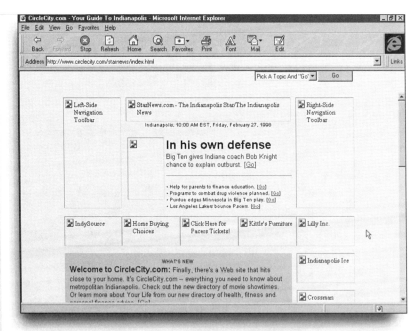

Protecting Your Privacy

You yourself are in the best position to assess your need for computer privacy at the local level. Do a lot of people use your home computer, or only you? Do you care if the other people who use your computer know what you've been looking at on the Internet?

There is also an Internet-wide privacy issue to consider. Whenever you send information to a site (such as entering keywords in a search engine), someone could intercept those keywords and find out what your interests are—in theory, anyway. The possibility is extremely remote (in fact, you stand a greater chance of being struck by lightning in the next 24 hours). But this slim possibility keeps some people awake at night.

SEE ALSO

➤ *For information about search engines, see page 407.*

Here are some settings you can use in the Options dialog box to make your system more snoop-proof.

Hiding Where You've Been

If you don't want other people who use your computer to be able to find out what Internet sites you've visited, there are some steps you can take to cover your tracks using the Options dialog box:

- On the **General** tab, set the color for the **Visited** and **Unvisited** links to the same color so that a link that you have visited before is not obvious to someone else using your computer.

- On the **Navigation** tab, click the **Clear History** button to clear the list of sites that you've visited. (If you don't clear this, someone can click the **View History** button on this same page to see.) Do this regularly. In this area you can also choose the number of days to keep your history file. Choosing a larger number of days keeps larger lists of your surfing, while a shorter number of days cleans up your tracks on a more regular basis.

- On the **Advanced** tab (see Figure 20.10), you can control the storage of temporary Internet files on your hard disk. When you visit a page, its information is *cached* (temporarily saved) on your hard disk in a special temporary folder. That way, the next time you visit that page, it loads much more quickly because it pulls the saved copy unless the page has changed. The downside is that, as with your History list, people can look at your saved temporary files and know where you've been. To clear the temporary files, click the **Settings** button. In the dialog box that appears, click the **Empty Folder** button and then **Yes**. To prevent IE from saving temporary files in the future, click the **Never** option button.

FIGURE 20.10

You can clear your temporary files from here.

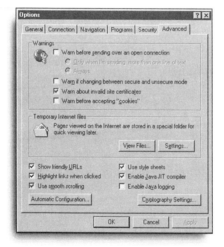

Now you can close all the dialog boxes and resume surfing, secure in the knowledge that your secrets will remain just that.

Be Warned About Outsiders

This section is mostly for the really paranoid. There are millions of people surfing the Internet, and most of them are visiting really ordinary sites. Unless you feel that you have somehow been targeted for surveillance, you can forget about people outside your home snooping on you.

If you're still reading, you must be worried, so here you go.

On the **Advanced** tab, choose which warnings you want to receive in the Warnings area. For example, you can set IE to warn you each time you send information over the Internet that someone could intercept, so you can assess your risk on a case-by-case basis.

On the **Security** tab, there is a section for *certificates* (see Figure 20.11). Certificates are like passcodes that prove that content is coming from a legitimate source. For example, when you download a file that appears to be coming from Microsoft, how do you know that some evil foreign government is not actually sending the file and pretending to be Microsoft? Microsoft sends a certificate with the download that says "Yes, it's really us." IE handles certificates more or less automatically, so you don't have to do anything with these controls; just feel good that they're there. (Advanced users can configure the use of certificates and even purchase their own digital certificates to positively identify them to others, but this is total overkill for the home user.)

Have a cookie?

One of the warnings in the Warnings area on the advanced tab is **Warn before accepting "cookies"**. A *cookie* is a little text file that is placed on your hard disk to keep track of the fact that you've visited this page before. They're used to identify frequent visitors, so you don't have to re-enter your information the next time you visit the site. Cookies make your Web browsing more convenient, but some people feel they are an invasion of privacy. If you mark the **Warn before accepting "cookies"** check box, each time a page tries to copy a cookie to your hard disk, a box appears so you can either accept or reject it.

FIGURE 20.11

Control the use of certificates, active controls, and more from here.

Also on the Security tab you'll find an **Active content** area with check boxes for the various kinds of active content you might encounter. Active content refers to programs that are designed to run over the Internet. You may have heard of Java, which is one common kind of active control. You can choose which kinds of

Safety level

Next to the **Active Content** check boxes on the **Security** tab is a **Safety Level** button that controls the types of sites from which your browser will accept active controls. Click on this button if you want to see the safety level settings. However, by default IE is set for the highest safety, so you should not have to ever change this.

controls you want to be able to use. For example, suppose a Web page you visit has an embedded Java application that plays a game with you. In theory, the person designing that Web page may be a malicious hacker who has written a program that will destroy the hard disks of people who play the game. You can prevent that from happening to you by disabling Java content. Of course, if you disable Java programs, you'll miss out on a lot of really cool games and other activities that are perfectly legitimate.

Limiting Content Access

Many parents wonder how they can prevent their children from visiting inappropriate Web sites. IE has a built-in content screening system. By default this system is turned off; here's how to turn it on.

Enabling content rating

1. On the **Security** tab, click the **Enable Ratings** button. A password box appears so you can password-protect your settings.

2. Type a password in the **Password** box, and then type it again in the **Confirm Password** box. Then click **OK**. The Content Advisor dialog box appears (see Figure 20.12).

Change the password

You can change the password from the **General** tab in the Content Advisor dialog box.

FIGURE 20.12

You can lock out certain kinds of sites from here.

3. In the Category box, click the category you want to work with—**Language**, **Nudity**, **Sex**, or **Violence**. A slide bar appears below the window.

4. Drag the slide bar to choose the tolerance level for the category. Figure 20.13 shows a tolerance level being set for Violence.

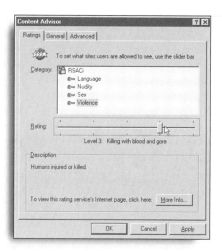

FIGURE 20.13.

Adjust the tolerance level for each category individually.

5. Repeat steps 3 and 4 for each category.

6. The settings you just set apply only to sites that have ratings. Unrated sites will all be blocked completely. If you want to allow access to unrated sites, continue on to step 7. Otherwise, click **OK**; you're done.

7. Click the **General** tab.

8. Click to place a check mark in the **Users can see sites which have no rating** check box. Then click **OK**.

When you turn on the Content Advisor, the **Enable Ratings** button becomes a **Disable Ratings** one instead. You can click that button to turn off the content screening at any time.

When someone tries to access a site that is forbidden based on the ratings, a message appears telling them that the site has been blocked by your browser's settings.

Additional surf security

You can buy other, more comprehensive site-blocking software to use along with Internet Explorer (such as NetNanny) that enables you to block sites based on specific keywords you enter. (For example, you could block out all sites that use "hot sex" as keywords.)

Working with Internet News and Mail

Reading your email

Replying to a message

Creating email messages

Keeping track of addresses

Reading a newsgroup

Posting messages to a newsgroup

What Are Internet Mail and Internet News?

Internet Mail is an email program through which you can exchange messages with others over the Internet. You can send a mail message to anyone for whom you have an address, and you can receive messages in the Mail program.

You can use Internet News to exchange ideas and information about business, politics, hobbies, and many other interests in some of the more than 15,000 public newsgroups on the Internet. *Newsgroups* (forums in which people exchange ideas on the Internet) enable you to contact others with similar, or completely different, ideas.

Usenet

You may hear newsgroups called Usenet groups. *Usenet* is the most popular network of newsgroup distribution, but it is by no means the only one. However, many people erroneously use the term "Usenet group" to refer to any newsgroup generically.

You can pose questions about your new computer or state opinions about the best type of dog to use in hunting grouse. You can discuss your home-decorating ideas or meet people who write science fiction short stories. There are literally thousands of forums you can search, read about, and visit time and again. The Windows Internet News application enables you to browse lists of available newsgroups, search groups for a topic or description, view a topic and related responses posted, and much more.

To use Internet Mail and News, you must have installed Internet Explorer 3 because Internet Mail and Internet News are accessory programs that come with it. You must also have a modem and an Internet connection. If you have Internet Explorer 4 (the newer version), you won't have Internet Mail and Internet News. Instead, you'll have a program called Outlook Express that serves the same purposes but is not covered in this book.

SEE ALSO

➤ For more information about getting started with Internet Explorer, see page 525.

➤ To configure an Internet connection, see page 400.

Opening and Closing Internet Mail and Internet News

You can start Internet Mail or Internet News as a separate application, or you can launch either of them from within Internet

Explorer. It all depends on what is most convenient at the moment; if you are already using IE, it's a simple matter to jump over to the mail or news program from there.

- To start these applications outside of IE, click the **Start** button, point to **Programs**, and then click on **Internet Mail** or **Internet News**.

- Within IE, open the **Go** menu and choose **Read Mail** or **Read News.**

If your Internet connection is not active, the Connect dialog box appears to connect you. Connect as usual.

SEE ALSO

➣ *To learn how to use the Connect dialog box, see page 403.*

Working with Internet Mail

When you start Internet Mail, your new messages may automatically appear. If they don't, or if you aren't sure, click the **Send and Receive** button on the toolbar. Any new messages appear in bold, as shown in Figure 21.1.

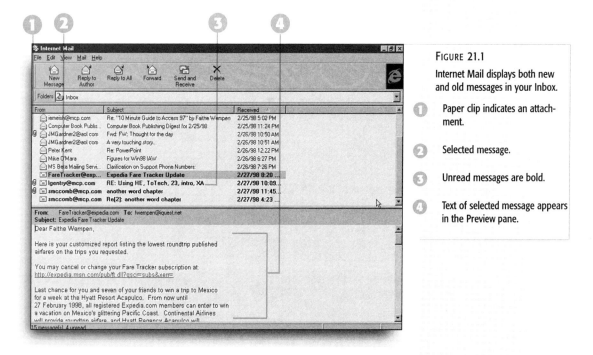

FIGURE 21.1

Internet Mail displays both new and old messages in your Inbox.

1. Paper clip indicates an attachment.

2. Selected message.

3. Unread messages are bold.

4. Text of selected message appears in the Preview pane.

The messages in your Inbox that are in bold type are messages that have not been read. Messages in regular type have been opened but remain in the Inbox until you either delete or move them to another folder.

Reading Mail

To read a message, you can select it in the upper pane of the Internet Mail window, and the message text is displayed on the lower pane. You also can double-click the message to open it so you see the text in a better view (see Figure 21.2).

FIGURE 21.2

View the message in its own window by double-clicking on it.

① AutoText entry pop-up.

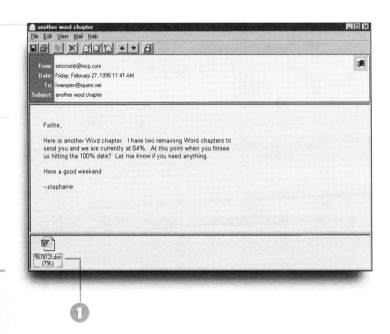

Mail management

The Inbox is where all new mail first arrives, but you have other mail folders as well. The Outbox holds your outgoing messages before they are sent, and the Sent Mail folder stores copies of your sent messages. To view a different folder, choose one from the drop-down list at the top of the Internet Mail window.

You can also create your own folders for mail management by opening the **File** menu and choosing **Folder**, then **Create.** You can then move selected messages from the Inbox to one of your created folders by opening the **Mail** menu and then choosing **Move To.**

Following are some other things you can do with open mail:

- To print an open message, choose **File** and select **Print**.
- To delete a message, choose **File** and select **Delete,** or press **Delete when the message is highlighted.**
- To close a message, open the **File** menu and choose **Close.**

- To read the next message in the list without closing the opened one, open the **View** menu and choose **Next Message**; to read the previous message, open the **View** menu and choose **Previous Message**.

If the message has an attachment, you'll see a paper clip next to it, as in Figure 21.1. When you open the message, the attachment appears in its own pane at the bottom, as in Figure 21.2. You can double-click on the attachment to open it. You can also save it directly to your hard disk without opening it by right-clicking the attachment and choosing **Save As** from the menu that appears.

Replying to a Message

You can reply to any message you receive, and Internet Mail automatically places a copy of the original message in your reply, separated from your text by a short, dashed line and identified with the > symbol preceding each line of the original message (including headers). When you reply to a message, the application also addresses the message to the original author and uses the subject of the original message as the subject of the reply, but with an RE: preceding the original subject (see Figure 21.3).

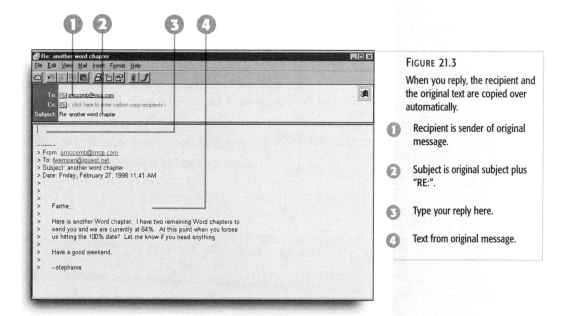

FIGURE 21.3

When you reply, the recipient and the original text are copied over automatically.

① Recipient is sender of original message.

② Subject is original subject plus "RE:".

③ Type your reply here.

④ Text from original message.

Want to reply to everyone?

If the original message was sent to more than one person, you can send the reply to each person who originally received the message by clicking the Reply All icon [icon] or choosing **Reply to All** from the **Mail** menu.

Replying to a message

1. In the open message to which you want to reply, click the Reply icon [icon] on the toolbar, or open the **Mail** menu and choose **Reply to Author**.

2. In the Reply message window (see Figure 21.3), add any names in the Cc area if you want to send a copy of the message to someone else.

3. Enter the text of your message above the original text.

4. When you're ready to send the message, click the Send button [icon] on the toolbar, or open the **File** menu and choose **Send Message**. If you're not connected to the Internet, Internet Mail stores your message in the **Outbox** and sends the message after you connect.

Creating Mail

You will probably also want to send your own, brand-new messages in Internet Mail. This process works basically the same as sending a reply, except you have to provide the address of the recipient(s) and the text for the Subject line.

Creating a new mail message

1. In Internet Mail, click the New Message button [icon] on the toolbar, or open the **Mail** menu and choose **New Message**. A **New Message** window appears.

2. In the **New Message** window, enter the address of the recipient in the **To** text box, or select addresses from the **Address book** (as explained in the section that follows these steps).

3. Click the **Subject** field and enter a topic for the message.

4. Click the message area and enter the text for your message (see Figure 21.4).

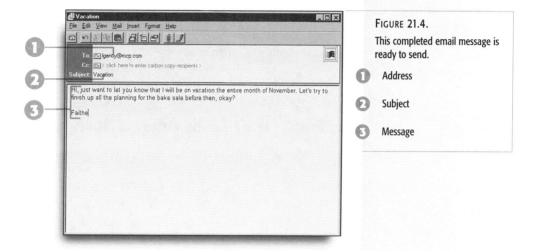

5. Choose **File** and select **Send Message** or click the Send button ⊡ on the toolbar when you're ready to send the mail. If you're not connected to the Internet, Internet Mail stores your message in the **Outbox** and sends the message after you connect.

You can also do the following things before sending a message:

- To set a priority, or level of importance, for the message, open the **Mail** menu and choose **Set Priority**, and then choose either **High**, **Normal**, or **Low**. The default priority is Normal.

- To attach a file, open the **Insert** menu and choose **File Attachment**, or click the Insert File button ⧉ on the toolbar. In the Insert Attachment dialog box, select the file you want to attach, and choose the **Attach** button. Internet Mail adds the file, represented by an icon, to your message.

- To format the message text, select the text and then open the **Format** menu and choose **Font** (to change the font) or **Align** (to change the alignment). You also can create bulleted text in your message by selecting the text, opening the **Format** menu, and choosing **Bullets**.

Working with the Address Book

The Address Book enables you to save the addresses of people to whom you send frequent emails so you don't have to look them up every time.

Adding a Name to the Address Book

What's in a name?

The name you enter in step 3 is purely for your own reference. If you don't want to bother with their entire name, or if you don't know it, just put something in the **First** field that will help you recognize their address on a list. For example, if the email address is for the sales staff at Acme Corporation, you might put Acme Sales as the first name and leave the other name fields blank.

Whenever you receive a message from someone, you can add that person's email address to your address book by displaying the message, then opening the **File** menu and choosing **Add To Address Book** and then **Sender**. You can also add people to your address book without having received a message from them. Follow these steps.

Creating a new address book entry

1. Open the **File** menu and choose **Address Book**. The **Address Book** window appears.

2. Click the **New Contact** button on that window's toolbar. A New Contact dialog box opens (see Figure 21.5).

FIGURE 21.5

Fill in any details about the new person that you want; email address is the only required field.

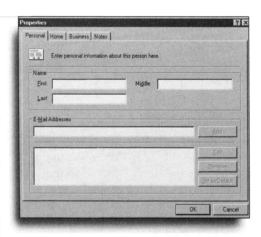

3. Type the person's **First**, **Last**, and **Middle** names in the fields provided.

4. Click in the **E-Mail Addresses** text box, and type the person's email address there. Then click **Add**.

5. (Optional) To record any extra information about the person, click one of the other tabs in the dialog box and fill in the other fields.

6. Click **OK**. The name is added to your address book.

Addressing Messages Using the Address Book

When addressing a message, you can click the index card next to the To: or Cc: field or click the Pick Recipients button 🐾 on the toolbar to display the Select Recipients dialog box. This box displays the names of everyone in your address book (see Figure 21.6). Click on the name of the person you want, and then click the **To** or **CC** button to copy that person's name to the appropriate list. When you are done adding recipients, click **OK** to return to creating your message.

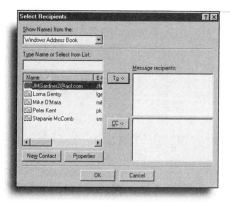

FIGURE 21.6
You can choose recipients from your address book for the emails you send.

Working with Internet News

As mentioned earlier, there are more than 15,000 newsgroups you can read with Internet News. To read one, you subscribe to it. (You can unsubscribe at any time.) When you are subscribed to a newsgroup, each time you start Internet News the new messages in that group are sent to your PC so you can read them.

Subscribing to Newsgroups

A long wait

Downloading an entire list of news-groups may take quite some time; luckily, you download the whole list once and then periodically add new lists to the current one.

More newsgroups later

If you want to subscribe to other groups (or unsubscribe to some), click the **Newsgroups** button on the Internet News toolbar to reopen the Newsgroups dialog box.

When you open Internet News for the first time, a dialog box appears asking if you want to view a list of available newsgroups. Choose **Yes** to continue. Then wait for the list of newsgroups to be transferred to your PC.

When the list of newsgroups finally appears, scroll through it and click on one to which you want to subscribe (see Figure 21.7). To narrow the list, type a subject in the **Display news-groups which contain** text box. Only the newsgroups that con-tain that word in their title appear on the list then. To return to the full list, remove the word from the text box. Then click the **Subscribe** button. Do this until you have picked out all the ones you want, and then click **OK** to read them.

FIGURE 21.7

Choose the newsgroups to which you want to subscribe.

1 Type a subject here to narrow down the list.

2 Click this tab to see the ones to which you've already subscribed.

3 Click **Unsubscribe** to unsub-scribe from a group.

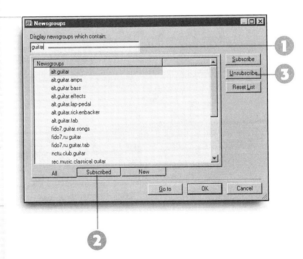

Viewing a Subscribed Newsgroup

To view the messages in a subscribed newsgroup, choose that newsgroup from the **Newsgroups** drop-down list at the top of the Internet News screen. The messages appear in the top pane. In the bottom pane, the selected message's text appears, just as in Internet Mail (see Figure 21.8). Click on the message you want to see in the upper pane to display it in the lower one, or double-click the message to display it in its own window.

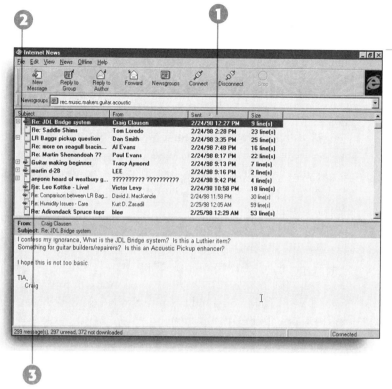

FIGURE 21.8

Newsgroup messages can be read just like email messages.

❶ Click on any column heading to sort by that column.

❷ Plus sign means there are replies; click on it to see them.

❸ Bold messages are unread.

Posting a Newsgroup Message

To post a new newsgroup message, simply create a new message, just as you would a new email message. The only difference is that you don't need to enter a recipient; instead you choose which newsgroup to post the message. Click the **New Message** button on the toolbar, or open the **News** menu and choose **New Message to Newsgroup**. Complete the message as you would any email message, with the subject and the text. Choose **File** and select **Post Message**, or click the **Post Message** button to send it.

You can also reply to any posted message in the newsgroup, and your reply will be also posted to the newsgroup for public reading. Just open the **News** menu and choose **Reply to Newsgroup**, or click the **Reply to Group** button on the

Managing messages

By default, only 300 messages are displayed at first. To see 300 more, open the **News** menu and choose **Get Next 300 Headers**.

If you get lost in all the messages, set up Internet News to show only the unread ones. To do this, open the **View** menu and choose **Unread Messages Only**.

If you want to get a group of messages out of your way without reading them, mark them as read. Simply select them and then open the **Edit** menu and choose **Mark As Read**. To mark all messages in the group as read (even the ones you haven't selected), use **Mark All As Read** instead.

toolbar. The Reply message window appears with a copy of the original message and the message's topic in the Subject area of the header. Enter your reply (just as with an email message), and then click the **Post Message** button on the toolbar, or open the **File** menu and choose **Post Message** to send it to the newsgroup.

To compose a new message to the group, open the **News** menu and choose **New Message to Newsgroup**. Complete the message as you would any email message, by entering the newsgroup's address (you can get it from the Newsgroups dialog box), the subject, and the text. Open the **File** menu and choose **Post Message** to send it.

You can do a lot more with the Internet Mail and Internet News programs—so much that we can't cover it all here. Fortunately, both programs are fairly intuitive. Explore the menu systems in these programs, and check out the Help options. Before you know it, you'll be sending public and private messages all across the Internet with the best of them.

Think before you post

The Internet is full of arrogant, ignorant people who post inflammatory, insulting messages to newsgroups. Don't be one of those people. Before you post, ask yourself: Is what I'm saying true? Is it kind? Is it helpful? If not, don't post it.

Keep in mind that whatever you post will be read—and criticized—by thousands of people. Posting in a newsgroup is not the same as sending a private email. If you have something to say that only one individual will be interested in, send a private email to that person instead of posting it to the newsgroup.

Exploring the Other Home Essentials

Microsoft Greetings Basics

Creating your first project

Making changes to text and graphics

Moving objects around

Adding a page border

Printing, saving, and opening projects

Finding add-ins on the Internet

What Is Microsoft Greetings Workshop?

Microsoft Greetings Workshop (Greetings Workshop for short) is an easy-to-use program that helps you create beautiful greeting cards, invitations, posters, calendars, photo frames, stickers, stationery—just about anything that's printed. If you don't have a color printer, you may end up buying one when you see all the fun, colorful items you can produce with Greetings Workshop.

Signing In

Experience level?

The experience level you choose sets the prompts in the program to the appropriate level of help for you. The examples in this chapter are based on the **Intermediate** level, so if you see slightly different prompts on your own screen, it may be because you have chosen a different experience level.

When you installed Microsoft Greetings Workshop, the installation program put a shortcut for it on your Windows 95 desktop, so all you have to do to start the program is double-click the shortcut. (If there's no desktop icon, open the **Start** menu and choose **Programs**, then **Greetings Workshop**, and **Greetings Workshop** again.

When you start the program, you're asked to sign in. That's because Greetings Workshop keeps track of each person's saved projects and preferences separately. If your name doesn't appear on the list, click **Add a name**. A dialog box appears where you can enter your name and experience level (see Figure 22.1). After you've entered the information, click **OK**.

FIGURE 22.1

The first time each person uses Greetings Workshop, he needs to identify himself.

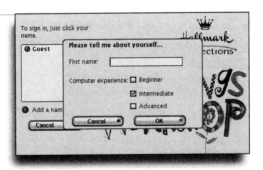

In the future, when you start the program, just click your name to log in.

Navigating the Program

If you are accustomed to businesslike programs like Word and
Works, you may be surprised and a bit taken aback by Greetings
Workshop, shown in Figure 22.2. Everything here is a cartoon,
and a talking dog guides you through each step of each project.
The mouse pointer is in the shape of a hand. When you pass the
pointer over an option "link," the link lights up. The Navigation
bar is at the bottom of the screen and contains the program's
Exit command.

To start a project, you just click one of these links, make choices
in the boxes that appear, and then plug in your customizations.
(You'll see this process at work several times later in this chapter.)

FIGURE 22.2

Greetings Workshop is its own
little cartoon universe. Click an
item on a shelf to create it.

1   Talking dog

2   Mouse pointer (hand)

3   Navigation bar

To lose the dog...

If you have some experience with other programs, such as Word or Works, you may find the program's controls (located on the toolbar and in the menu system) perfectly usable and the dog may seem annoying. If that's the case, ignore him, and the next time you log on, create a new user name and assign it an Experienced user level. The dog's involvement is minimized when you sign on this way.

Most of the things on the shelves are project types you can work on, but a few of the items are not projects. Here's a quick rundown of them:

- *Hallmark Papers*. If you bought special paper from Hallmark to use with Greetings Workshop, you can set it up here so anything you print will not bleed over on the edges of the drawings on that paper.

- *Go Online*. If you are connected to the Internet, you can click this link to jump to the Microsoft Greetings Workshop Web site, where you can download free add-ons.

- *Reminders*. You can set reminders for certain holidays so Greetings Workshop will prompt you to create cards for it. For example, you could set it to remind you about Valentine's Day a few days in advance.

- *Idea Book*. The program contains an entire book with advice about what projects are appropriate for what situations; you can read the book by clicking here.

- *Saved Projects*. Clicking here opens a list of the projects you have saved, so you can reopen and work on them.

Greetings Workshop's project types all sit on the shelves in Figure 22.2, waiting for you to select them. Each is fairly self-explanatory, so I won't list them all here. Instead, let's just try some out.

SEE ALSO

➤ *To learn how to download free add-ons for Greetings Workshop, see page 469.*

➤ *To learn how to work with saved projects, see page 469.*

Creating Your First Project

Let's start with a greeting card, because they're fairly straightforward. The skills you learn while creating this card can be applied to all the other projects.

Three types of cards can be created in Greetings Workshop: regular cards, announcements, and invitations. They all work the same way; the only thing that changes is the array of designs available. Let's start out with a regular birthday card, because everyone has a birthday.

Creating a card

1. From the main Greetings Workshop screen, click **Cards** (top shelf).

2. The dog asks how you want to get started, as shown in Figure 22.3. Click the card type you want (for example, **Birthday**) and then click **Continue**.

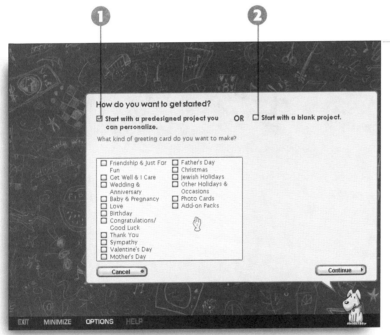

FIGURE 22.3

First, choose the type of card you want to create.

1 For your first project, you may want to work with a template.

2 Click here if you want complete creative control.

3. Depending on the card type, you are asked some other questions. For example, for the birthday card, you're asked to choose a recipient. Answer each question, clicking **Continue** to move on, until you arrive at the screen on which you get to choose the card (see Figure 22.4).

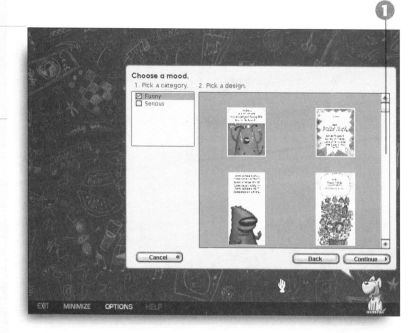

FIGURE 22.4

Choose the card design.

① Use the scrollbar to see more designs.

Card wording

When you click a card design, you see its text off to the right. Keep in mind that you can customize this text later, or even change it completely. Don't let the text be the defining factor on which card you pick.

On your own

If you want to add more stuff to the card, like a signature block, you can click the **Work On My Own Now** button to open the tools that enable you to do so. You won't learn about those tools until later in this chapter, however, so for now you might just stay on the beaten path.

4. Choose a mood for the card (for example, **Funny** or **Serious** in Figure 22.4) and then choose a card design from those that appear. Then click **Continue**.

5. Next you see the front of the card. Click the text on the card and make any changes to the text. Use the Backspace key to remove text, or highlight it and press Delete (see Figure 22.5).

6. Click the **Continue** button when you're ready to move to the inside of the card.

7. On the inside of the card, change the message if you want to. Just click the words on the card and edit them.

8. When you're done customizing the inside of the card, click **Continue**.

9. Now you see the back of the card, as shown in Figure 22.6. Change the text if you want. (For example, you might change "you" to the recipient's name in the phrase "Created just for you…".) Then click **Continue**.

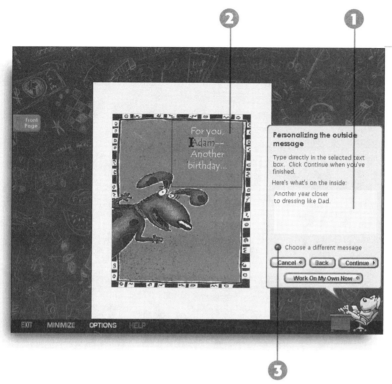

FIGURE 22.5

Type your own text here. You might choose to just change the recipient name, or you might make up your own text entirely.

1 This text is on the inside; it's strictly FYI here.

2 Customize the card front text here.

3 Click here to see some other suggested messages.

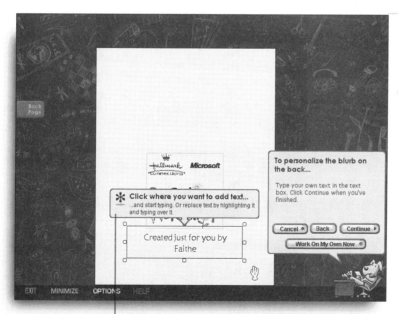

FIGURE 22.6

You can even customize the back of the card, where the company label usually goes.

1 If you see Help boxes like these, just click anywhere away from them to make them go away.

10. Now that the initial run-through is done, you get the whole palette of tools and choices for the card, as shown in Figure 22.7. Go on to one of the other sections in this chapter, depending on what you're interested in doing next.

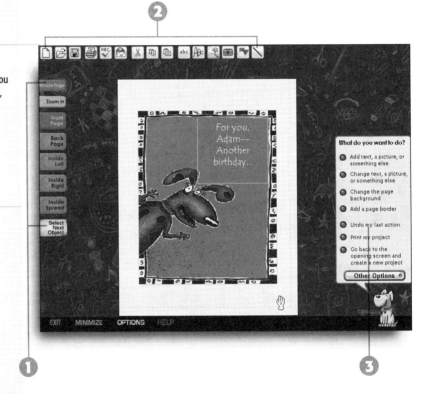

FIGURE 22.7

After the card has been built, you can further customize it, save it, print it, and so on.

1 Tabs

2 Toolbar

3 Option controls

SEE ALSO

➤ *To view the various sides of the card again (front, back, inside, and so on), see page 453.*

➤ *To change the font and font size, see page 453.*

➤ *To add something else to the card, see page 455.*

➤ *To resize, move, or copy text or graphics, see page 462.*

➤ *To print your card, see page 467.*

Moving Around in a Project

Notice in Figure 22.7, the tabs along the left side of the screen: **Front Page**, **Back Page**, **Inside Left**, and so on. Click one of these tabs to display that part of the card.

This can be really useful if you want to place something on a part of the card that is blank by default. For example, suppose you want to place a special message or picture on the inside left (behind the front cover). You can click the **Inside Left** tab to display that part of the card, and then add some text or a graphic as explained in the following sections.

The **Zoom In** and **Whole Pages** tabs toggle between looking at the whole card (the default) and viewing a close-up detail of part of it. When you click **Zoom In**, scrollbars appear so you can display different parts of the current page. Click **Whole Page** to zoom out again.

Changing Text

You already saw how to change existing text: Just click it to place the insertion point inside its box and then edit the text as you would in a word processor. Use the arrow keys to move the cursor, the Backspace to delete, and so on.

You can also add an entirely new text box. For example, suppose you want to add a new box under the inside message that says "Much love, Mom and Dad." There are two ways to do it. You can click the **Add Text** button in the talking dog's bubble and then keep responding to him until he tells you what to do (the no-brainer way), or you can just go ahead and add it (the fast way), as explained in the following steps.

Adding text

1. Click the **Add New Text Box** button ⎡abc⎤ on the toolbar at the top of the screen. A box appears saying "Your Text Here," in addition to some extra controls, as shown in Figure 22.8.

FIGURE 22.8

A new text box appears. You can modify and move it to fit your needs.

1 This Formatting toolbar appears.

2 **Add New Text Box** button.

3 The new text box.

Black box

Don't worry about the black outline around the text box. It won't print.

Wrong page

You cannot drag text boxes or other objects between pages on the card. If you realize you need to put the text box on a different page of the card, select it and click the Cut button to cut it, display the page on which it goes, then click the Paste button.

2. Type your own text, replacing the **Your text here**.

3. Select the text (hold down the left mouse button and drag across it, or press Ctrl+A) and then apply any formatting to it that you want. Hover over a button to get an explanation of what it does. Click a button to apply the format; if you don't like the results, click the button again to remove the format.

4. When you are finished formatting the text, click away from the text box to deselect it. Then reposition the mouse pointer over the border of the box, so the mouse pointer turns into a four-headed arrow with **MOVE** on it.

5. Drag the text box to the place you want it on the card. When you're finished, it might look something like Figure 22.9.

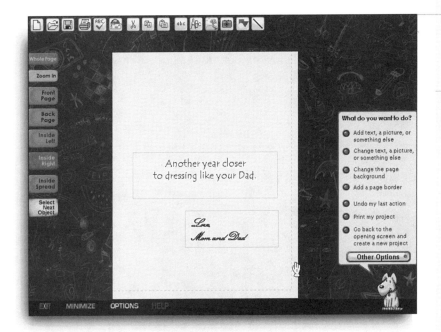

FIGURE 22.9
The added text has been formatted and positioned on the card.

Adding Non-Text Objects

Strictly speaking, everything is an *object* on your card (or other project). Each text box, each picture, is a separate piece. You have already seen how to add text to a card, so now let's take a look at what else you can add.

Adding a Picture

Picture is this program's word for clip art. If you have worked with clip art in Word or Works, you know that clip art is predrawn art that you can use to enliven a plain space or illustrate a point. Follow these steps to see and use what Greetings Workshop has to offer.

Adding a picture to your project

1. Click the Add New Picture button ![icon] on the toolbar. A box appears from which you can select the picture you want.

2. Click the category of picture you want. Samples of the pictures available for the first subcategory in that category appear (see Figure 22.10).

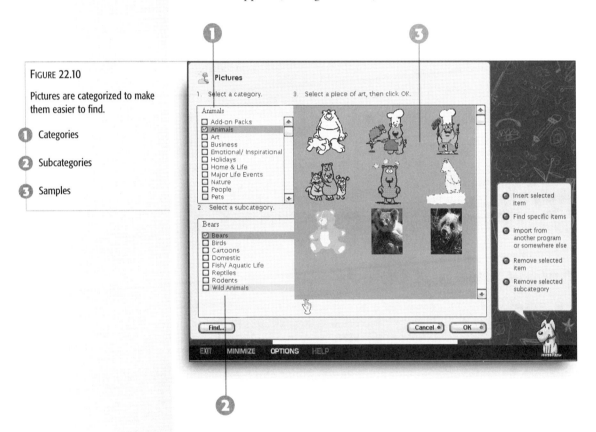

FIGURE 22.10

Pictures are categorized to make them easier to find.

1 Categories

2 Subcategories

3 Samples

3. Select a subcategory from the **Select a subcategory** list beneath the **Select a category** list. The available pictures change to show the ones for that subcategory.

4. Select the picture you want (scroll down to see others), and then double-click it to place it into your project.

5. Move or resize it as needed.

SEE ALSO

➤ *To move or resize your picture, see page 462.*

Adding a Photo

The distinction between a photo and a picture (that is, a piece of clip art) is rather fuzzy. For practical purposes, let's just say that *clip art* is anything that shows up in the categories when you insert clip art in Greetings Workshop, and a photo is any other piece of art, such as a *scanned image* or something you've drawn in an art program like Paint. That's not exactly accurate, but it's close enough without getting too technical.

Adding a photo is a lot like adding clip art, except it's not categorized. Click the Add New Photo ▣ button on the toolbar, and a list of photos appears in the default folder. You can look in other folders by clicking the **Add a Photo From Somewhere Else On My Computer** button to open a browsing window where you can select a different folder or drive.

All your photos in the chosen folder are listed, and you can preview them by clicking their names, as shown in Figure 22.11. When you find the one you want, click **OK**. It appears on your project.

SEE ALSO

➤ *You can work the photo just like any other object, see page 462.*

Adding Shaped Text

Shaped text is another name for *WordArt*, which you may have encountered in Word or Works. It's a neat little utility that takes regular-looking text and twists, bends, and otherwise manipulates it to look cool. You can spend many hours playing with this feature.

FIGURE 22.11

Choose from the pictures displayed, or display the contents of
a different folder.

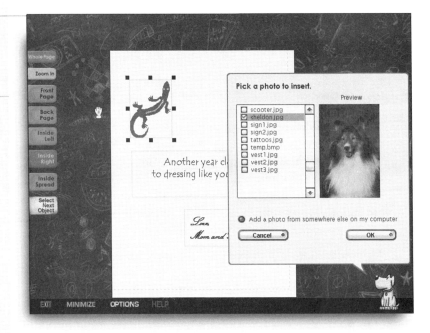

Experimenting with shaped text

1. You'll want to start with a blank canvas within the card
   you've been playing with, so click the **Inside Left** tab to display the inside left page (where there is currently nothing).

2. Click the Add New Shaped Text button 🔤 on the toolbar.
   A **Your text here** block appears, like when you were adding
   a regular text box.

3. In the **Type your shaped text here** box, type the text you
   want to use. Beneath this text box are a series of option buttons for manipulating your text (see Figure 22.12).

4. Click the **Change the shape** button, and a series of shapes
   appear as shown in Figure 22.13. The text conforms to that
   shape. Experiment with the different shapes until you find
   one you like, and then click **OK**.

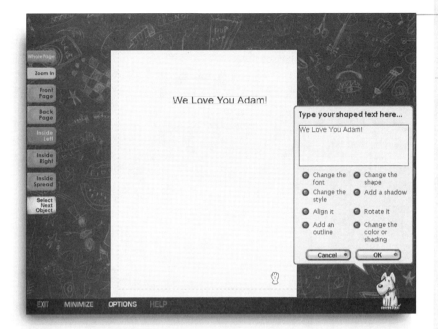

FIGURE 22.12
Replace the dummy text with
your own.

FIGURE 22.13
Pick a shape, and your text will
be squeezed into a corresponding
mold.

5. Click the **Change the Color or Shading** button. In the box that appears, you can blend the color for your text. Use the drop-down lists to choose a **Color One** and a **Color Two**; a selection of the two colors and shades in-between them appears, as shown in Figure 22.14.

6. Click one of the colors displayed, and then click **OK**.

7. Explore the other option buttons to change the font, style (bold, italic, and so on), rotation, shadow, and so on. Each is fairly self-explanatory. For practice, try setting up the text to be Arial Black font, bold, and with some kind of shadow.

8. Click **OK** when you are done working with the shaped text. Black squares appear around the text, and the dog displays a different menu of choices. You can experiment with them, or skip directly to the "Manipulating Objects" section later in this chapter.

Drawing Lines and Shapes

Greetings Workshop comes with some basic drawing tools, but don't get your hopes up too high—these are not sophisticated tools that you are going to be able to use to get fancy results. Rather, they enable you to create basic lines and shapes to enhance the other parts of your project. For example, you could add a line to separate one section of text from another, or you could add a circle around a picture. That sort of thing.

To add a shape, click the Add New Shape button 🔽 on the toolbar. A pop-up list of all the available shapes appears as shown in Figure 22.15. Click the one you want, and presto, it appears on your page. You can then move it and resize it as needed. The next section explains moving and resizing.

FIGURE 22.15
Choose the shape you want from this group.

A line works basically the same way. Click the Add New Line button ╲ on the toolbar, and a new line appears on your page right away. A **Thickness** control also appears near the toolbar, which you can use to choose the line thickness (see Figure 22.16). Click the black box next to the **Thickness** control to choose a different color. After placing the line, you can move it, rotate it, or whatever.

Manipulating Objects

The default placement of objects is seldom the right placement. The generic elements you add, like shapes, clip art, lines, text, and so on, need to be modified to work well on your page. In this section, you'll learn how to do just that.

Resizing an Object

One way to resize an object is to select it, and then click **Resize It** when the dog asks you what you want to do to it. A slide bar appears. Drag the slide bar up to make the object larger or down to make it smaller. Real basic stuff, eh? The problem with that procedure, however, is that you can't resize in only one dimension at once. For example, you can't make it taller without making it wider. To resize an individual dimension, you must resize using the following alternate procedure.

Resizing an object

1. Click the object so selection handles (squares) appear around its border. They can be either black, as in Figure 22.17, or white, depending on the object type.

FIGURE 22.17
A selected object is surrounded by selection handles.

1 Handles

2. Point the mouse pointer at one of those handles, so the mouse pointer turns into a double-headed arrow with **RESIZE** over it.

3. Hold down the left mouse button and drag the handle to change the size of the object. A dotted outline shows where the new dimensions will be.

4. When you're done, release the mouse button and the object changes to its new size.

Resizing tips

You can drag a side handle to resize in one dimension, or you can drag a corner handle to resize in two dimensions at once. To maintain the *aspect ratio* (the proportion of height to width), hold down the Shift key on the keyboard as you drag.

Repositioning or Moving an Object

First, let's get our terms straight. I'm using the term "reposition" here to mean moving an object around on its same page. I'm using "Moving" to mean transferring the object from one page to another. Got it?

To reposition an object, just point the mouse pointer at its middle, so the pointer turns into a four-headed arrow that says **MOVE** under it. Then drag the object to a different spot.

To move an object to another page, you have to use the cut-and-paste method. Select the object (by clicking it), and then click the Cut button ✂ on the toolbar. Then use the tabs on the left side of the screen to display the page where you want it to go and click the Paste button 📋 on the toolbar. The object will probably not be pasted at exactly the right spot on the new page, so you will likely have to reposition it after it gets there.

Rotating and Flipping an Object

Depending on what object you have selected, you may see rotating and/or flipping buttons on the toolbar at the top of the screen. Click the object to select it, and then click one or more of these buttons:

- ◁ *Flip Vertical*. Flips the object top-to-bottom so it's upside-down.

- ▲ *Flip Horizontal*. Flips the object side-to-side so it's a mirror image of itself.

- ↻ *Rotate Left*. Rotates the object 15 degrees to the left each time you click it. So, for example, if you want the object rotated at a 45 degree angle, click this button three times.

- ↺ *Rotate Right*. Same as **Rotate Left**, except, obviously, it rotates the other direction.

Cropping an Image

Some objects, like photos for example, allow cropping. This means you can eliminate some of the outside of the image and show just a certain part of it. For example, look at Figure 22.18. The image on the left is the original, and the one on the right is a cropped and resized copy. The cropping makes the important part of the image more noticeable.

FIGURE 22.18
Cropping can improve a picture with too much extraneous detail.

Cropping an image

1. Select the object, and then click the Cropping button ⊞ on the toolbar.

2. Position the mouse pointer over one of the selection handles, so the word **CROP** appears.

3. Drag the selection handle to crop the object. Repeat for each side of the object until it is cropped the way you want it.

4. Click the Cropping button ⊞ again to turn cropping off.

No **Cropping** button?

If you don't see the Cropping button ⊞, make sure an object is selected that allows cropping. You can crop only pictures and photos.

Changing the Object Color

Some objects allow you to change their color and line thickness. These special controls appear as drop-down items on the toolbar when you've selected a shape to which the effect can be applied. Just click the control to open an array of samples, then click the sample you want to use.

No border

If you don't want a line around the outside of a shape, set the **Line Color** to the same color as the **Shape Color**. That way the border will blend in.

Adding a Page Border

Page borders are a type of picture, but instead of hogging the center stage, they play a supporting role around the edge of the page. There are several kinds of page borders; some are banners that run across the top and bottom of the page; others are graphical lines or little repeated pictures.

The easiest way to add a page border is to work with the talking dog. (I'll bet there aren't too many occasions in your life when someone tells you *that*, eh?)

Adding a page border

1. On the dog's **What Do You Want to Do?** list, click **Add a Page Border**. This opens a box of borders from which you can choose.

2. Choose a border category from the **Choose a category** drop-down list at the top of the box. (You can always choose a different one anytime in the process.)

3. Click a border name that you're curious about, and it gets applied to your page so you can see a preview of it. If you don't like it, try another, until you've found a good one. Figure 22.19 shows the one called **Map Pins**.

4. If you want to make the border larger or smaller, change the number in the **Set the border width to** box.

5. Click **OK** to accept the border.

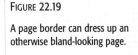

FIGURE 22.19

A page border can dress up an otherwise bland-looking page.

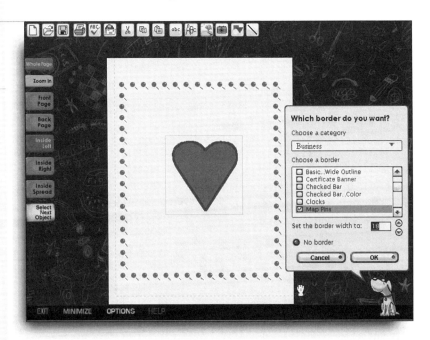

Printing Your Work

You can print your work not only when you're finished, but at any time along the way, to see what progress you're making. The onscreen display is pretty close to what the printout will look like, but sometimes it's nice just to hold the thing in your hands and admire it while you're thinking up ideas for the final touches.

Printing your project

1. Click the Print 🖨 button on the toolbar, or click the **Print My Project** button in the dog's bubble.

2. If you have not yet saved your project, the dog asks whether you want to save it. Click **Yes** (and follow the directions for saving in the "Saving a Project" section later in this chapter), or click **No** if you don't want to bother with that now. You can always save later.

3. The bubble above the dog's head shows the default printer and indicates that one copy will be printed. If that's okay, click **Continue** to print. (You can change the number of copies if you want more by clicking the little green up arrow next to the **Number of Copies to Print** text box or by typing a different number in there.)

4. Wait for the printout. If it looks okay, click the **OK** button onscreen. If it doesn't, click the **Fix Printing Problems** button and follow the prompts.

5. If you are printing a two-sided project, follow the dog's prompts to reinsert the paper correctly in your printer, and then click **Continue** to print the second side.

Color or black-and-white?

If you have a color printer, by all means use it for your final printout. Greetings Workshop projects make extensive use of color, and you won't get the same cool results on a black-and-white printer. However, if you have both a black-and-white and color printer, you might want to use the black-and-white for your in-progress drafts because the cost per page is lower. (You don't want to use up all your expensive colored ink on a rough draft.)

When it's time to print the final copy, consider using some of that special glossy paper available for inkjet printers. It's expensive, but it makes the printouts look great.

Use a different printer

If you have two printers, you can switch between them by clicking the **Click Here to Change Printer Setup** button. In the resulting dialog box, you can choose a different printer from the **Name** drop-down list.

First-time two-sided printing

The first time you print a two-sided project, the dog may ask you to do a test. Go ahead and do it, following his directions. This will test how the paper must be fed into your printer the second time through. (Every printer does it differently, so you really do have to go through the test to find out how yours works.)

Saving a Project

Whenever you print an unsaved project, the dog asks whether you want to save it. That's one way to save. Another is to click the Save button 🖫 on the toolbar at any time.

Each time you issue the **Save** command, a Save dialog box appears, as shown in Figure 22.20. The first time, a default name for the project appears. You should change this to something more specific (like Birthday Card for Adam). Then click **OK**. Your project is saved. When you click the Save 🖫 button again, the Save dialog box reopens, and you can click **OK** to save your most recent changes or type a different name to save it under a new name. You might do this, for example, if you wanted to base a new project on an existing one.

FIGURE 22.20

Change the default name for the project to something more meaningful and specific.

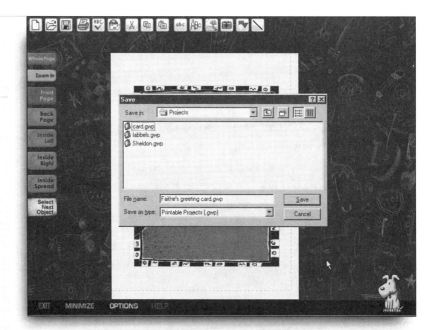

Opening a Saved Project

You can open a saved project in either of two ways:

- You can click the **Saved Projects** drawer from the main screen.

- You can click the Open Project 🖼 button on the toolbar at any time.

Either action opens a list of your saved projects. Click the project you want to open, and then click the **Open It** button to open it.

If you have a project stored in a different location (for example, on a floppy disk), you can access that location by clicking the **Open a Project on a Floppy Disk or Somewhere Else** button.

You can delete a saved project by clicking the project name in the Save dialog box and then clicking the **Delete a Selected Project** button.

Exploring the Microsoft Greetings Workshop Web Site

Greetings Workshop comes with some wonderful designs and art, but there is even more good stuff out there, absolutely free for downloading. The goodies are called *add-on packs*. All you need is a modem and Internet Explorer.

You already know how to use Internet Explorer—so all you need to know is "how do I get this good stuff?" Easy.

Downloading add-ons for Greetings Workshop

1. Start your Internet connection.

2. On the main screen of Greetings Workshop, click the **Go Online** button (the picture of the telephone). Internet Explorer opens and displays the product home page.

3. Click the **Add-On Packs** hyperlink on the Web page that appears.

4. Click the **Version 2** link. (Home Essentials 98 comes with version 2 of Greetings Workshop, so those are the add-on packs you want.)

5. Click one of the links on the Version 2 page. (The exact offerings may vary; the day I visited there were four packs.)

6. A page appears explaining the pack's content and providing instructions. Open the **File** menu and choose **Print** to print these instructions if you want them to refer to later.

Using Microsoft Encarta

Looking up articles

Playing media clips

Exploring interactive activities

Playing the MindMaze game

Finding more resources online

Starting and Exiting Encarta

After you have installed Encarta, starting the program is a simple affair. The only catch is that you have to have Disc #3 or #4 of the Home Essentials 98 CD set in your CD-ROM drive. (Those are the two Encarta discs.) Disc #3 contains most of the reference articles; Disc #4 has many of the extra features.

When you pop in one of the two discs, Encarta should start automatically. (The Home screen you'll see appears in Figure 23.1.) If it doesn't, you can either remove the disc and reinsert it or choose **Start**, **Programs**, **Microsoft Reference**, **Encarta 98 Encyclopedia**.

FIGURE 23.1

Encarta's Home screen points you in various directions.

When you're ready to exit Encarta, click the **Close (X) button** in the top-right corner to close its window.

SEE ALSO

➤ *To learn about installing Encarta, see page 522.*

How Encarta Is Organized

Encarta is basically a giant *database* of information, complete with pictures, sounds, video clips, and more. You can access the information in a variety of different ways.

- **Encyclopedia articles**. This is the main section where you go to look things up.
- **Media features**. All the multimedia (sound, video, and so on) items are linked to this area so you can browse them at a glance.
- **Online features**. This area connects you to the Microsoft Internet site, where you can look up more topics and download enhancements.
- **Tools**. These enable you to maximize your encyclopedic experience. There's a dictionary, a simple word processor, and a few other items, all of which are fairly straightforward and self-explanatory. You access the tools from the **Features** menu inside the encyclopedia, which you'll see in the following section.

The links on the Home screen in Figure 23.1 correspond somewhat—but not exactly—to the preceding list. The first three items are the same. You can go to the encyclopedia, to the list of media features, or to the online features by clicking the corresponding links. (The **Tools** area is different; you can't get to the tools without going through one of these other areas.)

The other two links on the Home screen are **MindMaze** and **Overview**. *MindMaze* is a trivia game that takes facts from the encyclopedia. (You'll learn how to play it later in this chapter.) *Overview* is a tour of the Encarta program that shows you, in a general way, what it can do.

Word processor?

Because you have two good word processors in your Home Essentials package—Works and Word—you will probably never need the word processor built in to Encarta. You can safely ignore it.

Looking Up a Topic

The library of encyclopedia articles is the largest part of Encarta, and also the part with the most complicated controls. Click the **Encyclopedia articles** link on the Home screen (refer to Figure 23.1), and then see Figure 23.2 for a quick tour.

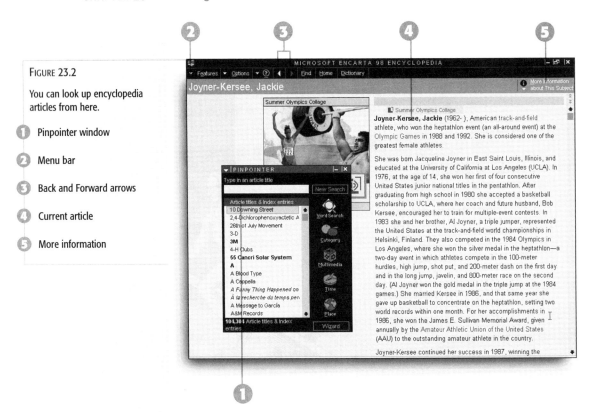

FIGURE 23.2

You can look up encyclopedia articles from here.

1. Pinpointer window

2. Menu bar

3. Back and Forward arrows

4. Current article

5. More information

The screen elements you see are as follows:

- *Pinpointer*. This is the main search tool for looking up articles. (We'll look at it in more detail shortly.)

- *Menu bar*. Each of the words on the black bar at the top open a drop-down list. For example, **Features** contains a list of the Encarta sections (like Media, Online, and so on), and **Options** contains a list of things you can do to the current article (print it, save it, and so on). **Home** returns you to the home screen.

- *Arrows*. Also on the menu bar are left and right-pointing arrows. These are like Forward and Back buttons in a Web browser.

- *Current article*. When you go into the Encyclopedia area, the last article you looked up appears (a default article the first time). Word or phrases in red are links to other articles.

- <u>*More Information*</u>. Click at the right end of the menu bar to open a list of other places you can look for information on the topic.

Looking up a topic

1. From the Home screen, click **Encyclopedia articles**, if you have not already done so. An article appears (refer to Figure 23.2).

2. If you do not see the Pinpointer window, click the **Find** link on the menu bar to display it.

3. In the **Type in an article title** box on the Pinpointer, type the subject you want to look up.

   The list of subjects narrows to show only those with your search words in them as shown in Figure 23.3 (be patient— this can take up to 30 seconds).

4. On the list of topics in the Pinpointer, double-click any of the bold entries that interest you. That article appears and the Pinpointer window goes away. (Remember, you can reopen it by clicking **Find** on the menu bar.)

SEE ALSO

➤ *If you aren't sure what the Forward and Back buttons in a Web browser do, see page 404.*

No plural

Almost all subjects are singular in Encarta. Avoid adding "s" to the end of the topic you are searching for, or Encarta may not be able to locate what you want.

FIGURE 23.3

Typing words in the Pinpointer box narrows down the list of topics.

Why only bold entries?

Bold entries represent actual articles. Non-bold entries represent information in articles on different subjects. If you choose a non-bold entry on the list, a submenu may appear asking you to choose an article.

Working with an Article

When the article you want is displayed, check out some of the things you can do with it. To start, open the **Options** menu. This displays a list of the things you can do to the currently displayed article (see Figure 23.4). Click away from the menu to close it after you've had a look.

FIGURE 23.4

Use the **Options** menu to act upon the article.

How about a couple of demos? The following sections explain some of the things you can do while reading articles. The assortment here is by no means comprehensive; you can do a lot more in Encarta than can fit in this chapter. These ideas should get you started.

Copying an Article

Let's say you want to copy a part of the article into your word processor so you can save it.

Copying an article into a word processor

1. If you want to copy only certain text, select it by dragging across it with the left mouse button held down. If you want the whole article, you don't need to do this.

2. Open the **Options** menu and choose **Copy**. A list of copying options appears: **Text Selection**, **Whole Article**, **Image/Frame**, and **Caption**.

3. If you selected text in step 1, click **Text Selection**. If you didn't, click **Whole Article**. The text is copied to the Windows Clipboard.

4. Open your word processing program (use the **Start** button). You don't need to close Encarta.

5. In the word processor, open the **Edit** menu and choose **Paste**. The material appears in the word processor.

Printing an Article

You can print part or all of the article. If you want to print only part of it, select that part first. Otherwise, just go ahead and open the **Options** menu and choose **Print**. A submenu with the same four choices that you saw in the preceding section appears: **Text Selection**, **Whole Article**, **Image/Frame**, and **Caption**. Click the one that describes what you want to print, and presto, a hard copy appears on your printer.

Using Article View Options

The **Views** command on the **Options** menu lets you choose among various views of the article. Some views show the pictures; some don't. Some show the outline of the article; some don't. Changing the view is most useful when working with large articles that contain their own outlines; for a short article you may not be able to tell much difference between some of the views. The default view, **Main**, shows graphics and text but not the outline. See Figure 23.5 to see Main, Outline view—a view that incorporates all three of the main elements: Outline, Graphics, and Text.

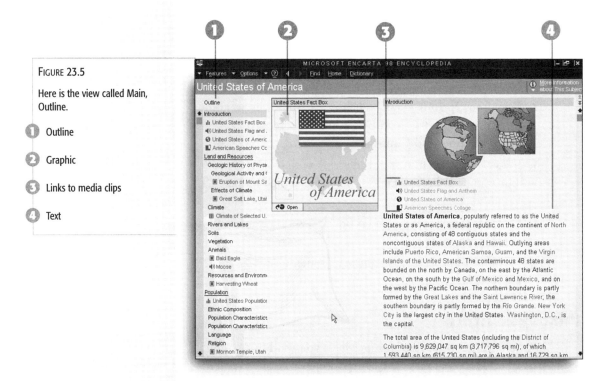

Callouts numbered 1, 2, 3, 4 above the Encarta screenshot

FIGURE 23.5

Here is the view called Main, Outline.

1 Outline

2 Graphic

3 Links to media clips

4 Text

Viewing test

If you want to check out an article where using the various **Views** options makes a big difference, look up United States of America, the article shown in Figure 23.5.

The Media Gallery

To see a full listing of the media included in Encarta, open the **Features** menu, choose **Media Features**, and then choose **Media Gallery**. You can play around with the listings in this gallery to get an idea of how each media type is controlled.

You can also change the text size from the **Options** menu. Just open the **Options** menu, choose **Text Size**, and then click **Small**, **Medium**, or **Large**. **Small** is the default, but **Medium** or **Large** may be easier to read, especially for people with less-than-perfect vision.

Working with the Media Clips in an Article

Many of the articles have at least one media clip (a picture, a video, a sound, and so on), others have many clips. Encarta media clips include sound, video and film clips, tables, maps, photos, and collages (these can include several of the other media clip types). Let's look at the United States of America article to test some of the controls.

Controlling media clips in an article

1. Display any article (in this example, we are using the United States of America article). A list of media clips (one or more) appears at the top of the article. The first media clip in the list is selected, and its media control box appears in the article window (see Figure 23.6).

Insert next disc

See that little picture of a disc with an arrow under the picture in Figure 23.6? That means the clip material isn't on the Encarta CD in your CD-ROM drive. To display that content, you have to swap discs. If your system has two CD-ROM drives, put one Encarta disc in each to avoid disc-swapping.

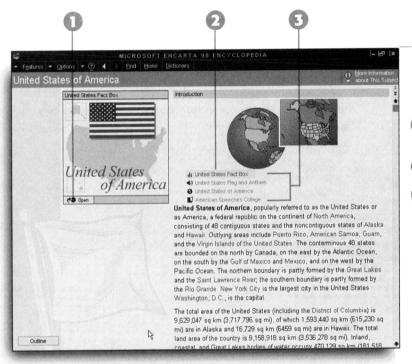

FIGURE 23.6

You can display only one media clip at a time; here the United States Fact Box clip is selected.

❶ This indicates you will have to swap discs to view the clip.

❷ The selected clip is highlighted.

❸ List of media clips for the article.

2. The controls that appear in the media box vary, depending upon what type of media clip you've opened. In this example, click the **Open** button in the Fact Box media box to open the clip.

3. Click any of the links in the Fact Box to read its information (see Figure 23.7). When you're done, click the **Close** (**X**) button in the top-right corner of the Fact Box to close it.

FIGURE 23.7

Some entries, especially those for countries, have fact boxes.

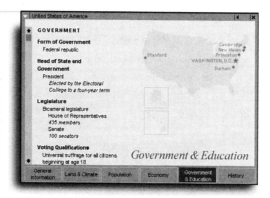

4. Click a sound or video clip (such as the United States Flag and Anthem clip in our example); the media box opens and displays controls that enable you to stop, play, and move forward or backward in the sound clip (see Figure 23.8).

FIGURE 23.8

Sound and video clips have controls like the ones shown here.

1 Play

2 Stop

3 Fast Forward

4 Fast Reverse

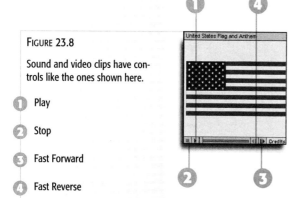

5. Click the **Play** button (the right-pointing arrow) to play the clip (when the clip is playing, a **Pause** button replaces **Play**). A slider bar tracks the progress of the sound clip as it plays.

6. Click a **World Maps** link (such as the United States of America link in our example); the map media box appears. When you have the correct disk in the CD-ROM drive, your pointer changes to a magnifying glass.

7. Position the pointer on the map and click to zoom into a full map window (see Figure 23.9). The pointer changes to a hand.

8. Click a map location; a drop-down menu that offers options for viewing or learning about that location appears. Click any option; click the **Close** (**X**) button to close the enlarged map media box.

9. When you're done with the map, click the **Close** (**X**) button in its right-top corner to close it.

10. To view the collage media clip in this example, click **American Speeches Collage**.

11. Click the **Open** button (or click anywhere within the box) to open the collage.

12. Use the arrow controls at the top of the presentation window to control your movement through the presentation (see Figure 23.10). As you pass your mouse pointer over the screen, it changes to a hand on which you can click to receive other information. If it changes to a speaker, an audio clip plays automatically if you hover there momentarily. Other onscreen instructions may appear to guide you through the presentation.

More mapping

You can do a lot more with the map controls than I have room to tell you about here. Experiment on your own with the menus, or see the Encarta Help system. To open the Help system for the map, click the down-pointing arrow in the map's top-left corner and choose **Help** from the menu that appears.

FIGURE 23.10

Use the arrow buttons in the top corners to navigate the collage.

1   Scroll backward

2   Jump backward

3   Jump forward

4   Scroll forward

13. When you're done viewing the presentation, click the **Close** (**X**) button in its top-right corner to close it.

Finding the Clips You Want: Encarta Search Tools

On the right side of the Pinpointer window are a series of option buttons for Encarta search tools. These search options help you narrow down your search for articles:

- **Word Search**. Enables you to search for a particular word in the full text of all articles. (Warning: This takes a while.)

- **Categories**. Searches for articles based on their topic, and eliminates "false hits" on articles with similar names. For example, suppose you are looking for information about outer space; if you search for "Space" your search results will include articles about physics. Narrowing the search down to the Social Science/Astronomy & Space Science category would prevent this.

- **Multimedia**. Finds a list of articles on a given topic that contain a specified type of media. For example, you may search for only those articles on the Civil Rights movement that contain video clips.

- **Time**. Searches for articles that relate to a specific period of time, which you can specify on a timeline within the option.
- **Place**. Finds all articles dealing with a particular region or country, type its name here to limit the search.

There isn't room in this chapter to cover each of these sophisticated search tools in detail, so let's pick just the most fun one to look at: **Multimedia**. Just as some people flip through magazines quickly just to find the cartoons, some people want to flip through Encarta looking only for the cool media clips. You can browse all the clips quickly through the Pinpointer. Just click the **Multimedia** button in the Pinpointer window to open a submenu of media types (see Figure 23.11). Then click the type you want, and the list of articles narrows to show only articles containing that kind of media clip.

FIGURE 23.11
You can find out quickly which articles have which type of clips through this Multimedia list.

When you're really looking for a specific type of information on a topic, you can use subsequent searches to narrow the results of the first. For example, you can search for articles by category, then time, then place, then media to really produce a specific list of articles—or cut the search short at any point along that way to get a longer (but less specific) list of articles. To "layer" your searches in this manner, do not click the **New Search** button in the Pinpointer window between searches.

When you're finished browsing based on a criterion or set of criteria, make sure you click the **New Search** button in the Pinpointer window before you start looking for another topic.

New search!

Forgetting to click **New Search** is a common user mistake. If you ever search for a topic that you know must be in Encarta but come up empty, one of the first things to check is that there are no limiting criteria still in place from a previous search.

Otherwise, your subsequent search will be based on the criteria you set for the previous search.

The final search tool is the **Wizard**. Click the **Wizard** option, and a box appears asking you for information about what you're looking for. Enter the information and follow the prompts, and the Wizard produces a list of articles you should look at.

Exploring the Media Features

You could spend years—literally—looking through just the articles in Encarta, but other neat features are also worth a glance.

Media features are video presentations that combine a variety of media to explain broad topics. You can think of them as a kind of "extra credit report." Some of them you have already seen glimpses of in the encyclopedia articles. For example, you have already worked with a timeline earlier in this chapter when you explored the United States media offerings. You can display a list of media features from two points: from within an Article, open the **Features** menu and choose **Media Features**; or, from the **Home** screen, click the **Media features** link. A list of media feature types appears. Access this list from the **Home** screen to see a brief explanation of what each type offers.

You may have already experimented with some media features. In "Working with Media Clips in an Article," earlier in this chapter, you worked with a Collage that explored American speeches and a World Map of the United States. The following sections walk through a few of the other media features offered by Encarta.

InterActivities

InterActivities, the first Media Feature, is a group of animated reports you can play with. As their name implies, they are interactive; you can click various parts of the reports to get more information.

As an example, let's look at the Climate Chart.

Displaying climate charts

1. From the Home screen, click **Media features**, then choose **InterActivities**. Or, from the Encyclopedia, open the **Features** menu and choose **Media Features**, and then **InterActivities**.

2. Click the **Climate Chart** link. A climate graph for the first state (alphabetically) appears: Alabama.

3. If you want to see a different state's climate graph instead, open the **drop-down list** in which Alabama is currently displayed and choose a different state.

4. (Optional) To compare climates for several states, choose the other states from the additional drop-down lists at the bottom of the window. Figure 23.12 shows four states being compared.

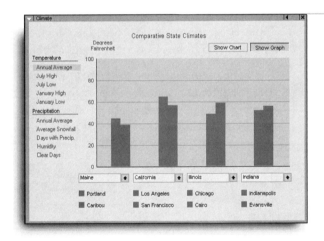

FIGURE 23.12
This InterActivity compares the climates in up to four states at a time.

5. To view different data on the graph, click one of the links to the left of the graph. For example, click **July High**.

6. (Optional) To view the data as a chart (that is, columns of text and numbers) rather than a graph, click the **Show Chart** button in the top-right corner of the window.

7. When you're finished playing with the climate chart, click the **Close (X)** button in its corner to close it.

Many other InterActivities are available; the following list explores just a few. Most have self-explanatory controls; just click the Instructions button on each one to get started with it:

- **Exploring Fractals**. An explanation with exercises. You can create your own fractal trees, zoom through layers of magnification of a fractal image, and examine some fern leaves that show fractals in nature.
- **Natural Wonders**. Explore the wonders of the world through an interactive map, then try the game to test your knowledge.
- **World Languages.** In one of the most interesting of Encarta's InterActivities, you can hear common phrases pronounced in any of dozens of languages.

Topic Treks

Topic Treks are yet another way to explore. You start with a certain theme, and then view articles and clips having to do with it.

The basic premise is this: You choose a category, and an article appears about one person, place, or thing in that category. For example, Young Achievers showcases several people who became famous or powerful early in life. It's just like reading an ordinary article in Encarta, except the Topic Trek box is floating alongside. When you are ready to go on to the next article, just click the **Next** button in the Topic Trek box (see Figure 23.13).

Timeline

Timeline, as the name implies, provides a timeline of world history. It is a great exploration tool that helps you see how events fit together in the grand scheme of things (see Figure 23.14).

To use the timeline, just scroll through (using the horizontal scrollbar at the bottom of the window). You can also find a certain event by clicking the **Find an Event** button and then choosing the event from the alphabetical list that appears.

When you see an event on the timeline that interests you, double-click it to see more information.

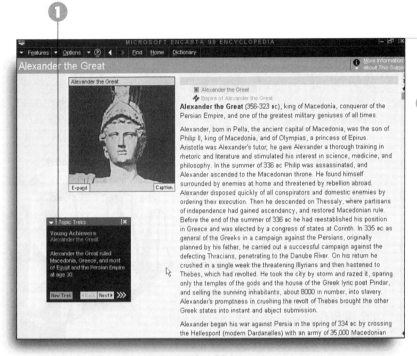

①

FIGURE 23.13

Topic Trek leads you through a series of articles.

① Topic Trek window

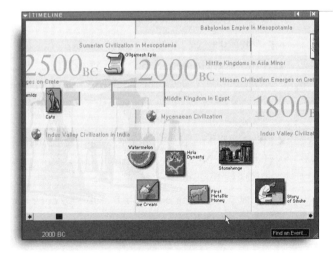

FIGURE 23.14

A timeline puts historical events into perspective.

Playing MindMaze

If you like Trivial Pursuit, you'll love **MindMaze**. It's a great "test-your-knowledge" game designed for all ages. You can play it at any of three degrees of difficulty. Level 1 is appropriate for kids and for adults who either have not had a whole lot of education or who enjoy winning easily. The difficulty level progresses all the way up to Level 4, for people who find the questions on Jeopardy insultingly easy.

The object of the game is to get to the top of the castle and answer the necessary questions to break the castle curse. To do this, you move through rooms in a castle to a stairway leading up. Each time you want to pass through a doorway, you have to answer a question correctly. (You get points along the way for correct answers, and speed of answering counts.) When you go up a stairway, you're on the next level, and you do the same thing again—navigate toward the stairway to an even higher level. Finally (presumably), you reach the top of the castle and break the curse, thus winning the game.

Along the way, you see various people and animals in the rooms. You can click them to "talk" to them (they talk to you, but you can't really interact), but talking to them is not an integral part of the game. It's just there to add interest.

Play MindMaze

1. From the Home screen, click **MindMaze**. Or, from the encyclopedia, open the **Features** menu, choose **Media Features**, and then choose **MindMaze**. The first thing you see is the entry door.

2. If you haven't played before, you need to enter your name. Click the **New Player** button, and then type your name and press Enter.

3. Click your name on the list, and then click the front door to enter the castle.

4. Now you're in the main playing area. Click the doorway that you can see through the bars, to reach the screen shown in Figure 23.15. The parts of the screen work as follows:

Map. You are the dot. Your goal (the next level's staircase) is the bracket. Each time you move through a room, the dot moves to a different square. This is how you can tell which room you should go to next. Like a maze, however, not all paths go through; some are dead ends. You may sometimes have to backtrack.

Choose Area of Interest. This lists the available question categories. Click the one you want, or click **All Areas** for a variety.

Level. Choose 1, 2, 3, or 4, depending on your knowledge level. You might want to start with 1 just to get the hang of the game.

Picture. This shows you what you're "seeing." You can click any person to show a blurb of what they're saying, or click any door to go through it. (You will have to answer a question first, of course.)

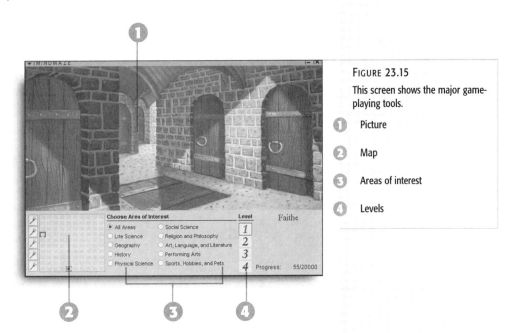

FIGURE 23.15

This screen shows the major game-playing tools.

1   Picture

2   Map

3   Areas of interest

4   Levels

5. Click one of the doors. (Try the one on the left, for starters.) The view changes again. Now you're in a room.

6. (Optional) If there's a character in the room, click him or her. Some text appears showing a message. Click away from it to get rid of it. Some rooms contain objects that link you to articles; when your pointer turns to a hand over one of these objects, click to see the associated information.

7. To leave the room, click a door. If you have not been through this door before, a question appears (see Figure 23.16).

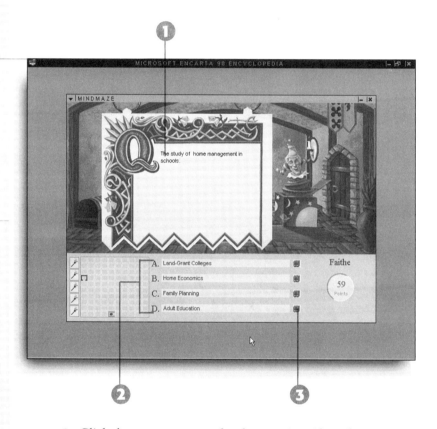

FIGURE 23.16

Answer the question by clicking answer **A**, **B**, **C**, or **D**.

1 Question

2 Possible answers

3 Click a book to look up the answer in the encyclopedia.

Guess again!

After two wrong guesses, the question goes away. Click that same door again for a new question. You can click the books icon next to any of the answers to see an encyclopedia article about that answer. This can help you determine which answer to pick.

8. Click the correct answer for the question, if you know it. If you don't, guess. (Incorrect answers just lower the points you get when you reach the right answer.) If you get it right, a box pops up to inform you of how many points you received for the correct answer. Click **OK** to move to the next room.

If you're wrong, a box appears telling you that you were incorrect and you can try again. Click **OK** to get rid of it and guess again.

9. In the next room, pick the door that looks most likely to take you in the direction you need to go. Consult the map as needed.

10. Keep moving through the rooms until you come to the staircase. Then click it to go up to the next level.

11. Keep playing until you win or get tired!

If you need to quit for awhile, you can come back later and pick up where you left off. Just click the **Close (X) button** in the window's corner to end the game. The next time you return, choose your same name again at the entry door, and you'll be whisked back into exactly the same spot.

Going Online with Encarta

Even with Encarta's two CDs' worth of information (over 1.2 gigabytes in all), you may find that you need more information on a topic. Perhaps you are looking up some obscure town that Encarta has only a paragraph or two about, or maybe you want up-to-the-minute info and your copy of Encarta is several months old. Whatever the case, you will want to check out the online component to Encarta.

You can get at these online features in several ways. You can open the **Features menu and choose the Online Features** command in the encyclopedia, or you can click **Online features** on the Home screen. Your choice; you end up at the same place.

Here's a quick rundown of the features, all of which you should have no trouble at all exploring on your own:

- **Yearbook**. Use this to manage updates to Encarta to keep your copy up-to-date. Encarta comes with the July 97 update preinstalled; click the Directory button on the Yearbook screen to see these updates.

    To get more updates, click **Downloads**, and then click **Update Encarta**. (Note that this is not a free service; you must buy a subscription for $19.95 a year to be entitled to updates. Full information appears when you click **Update Encarta**.)

Torches light the way

The five torches at the left are "cheats" that show you the floor's map along with the correct path to the stairway. Each time you click a torch, it is "used up," so use your torches wisely.

Online?

Online means connected to the Internet. If you don't have an Internet connection, you won't be able to take advantage of this feature unless you get one.

- **Web Links**. This is an assortment of *links* to Web pages with more information on them about selected topics. To display them, click the **Directory** button at the bottom of the Web Links screen. These can also be updated with a download if you have a Yearbook subscription.

- **Downloads**. The same as clicking **Yearbook** and then **Downloads**.

- **Encarta Online**. This opens Internet Explorer and displays the Microsoft Encarta Web site, where you can look up additional articles using the Microsoft Concise Encyclopedia (the free version). You can also explore teachers' resources and a spotlight topic that changes frequently. Figure 23.17 shows the Topic Archive in the teachers section.

FIGURE 23.17

Encarta Online provides a teachers area with ideas for lesson plans based on Encarta articles.

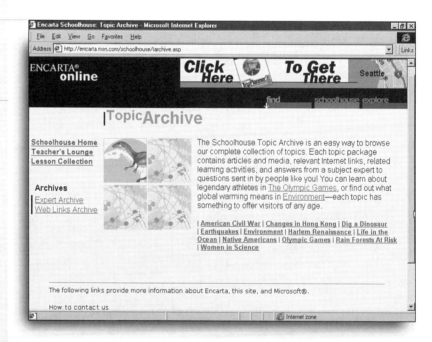

- **World Wide Web Tips**. This link opens a help screen with general information about the Internet. It's good for those who don't have an Internet connection yet and aren't sure how to get started.

■ **Online Library**. This also opens IE, and displays a page advertising this extra-charge service. Using the Online Library you have access to over 800 periodicals. You can get a free trial through this Web page, but to subscribe costs $6.95 per month or $34.95 for six months.

SEE ALSO

➤ *For information about getting an Internet connection, see page 400.*

➤ *Some of Encarta's online features require the use of Internet Explorer. If you aren't sure how to use that, turn back to Chapters 19 through 21 which start on page 399.*

Life after Encarta?

As you are searching for more sources of information, don't forget the Internet itself. It's a vast, varied web of information, and the free sources online greatly outnumber the Encarta information and Microsoft's extra-charge update information combined. Turn back to Chapters 19 through 21 and try searching for the topic you want using one of the Internet search engines such as Yahoo! or Excite; you may turn up some of your best information that way, without even using Encarta.

Playing Games in the Puzzle Collection

Toolbar all the time?

If you want the Puzzle Collection toolbar to be displayed automatically each time you start Windows, create a shortcut for it in your Startup group. To do so, right-click on the Start button and choose **Open**. Then double-click on the Programs icon and then on the Startup icon to open the Startup folder. Right-drag the Puzzle Collection icon from your desktop into this folder, and choose **Create Shortcut Here** from the menu that appears when you drop the icon there. Now close all the open windows and restart your computer (**Start, Shut Down, Restart**). The Puzzle Collection toolbar automatically opens.

Displaying the Puzzle Toolbar

To play one of the games in the Puzzle Collection, you fire up a special toolbar containing an icon for each game. Then you run the game by clicking its icon. To open the Puzzle Collection toolbar, do one of the following:

- Click the **Play the Puzzle Collection** icon on your desktop, if one is there.
- Choose **Start, Programs, Microsoft Games, Puzzle Collection**, Play the Puzzle Collection.

Either way, you open a floating toolbar on your Windows desktop, as shown in Figure 24.1. From there, just point to an icon to see which puzzle it opens. Find the puzzle you want to play, and click its icon to open it.

To close the Puzzle Collection toolbar, just click the **Close** button (X) in its corner, as with any other window.

FIGURE 24.1

The Puzzle Collection toolbar gives you quick access to all 10 of the games.

Controlling the Games

While playing any of the Puzzle Collection games, you can pause by minimizing the window, switching to another program, or clicking the **Pause!** command on the menu bar.

To resume a paused game, reopen the game window if minimized, and make it the active window. Then click the mouse on the paused play area or click the **Play!** command on the menu bar.

Setting the Game Options

All the games have similar options that you can select with the **Game**, **Options** command. This opens a dialog box where you can perform these functions:

- Enter your name (in case you get a high score)
- Turn the background music off or on (on by default)
- Turn the sound effects off or on (on by default)
- Choose your starting level (1 is the default)

Figure 24.2 shows the Options dialog box for Fringer.

FIGURE 24.2
You can set options for each game with its **Game, Options** command.

Playing Fringer

The object of Fringer is to straighten out knotted ropes (see Figure 24.3). You untwist a knot by positioning the cursor (using the right and left arrow keys) over a spot where two ropes are crossed, and you then press the spacebar to untwist them. When a rope is completely straightened out, it disappears. When you get rid of all the ropes, you start a new level.

Screens are broken into levels, with three screens for each level. When the level changes, the background picture changes and the play gets more difficult. You can tell what level and screen you're on by the indicator in the corner; in Figure 24.3, notice the player is in Level 1-1.

Each time you press the space bar (or the Up Arrow), the direction of the twist changes—right-over-left or left-over-right; you can tell by the slant of the cursor. For example, in Figure 24.3, the cursor points toward the left, aligning with the left-over-right twist.

You need to act quickly because a sliding bar pushes the knots down every few seconds. When a knot reaches the bottom, you lose.

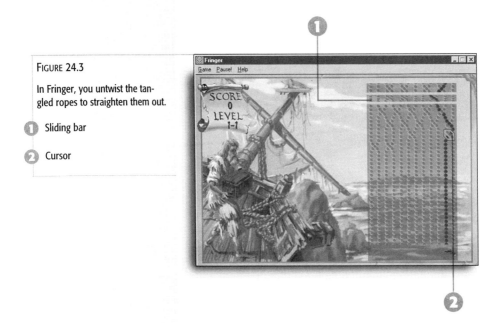

FIGURE 24.3

In Fringer, you untwist the tangled ropes to straighten them out.

1 Sliding bar

2 Cursor

If the two ropes involved in a twist are the same color, it doesn't matter which direction you untwist them; right-over-left and left-over-right both work equally well. However, if the ropes are different colors, you must pay attention to which way they need to be untwisted and work on that twist only when the cursor points in the correct direction. In the beginner levels, almost all the ropes are the same color, but in higher levels they are almost all different. Notice in Figure 24.3 that the knot the cursor is on is a left-over-right knot. Because the ropes are different colors, it makes a difference here.

Fringer Playing Strategies

As in most games in the Home Essentials puzzle collection, Fringer involves a certain level of strategy. The best way to learn any game's strategy is to play it. These Fringer strategies are just an example of some of the playing tips you'll learn as you become more experienced with playing games in the puzzle collection.

If you untwist a knot with sparkles around it, you get a bonus "token." You use the tokens to reverse the direction of the cursor. Bonus tokens appear along the sides of the play area. In Figure 24.4, for example, you see one bonus already accumulated (the gun symbol to the left of the play area) and several more sparkling knots waiting to be untied. You must act quickly on a sparkling knot; the sparkles disappear after the knot has moved approximately 1/3 of the way down the playing field.

FIGURE **24.4**

Untwist sparkling knots to get bonuses.

When a candle appears next to the play area, two red dots also appear: one at the top and one at the bottom (see Figure 24.5). Notice the rope at the top on which the red dot sits, and then try to twist the ropes so that that same rope aligns with the red dot at the bottom. When the same rope runs from dot-to-dot, that rope disappears the next time the sliding bar pushes the knots down. This can be a real life-saver if you have used up all your bonuses and still have knots to untie with the cursor pointing the wrong way! Sometimes if you wait a few seconds, the red dots and candle appear and help you save yourself.

Tips for accumulating bonuses

You will probably get to the point where you can complete level 1 very fast, even before any sparkles appear. This is a mistake; use the easy play in level 1 to accumulate bonuses for later, harder levels.

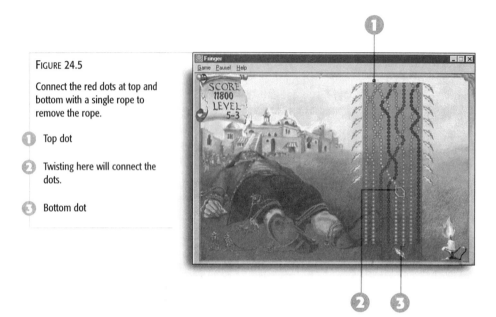

FIGURE 24.5

Connect the red dots at top and bottom with a single rope to remove the rope.

 Top dot

② Twisting here will connect the dots.

③ Bottom dot

When a paintbrush appears to the side of the play area (see Figure 24.6), you can press **Enter** to change the colors of all the ropes. This can help you because some twisted ropes that were formerly different colors might come out being the same color, making them much easier to untwist. But this trick can also hurt, because it can change two ropes to different colors that were formerly the same!

FIGURE 24.6

Press Enter when you see this paintbrush to change the rope colors.

① Paintbrush

Playing Finty Flush

Finty Flush is a marble game. The object is to fill up trays of marbles all in the same color; when do you that, the tray gets dumped out and is empty again so you can put more marbles in it. When you fill three grids, you get a bonus point and move to the next level. As you work, the top area continues to fill up with more columns of marbles. When the top area is full, the game is over.

Here's the general idea:

Filling a marble tray in Finty Flush

1. You have two areas: top and bottom. On the top are columns of marbles (see Figure 24.7). Click the left and right arrow buttons to align the column you want with the down arrow button.

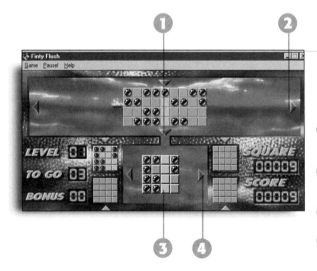

FIGURE 24.7

Align the marbles on top with the spaces to be filled on the tray at the bottom.

1. Click the down arrow button to transfer the marbles.

2. Top arrows move the columns on top to right or left.

3. Click the active tray to rotate it.

4. Bottom arrows move the tray from side to side.

2. On the bottom are empty trays waiting to be filled. Choose the tray you want to use by clicking on its image on the side, and then rotate the active tray (the one in the middle), if needed, by clicking on it. One click rotates the tray 90 degrees. A left click rotates to the left (counterclockwise), while a right click rotates to the right (clockwise).

3. As needed, use the right and left arrow buttons next to the active tray to move it from side to side to align with the hole from which the upper marbles are coming.

4. When everything is aligned, click the down arrow button to slide the chosen marbles into the chosen spot on the tray.

5. Repeat steps 1 through 4 to try to completely fill a tray with marbles.

If you try to put a marble into a spot on a tray that already is filled, it will cost you a bonus point. If you are out of bonus points, the row simply won't go, and another column of balls will be added to the upper grid, making matters even worse for you. When a ball drops to a spot occupied by another ball, both disappear, leaving an empty space. You can use this strategically to clear out some spaces to make room for balls that are waiting in the upper grid.

At level one, all the marbles are the same color, but as you get into higher levels, you have more colors to work with. A tray can be cleared only if it is completely full of marbles of all the same color, so you must avoid putting marbles of different colors into a tray.

In higher levels, sometimes a paint palette or a blot appears instead of one or more balls in one of the columns. Drop a paint palette onto a ball to change the ball's color to the color dominating the rest of the grid. This works well for correcting errors where you have put the wrong ball color in a tray. Dropping a blot onto a ball removes it.

Playing Mixed Genetics

Here's the premise of Mixed Genetics: the lab creatures have mixed-up genes so that, for example, an elephant might have a crab's head or claw. The goal is to combine, or "breed," three creatures so that they form one pure animal with no odd parts.

Breeding Basics

When you combine three animals, two or more animals who have a characteristic pass that characteristic on to an offspring. If all three creatures have a different characteristic for that body part, it's random chance which one the offspring will get.

An example will make this clearer. In Figure 24.8, the three animals on the bottom row are one body part away from being pure elephants. By "breeding" them together, you can make one pure elephant. Why? Look at each body part in turn: head, body, left arm, right arm, left leg, and right leg. Notice that among the three, there are two good elephant parts and one crab part for several body parts. When you breed these creatures, the two elephant parts will be dominant and a pure elephant will emerge.

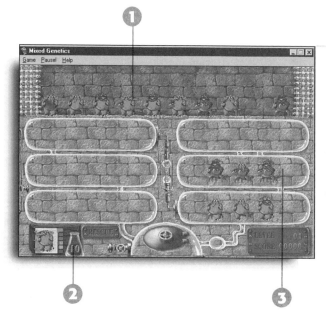

FIGURE 24.8

Breed three animals together to make "pure" ones.

1 New animals appear in the holding area.

2 Beaker shows number of pure-breds needed to complete round.

3 You can drag animals into these test tubes for breeding.

To breed a group together, you right-click on the middle one. The resulting offspring appears "stuck" to your mouse pointer, so you can drag it where you want it. If it's complete, the hatch at the bottom of the screen opens and you can drop the animal in the hatch. The counter in the beaker to the left of the hatch shows how many animals you have to drop into the hatch to move to the next level.

Ready to try it out? Follow these steps.

Breeding a pure animal in Mixed Genetics

1. Start the Mixed Genetics program. A new game starts.

2. In the "waiting area" at the top of the screen, identify three animals that are one body part shy of being a purebred elephant. Make sure you pick three that are different; you can't breed two of the same. For example, you might find one with a crab head, one with a crab left foot, and one with a crab right foot, like the ones in Figure 24.8.

3. Drag each of the identified animals into one of the test tube rows, as in Figure 24.8, so they are side by side.

4. Right-click on the middle animal. A perfect elephant appears, stuck to your mouse pointer, and the hatch opens.

5. Position the pure elephant over the hatch, and click to drop it there. Notice that the animals you just bred now have red hearts on their bodies. This indicates that they have been bred once.

6. Right-click again on the same middle animal, and drag the resulting perfect elephant again into the hatch. Notice that now the animals have black hearts on their bodies. This indicates that they have been bred twice.

7. Right-click once more on the same middle animal. The breeding animals disappear, because they can be bred only three times before they die. Once again drag the perfect one to the hatch.

8. Repeat the procedure, identifying three other animals, until the number in the beaker reaches zero and you start a new level. You may want to try for a purebred crab this time.

Breeding with Pure Specimens

The biggest tip I can give you for this game: sometimes it is advantageous not to immediately drop a pure animal into the hatch. You may want to use it once or twice to breed with other animals before you put it down the hatch. (Don't use it three times for breeding, though, or it will die before you get credit for it.)

Breeding pure animals from other pure ones

1. Perform a breeding, as in the preceding steps, so that you have a pure animal, but don't drop it in the hatch. Instead, drop it in a test tube row.

2. Find two different animals that are perfect specimens of that type except for one body part, and place them next to the perfect one.

3. Right-click on the middle animal, creating another perfect one. Set this animal aside in a test tube row rather than drop it down the hatch.

4. Right-click again on the middle animal, and drop the resulting perfect animal down the hatch. Now the original breeders have black hearts.

5. Take the perfect black-hearted creature and drop it down the hatch.

6. Drag the waiting perfect creature into the spot formerly held by the old perfect breeder.

7. Right-click on the triad again, producing yet another perfect creature. Set it aside.

8. Drag the red-hearted perfect creature into the hatch.

9. Repeat this process as needed, using perfect creatures to breed more.

The game is fairly easy when you are working with only two species—elephants and crabs. But as you progress through higher levels, there will be more species (up to eight), and more body parts will be wrong on each creature. By level 10, you will be working with eight different creature types, and each animal may have body parts from up to six types at once! When you get to this level, you may have to do "interim breeding." In other words, you may have to breed some creatures that you know will not produce a perfect offspring, simply to get a creature that is closer to perfect than what you have. You then use these "closer" creatures to breed something even better, until finally you produce a pure specimen.

Playing Rat Poker

Rat Poker is a pretty simple game. The object is to line up rats in certain combinations to send them marching out the door and get points. For example, in the first round, you need to get three rats of the same color in a row. When you do so, the rats leave the playing area and you get some points. More rats are constantly entering the playing area. When the playing area is so full of rats that no more can enter, the game is over.

The Basic Game

The rats march around in a clockwise pattern, past one or more traps, as shown in Figure 24.9. Each trap can hold only one rat at a time. You can capture any rat as it passes by a trap by pressing the space bar. You can then release the rat at any time by pressing the space bar again. For example, suppose you have two orange rats, then a red one, then another orange. You could trap the red one, forming three orange ones in a row, as in Figure 24.9. Then after the orange ones have passed, you could release the red one, or wait until another red one passes to release it, forming a pair.

If another rat passes by the trap at the same moment that you release one, the two rats swap places. If you release a rat when no other rat is passing by, it simply releases it, leaving the trap empty.

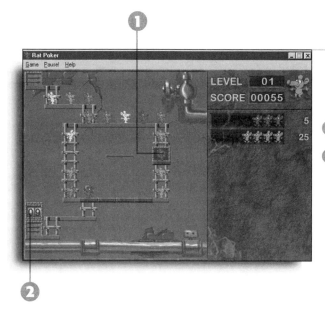

FIGURE 24.9

In Rat Poker, you trap and release rats strategically to form groups of same-colored rats.

1 Trap

2 Number of rats needed to clear level

Higher Levels, More Traps

When the specified number of rats have escaped (the number on the counter on the left—17 in Figure 24.9), you start a new level. On higher levels, there are multiple traps, and you switch which trap is active by pressing Tab.

Some levels also have a swinging arm that you control with the arrow keys that can transfer a rat between one trap and another. For example, in Figure 24.10, I can move the rat from the top trap to the side one by pressing the right arrow key twice to swing the arm clockwise, moving the rat to the other trap. (The left arrow swings it counterclockwise.) Notice also in Figure 24.10 that the list of valid rat combinations (on the right) has expanded, so you can get more points for making more complicated combinations (for example, three of one color immediately followed by three of another is worth 150 points).

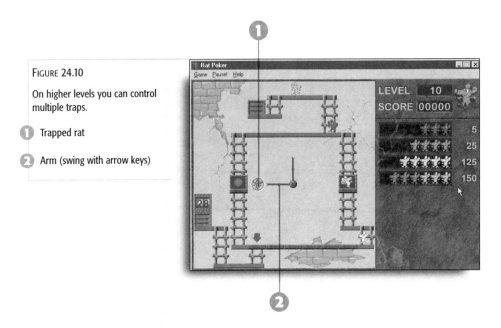

FIGURE 24.10

On higher levels you can control multiple traps.

① Trapped rat

② Arm (swing with arrow keys)

Higher levels also bring some special rat features:

- White rats are wild cards. They substitute for any other color.

- A single gray rat following a valid combination prevents that combination from scoring and escaping.

- A rat with a plus sign on him doubles the score for any combo that uses him.

- A rat with a minus sign halves the score for any combo that uses him.

Playing Lineup

Lineup is sort of like Tetris. You have various shapes made up of balls (it's a sports-themed game), and you try to place the shapes on the field to form a complete line from one end of the field to another. When you do so, all the shapes that formed the line disappear. When you fail to place the next shape quickly enough and create a backlog of five shapes waiting, you lose.

Check out Figure 24.11. Six shapes have been placed, and a full line across the field is almost complete. I can now place the next shape (the bottom-most one to the right of the field) in the empty area to complete the line.

Each shape to be placed has one ball that's highlighted. In the next shape to be placed in Figure 24.11, this is the rightmost ball on the bottom of the shape. Wherever you click the field, that ball will be placed, and the other balls will be placed in the shape around it.

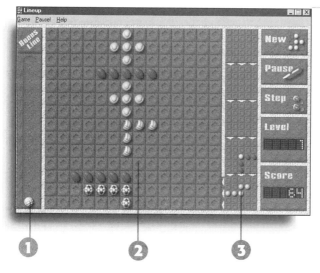

1 **2** **3**

FIGURE 24.11

Complete full lines of balls across the field to make the shapes disappear, clearing the way for more.

1 Golf balls indicate bonuses.

2 Click here to place the next shape's highlighted ball in this spot.

3 Highlighted ball in the next shape to be placed.

Bonus Balls

When you clear the entire playing field, complete two lines at once, or make a line out of all one kind of ball, you get one or more bonuses (a golf ball) in the trough on the left side of the playing field (see Figure 24.11). You can cash in your bonuses in any of the following ways:

- Click a piece on the playing field to remove it.
- Click the next piece to be played to rotate it.
- (Higher levels only) Click a dirt patch to remove it (requires three bonus balls).

Special Objects

On higher levels, special objects appear on the field, and you must surround them completely with balls to remove them and activate their special properties. Until you remove the objects by surrounding them, they are merely impediments that don't count toward a completed line and that prevent you from completing the line on which they're located. These objects include the following:

- *Clock*. Stops the clock temporarily so that no new pieces are added to the line of waiting pieces.
- *Scorecard*. Surrounding it adds points to your score.
- *Medal*. Surround it to clear the playing field.
- *Garbage can*. Adds a dirt patch to the field every time you remove a line from the field while it is there. When you see a garbage can, surround it to remove it before completing any more lines.
- *Dirt patches*. Remove them by surrounding a garbage can. Every time you surround and remove a garbage can, one dirt patch comes off. You can also click a dirt patch to remove it, but it costs three bonus balls.

Strategies for Lineup

Here are some winning strategies:

- As tempting as it is, don't try to fill in areas with balls. Concentrate instead on completing lines as soon as possible.
- When possible, build lines from the edges inward. The center area offers greater flexibility for placing pieces than the edges.
- Work ahead by looking at what pieces are coming up. If you are playing so fast that you are having to wait for upcoming pieces to display, click the **Step** button to display the next one in line immediately.
- Save your bonus golf balls! You will need them for the higher levels. Do not use them unless it's absolutely necessary.

Playing Jewel Chase

In Jewel Chase, you are a jewel thief who runs around collecting loot. When you've gathered up all the loot on a level, you run for the exit to "escape" to the next one. You are competing against a rival thief (controlled by the computer) who is also after the same goods.

You can move only among squares of the same color. To transition between colors, you move onto a "half-and-half" square that is a mixture of two colors. From there you can move to squares that are the second color. For example, suppose the playing field is made up of red and blue squares, and the staircase to the next level is on a red square. First you gather up all the loot on the red squares, and then you move onto a square that is half blue and half red. From there you can go to the blue squares and get the loot there. Then you head back to the red/blue square, and then back to the red ones, and to the staircase to the next level (see Figure 24.12).

Training mode

This game can be a little tricky at first, racing against the computerized opponent. A good way to get your bearings is to put the game into Training mode. That way you can complete a few levels without the opponent. To do so, choose **Game** and then **Options** and set the difficulty level to Training.

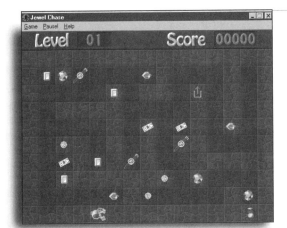

FIGURE 24.12

Gather up the loot and then get out of there!

You use the arrow keys to move from square to square. If you move in a direction where the next square is the wrong color, you automatically jump to the next correct-colored square in that direction. For example, suppose there are three squares from left to right: red, blue, red. You are on the leftmost one. You press the right arrow key. You jump over the blue square and move to the other red one.

Jewel Thief Strategies

It's important to accumulate points in this game by picking up loot, but the essential part of each level is to exit it before your computerized opponent does. If you fail to do this, your game is over. Therefore, you need to strategize a bit. Don't go far away from the staircase to get the last gem if your opponent is near it, or he may escape out the stairs before you, and then the few points you got from that last gem will be for naught.

In higher levels, you can pick up other objects besides loot—bombs and keys, for example. These open locked areas on the screen. Again, use these strategically. Don't unlock a gate leading to an area with lots of loot if your opponent will be able to get there before you and get it.

Playing Color Collision

In Color Collision, you control a wispy little line called a *color collider* that bounces around the screen. Use the arrow keys to direct it.

FYI...

Ever wonder how Color Collision determines what color the collider will be next? It's the color of the inside of the circle that it most recently touched. For example, if the color collider is red and you hit a red circle with a green interior, the color collider will be green next.

Your immediate goal is to hit an object with a border that matches the current color of the collider (see Figure 24.13). (Its color changes every time you hit something.) If you hit an object with the correct border color, the collider disappears. If you hit an object with the wrong color border, it changes into a stick of that color. If you hit the wrong color stick, you lose a life. You have three lives, and then the game is over. (However, you can earn more lives as you go; see the section on "Collecting Bonuses" on the next page.)

Notice the little balls along the left side of the screen? Every time you hit a correct-colored item, one of them disappears. When they're all gone, the level is over and you move on to the next level (where things get harder).

If you get a stick on the screen, be careful not to hit it unless the collider color matches it! When you hit a stick of the right color, it disappears, but another stick appears somewhere else on the screen. You have to hit five sticks of the right colors to get rid of them.

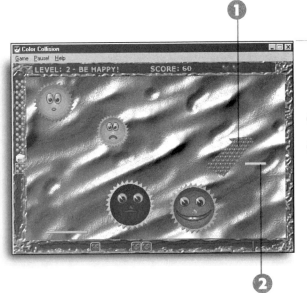

FIGURE 24.13

In Color Collision, you try to hit objects of the right color and avoid those of the wrong color.

1 Color collider

2 Stick

Collecting Bonuses

Each level has its own theme and its own opportunity to earn bonus points. A box pops up at the beginning of each level explaining the theme and its bonus structure. The bonuses differ depending on the level and how many other bonuses you have already earned on the level. Your bonus might be one of these:

- *Heart*. An extra life.
- *Gold coin*. Extra points.
- *Ice*. Freezes all circles except those of the color matching the collider, so the collider bounces off them harmlessly.
- *Palette*. Changes the colors of all circles and sticks.
- *First-aid kit*. Changes all sticks back to circles.
- *Bomb* (looks like a big blue ball). Blows up five green balls, putting you closer to clearing the level.
- *Question mark*. Mystery bonus, can be any of the above.

When you earn a bonus, you don't collect it immediately; it's placed somewhere within the rack of little green balls. When you've cleared away all the balls below it, you earn the bonus by hitting a correct-colored object, the same way that you earn a regular green ball.

Playing Charmer

In Charmer, your job is to coax the snakes in the pots to rise up to the vine above them. When their heads hit the vine, they—and their pots—disappear (see Figure 24.14). When you've gotten rid of all the pots, you've finished the level.

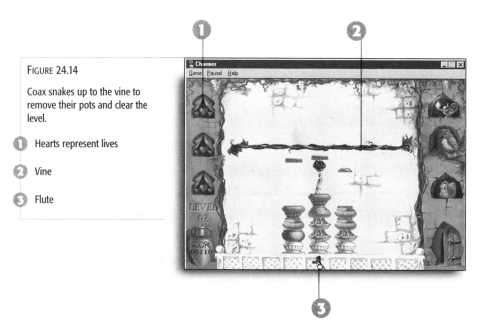

FIGURE 24.14

Coax snakes up to the vine to remove their pots and clear the level.

1 Hearts represent lives

2 Vine

3 Flute

Flutes, Falling Lids, and Bonus Lives

You charm a snake by positioning the flute under the pot. Move the flute with the right and left arrow keys. There are three different flutes you can play to charm the snakes, and you switch among them with the space bar. Each snake prefers one flute over the others and will rise faster when he hears it, so with each snake you charm, you should switch among the flutes to discover which one makes the snake rise fastest.

Sometimes a lid will fall off the vine and start down toward the pot. Make the snake in the pot rise up to hit the lid and push it back up. If the lid reaches the pot, you lose one of your hearts (lives) in the windows on the left. When you lose all the hearts, your game is over.

There is only one way to recover your lost lives. When you get rid of a pot (by charming the snake up to the vine) while the parrot is squawking, you get one of your hearts back if you have lost any.

Playing Spring Weekend

If you like spatial games such as the Rubik's Cube, you'll like Spring Weekend. In this simple game, you rotate pieces to match a given pattern. When you click an object, all the objects in a circle around it rotate one space counterclockwise (left-click) or clockwise (right-click).

Let's take a look at a sample Level 1, shown in Figure 24.15. You need to match the big circle (on the left) to the sample (on the right). To do so, right-click the second flower in the third (middle) row, rotating the rose into the correct position.

Mysterious man

Periodically, a man appears in the door at the bottom right corner of the screen. While he is there, the snakes retreat quickly back into their pots the moment you move the flute from under their pot. (Ordinarily, a snake will glide slowly back down if you move the flute before he has reached the vine.)

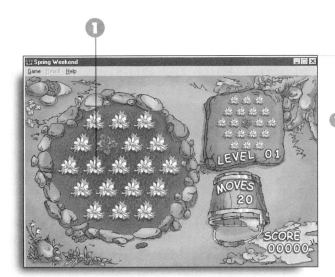

FIGURE 24.15

What would you do to make the left one match the right?

1 Right-click this flower to rotate all the ones around it clockwise.

Save your moves

Be judicious with your moves, because you get points for unused moves at the end of every round.

That sample took only one move, but you're allowed up to 20 moves on level 1. (At the beginning of each level, the game tells you how many moves you get.) For most other levels, you will need to plan your moves like a chess game.

Playing Muddled Casino

Muddled Casino, shown in Figure 24.16, is perhaps the hardest game in the Puzzle Collection—it definitely requires some strategy and planning! The object is to remove all the cards from the table in the order shown in the right-hand column. The bottom card in the column indicates the first card to remove. Once you've played through the Training levels, you bid against the house to win points. To break even, you need to remove six cards from each table. The game ends when you have fewer than 40 points to wager.

FIGURE 24.16

Try to move the cards toward the exit.

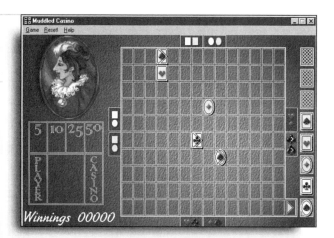

The training level starts with five cards on the table. The betting levels start with eight. The cards move in groups. You position a group so that you can remove a particular card, but you also must plan as you are moving the groups, keeping in mind the future cards you must remove and the order in which you must remove them. To remove a card, you slide it out the hole in the bottom right corner of the playing field.

Clear as mud, right? Actually it's not that bad. Try these steps.

Learning to play Muddled Casino

1. Find the card on the playing field that matches the bottom card on the left. This is the card you need to move to the outhole in the bottom left corner of the playing field.

2. You'll move the card there by sliding its entire group in one of the four directions. Identify the group to be moved, and click on the appropriate button to select it. (The group buttons are above, below, to the right, and to the left of the playing field.)

3. Press the arrow key that matches the arrow on your group button to move the group. Note that each group moves in only one direction; for example, the group consisting of red cards (hearts and diamonds) moves only to the left. If the group you've chosen doesn't move in the direction you need the card to move, choose a different group of which that card is a member.

4. To move the group, press the spacebar. You can't move a card toward another card in the same row, but otherwise any card can move anywhere.

5. If you get stuck, press Tab to knock a card off the table. You can tab a card off the table or into a black hole, but it costs you points.

When you get the hang of moving cards around, you'll be able to complete the training levels. At that point, you need to bid. To bid, click the chip with the point value you want to bet. The bid you make depends on how easily you think you can clear the table, based on the positions of the cards there. (They change every time.) An average bid might be 40 or 80. If you have more points later in the game, you can bid more. For each card you remove from the table, you win back a certain number of chips. To break even, you need to remove six of the eight cards from the table. For each card you Tab off the table, you lose the potential to win back chips for it. (That's why you can't Tab off more than two cards.)

Don't Tab too much

If you Tab more than two cards off the table, you will not have enough points to break even in the round.

Special Objects

As you advance to higher levels, special objects appear on the table.

- *Bumper*. Blocks any card from moving toward it. Experienced players can use it strategically.

- *Black hole*. Acts like a table edge, preventing the entire group from moving if a card would be moving into it. You can tab a card off into a black hole, the same as tabbing it off regularly.

- *Dice*. Appear in pairs. Slide a card into one die to make it appear at the location of the other one.

- *Joker*. An alternative exit. Sliding a card into the joker is the same as removing it from the table (and you get the points for it, unlike tabbing it off).

Tips and Hints

The key to this game, after you have mastered the basics, is to wager carefully. You need to accurately predict how easily you can clear the board. Wager as much as possible when you get an easy table (for example, if all the cards are near the exit). Wager less if the table looks difficult (for example, if cards are on opposite sides of the table or if the board has black holes that block cards).

When moving your cards around, try to group them in the center or toward the exit. It is harder to move a card group if individual cards are around the table edges.

Remember that you can't move a card toward another card (or bumper) in the same row or column. You can use these limits to your advantage by blocking certain cards from nearing the edge of the table or the exit before their turns.

A

Installing Home Essentials

Installation Demystified

When you get a new Windows-based program, you usually have to run a *setup utility* before you can use it. The role of the setup utility varies from program to program, but some common things that setup utilities do include

- Copy the files used to run the program to your hard disk. Some programs, such as Word, copy all the necessary files; others, such as Encarta, leave some of them on the CD and require you to pop the CD into your drive every time you want to use the program.

- Register the program with Windows, letting Windows know how to handle the data files for the program. For example, Word registers its document extension (.doc) with Windows, so when you double-click a file with a .doc extension, Word starts automatically.

- Install special *drivers* and *system files* that interact with Windows to help the program run. Some of these drivers must be loaded each time Windows starts; if you install a program that uses these, you will be prompted to restart your computer after the setup utility has finished its work.

- Set up a command on the **Start** menu, and sometimes a *desktop shortcut*, too, that makes it easy for you to start the installed program.

Starting the Home Essentials Setup Program

Home Essentials is actually a bundled group of products, rather than one *integrated program*. Therefore, its setup program consists of links to the separate setup programs for each product. The setup programs have some things in common, but each is a little different. This appendix covers each of them separately.

The Home Essentials setup screen (see Figure A.1) should appear automatically when you put Disc #1 of the Home Essentials CD set in your CD-ROM drive. If it doesn't appear automatically, follow these steps:

1. Double-click the **My Computer** icon on the desktop.

2. Double-click the icon for the CD-ROM drive containing the CD.

FIGURE A.1

You can access each of the individual setup programs from this Microsoft Home Essentials setup window.

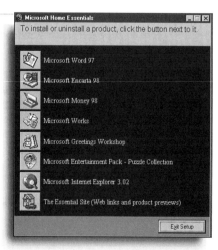

If that doesn't work, right-click the icon for the CD-ROM drive and select *AutoPlay*.

If that doesn't work, right-click the icon for the CD-ROM drive and select **Open**. Then in the window that appears, double-click the **Setup.exe** icon.

Installing Word 97

Word 97 is the most expensive and complex program in the Home Essentials suite, so Microsoft has taken extra care with its installation procedure. Before installing Word 97, you must locate the 11-digit CD key on the back of the Home Essentials CD-ROM case. It's on a bright yellow sticker that says CD KEY. If for some reason yours has been removed, you'll need to call Microsoft (800-426-9400 is the Sales Information line) and ask them what you can do about it. If a family member removed it, Microsoft may be able to issue you a different number; if your copy came without one, you may have unwittingly bought a bootleg copy and Microsoft would like to know where you got it.

To install Word, just click the **Microsoft Word 97** icon in the setup program and follow the onscreen steps. When prompted, enter your name, company name, and the CD key.

After entering the CD key, your product ID number will appear. It's a good idea to write this number down on paper somewhere, even though you can display it at any time from within Word by opening the **Help** menu and choosing **About Microsoft Word**. That way, if for some reason Word isn't working, you can call Microsoft Technical Support and get help. (They won't help you without a valid product ID number.)

When prompted for the location, just click **OK** to accept the default. When asked what kind of installation you want to do, choose **Typical**. After you do that, A short list of options appears for your installation (see Figure A.2). Notice that **Typical Word Components** is already checked; the other two options are **Web Page Authoring (HTML)** and **Converters for Use with Lotus Notes**. If you feel you will need either of these items, click the check mark next to the one you want.

Typical versus Custom

If you choose **Custom** instead of **Typical** installation, your list of choices is much more extensive than just the two check boxes. I don't recommend a Custom installation except for experienced users who know exactly what components they want.

FIGURE A.2

Even if you choose the **Typical** installation, you still have a couple of choices to make.

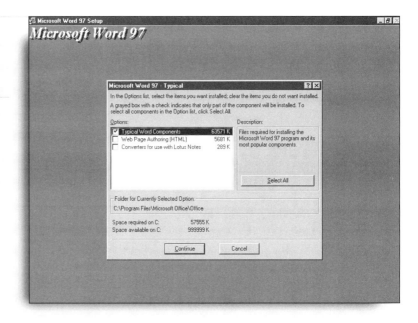

SEE ALSO

➤ *To learn how to use Word 97, see Part II of this book, which begins on page 159.*

Installing Encarta

CD unreadable?

If you get a message that it can't read the drive, wait a few seconds and retry. Sometimes a disc requires a few seconds to come up to speed in a drive before the computer can read from it.

Encarta setup is easy. The only glitch (and it's a minor one) is that you have to pop in Disc #3 of the Home Essentials set, because that's the Encarta disk.

Encarta is such a big program that it wouldn't be practical to copy all of it to your hard disk, so the installation program copies only enough of the files to start up the interface. The rest of the files remain on the CD. That's why you need the CD in the drive at all times when you're running Encarta. Without the data from the CD, Encarta can't work its magic.

To install Encarta, just click the **Microsoft Encarta 98** button on the setup screen and follow the onscreen prompts.

SEE ALSO

➤ *To learn how to use Encarta, see page 471.*

Installing Money 98

The Money 98 installation program is fairly straightforward and without peril. Just click the **Microsoft Money 98** button on the setup screen and follow the steps. If you want to use Money 98's online features, you will also need to install Internet Explorer 3.02, as explained later in this appendix.

SEE ALSO
➤ *Money is covered in Part III, "Using Money," of this book, which starts on page 305.*

Installing Microsoft Works

Works is another fairly easy program to install. The only question that you may not have seen before is whether you want a shortcut on the desktop. Basically, this puts a shortcut icon that starts Works in plain sight for you, so you don't have to use the **Start** menu to run it. This is very handy, and I recommend it unless your desktop is already jam-packed with shortcut icons.

Just click the **Microsoft Works** icon in the setup program to start the ball rolling, and follow the onscreen prompts. When asked whether you want a **Complete Installation** or a **Custom Installation** (see Figure A.3), click **Complete Installation**. When asked whether you want to create a shortcut for Works on the desktop, click **Yes**.

SEE ALSO
➤ *You'll learn all about Works in Part I, "Using Works," which begins on page 1.*

Two versions of Money

The version of Money 98 included with Home Essentials is the basic one. You can buy a fancier version called Money 98 Financial Suite separately if you want. If you have already installed the Financial Suite version, don't install the version on the Home Essentials CD. If you do, it will overwrite the better version with the lesser one.

Who needs Custom installation?

If you're running out of hard disk space, you might consider choosing **Custom Installation** instead of **Complete Installation**. Custom lists all the optional components included in Works and lets you choose which ones you don't want installed (such as clip art, for example).

FIGURE A.3
Complete Installation is the right choice for most users.

Installing Microsoft Greetings Workshop

Like Encarta, Greetings Workshop has its own separate CD that must be in your CD-ROM drive for the program to operate. It also requires its own special CD for installation.

To install, click **Microsoft Greetings Workshop** on the setup screen and follow the prompts. When prompted, click the button for either **Typical** or **Minimal** installation, depending on what you want. Typical is better if you have at least 80MB of spare hard disk space because it makes the program run faster. Both options require you to have the CD in the drive whenever you use the program.

SEE ALSO

➤ *To find out how to use Microsoft Greetings Workshop, see all of Chapter 22 beginning on page 444.*

Installing Microsoft Entertainment Pack

The Entertainment Pack Puzzle Collection has a completely different installation program interface than the others. It's sort of a swirly tan and brown affair, very exotic, and non-businesslike (which, if you think about it, is more appropriate anyway for something as fun as puzzles).

After you've selected **Microsoft Entertainment Pack – Puzzle Collection** from the Home Essentials setup window, follow the onscreen prompts until you reach the screen that asks whether you want to install into the default folder. The following steps outline the remainder of the installation steps.

Installing Microsoft Entertainment Pack

1. Click **OK** to accept the default folder for installation.

2. A message appears saying that the folder does not exist and asking whether you want to create it. Click **Yes**.

3. Click **Typical** to install all the games.

4. Wait for the files to be copied to your hard disk; when you see a message asking whether you want a shortcut on the desktop, click **Yes**.

5. When asked whether you want to register online, click **Yes** or **No**, as desired. (If you don't have a modem, you must select **No**.)

6. If you chose **Yes** in step 5, work through the registration screens, following the prompts. If you chose **No** in step 5, go on to step 7 now.

7. When you see a message that setup has completed successfully, click **OK**.

8. Back at the wavy tan screen, click **Exit** to leave the setup program.

SEE ALSO

➤ *You'll learn how to play all these great puzzle games in Chapter 24, which starts on page 495.*

Installing Internet Explorer 3.02

Home Essentials comes with two months of free Internet access from MCI, but to take advantage of it, you will need a Web *browser*. Fortunately, that's just what Internet Explorer is. A Web browser is a program that lets you read the "pages" that people and companies have posted on the Internet. Internet Explorer also comes with auxiliary programs that handle your email and let you read newsgroups.

You may also want to install Internet Explorer 3.02 (IE3) even if you aren't interested in the MCI offer. You can use IE3 with any Internet service provider.

Installing Internet Explorer 3.02

1. From the Home Essentials setup window, click **Microsoft Internet Explorer 3.02**.

2. If you want to take advantage of the MCI two-month free Internet trial, click the **MCI** button and follow the prompts. (You'll catch back up to these steps after the signup.) Otherwise, click the **Upgrade Only** button and continue to step 3.

SEE ALSO

➤ *You'll understand more about Web browsers, email, and newsgroups after you read Part IV, "Using Internet Explorer," which begins on page 397.*

Newer version available

Internet Explorer 3.02 is not the latest version of the program—you can download version 4 from Microsoft's Web site for free (`http://www. microsoft.com/ie`), or you may already have it. However, be aware that some programs may not coexist well with Internet Explorer 4.0–in particular, you cannot use Microsoft Money 98's online banking or bill paying features with IE4 unless you download and install a special 128-bit patch for it. Little quirks like that are the main reason Home Essentials comes with version 3.02 instead.

If you already have Internet Explorer 4 installed on your system…

Leave it; don't try to install version 3.02 from the Home Essentials CD. Uninstalling IE 4 can be a real hassle, and the two versions cannot coexist on the same computer. If you have IE 4 on your computer, download the 128-bit patch that enables you to use Money 98's online banking and bill-paying feature (you'll find more information about this patch in Chapter 18, "Investigating Online Banking and Bill Paying").

Desktop icon

If you have already installed some of the other components of Home Essentials, you might see an icon on your desktop called **Setup for Internet Explorer 3.02**. You can double-click this icon to start the IE setup program; it has the same effect as starting the following steps at step 3.

Newer files?

If you see a message about a file being copied that is older than an existing file on your system, you should always choose **Yes** to keep the existing file.

Your Internet connection

Some Internet connections are through local area networks or direct connections, but at home, you'll probably have a dial-up connection. If you use an online service, you log on to that system and then minimize that program's window. If you use an Internet service provider, you probably connect using Windows 95's Dial-Up Networking, which is set up when you set up your Internet connection with Internet Explorer in Chapter 19, "Surfing the Internet with Internet Explorer."

3. Read the license agreement, and then click **Yes**.

Wait for the files to be copied to your hard disk.

4. When a message appears that your computer needs to be restarted, click **Yes** to allow it.

Installing the Essential Site Link

If you install Internet Explorer, you can also install a shortcut on your **Start** menu to the Home Essentials Web site. The resulting shortcut accesses a Web page on the *Home Essentials* CD, which in turn contains links to the Microsoft Home Essentials Web site on the Internet. At that site, you can download updates and additions, read about new products, get project ideas, and more.

To install the link to the Home Essentials Web site

1. If you want to view the Home Essentials Web site immediately after this setup, start your Internet connection now.

2. From the Home Essentials setup window, click **The Essential Site (Web links and product reviews)**.

3. Follow the onscreen prompts to install the needed files.

4. When a message appears asking if you want to view the site after setup, click **Yes** or **No** as desired. If you choose **Yes**, make sure your Internet connection is active—you'll need to be connected momentarily.

Wait for the needed files to be copied to your hard disk.

5. If you chose **Yes** in step 4, a Web page appears in Internet Explorer (see Figure A.4). If you chose **No**, skip to step 8.

6. Click the **Visit the Home Essentials Web site** hyperlink. (Hint: Look for underlined words.)

7. Explore the Web site as desired; when you're finished, close Internet Explorer and terminate your Internet connection.

8. When you see the message that the setup program has completed successfully, click **OK**.

SEE ALSO

➤ *For more information about using hyperlinks, see Chapter 19, "Surfing the Internet with Internet Explorer," which begins on page 399.*

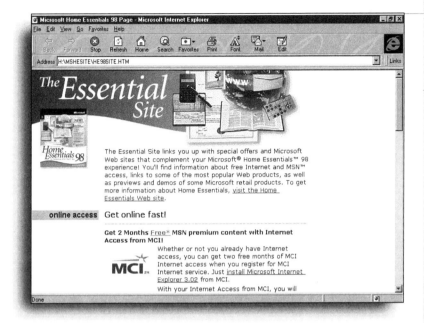

The Microsoft Home Essentials page provides a link that connects you with the live Microsoft site online.

Exploring the Home Essentials Web Site

What's the Essential Site?

When you installed the rest of the Home Essentials programs, you may have also installed something called the Essential Site, probably more out of curiosity than anything else. The Essential Site is an HTML document that the installation program copied to your hard disk. You can view it with Internet Explorer. It contains hyperlinks to various goodies on the Internet that relate to the applications in your Home Essentials suite. For example, one pointer on the Essential Site page directs your Web browser to the online support page for Home Essentials.

SEE ALSO
➤ *For more information about installing the Home Essentials programs, see page 519.*

Viewing the Essential Site Page

You do not have to be connected to the Internet to view the Essential Site because it is stored on your hard disk rather than the Internet. However, if you click on any of the hyperlinks on this site, you will be prompted to start your Internet connection at that point if it is not already running.

SEE ALSO

➤ *To view the Essential Site page in Internet Explorer, you must have Internet Explorer installed. If you don't, see page 525.*

Viewing the Essential Site page

1. Click the **Start** button, select **Programs**, and click **Microsoft Essentials Site**. Internet Explorer opens with the opening page displayed (see Figure B.1).

FIGURE B.1

The Essential Site is actually a Web page full of hyperlinks to various resources.

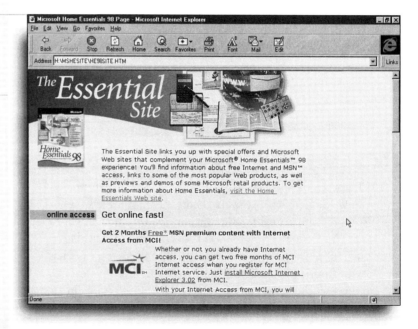

2. Read the information on the page, and when you are interested in checking out one of the topics, click its hyperlink.

3. When you are finished, close Internet Explorer and terminate your Internet connection if you started one and it does not terminate automatically.

SEE ALSO

➤ *For help on shutting down your Internet connection, see page 414.*

Table B.1 lists the links on the Essential Site page and what each will do for you.

TABLE B.1 **Essential Site links**

Area	Purpose
Visit the Home Essentials Web site	Displays a very useful support site at Microsoft devoted to Home Essentials.
Online access	Sets you up with free and discounted Internet offers from MCI and the Microsoft Network.
Web products	Points you toward online demos and information about various Microsoft products.
Retail products	Provides links to advertisements for other Microsoft software you might want to buy.

Glossary

128-bit security Extra security for data sent via the Internet; available in the United States only. The default security is 40-bit. You must have the 128-bit patch for Internet Explorer 4.0 to use Microsoft Money's online banking and bill payment.

401(k) A retirement plan through your employer. You make contributions, and sometimes the employer does, too. Contributions are not taxed, but withdrawals are.

Absolute reference A reference to a spreadsheet cell that, when copied to a different cell, retains its original reference. Absolute references are denoted with dollar signs in formulas, such as A5.

Account In Money, any bank or brokerage account, or a non-bank holding such as petty cash.

Account details In Money, the details about an account, such as the account number, name and address of the bank, and opening balance.

Account number The unique identifier for a bank or brokerage account.

Active cell In a spreadsheet, the cell that is currently selected. All commands issued apply to the active cell, and the active cell's content appears in the formula bar.

Address book In Works and some email programs (such as Internet Mail), a list of addresses (physical or email, or both) from which to pick recipients.

Alignment The way text in a paragraph or a cell positions itself in relation to the margins or edges. Alignment options include left-aligned, right-aligned, and centered.

Amortization chart A chart that shows the split of each payment between the principal and the interest of the loan. As time goes by, more of each payment progressively goes toward principal and less toward interest.

Arguments In a spreadsheet function, parameters that tell the function what cells to operate on and how. For example, the =SUM function's arguments are the names of the cells whose contents should be added.

Arithmetic operators Math symbols in a formula that tell a spreadsheet how to calculate. Arithmetic operators include

+ (addition), - (subtraction), * (multiplication), and / (division).

Attachment A binary file attached to a text-based email message. For example, you could send a text email to your boss, along with an attached Word file containing a report.

AutoComplete In Word, a feature that automatically completes a word or phrase based on the first few letters.

AutoCorrect In Word, a group of features that automatically correct typing and formatting errors. The features included under AutoCorrect include AutoFormat, AutoComplete, and AutoText.

AutoFit A feature in the Works spreadsheet program that automatically changes the width of a column to exactly fit the longest line of text in it.

AutoFormat In Word, a feature that applies certain formatting, such as creating automatic bulleted or numbered lists or converting email addresses to active hyperlinks.

AutoFormat As You Type Special AutoFormat settings that apply the changes automatically as you type, rather than waiting for you to issue the AutoFormat command.

AutoPlay A Windows 95/98 feature that automatically runs a CD-ROM when you place it in your PC.

AutoShape A drawing tool in Word and other Microsoft products that enables you to place pre-drawn shapes, such as arrows, starbursts, and complex shapes.

AutoSum In the Works spreadsheet, a toolbar button that automatically applies the =SUM function and guesses which cells you want to sum based on the active cell position.

AutoText In Word, a means of storing frequently typed phrases and paragraphs and inserting them into a document with a few keystrokes.

Backup To copy important files from your PC's hard disk to an alternate location, such as a floppy disk or tape drive, in case something happens to the originals.

Balancing In Money, to reconcile a bank account with the statement you receive.

Bank Online The former name of the online banking portion of CheckFree, an online banking and bill payment service.

Bill Calendar In Money, a calendar that helps you track when your bills are due and reminds you to pay them.

Boilerplate Material that is standard among many documents, such as a standard closing to a business letter.

Bond An agreement by the issuer to borrow money and then pay it back with interest on a certain date. Bonds are often issued by governments and sometimes by companies.

Bookmark *See* **Favorite places**.

Border A line or box drawn around certain paragraphs (in a word processor) or cells (in a spreadsheet).

Cache A storage area for information from a program that keeps the information readily available in case it is used again. For example, Internet Explorer caches recently visited Web pages.

Capital gain The profit you make when you sell a security (such as stock) or other investment (such as real estate) for more money than you initially paid.

Category In Money, a means of classifying income and expenses for reporting purposes.

Cell The intersection of a row and a column in a table or spreadsheet.

Cell address area In the Works spreadsheet, the area to the left of the formula bar where the address of the active cell appears.

Certificate On the Internet, a verification code sent to your Web browser designed to ensure that software being downloaded or run is from the source it claims to be from.

Certificate of Deposit (CD) Like a bond, but purchased from a bank. You agree to let the bank use your money for a certain period of time, and the bank agrees to return it with interest on a certain date.

Character formatting Any formatting that affects individual words and characters rather than entire paragraphs or pages.

Character styles Styles (in Word) that apply character formatting, such as font changes and attributes.

Chart A graphical representation of spreadsheet or other numeric data.

CheckFree An online banking and bill-paying service that you can sign up to use with Money.

Clip art Pre-drawn artwork that you can use in your documents, for example, in Word and Works.

Clipboard A holding area in Windows where copied or cut material waits to be pasted.

Column header The button with the shaded letter at the top of a spreadsheet column.

Commission fees Brokerage fees that you pay when you buy or sell a stock or other security.

Communications program A program that uses your modem to help your computer connect to and communicate with other computers over phone lines.

Concepts In Money, broad groups into which certain categories are divided.

Context sensitivity The capability of a Help system to determine what you are working on and then provide help based on the context.

Contiguous Touching one another. For example, a block of cells together in a spreadsheet consists of contiguous cells.

Cookie A small file placed on your hard disk when you visit a Web site. The information in the file feeds back to the originating Web site when you visit it on subsequent occasions, letting the site owner know that you are the same person who has visited before.

Criteria In a database filter, the specifications that data must meet to be included. For example, if you are filtering out all addresses in the 46240 zip code, having a 46240 zip code is the criterion.

Crosshair A "plus sign" cursor used to help align the mouse pointer precisely when drawing or placing graphics.

Cursor The insertion point in a word-processing document, or the thick border denoting the active cell in a spreadsheet. Sometimes erroneously used to mean the mouse pointer.

Database A file created with a database program.

Database program A program that helps you organize and manipulate data (such as addresses, phone numbers, descriptions, and so on).

Decimal tab A tab stop that aligns the data with the decimal point. For example, you might use a decimal tab stop to align a column of numbers that had varying numbers of digits before and after the decimal point in them.

Desktop publishing Page layout done in a computer application. For example, when you design a newsletter layout in Word, you are doing desktop publishing.

Desktop shortcut An icon on your Windows desktop that provides a shortcut to running a program or opening a document or window.

Dialog box A window that appears when you select certain commands prompting you for more information. For example, when you choose File, Print, a Print dialog box opens.

Dividend Profit-sharing that you get from the company in which you hold stock.

In addition to the profit you might make by buying stock at a low price and selling it at a high price, you also may receive quarterly dividend payments from the company for each share you hold, if the company is doing well.

DNS address Stands for Domain Name Server address, one of several numeric settings that your Internet Service Provider may need you to specify in your Dial-Up Networking setup.

Download To transfer files from a remote computer to your own (usually through a modem).

Drivers Utility files that help Windows communicate with your system's hardware. For example, a driver tells Windows how to talk to your modem. Another driver tells Windows how to work with your video card.

Drop-down list A list in a dialog box that drops down to display its choices when you click on the down-pointing arrow to its right.

Easy Filter In Works database, one of two methods of filtering data. Easy Filter is the simple, easy-to-use method; Filter by Formula is the other, more complicated method.

Easy Text A text-insertion feature in Works that operates like AutoText does in Word. *See* **AutoText**.

Electronic mail *See* **email**.

Electronic payment (E-Pay) A bill payment you make through a bill-paying service such as Checkfree rather than by writing a check yourself.

Email Electronic messages sent and received on the Internet.

Email client A program that helps you send and receive email on your PC (for example, Internet Mail, which comes with Internet Explorer 3.0).

Favorite places A list of saved Internet addresses (URLs) in Internet Explorer that you can quickly access to visit those sites.

Field code A code in a database or word-processing document that substitutes a variable value when printed. For example, the code &p in a header or footer inserts the correct page number on each page of the document.

Fields Text boxes or lists where you enter data or settings. For example, when you fill out a form, each individual text box (such as the one for Name or Address) is a field.

Filter A set of criteria applied to data (for example, in a Works database) so that only the data you want is displayed. For example, a filter could weed out all addresses that do not have a certain ZIP code.

Filter by Formula In Works database, one of two methods of filtering data. Filter by Formula enables you to create complex filters using multiple criteria. The other method is Easy Filter, a simpler filter type designed for beginners.

Font A typeface, or style of lettering. Fonts that come with Windows include Courier, Arial, and Times New Roman.

Font style The attributes applied to characters, such as bold, italic, and underline. Do not confuse these with character style, which is a named style in Word that applies pre-specified fonts and font styles to text.

Footer Repeated text at the bottom of each page of the document, such as the company name or the date the document was printed.

Formatting Attributes you apply (usually to text) to change its appearance. Formatting can include font and size changes, bold, italic, and underline, and indenting.

Formula In a spreadsheet, a notation in a cell that tells the program to process a function or perform a math operation with arithmetic operators. For example, =A1+A2 adds the contents of cells A1 and A2.

Formula bar The area above the column headers in a spreadsheet that shows the current content of the active cell.

Forum An area of the Internet that enables people to exchange ideas about a topic of interest.

Function A named math operation that you can apply in a spreadsheet. For example, Works includes =SUM, which sums the contents of cells, and =AVG, which averages them.

GIF A graphics format popular on the Internet. GIF stands for Graphics Interchange Format, and was originally developed for and popularized on the CompuServe online service.

Graph *See* **chart**.

Graphics filter A utility built into an application (such as Word or Works) that enables it to open and use graphics files in various formats, such as PCX and BMP.

Grayed out Currently unavailable commands or controls. The name comes from the fact that they often appear in gray letters rather than black ones.

Gridline In a spreadsheet, the gray lines onscreen that separate each row and column. These may or may not print, depending on the settings you have specified.

Gutter The whitespace between two columns in a multicolumn layout, or the whitespace between the text and the binding in a book.

Handles Black or white squares onscreen surrounding a selected graphic image. You can resize the object by dragging the handles. Handles do not print.

Hanging indent An indent where the first line of the paragraph starts farther to the left than the subsequent lines.

Hard page break A page break that you enter with a command, as opposed to one that occurs naturally (soft page break).

Header Repeated text at the top of each printed page, such as the company name or the name of the document.

HTML Stands for Hypertext Markup Language, the formatting scheme used to create Web pages.

Hyperlink A link to a Web page, usually on the Internet. Hyperlinks usually appear as underlined text in a different color than the surrounding text. Clicking on a hyperlink opens the page that it represents.

Increment button Small up and down arrow buttons next to a text box in a dialog box. Click these buttons to increment the numeric value in the text box up or down.

Indent The amount that an individual paragraph is moved in or out from the rest of the document's margins. For example, some people like to indent the first line of each paragraph by five spaces.

Individual retirement account (IRA) A generic term that covers a wide variety of tax-deferred retirement plans. An individual can open an IRA for himself through a bank or brokerage, or an employer can provide an IRA plan. Contributions may be tax-deductible, and earnings may be tax-deferred.

Inline picture A graphic embedded in a document that is treated like an individual character. For example, if the graphic were embedded between two words and those words moved on the page, the graphic would move, too. Compare to a floating picture, which moves independently of the text on the page.

Input form In the Works database, the form you use in Form view to input new records into the database.

Insert mode A typing mode in a word processor in which existing text moves over to make room for additional text you type. Compare to Overtype mode.

Insertion point The flashing vertical line onscreen that indicates where text you type will appear. Also called the cursor.

Integrated program A program that combines several functions in one interface. Works is an example of an integrated program.

Internet A vast network of interconnected computers all over the world.

Internet service provider (ISP) A company that provides access to the Internet to consumers for a monthly fee.

Investment In Money, an investment is a stock, bond, CD, or other security that you buy or sell.

Investment account An account in Money that tracks all your investments with a single brokerage or bank.

IP address Stands for Internet Protocol address. One of several numeric settings that your Internet service provider may need for you to specify in your Dial-Up Networking setup.

ISP *See* **Internet service provider**.

Java A programming language that creates programs that can be run from Web pages, regardless of the type of computer you are using (PC or Macintosh).

JPEG A graphics format that is popular on the Internet. JPEG stands for Joint Photographic Experts Group. JPEG files are smaller than other formats (such as GIF), so they are popular for displaying graphics on Web pages.

Justified An alignment option that aligns a paragraph's text with both the right and left margins, inserting extra space between words and letters as needed so that each line begins and ends in exactly the same spot.

Keogh A retirement plan for self-employed people. It works much like other IRAs: Contributions are tax-deductible and earnings are tax-deferred, but withdrawals are taxable.

Landscape A page orientation in which the page is wider than it is tall.

Launch To start an application.

Leader Repeated dots or other characters between text and the next tab stop, to help the readers' eyes follow the line. This is common in tables of contents.

Link A connection between two files in Works, Word, or any other Windows-based program. Typically, one file is linked or embedded into another, such as a graphic in a word-processing document. Whenever the source (the original graphic, for example) changes, the copy in the document changes too. *See* **Object linking and embedding**.

Mail merge A technique that takes names and addresses from a database or other list and combines them with a standardized form letter to produce "personalized" copies for each recipient.

Mail server A computer set up by an Internet service provider that handles incoming and outgoing email for its subscribers.

Manual page break *See* **hard page break**.

Mass mailing A group of letters or other documents created with a mail merge.

Menu bar The bar across the top of most Windows programs listing the names of menus that can be opened.

Merge To combine data from two or more files or programs. For example, you can merge addresses from a Works database with a form letter from the Works word processor.

Merged cells Two or more cells in a table or spreadsheet that have been combined to form a single, larger cell.

Modem A device in (or attached to) a computer that converts computer data to analog signal (sound) that can be sent over phone lines, and that receives such data from other computers, translating it back into computer data.

Money market fund A type of mutual fund that invests in short-term securities, such as T-bills. You can choose to have your invested cash in a brokerage account put into a money market fund so that it continues to earn while you are deciding what stocks to buy with it.

Mutual fund A collection of stocks, bonds, and other securities managed by an investment professional. You buy shares

in a mutual fund as if it were a single stock.

Negative indent *See* **Outdent**.

Newsgroups Public discussion forums on the Internet where users can post public messages and read messages posted by others. Examples are computer consulting newsgroups, a dolphin newsgroup, an Irish music newsgroup, and so on.

Normal document template The default template used to start new documents in Word. Also called blank document.

Object Any bit of text or graphics (or a whole file) that is copied, linked, or pasted into a document in a Windows-based application.

Object linking and embedding (OLE) The process of creating dynamic links between data. For example, you might include a chart from Works in a Word document with a link so that when the chart changes in Works, the copy in the Word document changes, too.

OLE *See* **Object linking and embedding**.

Online Layout view A special view in Word in which you can see all the document's headings in a panel to the left of the main document window.

Opening balance The amount of money that you start with in a Money account. You must enter all transactions that have occurred between the opening balance and the present balance.

Operator *See* **arithmetic operator**.

Orientation The direction that text runs on a page: across the short edge (portrait) or the long edge (landscape).

Outdent A negative indent, where a particular paragraph begins to the right of the right margin or to the right of the rest of the paragraphs in the document.

Overtype mode A typing mode in which text you type replaces any text that is already there to the right of the cursor.

Paragraph code An invisible code placed in a document by pressing the Enter key on the keyboard, indicating that a new paragraph should begin.

Paragraph formatting Any formatting that affects entire paragraphs rather than individual letters or words.

Paragraph styles Styles (in Word) that affect the entire paragraph rather than just individual letters or words. For example, a style might set the indents for a paragraph or the line spacing.

Path The location of a particular file on your hard disk. Paths are written with the driver letter first, followed by each level of folder. For example, c:\Windows\System\thisfile.dll is in the System folder, which is in the Windows folder, which is on the C drive.

Pay Online The former name of the bill-paying portion of the Checkfree banking and bill-payment service.

PIN number A secret code that you use like a password to identify yourself when doing online banking or bill payment in Money.

Points A measurement of type size. A point is 1/72 of an inch. Can also be a measurement of blank space; for example, in Word, a paragraph can be set to have 12 points of space before or after it.

Populate To enter or import data records into a database.

Portrait A page orientation in which the page is taller than it is wide.

Printer font A font that is built into your printer so that you can use it with any PC to which the printer is attached.

Properties Additional ways to categorize Money transactions. They work like categories and are optional to use.

Reconciling To compare the balance on your bank statement to the balance for an account in Money and then correct any discrepancies.

Records Data in a database. For example, in an address database, each person's set of data (name, address, phone number) is a record.

Register In Money, the area where you enter transactions for a particular account.

Registered retirement savings plan (RRSP) A Canadian retirement savings plan. As in other plans, contributions are tax-deferred, but withdrawals are taxed.

Relative reference In a spreadsheet formula, a cell reference that changes when copied to a different location. By default, all formulas use relative references. *See* **Absolute reference** for an alternative.

Retirement account In Money, any account that tracks investments for retirement.

Rollover A direct transfer of funds from one investment to another. For example, when changing retirement plans, you roll over the funds to the new plan rather than cashing out the old one to avoid paying taxes on the withdrawal.

Routing number The number on a check that identifies the bank.

Row header The gray button to the left of each row in a spreadsheet containing the row number.

Sans serif A font without little "tails" on the letters. Block lettering is an example of sans serif. The opposite of serif, which is a font that does have tails on the letters.

Scalable Capable of being resized. For example, TrueType fonts in Windows are scalable because you can use them at any size, from very tiny (8 points) to very large (72 points).

Scanned image An image acquired by using a scanner. These are almost always bitmap images and may be saved in any of a variety of formats, such as TIF, JPG, GIF, PCX, or BMP.

Scanner A device (much like a copier) that scans documents and images and then imports them into your computer in digital format so you can modify and save them.

Screen font A font designed specifically to be displayed on your screen. Some printer fonts and other fonts require complementary screen fonts so that your preview of your work onscreen does not appear jagged. TrueType fonts do not require screen fonts, as they work equally well when printed and when displayed on the screen.

Scroll bars Bars along the right and bottom edges of a window that enable you to scroll the display to see parts of the document or window that are not currently visible onscreen.

Search criteria In a database filter or a Search utility in another application, the keyword(s) or criteria used to narrow a list or locate specific text.

Search engine A Web site (usually a sophisticated, commercial one) providing a service that helps users find other Web sites on the Internet.

Section A division in a Word document that has its own margin and column settings—and possibly its own headers and footers, too. Section breaks enable a single document file to have different margins, columns, and so on, in different spots.

Serialized A data type in a database that increments the value in the field for each record. For example, you might have a Record Number field that automatically numbers the records: 1, 2, 3, and so on.

Serif A type of font that uses little "tails" on the letters to improve readability. The term "serif" can also apply to the little tails themselves.

Server A computer that provides information or performs services for other computers.

Setup utility A program that helps you set up another program to run on your computer.

Shortcut icon An icon (often on the Windows 95 desktop) that provides a pointer to an application or a document. You can double-click a shortcut icon to quickly open that program or document.

Simplified employee pension (SEP) A type of IRA retirement plan for small-business owners and the self-employed. Contributions are tax-deductible, and earnings are tax-deferred.

Smart quotes A feature of Word that converts straight quotation marks " to marks that point to the right or left, depending on their position in the sentence: "Smart Quotes."

Soft page break A page break that occurs naturally in a multipage document. If you add or remove text, a soft page break adjusts itself. In contrast, a hard page break, which you insert yourself, does not automatically adjust.

Sort To arrange data according to certain criteria. For example, you might sort an address database alphabetically by the last name of the people, from A to Z.

Special character A character not found on a standard keyboard, such as a copyright symbol ©.

Split In Money, to divide a transaction's amount between two or more categories.

Spreadsheet program A program that helps you track and calculate numbers in a grid of rows and columns.

Static The opposite of dynamic. A static copy of an object is not automatically updated when the original changes, while a dynamic copy is.

Stock Shares of ownership in a company. Stocks fluctuate in value on a daily basis and sometimes pay quarterly dividends.

Style Most commonly refers to a named set of formatting in a word processor. Can also refer to the attributes applied to a character, such as bold, italic, and underline.

Style Gallery An area in Word where you can view and transfer styles from various templates.

Style sheets An obsolete term for a type of template that held only styles. In earlier versions of Word, you could attach a style sheet to a document to make a list of styles available. (Now you would attach a template to do this.)

Styles Named formatting that you can apply to text in Word. For example, you might have a style called Heading 1 that formats text as 18-point bold Arial text with a ½-inch indent.

Subcategory In Money, a category within a category. For example, in the Home category you might have subcategories for Utilities, Rent, and Maintenance.

Subscribe Subscribing to a newsgroup (for example, Internet News) tells your news readers that you want to monitor the newsgroup and see the new message headings in it each time you log on to the Internet.

Symbol A printed character that is not a regular letter or number. Some symbols appear on a normal keyboard, such as * and $; others are special characters.

Syntax rules Rules for writing formulas and functions in a spreadsheet program so that they execute properly.

System files Files on your PC that start the PC and help keep it running.

Tab stop A marker for a paragraph that determines where the insertion point will move when you press the Tab key.

Table A grid of rows and columns, similar to a spreadsheet grid, in a word-processing document.

TaskWizard An easy-to-follow series of dialog boxes in Works that prompts you for information to help you create various kinds of documents, such as letters and invoices.

Tax reporting Reports in Money that help you figure out your tax deductions and liabilities.

Tax-deductible You can deduct the amount you contribute from your income that you report to the IRS.

Tax-deferred You don't have to pay taxes on the income until you withdraw it from the plan.

Template A set of styles, margins, boilerplate text, and other formatting on which you can base new documents.

Text wrapping *See* **Word wrap**.

Texture A graphic image of a certain surface type, such as wood or granite, that you can apply to text or an object in place of a color.

Title bar The colored bar across the top of a window that shows the program name.

Toggle button A button or command that works like a light switch, changing its state each time you activate it.

Toolbar A row of graphic buttons along the top or bottom of a window that provide shortcuts to common menu commands.

Tools In Works, Tools refers to the individual program components, such as Word Processor, Spreadsheet, and Database.

ToolTip A note that pops up when you position your mouse pointer over a toolbar button or other control, explaining that object's purpose.

Transactions In Money, any activity that results in a change of the balance in an account. Transactions include deposits, withdrawals, and transfers.

Treasury bill (T-Bill) Money that the United States government borrows from the purchaser for exactly one year.

Treasury bond (T-Bond) Like a treasury bill, except the duration is 10 years or more.

Treasury note (T-Note) Like a treasury bill, except the duration is two to 10 years.

TrueType A scalable type of font available in Windows programs. TrueType fonts have many advantages over other fonts, and most Windows users prefer to use them exclusively. Windows 95 comes with several TrueType fonts, and Home Essentials comes with many more, which are installed automatically when you install Word.

Typefaces *See* **Fonts**.

Uniform Resource Locator *See* **URL**.

Unprintable area The area at the edges of a piece of paper (usually about ¼-inch on all sides) on which the printer cannot print. Only the most high-quality printers do not have this limitation. The capability of printing all the way to the edges of the page is called *bleeding*.

Unvisited hyperlink A hyperlink that you have not yet explored on a Web page. Unvisited hyperlinks are usually a different color than visited ones so you can tell them apart.

URL (pronounced "Earl") An acronym for Uniform Resource Locator, which is the electronic address of a Web page (for example, `http://www.mcp.com`) or other Internet resource. Entering an URL in your Web browser tells the browser to find and display the page at the address.

Visited hyperlink A hyperlink that you have already explored on a Web page. *See* **Unvisited hyperlink**.

Web browser A software program that enables you to navigate documents, or pages, on the Web. With most browsers, you can view both text and graphics in documents authored in the HTML format. The most popular browsers are Netscape Navigator and Microsoft Internet Explorer.

Web page An HTML document on the Internet that has its own unique address. (The term *page* does not refer to a printed page; a single Web page might take many sheets of paper to print.)

Web site A page or collection of pages on the World Wide Web that you can view with your Web browser.

Weight The thickness of the letters in a typeface. For example, the Arial typeface comes in several weights, including Light, Regular, and Black (heavy).

Wizard Any helper program that walks you through a complicated procedure with a series of question-and-answer dialog boxes.

Word processor A program that helps you type and format text. Word is a word processor, and Works contains a word-processing tool also.

Word wrap The feature in a word processor that automatically starts a new line of text when you reach the right margin of a line.

WordArt A feature in Word and Works that enables you to create stylized text in a variety of shapes and orientations, often with special shading, textures, or 3D effects.

Worksheet *See* **Spreadsheet**.

World Wide Web (WWW) The graphical portion of the Internet, consisting of a vast network of interlinked Web sites.

Index

Works databases,
121-122, 144-148
adding fields, 145-146
filtering records, 147
fonts, 144-145
grouping records,
146-147
naming, 144-145
orientation, 144-145
previewing/printing,
148
Report View, 144
sorting records, 146
summary options,
147-148

researching topics
(Encarta), 473

resizing
drawn objects, Word
documents, 278
spreadsheet
columns/rows, Works,
106-108
tables
Word, 257-258
Works word processor,
69-70
WordArt
Word, 276
Works documents,
49-50

responding. *See replying*

Retail products link
(Essential Site Web
page), 531

retirement accounts
(Money), 312, 317. *See*
also investment accounts
(Money)

reversing actions. *See*
undoing; Redo

reviewing
AutoFormat changes,
Word documents,
217-218
budgets, 378-379
How I'm doing report,
379
My Budget report, 378

revolving charge
accounts. *See* credit card
accounts (Money)

rotating
greeting card objects,
464
Word graphics, 279-280

RTF (Rich Text Format),
converting files into
Word, 169

rulers
Word, 210-211, 257
displaying, 210
setting tab stops,
210-211
Works word processor
displaying, 20
setting tab stops, 52-54

rules, Web pages,
292-294

running applications. *See*
starting

running heads. *See* head-
ers/footers

S

Safety Level button
(Internet Explorer), 428

sans serif fonts, 195

saving
articles, Encarta, 476-477
email addresses to
(Internet Mail),
438-439

Greetings Workshop
projects, 468-469
styles, Word, 224-225
Web site address,
Favorite Places, 411
Word documents,
167-169
as HTML, 288
as templates, 230-231
file formats, 169
My Documents folder,
168
opening saved docu-
ments, 168-169
settings, Normal tem-
plate, 163-164
Works
databases, 127
word processor docu-
ments, 37-38

savings accounts (Money),
313-314

scalable fonts, 201. *See*
also fonts

scanned images
Greetings Workshop
photos. *See* photos,
Greetings Workshop
inserting into Word
documents, 268

scatter (XY) charts,
Works spreadsheets,
113-115. *See also* charts

screen fonts, 201. *See also*
fonts

scrolling. *See also* navigating
Word, scrollboxes, 174
Works
spreadsheets, 77-78
word processor docu-
ments, 24-26